Voices of Intimate Partner Homicide

In the United States and most parts of the world, law, policy, policing, and prevention work addressing domestic and intimate partner violence is created and enacted based on a violence model. Likewise, it is generally believed that all victims of intimate partner homicide are victims of intimate partner violence, through physical abuse, prior to the incident of homicide, and that this violence is reported beforehand.

Voices of Intimate Partner Homicide takes a critical look at these misconceived notions and sheds light on multiple non-violent forms of controlling behavior that precipitate intimate partner homicide. The book bases its critical examination on a content analysis of court-filed Petitions for Injunction for Protection Against Domestic Violence. Through these records, as well as corresponding police and homicide reports, the accounts of the victims, and their relationships with their offenders, come to life. Recurring coercive control tactics are coded and analyzed across multiple accounts, including intimidation, isolation, and humiliation, to illustrate the ways in which individuals are threatened prior to homicide and the true extent of harm that happens in the absence of physical violence. Considering the victim's responses, as well as their interaction with law enforcement and the court system prior to their death, the author challenges current legal and policy initiatives made to address and protect victims from intimate partner violence and argues that non-violent controlling behaviors deserve more attention in lethality risk assessments that are utilized throughout the United States.

For practitioners, advocates, researchers, and students, this book provides an intimate and important account of the causes and consequences of intimate partner violence prior to homicide and a rare window into the victim's overall experience.

Donna J. King, Ph.D., J.D., is an IPV survivor and President/Director for Victims' Safe Harbor Foundation, Inc., a 501(c)3 social impact organization that provides legal, educational and policy services on domestic violence and child abuse. She received her Ph.D. in Sociology from the University of Central Florida, where her areas of expertise focused on domestic violence, social inequalities, law and society, gender, and criminology. She also holds a juris doctorate from the Florida Agricultural & Mechanical University College of Law and is a Florida licensed attorney in good standing.

"*Voices of Intimate Partner Homicide* grew out of Dr. King's dissertation. It is an important addition to the literature in the area, as the depth of research exposes the seriousness of non-violent coercive control tactics and the part they may play as precursors to intimate partner homicide. Non-violent coercive control tactics must be included in the definition and as indicators of intimate partner homicide on lethality risk assessments.

Whether you are new to the study of intimate partner violence or have researched the area for years, by reading this book like me, you are bound to gain new insights into abusive relationships!"

Dr. Lin Huff-Corzine, *Emerita Professor, Department of Sociology, University of Central Florida*

"*Voices of Intimate Partner Homicide* by Donna King, Ph.D., J.D., is a 'must read' for all domestic violence advocates. Its publication coincides with the unrolling of the White House National Plan to End Gender-Based Violence and will contribute substantially to the body of knowledge that will help to end family and intimate partner violence and murder."

Connie Valentine M.S, *co-founder of California Protective Parents Association*

"Systems interacting with targets of coercive controllers have skated along for a half-century, utilizing incomplete, outdated information to build stale practices, policies, and laws that have done more to endanger than to help. Family courts, the ultimate gatekeepers for victim safety, are behind decades in utilizing the available obsolete information; lives are being snuffed out in the information gap.

Enter *Voices of Intimate Partner Homicide*, the bible you didn't know you need, to enumerate just how lethal coercive controllers are. The knowledge gained here is your 'know better,' so you can 'do better.' Lives everywhere are dependent on you doing just that."

Kathy Jones, *Creator of The Maze of Coercive Control, Mother Justice Network*

"*Voices of Intimate Partner Homicide* is one of the first of its kind to acknowledge and provide data regarding coercive control and its precursors to homicide in Domestic Violence. Domestic Violence is a complex and multidimensional issue and *Voices of Intimate Partner Homicide* brings darkness to light by providing extensive research on how coercive control is more dangerous than often acknowledged. A good read for those working with survivors, as well as those trying to create an understanding of Coercive Control."

Linda L. Parker, *Ph.D. President and CEO of Women In Distress of Broward County*

Voices of Intimate Partner Homicide
An Exploration of Coercive Control and Lethality

Donna J. King

NEW YORK AND LONDON

Designed cover image: Erich Martin

First published 2024
by Routledge
605 Third Avenue, New York, NY 10158

and by Routledge
4 Park Square, Milton Park, Abingdon, Oxon, OX14 4RN

Routledge is an imprint of the Taylor & Francis Group, an informa business

© 2024 Donna J. King

The right of Donna J. King to be identified as author of this work has been asserted in accordance with sections 77 and 78 of the Copyright, Designs and Patents Act 1988.

All rights reserved. No part of this book may be reprinted or reproduced or utilised in any form or by any electronic, mechanical, or other means, now known or hereafter invented, including photocopying and recording, or in any information storage or retrieval system, without permission in writing from the publishers.

Trademark notice: Product or corporate names may be trademarks or registered trademarks, and are used only for identification and explanation without intent to infringe.

ISBN: 978-0-367-56388-2 (hbk)
ISBN: 978-0-367-56386-8 (pbk)
ISBN: 978-1-003-09748-8 (ebk)

DOI: 10.4324/9781003097488

Typeset in Sabon
by KnowledgeWorks Global Ltd.

Details of the cases reported in this book are based upon facts available at the time of writing and readers should be mindful of any subsequent updates.

This book is dedicated to those who lost their lives to intimate partner homicide, as well as all the intimate partner violence victims who struggle every day to survive horrific acts of physical violence and non-violent tactics of coercive control.

Contents

Acknowledgments — xiv
List of Abbreviations — xv

Introduction — 1

Davenport v. Davenport 1
Significance of the Research 8

PART I
The Gender Identity of Coercive Control — 19

1 Women's Rights, Domestic Violence, and Intimate Partner Violence — 21

Explaining the Inexplicable: The Difficulty in Defining "Intimate Partner Violence" 21
Gender and Intimate Partner Violence: Legislating against Patriarchal Violence 23
The Gender Asymmetry of Coercive Control 28

2 Not All Intimate Partner Violence Is Created Equal — 33

Coercive Control's Impact on the Intimate Partner Violence Victim 34
Intimidation 34
Isolation 37
Humiliation 39
Power and Control 40

    Fearful of the Future 43
    Resistance to Abuse 44
    Abuser Mental Illness 45
    Physical Violence 46

3 Assessing the Risk: Understanding an Intimate Partner Violence Victim's Risk of Death   51

    The Risk of Leaving: She Knows He's a Threat, but Does Anyone Else? 51
    The Role of Intimate Partner Homicide-Suicide in Intimate Partner Homicide 52
    The Disillusionment of the Protections of an Injunction for Protection against Domestic Violence: Why and When Are They Important to Intimate Partner Violence Victims? 54
    Litigation Abuse or Judicial Terrorism®? 55
    Gender Bias in the Courts 58
    Litigation and Coercive Control: Not Every Petition for Injunction for Protection against Domestic Violence Is the Same 59

4 Understanding Intimate Partner Homicide Victims from Their Own Data   64

    Methodology for Data Collection: Sourcing Public Records 64
        The Florida Department of Law Enforcement Uniform Crime Report-Supplemental Homicide Report Data 65
        Florida Local Law Enforcement Agencies 66
        The Florida County Courthouse 68
    A Comparison of Intimate Partner Homicide Studies 69
    Theorizing Intimate Partner Violence and Intimate Partner Homicide 73
    Black's Theory of the Behavior of Law 74
    Bellew's Explanation of the Intimate Partner Violence Socioeconomic Divide 75
    Theoretical Implications from the Avakame et al. (1999) Study 76

PART II
Voices of Intimate Partner Homicide Victims   83

5 The Torture of Coercive Control   85

Intimidation 89
  Animal Abuse 91
  Harassment 93
  Surveillance 95
  Threats 96
  Threatens Friends and Family 99
  Weapons 101
Isolation 103
  Economic Control 107
  False Imprisonment 109
  Financial Control 112

6 The Insidious and Omnipresent Coercive Control   125

Humiliation 125
  Degradation 126
  Name Calling 128
Power and Control 130
  Child Abuse 134
  Violent Acts toward Family and Friends 137
  Taking Children from Victim 137
  Deprivation of Necessities 142
  Psychologically Controlling 143
  Verbal Abuse 147
  Household, Clothes, and Personal Belongings
    Destroyed 149

7 When the Intimate Partner Violence Victim Resists the Abuse   165

Fearful of the Future 165
  Fear of Children's Safety 166
  Pregnant 170
Resistance to Abuse 172
  Helping Abuser 177
  Separated or Estranged 181

  Abuser Mental Illness 183
   Drinking Alcohol 188
   Drug Use 192
   Paranoia 195

 8 Physical Violence, the Ultimate in Power and Control? 213

  Physical Violence 213
   Nonfatal Strangulation 217
   Rape and Sexual Abuse 220
  Familicide and the Family Annihilator 222
  Judicial Terrorism® Revisited 232

PART III
Regulating Coercive Control: Lessons from Intimate Partner Violence and Intimate Partner Homicide Data 255

 9 The Frequencies of Coercive Control 257

  Demographics of Intimate Partner Homicide Victims 263
   Native Americans 264
   Asian Americans and Pacific Islanders 264
  Multiple Petitions for Injunction for Protection Against Domestic Violence 265
  Abuser Mental Illness Disclosed 266
  The Intimate Partner Violence Victim's Resistance to Abuse 267
  The Effectiveness of Orders of Injunctions for Protection Against Domestic Violence 268
  The Interactions of Coercive Control Tactics 270
   Qualitative Frequency Interactions 270
   Quantitative Methods Results 271

 10 Coercive Control Legislation and Reimagining Lethality Risk Assessment for Intimate Partner Violence 293

  Coercive Control Legislation in the United States 293
   Addressing the Legislative Gaps of Coercive Control 293

Reimagining Intimate Partner Violence Lethality Risk Assessments 300
Reallocating Intimate Partner Violence Resources 301

11 Conclusion   307

Limitations to the Study 309
Future Directions for Research 311
One Final Word 313

Appendix: Codebook – Coercive Control Themes and Subthemes   316
Index   320

Acknowledgments

This study would not have been possible without the dedication and support of many extraordinary people. First, *Dr. Lin Huff-Corzine*, my major professor and dissertation chair, is the reason this book is a reality. Without her vision, this project would not have occurred. Second, I would like to thank Kathy Jones for her support since the time of my dissertation and for her fabulous Maze of Coercive Control. She has shaped my views on the non-violent tactics of coercive control since I was in law school.

My family, including my *mom, dad, stepmother, daughters, and stepsons*, was an incredible support system as I worked throughout my Ph.D. program and on this book. I could not have done any of it without their steadfast love and inspiration. I especially want to thank my husband, *Dayton King*, who has been my biggest moral supporter throughout the writing of this book. I also have many friends who have provided tremendous encouragement throughout this process, and I want to thank them as well. They know who they are, and I am forever indebted to them for all their undying support and encouragement.

To the many domestic violence and legal professionals who have encouraged and supported me as I have been writing this book, thank you. The work you do daily is critical, and I hope this book assists you in your endeavors.

Dad, this is my encore. I know you are watching.

Abbreviations

Be-On-the-Look-Out	BOLO
Dissolution of Marriage Action	DOM
Domestic violence	DV
Florida Department of Law Enforcement	FDLE
Uniform Crime Report Supplemental Homicide Report	UCR-SHR
Florida Department of Children and Families	DCF
Final Judgment of Injunction for Protection against Domestic Violence [with Minor Children]	final injunction
Injunction Court	court
Intimate Partner Homicide	IPH
Intimate Partner Homicide-Suicide	IPHS
Intimate Partner Violence	IPV
Lesbian, Gay, Bisexual, Transgender, Queer, Questioning, Intersex, Asexual, and (expanding)	LGBTQIA+
National Crime Victimization Survey	NCVS
National Family Violence Surveys	NFVS
Office of Violence Against Women at the United States Department of Justice	OVW
Petition for Injunction for Protection against Domestic Violence	petition for injunction
Temporary Injunction for Protection against Domestic Violence	temporary injunction
Variance Inflation Factor	VIF

Introduction

Davenport v. Davenport

On March 29, 2004, Deborah Davenport filed a petition for injunction for protection against domestic violence [hereinafter *petition for injunction*] against her husband, Joseph.[1] In her petition, she explained that, on March 28, 2004, Joseph came home drunk and was angry because she did not have dinner ready for the family; they had three children.[2] He believed she should have had dinner ready when he got home.[3] As she continued to describe in her petition, the family was sitting around the dinner table as Joseph commanded they do on a regular basis.[4] But that night, he informed the children that the he and Deborah were getting a divorce and that he was moving to New Jersey without the children.[5] Deborah recounted Joseph's demands that the family share how they felt about the situation in that moment, while they sat there eating dinner, whether they wanted to or not.[6]

As this continued to take place, Joseph became louder and more insistent that the family participate in his demands.[7] To ensure their compliance, Deborah detailed in her petition how Joseph put a bullet to each one of their heads.[8] He told the family which one of them would be killed first; his plan was youngest to oldest.[9] But he planned to spare the oldest because she had a job.[10] He would kill Deborah with two bullets because the divorce was her fault.[11] He told them he would try to shoot himself twice in the process of killing himself.[12] She explained that it was clear to her that the children were being tormented; but he continued even though they were all crying.[13] He repeatedly stated the day and month and told them to remember the date on the calendar because it would be their last day on earth.[14] He wanted them to know that their deaths would make front-page news the next morning and how their house would be a crime scene.[15] But he went to use the bathroom; telling them "if [they] wanted to make a 'run for it', 'now would be the time.'"[16] So, Deborah and the children ran out of the house and drove away to safety.[17]

DOI: 10.4324/9781003097488-1

Introduction

On March 29, 2004, the day Deborah's petition for injunction was filed, she was granted an *ex parte*[18] temporary injunction for protection against domestic violence [with minor children] [hereinafter *temporary injunction*].[19] On April 8, 2004, after notice to Joseph, a hearing was held in which the court entered a final judgment of injunction for protection against domestic violence [with minor children] [hereinafter *final injunction*], which did not expire without further order of the court.[20] Nevertheless, on April 21, 2004, Deborah filed a motion for modification of the injunction for protection she had against Joseph, stating that she wished to have the final injunction, issued just 13 days prior, changed because he received help for his alcohol and anger issues.[21] She also explained that she wanted to work on her marriage.[22] On April 8, 2004, her motion resulted in dismissal of the final injunction against Joseph.[23] Because the final injunction was dismissed, on July 1, 2004, Joseph received an order from the court releasing his firearms.[24]

The couple lived together as husband and wife for the following eight years, seemingly without incident or any reports of physical violence to law enforcement or the court. However, on July 1, 2012, Deborah and the children, now much older, moved out of the marital residence because she was considering divorce and told Joseph she wanted one month to consider the situation.[25] But on August 1, 2012, during the early morning hours while she was leaving for work, Joseph kidnapped Deborah from the home where she was living with the children.[26] He drove her to the marital residence, shot, and killed her.[27] He died by turning the gun on himself.[28] Both Deborah and Joseph were found lying together in bed, face up, naked.[29] Deborah had several wounds that indicated she had been beaten prior to her death.[30]

It is difficult to know exactly what type of relationship Deborah and Joseph experienced for the eight years between the dismissal of the final injunction and release of firearms in 2004 and their deaths in 2012. It is possible they lived free of physical violence and threats of physical violence during that time. However, it is also possible that, if there were such episodes of physical violence or threats thereof, they went unreported to law enforcement and the court. Other types of intimate partner violence (IPV)[31] Deborah described in her petition for injunction, which are not related to physical violence or the threat thereof, are non-violent tactics of abuse that occur during the daily lives of abuse victims throughout the United States and the world.[32] These tactics are utilized by the IPV abuser against their victim on an ongoing basis to invoke power and control, and, often, to terrorize their victim without the need for physical violence to accomplish the goal of exerting this power over their victim.[33]

Victims of abuse, especially women, from all socioeconomic levels throughout the United States and the world, living with and without children, married and single, suffer ongoing, torturous abuse, that frequently leads to death, often without being physically beaten by their abuser prior to the killing.[34] In 2020, the National Center for Injury Prevention and Control's Division of Violence Prevention at the Centers for Disease Control and Prevention reported how common IPV is by explaining that millions of people each year, both men and women, are affected by it at some point in their lifetime.[35] Women experience IPV at a much higher rate than men, i.e., "1 in 4 women and 1 in 10 men experience sexual violence, physical violence and/or stalking by an intimate partner during their lifetime with 'IPV-related impact' such as being concerned for their safety, PTSD [post-traumatic stress disorder] symptoms, injury, or needing victim services."[36] When considering its many forms, women experience IPV at consistently higher rates than men each year throughout the United States.[37]

A debate exists among experts regarding the experiences of IPV between the genders and its relative applicability to society's patriarchal gender norms.[38] The concept known as gender-symmetry, or conversely gender-asymmetry, is the cornerstone of this debate.[39] The debate about whether gender-symmetry or gender-asymmetry is applicable to a particular IPV situation is, generally, contextualized in relation to *situational couple violence* because the data for such are contained within general survey data.[40] But Johnson (2010) explains that biases exist within these "representative survey samples" that create the illusion of a gender-symmetric perpetration of violence between couples.[41] Indeed, most researchers, practitioners, and academics understand IPV as a highly gendered combination of tactics of abuse, intended to exert power and control over another person, that may or may not include physical violence; in short, this continuum of abuse, used primarily by men, is known as *coercive control*.[42] In fact, Barlow and Walklate's (2021) recent study regarding risk assessments and coercive control found that 95 percent of coercive control victims were women and 93 percent of its offenders were men.[43] And Dobash and Dobash (2015) explain that intimate partner homicide (IPH) across the world is asymmetrical.[44]

This book acknowledges that both men and women, whether in heterosexual or same-sex relationships, experience IPV as victims and commit the same as offenders.[45] Indeed, this Introduction illustrates that family members can become collateral and/or covictims of coercive control, if not direct victims themselves. However, this book's focus, including its empirical research, is on IPV and IPH between heterosexual spouses. But this focus is not intended to minimize the effects of IPV or IPH within same-sex intimate relationships or among other forms of Lesbian, Gay, Bisexual, Transgender, Queer, Questioning, Intersex, Asexual, and (expanding) (LGBTQIA+) intimate partner relationships.[46]

IPV often presents in an ongoing, coercive, and controlling manner and has a much more devastating impact on its victim than physical violence alone, including the risk of lethality.[47] Many of the tactics utilized by an

IPV abuser to control their victim, which do not involve the use of physical violence, include isolation, intimidation, harassment, and power and control.[48] However, these tactics are the broader range of "themes" that help to explain how an abuser invokes control in the daily life of their victim. This book provides empirical data relevant to these themes and their corresponding "subthemes" to help further explain how an abuser utilizes the non-violent tactics of coercive control to micromanage their victim's everyday routine to eliminate their victim's sense of autonomy and self-worth. These themes and subthemes help to elucidate the victim's responses to their abuse, whether physical or non-violent, when attempting to free themselves from their abuser's power and control.

There is a lack of consensus about the causes of IPV, which stems from differing worldwide cultural accounts and explanations.[49] Little progress is being made toward the elimination of this devastating social epidemic, leaving many victims and their children without the services they desperately need.[50] Additionally, abusers who want to improve their circumstances might find themselves lacking the resources available to them to do so.[51] This is because, typically, abusers are only provided state funded intervention resources once they are under the court's jurisdiction, which generally only happens when they become physically violent toward their victim.[52] One reason for this is because there is little agreement among scholars, legislators, law enforcement, prosecutors, defense attorneys, judges, advocates and IPV program employees about how to universally define the collective of behaviors attributed to IPV, as well as to how to respond to this social problem that is among the list of the most misunderstood crimes.[53]

Understanding and classifying the types of physically abusive acts constituting physical and sexual abuse is easier achieved than accepting the concept of the continuum of behaviors that are the non-violent forms of IPV, also commonly referred to or known as financial, economic, mental, verbal, psychological, and/or emotional abuse, i.e., coercive control.[54] These intangible forms of coercive and controlling behaviors, which are continuously utilized by the abuser against the victim, have a very different and long-lasting effect on the victim when invoked through non-violent tactics rather than through physical violence or other criminal acts.[55] As a result, over time, the abuser is able to control the victim, even without being in the victim's presence, due to the overwhelming effect these non-violent tactics have on the victim. Indeed, the abuser maintains a sense of omnipresence over the victim once the abuser's coercive control is firmly established.

National, state, and local governments throughout the world employ different definitions in their recognition and prosecution of IPV or domestic violence (DV).[56] Many definitions include physical acts of violence because there is more universal agreement that IPV includes hitting, grabbing, choking, stabbing, etc.; and these acts are able to be easily legislated as single, isolated incidents.[57] Nevertheless, a need for legislating the non-violent tactics of coercive control exists and advocates around the world have argued for the implementation of criminal and civil laws to assist in curtailing their use by abusers against victims and other covictims.[58] Wright (2013) explains that some governmental bodies – such as the Office of Violence Against Women at the United States Department of Justice (OVW) and the United Nations – agree that IPV manifests itself in physical, sexual, and psychological abuse, occurring concomitantly rather than in isolation.[59] The behaviors embodying these forms of abuse are not mutually exclusive; yet they are often legislated and enforced as though they occur discretely.[60] Still, a uniform, all-encompassing definition, inclusive of the multitude of behaviors encompassing the continuum of coercive control's non-violent tactics that is accepted throughout the United States at the federal and state level, remains elusive.

Most U.S. state statutes regulating "domestic violence," "domestic abuse," "family violence," or "intimate partner violence" generally proscribe isolated incidents of physical violence, especially in the criminal law system.[61] The majority of U.S. state statutes do not address behaviors by an abuser in which the abusive acts occur over an extended period of time whereby the physical acts of violence may be non-existent or pale in comparison to the overall non-violent abusive behaviors.[62] Laws often utilize the terms DV, domestic abuse, family violence, or intimate partner violence interchangeably, adding to the difficulty of developing unity among governing bodies and law enforcement authorities to define all abusive behaviors, both violent and non-violent, occurring between intimate partners.[63] But, if any of these definitions included language covering the abusive behaviors that describe the non-violent tactics of coercive control, they might begin to protect the IPV victim who is suffering the torturous effects of this type of abuse that does not require physical violence for its effectiveness. And, in fact, a handful of civil U.S. state statutes are making advancements toward doing so; but there is much more work to be done.[64]

To provide broader protection that encompasses all victims of IPV, including those who experience non-violent tactics without any physical violence, it is necessary for legislators to understand that the non-violent forms of abuse may be just as devastating to the victim, if not more so in some cases, than the physical acts.[65] Accordingly, it is reasonable to think that, with such an understanding, legislators would seek to protect their citizenry from non-violent forms of abuse, similarly to how they have from the physically violent forms. Thus, the main research question posed in this mixed-methods exploratory study seeks to determine whether coercive control, exclusive of a prior reporting of physical violence to law enforcement or the court, presents a significant risk of death due to the killing of the heterosexual spouse by the other spouse.

Scholars from various academic disciplines and experts in related fields, including sociology, psychology, and law, have studied DV for decades, mostly focusing on its nonlethal forms; yet the murder of women by their intimate partners has attracted comparatively little attention.[66] During the last quarter of the 20th century, IPH research focused more on women as the perpetrators rather than as the victims, leading to the development of the battered women's defense.[67] But the problem of IPH of women persisted, as it does today.[68] Every day in the United States, three or more women are killed by an intimate partner, whether current, estranged, or former.[69] More recently, scholarly attention has started to focus on IPV and the potential of women as IPH victims.[70] Yet, the availability of reliable, unbiased, and generalizable data for studies about IPH is still difficult to obtain.[71] Thus, IPV and the murder of women by their abusive intimate partners needs to be studied together because women are more likely to become the victim of an IPH than any other category of homicide.[72]

The general notion is that an IPV victim, who is scared for their life from their intimate partner, would contact law enforcement or the judicial system to secure protection for themself (including their children) from their abuser; but this may not always be the case.[73] It is often assumed that a physically violent event between intimate partners would result in an intervention by law enforcement or by the victim choosing to leave the abuser; however, this is not necessarily the outcome of IPV.[74] Indeed, there exists an abundance of research that explains that many IPV victims, including those who ultimately become victims of IPH, do not report every act, or multiple acts, of IPV.[75] Yet, there also exists a plethora of research and academic literature linking the social issue of IPV to arrest rates and whether the policing of IPV is positively affecting the lives of IPV victims, especially the prevention of their death from IPH, suggesting that the victim did seek law enforcement's intervention.[76] Contrarily, there is a dearth of research and academic literature analyzing the experiences between an offender and the victim of an IPH prior to the killing, especially focusing on the long-term effects of coercive control on a victim, which are understood to be much worse than physical abuse alone.[77] This study begins to fill the empirical gap where the research on IPV arrests ends and the research into the lives of IPV victims and offenders, who become the IPH victims and offenders, begins. Indeed, this book follows the cases to a conclusion with explanations of the aftermath of the killings.

The theoretical framework stemming from the predominant body of literature, focusing on the risk factors for the lethality of women in relationships where IPV is present, is based on the notion of recidivism, meaning those who are repeatedly arrested for IPV or violent crimes are the most at risk for committing re-abuse or IPH.[78] The research interest in arrest rates stemmed from early 1980s research that concluded arresting abusers was the most effective method in reducing re-abuse, including over mediation and counseling.[79] Because of the implementation of mandatory arrest, mandatory prosecution, and proarrest policies, due to the passage of nationwide legislation against DV, many studies began to look at the efficacy of these policies.[80] However, these arrest-based studies only look to the impacts of the physical violence allegations between the intimate partners and the criminal justice response as opposed to their outcome-based implications on the IPV victim.[81] Yet, researchers, academics, and social workers understand that events in the life cycle of abuse, such as separation or the threat of separation, increases the likelihood of IPH.[82] Previous abuse, the presence of firearms, alcohol and drug abuse, jealousy and mental illness are just a few of the risk factors identified when determining lethality risks for victims of IPV; but much less is known about the risk factors for IPH.[83]

Unquestionably, protecting IPV victims from non-violent tactics of coercive control is a challenging and unresolved proposition because it is difficult to measure coercive control when definitions and regulations rely upon traditional norms and standards of physical acts of violence.[84] In fact, coercive control is rarely recognized by courts; and, if it is, it is simply to inform the court about the likelihood of future physical harm to its victims rather than using it solely as a basis for issuing a civil injunction to protect an IPV victim.[85] Rarely do the U.S. criminal and civil justice court systems consider episodes of IPV that do not include physical violence as offenses worthy of punishment or deserving of protection for the victim.[86] It is due to this inherent disregard for the most devastating forms of abuse, i.e., the non-violent tactics of coercive control, that this study was developed.

One goal of this study was to contextualize and operationalize coercive control, using secondary data collected from the Florida Department of Law Enforcement's (FDLE) Uniform Crime Report Supplemental Homicide Report (UCR-SHR), law enforcement records, and court documents for the years January 1, 2006, to June 30, 2016. Content analysis of the petitions for injunction between the IPH victim and offender spouses was conducted, employing NVivo 12 Pro, a qualitative social sciences software package. NVivo 12 Pro helped to analyze the petition for injunction narratives, filed with the clerk of courts throughout Florida by IPV victims, for the development of an understanding of the nature of the abusive intimate partner relationships between the heterosexual spousal couples involved in IPHs. Also, the raw data from the coding in NVivo Pro 12 were used in the quantitative phase of this study to determine the association between non-violent coercive control tactics and prior reporting of physical violence to law enforcement, as well as to the injunction court [hereinafter *court*]. Additional variables were also considered in the quantitative phase of the study using IBM SPSS®, an advanced statistical software analysis program.

In furthering the notion that an IPH victim, involved in a heterosexual spousal relationship, may or may not have reported physical violence to law enforcement or the court prior to their death, Donald Black's (2010) theory of *the behavior of law* is instructive.[87]

Significance of the Research

Prior to conducting this study, no large-scale, empirical study existed that documents coercive control rather than, or concurrent with, physical violence preceding an IPH.[88] Johnson (2010), in explaining the importance of examining the broader social context of IPV, "[made] a plea for an increased focus on qualitative research.[89] Wydall and Zerk (2020), who conducted a qualitative study on twelve victim-survivors of coercive control, echoed Johnson's sentiment by stating "there are very few qualitative studies that explore victim-survivors' lived experiences of coercive control when attempting to seek protection from the police and other criminal justice agents."[90] This study adds to the dearth of qualitative studies on IPV and coercive control by providing a comprehensive content analysis of the data derived from the petition for injunction narratives filed by IPV victims in sixty-two (62) cases filed with the clerks of court throughout Florida where the IPHs took place.

Block and Christakos (1995) explain that the particulars of an IPH rarely provide information about the intimate details of the relationship, as well as the events and circumstances that took place prior to the IPH.[91] However, the aim of this study was to accomplish just that, meaning it traced each case to elucidate the IPV victim's interactions with the abuser, as well as the criminal and civil justice system prior to the IPH. Since, historically, the IPH of women has received little academic attention because the focus was on physical violence, one goal of this study was to highlight the fact that emphasizing physical violence in an intimate partner relationship to identify high risk IPV victims may be misplaced.[92] In fact, most of the research involving lethality risks for IPV victims stems from the abusers' arrest data rather than from any type of IPH data.[93] This study distinguishes itself because it utilizes petitions for injunctions between the heterosexual spouses, meaning the IPV victims' data, as one of its sources for data collection to understand the relationship between the IPH victim and offender. However, it is essential for a full understanding of the data to clarify that, although the spouses in each case remain the same, the IPV victim and offender may not always be the same as the IPH victim and offender. Meaning, in some cases, the IPV victim became the IPH offender because the IPV victim killed their abuser.

It is important that these data were collected and analyzed to assess the efforts, or lack thereof, made by IPV victims, law enforcement authorities, and the judicial system, to protect victims prior to an IPH. Empirical literature analyzing the effects of legislation on IPV *beyond* the point of arrest is not readily available, if at all. Although recent literature is working to fill the voids, there is a dearth of information related to the non-violent tactics of coercive control and risk factors of IPH.[94] This lack of empirical literature also includes an analysis of enacted laws protecting against coercive control, including its non-violent tactics.[95] Most of the accessible research about coercive control legislation concerns the arguments for, or against, such laws rather than assessing the enforcement or efficacy of any such laws that are currently in place.[96] The goal of this study is to help fill the gaps in the existing empirical literature regarding IPV and IPH so that it will provide helpful data for future research into IPV and IPH, as well as coercive control for social science, legal, and criminal justice perspectives and implications.

Websdale (2010) describes the establishment of the National Domestic Violence Fatality Review Initiative, a federally funded fatality review board established in October 1999.[97] He explains that many fatality review boards begin by examining intimate partner homicide-suicides (IPHSs).[98] However, Dobash and Dobash (2015) discuss the problems presented with conducting IPH case studies, in particular, including that of fatality reviews because of the inability to generalize the results.[99] They explain that in-depth details about a small sample size of cases may be useful for local policies and practices, but it is not possible to use the results for making any conclusions regarding the population studied as a whole.[100] But this study seeks to provide both IPH case studies, which includes cases of IPHSs, and empirical research results that are generalizable.

Similar to other DV fatality reviews overseen by the National Domestic Violence Fatality Review Initiative, the Fatality Review Team was created in 2009 after a drastic increase in DV homicides in Florida.[101] The purpose of the Fatality Review Team is to identify means to improve responses to DV and to "support community partners and systemic services in ongoing efforts to reduce and prevent domestic violence homicides in Florida."[102] The team provides a report of comprehensively reviewed selected DV homicide cases "*or near homicides*" [emphasis added] from the state's complete set of DV homicide cases as provided by the FDLE's Uniform Crime Report.[103] The 2019 Florida Domestic Violence Fatality Review report analyzed 31 homicides that occurred between 2009 and 2018.[104] The resultant report is quite detailed; however, it lacks in the volume of cases for generalizability to the population for an empirical study.[105] For instance, the report covered an IPHS, which seems to have been hand selected for the purposes of presentation in the report.[106] Due to the nature of the Florida Attorney General's Statewide Domestic Violence Fatality Review Team, this is appropriate; however, it is possible that more IPHSs might need to be included in their sample of cases if the review team wants it to reflect more accurate statistics regarding the potential prevalence of IPHS in Florida. Caman et al. (2017) explain that:

> [a] deficiency in the scientific landscape of homicide is the systematic omission of homicide-suicide perpetrators from prominent datasets, as they are not charged or convicted. This results in increased risk of bias, especially related to IPH, as profound percentage of the IPH offenders commit suicide in connection to the homicidal act.[107]

Thus, one of this study's contributions is to add to the body of work that the state of Florida currently has regarding IPHs and IPHSs. Indeed, fatality review teams serve a very important purpose in detailing DV homicides throughout the state each year. However, this study provides valuable information for key stakeholders because it provides detailed case studies, and it is generalizable.

Part I of this book provides a comprehensive introduction to the concepts of DV, IPV, and coercive control. Through detailed explanations for defining these concepts, the policies behind their current legislation, and the gender debate surrounding IPV, the difficulty in promoting change becomes evident. The themes and subthemes of coercive control, as derived from this study, are detailed, as well as the risks an IPV victim faces when leaving their abuser. IPHS is discussed to prepare the reader for the cases that follow in later chapters. The process of filing for and obtaining an injunction for protection against DV is examined, as well as the complex process of litigation between an IPV victim and their abuser, which may be referred to as judicial terrorism®. The concept of gender bias in the courts is covered, culminating in the notion that judges, who render discretionary decisions in injunction cases, do not necessarily provide the most impartial treatment toward IPV victims in their courts. Finally, in Part I, the methodology and theory behind this study is discussed in detail.

Part II provides the sixty-two (62) case studies, broken down by each coercive control theme and subtheme, resulting from the content analysis from the qualitative phase of the study. Throughout this part of the book, the voices of the IPV victims, the majority of whom became the IPH victims, tell their stories of how they came to the court to ask for protection from their abusers. Every theme and subtheme are discussed throughout this portion of the book to help contextualize the information learned from each case study. Each story is told to its ultimate conclusion, beyond just the point of arrest, so a more thorough understanding of the case and its complexities may be understood, including the ensuing criminal trial and sentencing if relevant. Part III presents this study's qualitative and quantitative results and findings. The lessons learned from the IPH victims and the voices of the IPV victims who provided the data for this empirical research are reviewed and discussed. Additionally, the policy implications from these lessons are detailed so that progress toward improved protections for IPV victims may be accomplished, including changes in legislation and lethality risk assessments.

This study gives meaning to the lives of the IPH victims behind the incident report numbers on the FDLE's UCR-SHR and provides a deeper, richer understanding of the process law enforcement and judicial system personnel confront regularly in attempting to protect the IPV victim prior to an IPH. By doing so, it is possible to determine whether physical violence is the only, or even the most, important indicator of lethality risk for IPV victims, as is the current policy. The results of this study should have far reaching implications for lethality risk assessment policies for IPH and for IPV victims who request temporary and/or final injunctions or any other forms of legal assistance or protective services. Briefly stated, lives depend on finding answers to the questions posed in this book.

Notes

1 *See generally* Davenport v. Davenport, 2004-DR-1235 (2004) (Pet. for Inj. Against Dom. Viol.). In Florida, although the terminology may be different in other states, a civil court order for protection against domestic violence is referred to as an injunction for protection against domestic violence, which is obtained by filing a petition for injunction against domestic violence.
2 *See Id.* at 3.
3 *See Id.*
4 *See Id.*
5 *See Id.*
6 *See Id.*
7 *See Id.*
8 *See Id.*
9 *See Id.*
10 *See Id.*
11 *See Id.*
12 *See Id.*
13 *See Id.* at 4.
14 *See Id.*
15 *See Id.*
16 *Id.*
17 *See Id.*
18 BLACK'S LAW DICTIONARY 291 (Bryan A. Garner ed., 4th ed. 2011). "On or from one party only, usu. without notice to or argument from the adverse party" (BLACK'S LAW DICTIONARY 291 (Bryan A. Garner ed., 4th ed., 2011)).
19 *See* Davenport, 2004-DR-1235 (2004) https://scorss.citrusclerk.org/case (last visited August 21, 2021).
20 *See Id.*
21 *See Id.*; Davenport, 2004-DR-1235 (2004) (Motion for Modification of Inj. for Prot. Against Dom. Viol.).
22 *See Id.*

23 *See* Davenport, 2004-DR-1235 (2004) https://scorss.citrusclerk.org/case (last visited August 21, 2021).
24 *See Id.*
25 *See* Ventimiglia, 2012-00137133 at 8.
26 *See Id.*
27 *See Id.*
28 *See Id.*
29 *See Id.*
30 *See Id.*
31 In this book, "domestic violence," "domestic abuse," "family violence," and "intimate partner violence" are used interchangeably but predominately as "intimate partner violence," unless otherwise indicated. Generally, DV is used to describe behavior between family members other than intimate partners whereas IPV is used, specifically, to describe behavior between intimate partners. *See infra* Chapter 1, Explaining the Inexplicable: The Difficulty in Defining "Intimate Partner Violence".
32 *See About Us*, ICCC, https://theccc.international/about-us/ (last visited Jan. 27, 2023).
33 *See Id.*
34 *See* R. Emerson Dobash et al., *Lethal and Nonlethal Violence Against an Intimate Female Partner: Comparing Male Murderers to Nonlethal Abusers*, 13 SAGE PUBLICATIONS 329 (2007) https://doi.org/10.1177%2F1077801207299204; JODY RAPHAEL, SAVING BERNICE: BATTERED WOMEN, WELFARE, AND POVERTY (2000); EVAN STARK, COERCIVE CONTROL: HOW MEN ENTRAP WOMEN IN PERSONAL LIFE (2007); SUSAN WEITZMAN, "NOT TO PEOPLE LIKE US:" HIDDEN ABUSE IN UPSCALE MARRIAGES (2000); Sandra Walklate & Anna Hopkins, *Real Lives and Lost Lives: Making Sense of 'Locked In' Responses to Intimate Partner Homicide*, 14 ASIAN JOURNAL OF CRIMINOLOGY 129 (2019) https://doi.org/10.1007/S11417-019-09283-2; Sarah Wydall & Rebecca Zerk, *"Listen to Me, His Behaviour is Erratic and I'm Really Worried for Our Safety ...,"* 21 CRIMINOLOGY AND CRIMINAL JUSTICE 1 (2020) https://doi.org/10.1177/1748895819898513.
35 CENTERS FOR DISEASE CONTROL AND PREVENTION, PREVENTING INTIMATE PARTNER VIOLENCE (2020), https://www.cdc.gov/violenceprevention/pdf/ipv/IPV-factsheet_2020_508.pdf. *See also* National Coalition Against Domestic Violence, *Domestic Violence* (2020) https://assets.speakcdn.com/assets/2497/domestic_violence-2020080709350855.pdf?1596828650457.
36 National Coalition Against Domestic Violence, *supra* note 35 at ¶ 4; *accord* CENTERS FOR DISEASE CONTROL AND PREVENTION, *supra* note 35.
37 *See* WALTER S. DEKESEREDY & MARTIN D. SCHWARTZ, DANGEROUS EXITS: ESCAPING ABUSIVE RELATIONSHIPS IN RURAL AMERICA (2009); R. Emerson Dobash & Russell P. Dobash, *What Were They Thinking?: Men Who Murder an Intimate Partner*, 17 VIOLENCE AGAINST WOMEN 111 (2011) https://doi.org/10.1177%2F1077801210391219; Joan B. Kelly & Michael P. Johnson, *Differentiation Among Types of Intimate Partner Violence: Research Update and Implications for Interventions*, 46 FAMILY COURT REVIEW 476 (2008) https://doi.org/10.1111/j.1744-1617.2008.00215.x; National Coalition Against Domestic Violence, *supra* note 35; Brynn E. Sheehan et al., *Intimate Partner Homicide: New Insights for Understanding Lethality and Risks*, 21 VIOLENCE AGAINST WOMEN 269 (2015) https://doi.org/10.1177%2F1077801214564687.

38 *See* DeKeseredy & Schwartz, *supra* note 37; Molly Dragiewicz, Equality with a Vengeance: Men's Rights Groups, Battered Women, and Antifeminist Backlash (2011); Mary Ann Dutton & Lisa A. Goodman, *Coercion in Intimate Partner Violence: Toward a New Conceptualization*, 52 Sex Roles 743 (2005) https://doi.org/10.1007/s11199-005-4196-6; Michael P. Johnson, *Langhinrichsen-Rolling's Confirmation of the Feminist Analysis of Intimate Partner Violence: Comment on "Controversies Involving Gender and Intimate Partner Violence in the United States,"* 62 Sex Roles 212 (2010) https://doi.org/10.1007/s11199-009-9697-2; Jennifer Langhinrichsen-Rohling, *Controversies Involving Gender and Intimate Partner Violence in the United States*, 62 Sex Roles 179 (2010) https://doi.org/10.1007/s11199-009-9628-2.
39 *See* Johnson, *supra* note 38; Langhinrichsen-Rohling, *supra* note 38.
40 *See* Johnson, *supra* note 38.
41 *Id.* at 213.
42 *See, e.g.,* Gretchen Arnold, *A Battered Women's Movement Perspective of Coercive Control*, 15 Violence Against Women 1432 (2009) https://doi.org/10.1177/1077801209346836; Dobash et al., *supra* note 34; Catherine Donovan & Rebecca Barnes, *Re-tangling the Concept of Coercive Control: A View from the Margins and a Response to Walby and Towers (2018)*, 21 Criminology & Criminal Justice 242 (2021) https://doi.org/10.1177/1748895819864622; David Hirschel & Eve Buzawa, *Understanding the Context of Dual Arrest with Directions for Future Research*, 8 Violence Against Women 1449 (2002) https://doi.org/10.1177%2F107780102237965; Johnson, *supra* note 38; Andy Myhill, *Measuring Coercive Control: What Can We Learn From National Population Surveys?*, 21 Violence Against Women 355 (2015) https://doi.org/10.1177%2F1077801214568032; Stark, *supra* note 34.
43 *See* Charlotte Barlow & Sandra Walklate, *Gender, Risk Assessment and Coercive Control: Contradictions in Terms?*, 61 Brit. J. Criminol. 887 (2021) https://doi.org/10.1093/bjc/azaa104.
44 *See* R. Emerson Dobash & Russell P. Dobash, When Men Murder Women (2015) https://doi.org/10.1093/acprof:oso/9780199914784.001.0001.
45 *See* Johnson, *supra* note 38.
46 *See* Donovan & Barnes, *supra* note 42. *See also* Gender Sexuality Resource Center, *LGBTQIA+ 101*, https://www.gsrc.princeton.edu/lgbtqia-101.
47 *See* Dragiewicz, *supra* note 38; Sheehan et al., *supra* note 37; Stark, *supra* note 34; Walklate & Hopkins, *supra* note 34.
48 *See, e.g.,* Arnold, *supra* note 42; Donna J. King, *Naming the Judicial Terrorist: An Exposé of an Abuser's Successful Use of a Judicial Proceeding for Continued Domestic Violence*, 1 Tenn. Journal of Race, Gender, & Social Justice 153 (2012); Stark, *supra* note 34.
49 *See* Clare Dalton & Elizabeth M. Schneider, Battered Women and the Law (2001).
50 *See, e.g.,* John R. Barner & Michelle M. Carney, *Interventions for Intimate Partner Violence: A Historical Review*, 26 J. Fam. Viol. 235 (2011); Dalton & Schneider, *supra* note 49.
51 *See* Barner & Carney, *supra* note 50.
52 *See Id.*
53 *See* Hirschel & Buzawa, *supra* note 42; Daniel P. Mears, *Research and Interventions to Reduce Domestic Violence Revictimization*, 4 Trauma, Violence & Abuse 127 (2003) https://doi.org/10.1177%2F1524838002250764; *Domestic Violence 101: How Should a Law Enforcement Agency Respond?*,

13 Dispatch 10 (2020); Stephanie Riger et al., *Measuring Interference with Employment and Education Reported by Women with Abusive Partners: Preliminary Data*, 15 Violence and Victims 2 (2000) https://doi.org/10.1891/0886-6708.15.2.161; Claire Wright, *Torture at Home: Borrowing from the Torture Convention to Define Domestic Violence*, 24 Hastings Women's L. J. 457 (2013).

54 E.g., Marilyn McMahon et al., *An Alternative Means of Prosecuting Non-Physical Domestic Abuse: Are Stalking Laws an Under-Utilised Resource?*, *in* Criminalising Coercive Control: Family Violence and the Criminal Law (Marilyn McMahon & Paul McGorrery eds., 2020) https://doi.org/10.1007/978-981-15-0653-6_5; Julia Quilter, *Evaluating Criminalisation as a Strategy in Relation to Non-Physical Family Violence*, *in* Criminalising Coercive Control: Family Violence and the Criminal Law (Marilyn McMahon & Paul McGorrery eds., 2020) https://doi.org/10.1007/978-981-15-0653-6_6; Kristy Candela, *Protecting the Invisible Victim: Incorporating Coercive Control in Domestic Violence Statutes*, 54 Family Court Review 112 (2016).

55 See Margaret E. Johnson, *Redefining Harm, Reimagining Remedies and Reclaiming Domestic Violence Law*, 42 U.C. Davis L. Rev. 1107 (2009); McMahon et al., *supra* note 54; Mears, *supra* note 53; Stark, *supra* note 34.

56 See Candela, *supra* note 54.

57 E.g., *Id.*; Quilter, *supra* note 54; Wright, *supra* note 53.

58 E.g., Candela, *supra* note 54; Quilter, *supra* note 54; Stark, *supra* note 34; Wright, *supra* note 53.

59 See Wright, *supra* note 53.

60 See McMahon et al., *supra* note 54; Wright, *supra* note 53.

61 Wright, *supra* note 53 at 465; *accord* Quilter, *supra* note 54.

62 See Candela, *supra* note 54; Stark, *supra* note 34; Wright, *supra* note 53.

63 See Wright, *supra* note 53; Mears, *supra* note 53; Quilter, *supra* note 54.

64 See *Coercive Control Codification Matrix*, Battered Women's Justice Project (2022) http://bwjp.org/wp-content/uploads/2022/08/CC_MATRIX.pdf.

65 See King, *supra* note 48; Stark, *supra* note 34.

66 See Mari L. Aldridge & Kevin D. Browne, *Perpetrators of Spousal Homicide: A Review*, 4 Trauma, Violence, & Abuse 265 (2003) https://journals.sagepub.com/doi/10.1177/1524838003004003005; Cynthia Grant Bowman et al., Feminist Jurisprudence: Cases and Materials (4th ed., 2011); Dobash & Dobash, *supra* note 44; R. Emerson Dobash et al., *"Out of the Blue:" Men Who Murder an Intimate Partner*, 4 Feminist Criminology 194 (2009) https://doi.org/10.1177/1557085109332668; Myhill, *supra* note 42; Kathryn E. Moracco et al., *Femicide in North Carolina, 1991–1993: A Statewide Study of Patterns and Precursors*, 2 Homicide Studies 422 (1998) https://doi.org/10.1177%2F1088767998002004005; Mary Jane Mossman, *Feminism and Legal Method: The Difference it Makes*, *in* At The Boundaries of Law: Feminism and Legal Theory (Martha Albertson Fineman & Nancy Sweet Thomadsen eds. (1991); Stark, *supra* note 34.

67 See Dobash & Dobash, *supra* note 44; Moracco et al., *supra* note 66; Stark, *supra* note 34. Contemporarily, battered woman's defense or battered woman syndrome (BWS) is a complex legal defense strategy that, along with expert testimony and possible diagnosis of posttraumatic stress disorder (PTSD), helps to explain why a woman might kill her intimate partner even when, to another reasonable person, there appeared to be no imminent threat of

physical harm at the time of the killing. See STARK, *supra* note 34; Jessica R. Holliday et al., *The Use of Battered Woman Syndrome in U.S. Criminal Courts*, 50 J. AM. ACAD. PSYCHIATRY LAW 1 (2022). DOI: 10.29158/JAAPL. 210105-21.

68 See, e.g., DOBASH & DOBASH, *supra* note 44; National Coalition Against Domestic Violence, *supra* note 35.

69 See Lisa A. Fontes, *Domestic Violence Isn't About Just Physical Violence – and State Laws are Beginning to Recognize That*, THE CONVERSATION (May 12, 2021).

70 See DOBASH & DOBASH, *supra* note 44; Moracco et al., *supra* note 66.

71 See DOBASH & DOBASH, *supra* note 44; Johnson, *supra* note 38; Moracco et al., *supra* note 66.

72 See Moracco et al., *supra* note 66; Walklate & Hopkins, *supra* note 34.

73 See Edem F. Avakame, *"Did You Call the Police? What Did They Do?:" An Empirical Assessment of Black's Theory of Mobilization of Law*, 16 JUSTICE QUARTERLY 765 (1999) https://doi.org/10.1080/07418829900094361; Kara Bellew, *Silent Suffering: Uncovering and Understanding Domestic Violence in Affluent Communities*, 26 WOMEN'S RIGHTS LAW REPORTER 39 (2005); Mears, *supra* note 53; Moracco et al., *supra* note 66.

74 See Avakame, *supra* note 73; Bellew, *supra* note 73; Mears, *supra* note 53; Moracco et al., *supra* note 66.

75 See Jacquelyn C. Campbell et al., *Intimate Partner Homicide: Review and Implications of Research and Policy*, 8 TRAUMA, VIOLENCE, & ABUSE 246 (2007) https://doi.org/10.1177%2F1524838007303505; Mears, *supra* note 53; Moracco et al., *supra* note 66; Nick Butto, *The Front and Back Eds of Domestic Violence Murder: An Exploration of the Avenues for Change and an Introduction of the Domestic Violence-Murder Doctrine*, 107 GEO. L. J. 457 (2019).

76 See Campbell et al., *supra* note 75; Lorena Garcia et al., *Homicides and Intimate Partner Violence: A Literature Review*, 8 TRAUMA, VIOLENCE, & ABUSE 370 (2007) https://doi.org/10.1177%2F1524838007307294; Nancy Glass et al., *Violence: Recognition, Management and Prevention: Non-fatal Strangulation is an Important Risk Factor for Homicide of Women*, 35 THE JOURNAL OF EMERGENCY MEDICINE 329 (2008) https://doi.org/10.1016/j.jemermed.2007.02.065; Hirschel & Buzawa, *supra* note 42; Judith M. McFarlane, *Stalking and Intimate Partner Femicide*, 3 HOMICIDE STUDIES 300 (1999) https://doi.org/10.1177%2F1088767999003004003; Mears, *supra* note 53; NATIONAL INSTITUTE OF JUSTICE, U.S. DEPARTMENT OF JUSTICE, QUESTIONS AND ANSWERS IN LETHAL AND NON-LETHAL VIOLENCE: PROCEEDINGS OF THE SECOND ANNUAL WORKSHOP OF THE HOMICIDE RESEARCH WORKING GROUP (1992).

77 See Bellew, *supra* note 73; Moracco et al., *supra* note 66; Sheehan et al., *supra* note 37; STARK, *supra* note 34; Susanne Lohmann et al., *The Trauma and Mental Health Impacts of Coercive Control: A Systematic Review and Meta-Analysis*, 0 TRAUMA, VIOLENCE & ABUSE 1 (2023) https://doi.org/10.1177/15248380231162972.

78 See Dobash et al., *supra* note 66 (discussing the fact that "the best predictor of subsequent intimate partner violence is general criminal recidivism"); Laurie M. Graham et al., *The Danger Assessment: An Instrument for the Prevention of Intimate Partner Homicide*, in HANDBOOK OF INTERPERSONAL VIOLENCE ACROSS THE LIFESPAN (R. Geffner et al. eds., 2019) https://doi.org/10.1007/978-3-319-62122-7_145-1; Hirschel & Buzawa, *supra* note 42;

Radha Iyengar, *Corrigendum to "Does the Certainty of Arrest Reduce Domestic Violence? Evidence from Mandatory and Recommended Arrest Laws" [JPubEc 93(1–2), pp. 85–89]*, 179 J. OF PUBLIC ECONOMICS 1 (2019) https://doi.org/10.1016/j.jpubeco.2019.104098; Andrew R. Klein, *Lethality Assessments and the Law Enforcement Response to Domestic Violence*, 12 J. OF POLICE CRISIS NEGOT. 87 (2012) https://doi.org/10.1080/15332586.2012.720175; N. Zoe Hilton et al., *An Indepth Actuarial Assessment for Wife Assault Recidivism: The Domestic Risk Appraisal Guide*, 32 LAW HUM. BEHAV. 150 (2008) https://doi.org/10.1007/s10979-007-9088-6.
79 *See* Klein, *supra* note 78.
80 *See* BOWMAN ET AL., *supra* note 66; Hirschel & Buzawa, *supra* note 42; Klein, *supra* note 78.
81 *See* BOWMAN ET AL., *supra* note 66; Hirschel & Buzawa, *supra* note 42; Klein, *supra* note 78.
82 *See* DOBASH & DOBASH, *supra* note 44; Sheehan et al., *supra* note 37; LENORE E. WALKER, THE BATTERED WOMAN (1979).
83 *See* Jacquelyn C. Campbell et al., *Risk Factors for Femicide in Abusive Relationships: Results From a Multisite Case Control Study*, 93 AMERICAN JOURNAL OF PUBLIC HEALTH 1089 (2003) https://doi.org/10.2105/AJPH.93.7.1089; Sheehan et al., *supra* note 37; Jill Theresa Messing et al., *The Arizona Intimate Partner Homicide (AzIPH) Study: A Step Toward Updating and Expanding Risk Factors for Intimate Partner Homicide*, 36 J. OF FAMILY VIOLENCE 563 (2021) https://link.springer.com/article/10.1007/s10896-021-00254-9.
84 *See* Myhill, *supra* note 42.
85 *See* Hirschel & Buzawa, *supra* note 42; STARK, *supra* note 34. *See also Coercive Control Codification Matrix*, *supra* note 64.
86 *See Coercive Control Codification Matrix*, *supra* note 64.
87 *See generally* DONALD BLACK, THE BEHAVIOR OF LAW: SPECIAL EDITION (2010).
88 *See* Bellew, *supra* note 73; DOBASH & DOBASH, *supra* note 44; Wydall & Zerk, *supra* note 34.
89 Johnson, *supra* note 38 at 216.
90 Wydall & Zerk, *supra* note 34 at 11.
91 *See* Carolyn Rebecca Block & Antigone Christakos, *Intimate Partner Homicide in Chicago Over 29 Years*, 41 CRIME & DELINQUENCY 496 (1995).
92 *See* Aldridge & Browne, *supra* note 66; DOBASH & DOBASH, *supra* note 44. Although much work still needs to be done, since the time of completion of this study, there has been a positive shift toward academic research and broader acknowledgement of the non-violent aspects of abuse and its harms, including adding to the research base of coercive control.
93 *See* Hirschel & Buzawa, *supra* note 42; Messing et al., *supra* note 83.
94 *See* Viveka Enander et al., *Before the Killing: Intimate Partner Homicides in a Process Perspective, Part I*, 5 J. OF GENDER-BASED VIOLENCE 59 (2021) https://doi.org/10.1332/239868020X15922355479497; Jacqueline Harden et al., *Examining Attempted and Completed Intimate Partner Homicide: A Qualitative Synthesis*, 34 VIOLENCE AND VICTIMS 869 (2019) https://doi.org/10.1891/0886-6708.vv-d-18-00128; Jennifer Chopra et al., *Risk Factors for Intimate Partner Homicide in England and Wales*, 30 HEALTH AND SOCIAL CARE COMMUNITY E3086 (2022) https://doi.org/10.1111/hsc.13753.
95 *See* Dee-Dee Kanhai, *Not All Bills are Created Equal: A Review of Coercive Control Legislation*, ACECC (Nov. 13, 2020).

96 *See* Kristin L. Anderson, *Gendering Coercive Control*, 15 VIOLENCE AGAINST WOMEN 1444 (2009) https://doi.org/10.1177/1077801209346837; Arnold, *supra* note 42; Cheryl Hanna, *The Paradox of Progress: Translating Evan Stark's Coercive Control Into Legal Doctrine for Abused Women*, 15 VIOLENCE AGAINST WOMEN 1458 (2009) https://doi.org/10.1177%2F1077801209347091; Evan Stark, *Re-Presenting Women Battering: From Battered Woman Syndrome to Coercive Control*, 58 ALB. L. REV. 973 (1995); STARK, *supra* note 34; Evan Stark, *Rethinking Coercive Control*, 15 VIOLENCE AGAINST WOMEN 1509 (2009) https://doi.org/10.1177/1077801209347452.
97 *See* NEIL WEBSDALE, FAMILICIDAL HEARTS: THE EMOTIONAL STYLES OF 211 KILLERS (2010) https://doi.org/10.1093/acprof:oso/9780195315417.001.0001.
98 *See Id.*
99 *See* DOBASH & DOBASH, *supra* note 44.
100 *See Id.*
101 *See* Faces of Fatality, *Report of the Attorney General's Statewide Domestic Violence Fatality Review Team* (2019) https://www2.myflfamilies.com/service-programs/domestic-violence/docs/FACES%20OF%20FATALITY%20IX.pdf. *See also* About NDVFRI, *The National Domestic Violence Fatality Review Initiative*, NDVFRI https://ndvfri.org/about/ (last visited June 14, 2023).
102 Faces of Fatality, *supra* note 101.
103 *See Id.*
104 *See Id.*
105 *See Id.*
106 *See Id.*
107 Shilan Caman et al., *Trends in Rates and Characteristics of Intimate Partner Homicides Between 1990 and 2013*, 49 J. OF CRIMINAL JUSTICE 14, 19 (2017) https://doi.org/10.1016/j.jcrimjus.2017.01.002.

Part I
The Gender Identity of Coercive Control

This part addresses the gendered world of intimate partner violence (IPV) and the difficulty in defining it, legislating against it, and working to regulate acts of abuse that are non-violent in nature, such as the non-violent tactics of coercive control. The Domestic Abuse Intervention Program's Power and Control Wheel and The Maze of Coercive Control: The (New!) Recreated Power & Control Wheel are introduced as visual tools for understanding IPV and coercive control. In this part, coercive control is introduced, and its eight themes and twenty-seven subthemes, derived from this study, are thoroughly presented and explained. The IPV victim's perspective is provided to help explain the difficult decision-making process that one goes through in determining whether to leave an abusive intimate partner relationship, as well as whether to file for an injunction for protection. The effectiveness of the injunction for protection process is discussed, as well as gender bias in the courts. The concept of judicial terrorism® is introduced to ensure that it is understood that the non-violent tactics of coercive control are able to be effectively deployed in a judicial proceeding.

1 Women's Rights, Domestic Violence, and Intimate Partner Violence

Explaining the Inexplicable: The Difficulty in Defining "Intimate Partner Violence"

Defining "intimate partner violence" (IPV) is a daunting task; and there is little agreement among scholars and legislators in doing so, making consistency and comparisons across policies and evaluations extremely difficult.[1] It is a process that begins with a subjective viewpoint but ends with an objective description of an act by one person against another who, in the case of IPV, were intimate with each other, presumably without violence or any other form of abuse.[2] But often, even intimacy becomes terrifying or violent; and the need to comprehensively define the cornucopia of behaviors that encompass IPV is needed.[3] One reason for the inconsistency in defining IPV is due to the perceived reason for the definition, whether social or legal.[4] Depending on the purpose for which the IPV definition is used and for which governing body, organization, or entity throughout the world the definition is provided, legally, it is meant to recognize and prosecute IPV, as well as to protect its victims.[5]

During the 1970s and 1980s, as domestic violence (DV) research and battered women's shelters helped to change society's perspective regarding the fact that DV offenders should be held criminally liable for their actions rather than believing that DV was a private family matter where men were entitled to physically dominate their household, it became more understood that DV is the result of a manifestation of societal power differentials between men and women.[6] This new perspective required new ways of describing the behaviors, not just physical violence, that manifest the gender imbalance between men and women, requiring more terminology for DV other than simply "domestic violence."[7] The type of intimate violence that refers to society's gender imbalance and patriarchal values where it is generally acceptable for men to physically dominate women and subjugate them in other ways is referred to as IPV.[8] Thus, DV has taken on a more nuanced perspective for legal purposes where it often refers to violence among the

DOI: 10.4324/9781003097488-3

entire family as opposed to just intimate partners.[9] IPV is understood to refer to only those people who engage in intimate relationships; thus, the term "intimate partner violence."[10]

Most commonly utilized IPV definitions include physical acts of violence without the inclusion of other non-violent tactics of abuse.[11] One of the reasons for this overuse of the physical violence definition is the fact that the most understood form of IPV is situational couple violence, which typically manifests in the form of physical violence and does not continue beyond a single, isolated incident.[12] Yet, IPV is understood as a pattern of coercive control that often does not include physical harm.[13] Academics, such as Lininger (2009) and Sev'er (1997), utilize the term "violence" as an incorporation of intentional physical acts of violence against the body, as well as controlling and degrading behavior against a woman's personhood, including her psychological well-being.[14] And in its 1994 Declaration on the Elimination of Violence against Women, the United Nations provides a comprehensive definition of "violence against women," which includes "coercion or arbitrary deprivation of liberty" and "results in, or is likely to result in ... suffering to women."[15] What is more, when politics play a role in defining such terms, the chances of success of being able to broaden the definitions seem to be less likely. For example, the Trump Administration removed elements of coercive control that were previously included by the Obama Administration in its definition of domestic abuse.[16] Under the Trump Administration, the definition had wording that specifically limited the definition to "harms that constitute a felony or misdemeanor crime," harkening back to those discrete acts of physical violence.[17]

Now, under the Biden Administration, the Office of Violence Against Women at the United States Department of Justice's (OVW's) definition of DV is broader than ever, including "a pattern of abusive behavior ... to gain or maintain power and control over another intimate partner."[18] It continues to define the term as being "physical, sexual, emotional, economic, psychological, or technological actions or threats of actions or other patterns of coercive behavior that influence another person within an intimate partner relationship. This includes any behaviors that intimidate, manipulate, humiliate, isolate, frighten, terrorize, coerce, threaten, blame, hurt, injure, or wound."[19] Indeed, at the federal level, for anyone who may look to the OVW for guidance, this definition is comprehensive and instructive. Nevertheless, DV experts detail the fact that most state laws within the jurisdiction of the United States define DV very narrowly, excluding coercive control and its non-violent tactics; and many state laws are doing an inadequate job of protecting victims of IPV given its prevalence.[20]

Gender and Intimate Partner Violence: Legislating against Patriarchal Violence

The Women's Rights Movement of the 1960s and 1970s ushered in the DV Revolution.[21] Within the argument for women's civil rights, there exists an assertion for greater regulation and enforcement against IPV because of its "political, social, cultural, and structural context."[22] It was within this context that Lenore E. Walker (1979) developed the ground-breaking concept of "The Cycle Theory of Violence."[23] Walker (1979) explains that IPV moves through stages called the tension-building stage, when minor battering incidents occur, to the acute battering incident, whereby the tension-building incidents become more frequent and out of control to the point that the batterer and the victim are no longer able to prolong the inevitability of a major battering incident.[24] The final stage identified by Walker (1979) is the kindness and contrite loving behavior stage when the battered woman's victimization becomes complete through the batterer's cries for forgiveness and promises of changed behavior.[25]

Then, in 1984, the Domestic Abuse Intervention Project developed the Power and Control Wheel to describe women's experiences in abusive relationships.[26] Battering, as they argued, was just one form of IPV.[27] The pattern of actions is one that involves intentional control of the intimate partner.[28] Thus, the Power and Control Wheel includes coercion and threats, intimidation, emotional abuse, isolation, and economic abuse in its list of forms of abuse.[29] When looking at the wheel, it is meant to be interpreted from the outside in, with physical violence and sexual violence as the ultimate driving force holding the wheel together, meaning "this violence is the rim of the wheel." "'[P]ower and control' are in the center of the wheel. A batterer systematically uses threats, intimidation, and coercion to instill fear in his partner. These behaviors are the spokes of the wheel."[30] Now, the Power and Control Wheel is one of the most widely used and well-known visual tools to help describe the dynamics of DV (Figure 1.1).

Later, in 2011, the Maze of Coercive Control was created by Kathy Jones to depict the complexities of coercive control that are not adequately conveyed through the original Power and Control Wheel (Figure 1.2).[31] In order to focus on the non-physical violence aspects of abuse a victim endures, Jones created her Maze as a visual tool "that demonstrate[s] ... abuse is more than physical."[32] Indeed, as a visual tool, the Maze of Coercive Control is one of the best aids to succinctly show the chaos an IPV victim deals with when coercive control enters their life on an everyday basis. She took care to include many of the facets of an IPV victim's life that are encompassed by coercive control so that those who have not experienced it would understand or imagine it, including medical neglect, spiritual conflict, and legal harassment.[33] As Jones (2023) explains, "The wheel is confusing and

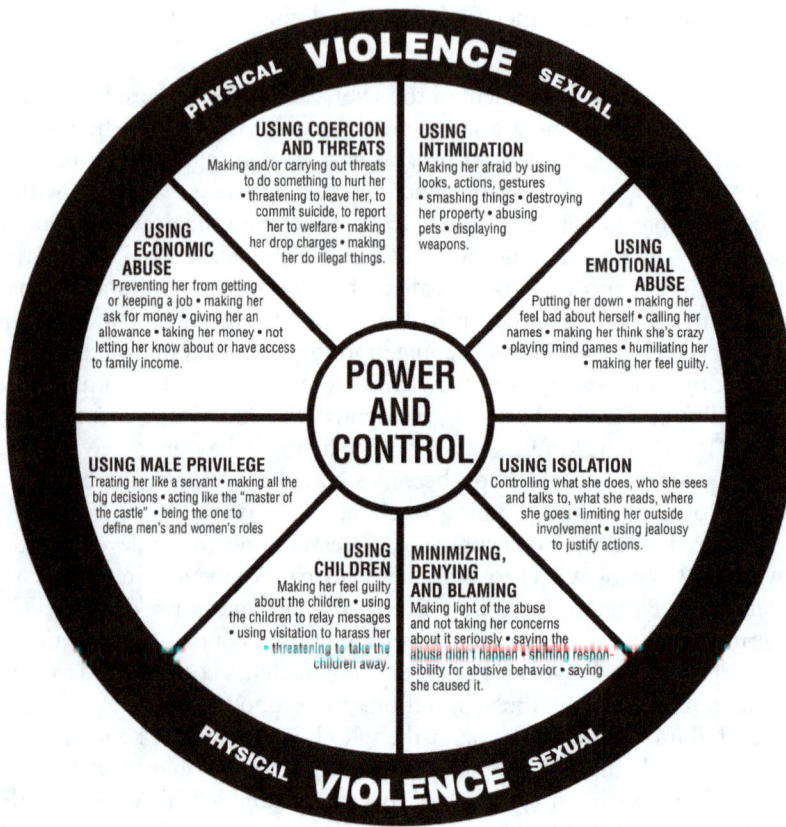

Figure 1.1 The Domestic Abuse Intervention Program's Power and Control Wheel

overwhelming to look at, but that's the point: if it is confusing and overwhelming for people with no traumatic experience to wade through, how much more intimidating must all of this be for victim/survivors?"[34]

To successfully legislate against DV, society and the law must adequately recognize and identify all forms of IPV.[35] The continuum of abuse that includes all forms of coercive control should be properly regulated and enforced. To do so, state laws should encompass the broad spectrum of coercive control tactics in their regulation. To accomplish this, legislators must understand the lack of enforcement against all forms of IPV, including

Women's Rights and Gender Violence   25

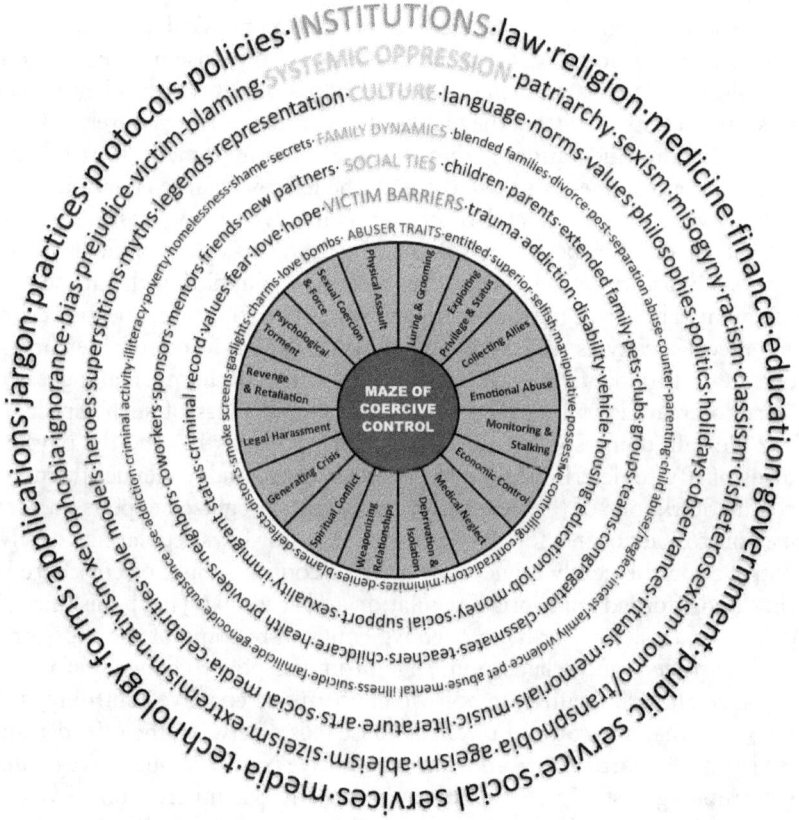

Figure 1.2 The Maze of Coercive Control: The (New!) Recreated Power & Control Wheel

abuse without physical violence, which causes victims to be at risk of great harm by their abuser, including, but not limited to, death.[36] However, it is important to recognize that lawmakers and the public for whom they serve, generally, lack an understanding of the dynamics of an intimate relationship that involves abuse, let alone one that only encompasses the non-violent tactics of coercive control. Thus, advocating for legislation to help improve protections for an IPV victim for all forms of abuse is imperative, especially when no physical violence or threat thereof is present, to prevent both those intimate partner homicides (IPHs) that have prior reported physical violence and those IPHs without a prior record of reported physical violence.

Very few laws focus on the broad range of continuous abusive behaviors that allow IPV to manifest into a woman's loss of self-worth, identity, and physical integrity.[37] Indeed, the tactics of coercive control are rarely simplistic in their implementation, making them even more difficult to regulate.[38] Coercive control does not comport with the narrow characterization of the physical violence of IPV and those harms involved.[39] Experts understand that the motivation behind IPV is multifaceted, making it difficult to unequivocally ascertain the abuser's intention for committing the abuse.[40] In fact, many scholars argue that coercive control is a political crime, or a crime that affects society as well as the individual.[41] Similar to political terrorism, coercive control deprives its victims of liberty and autonomy, making it necessary to create laws that consider an IPV victim's loss of such aspects of their life.[42] In doing so, it requires law makers to look beyond the physical harms of IPV to determine how to decontextualize and de-gender them.[43]

Evan Stark, one of the best-known and most recognized experts on coercive control, advocates for the implementation of laws regulating coercive control and vehemently argues that coercive control should be considered a crime and afforded appropriate regulation and accompanying punishment.[44] Because of this, his works on coercive control are some of the most analyzed, criticized, and relied upon.[45] He promotes policy change that would recognize and criminalize the non-violent forms of coercive control regardless of whether any form of physical abuse exists between the offender and his victim.[46] In particular, Stark believes coercive control should be regulated as a crime against a person's liberty because its victims remain in virtual prisons while under their abusers' control.[47] In fact, he was instrumental in providing expertise in the United Kingdom in their effort toward criminalizing coercive control, something that has been in place since 2015.[48]

Tuerkheimer (2004) supports Stark's assertions by stating that criminal statutes throughout the United States "are inapt and require an overhaul to capture the practice of domestic violence."[49] She asserts that victims' accounts of the battering they survive are not included in existing legal and extralegal structures.[50] Tuerkheimer (2004) explains that women's accounts of abuse are the most accurate form of evidence in determining the forms of DV that should be regulated.[51] In fact, both Stark and Tuerkheimer developed their views because of the patterns of abusive behavior they began to understand from their abused female clients who repeatedly described similar accounts of the violence they endured and escaped.[52] These are the ongoing patterns of abusive behavior that criminal law does not consider in its regulation and punishment for the perpetration of DV.

Hanna (2009) is one of Stark's toughest critics.[53] She argues that it is difficult to convert the results of social science research, such as that of coercive control, into legal doctrine.[54] She explains that social theory does not always transform directly into legal practice.[55] Hanna (2009) explains that, theoretically, expanding DV laws to include coercive control and its non-violent tactics might provide better safeguards for women who are disqualified from legal protection from their abusers because their abuse does not fit the category of physical violence.[56] However, she explains that separating situational couple violence from coercive control may be very difficult for law enforcement and the criminal justice system.[57] Hanna (2009) comprehensively critiques Stark's (2007) advocacy for new coercive control laws, which are presented in his book, "Coercive Control: How Men Entrap Women in Personal Life."[58] Also, Hanna (2009) does not agree with Stark's (2007) belief that victims will readily testify against their abusers, which is necessary to provide the detailed evidence of the unique techniques utilized in coercive control's non-violent tactics.[59] Without such testimony, Hanna (2009) asserts it is nearly impossible to obtain convictions of abusers who exclusively employ coercive control's non-violent tactics.[60]

Hanna (2009) raises valid points about the potential difficulties in prosecuting coercive control, including the expense of providing expert witnesses to help explain its dynamics.[61] However, she does not offer solutions for working with victims to encourage them to testify or to curtail expert witness expenses.[62] Nevertheless, she definitively agrees that coercive control poses societal and political challenges as a crime against women's freedom and autonomy.[63] Hanna (2009) also acknowledges that coercive control denies women full equality and citizenship but suggests that laws regulating it may cause more problems for its victims than the number of issues they resolve.[64] She believes Stark's (2007) advocacy for new laws governing coercive control is both optimistic and naïve by not accounting for the realistic difficulty in prosecuting such crimes.[65]

But does difficulty proving a crime make it any less of a crime?[66] Absolutely not. Should society turn its back on victims who may be at risk of death simply because prosecuting the crimes perpetrated against them is *inconvenient*?

Instead of ignoring coercive control victims, more stringent laws that include coercive control regulation, especially for the non-violent tactics of coercive control, need to be developed. Law enforcement needs to respond with arrests for IPV violations that include actions without physical violence, and prosecutors need to prosecute cases that have the evidence to support convictions against IPV abusers. There is a multitude of academic literature supporting the notion that prior physical violence, or a tendency thereto, between intimate partners is one of the best indicators that IPH may take place; however, the unresolved proposition of protecting victims of IPV from the non-violent tactics of coercive control has left a chasm to fill the empirical literature.[67]

The Gender Asymmetry of Coercive Control

The type of abuse women experience from men who assert their patriarchal privileges with which coercive control is identified is particularly gender-asymmetrical, meaning it is not experienced in a similar manner by both genders.[68] The concept of gender symmetry and violence in intimate partner relationships is one that has been debated for several decades.[69] However, recently, theorists and researchers have attempted to find common collective ground.

Dragiewicz (2011) explains that abusers utilize patriarchal gender norms to justify their IPV.[70] She also asserts that such norms are important for society's general acceptance of violence against women.[71] Masculinity is usually associated with violence because men use it in their day-to-day lives more than women; thus, their violence against women is sewn into the fabric of American life, making it explicitly condoned or generally ignored.[72] Other authors, such as Berns (2004), suggest that the media is largely responsible for society's ambivalence and indignation toward IPV.[73] In fact, Waller (2010) points out that the mainstream media turns a blind eye on the every-day abuses women face, allowing such disgraces as IPV to go unchecked not only by law enforcement and the courts but by society at large.[74] Waller (2010) explains that some stories are simply too dark and too extreme for the media to cover because the public will not be interested in these types of IPV stories.[75]

Dutton and Goodman (2005) explain how some studies argue that IPV is a gender symmetrical offense, meaning that men are victims of violence perpetrated by women offenders just as often as women experience violence inflicted by men.[76] However, there is a recognition that IPV should be broken down into different typologies; and when discussing gender symmetry, violence is the measurement between the man and the woman in the intimate relationship.[77] Indeed, Dutton and Goodman (2005) explain that, because violence has historically been the measurement in most IPV studies, it is difficult to come to a consensus on the gender debate due to the fact that IPV is so much more complex than violent acts alone.[78] Generally, it is recognized that the type of IPV most closely associated with coercive control is gender asymmetrical and is usually perpetrated by the male in the relationship.[79] Additionally, because gender symmetry is measured by violence, the typology most generally known as situational couple violence is recognized more as one that is gender symmetrical because men and women do engage in violence perpetration.[80]

Coercive control does not focus on *actual* violence for its effectiveness; thus, whether physical violence between the couple is reported is not relevant to the existence of IPV between the couple.[81] However, because coercive control is usually perpetrated by men in heterosexual relationships, it is important to consider the violence a woman may use in resistance to her abuser's violence.[82] Kelly and Johnson (2008) term this type of violence by women "Violent Resistance" and make it clear that they do not classify similarly to the legal term of art definition of "self-defense," even though the two terms may have similarities.[83] Violent resistance is any type of violence a woman uses "as an immediate reaction to an assault and that is intended primarily to protect oneself or others from injury," which does correspond to the layperson's understanding of self-defense.[84] IPV victims who employ this type of resistance to abuse may feel empowered and decide to separate from their abuser once they begin to resist coercive control, or they may determine that it worsens their situation.[85] Thus, resistance to abuse, whether violent or not, is a personal choice the coercive control victim must navigate while ensuring their and their children's safety.

Notes

1 *See* David Hirschel & Eve Buzawa, *Understanding the Context of Dual Arrest with Directions for Future Research*, 8 VIOLENCE AGAINST WOMEN 1449 (2002) https://doi.org/10.1177%2F107780102237965; Daniel P. Mears, *Research and Interventions to Reduce Domestic Violence Revictimization*, 4 TRAUMA, VIOLENCE & ABUSE 127 (2003) https://doi.org/10.1177%2F1524838002250764; Stephanie Riger et al., *Measuring Interference with Employment and Education Reported by Women with Abusive Partners: Preliminary Data*, 15 VIOLENCE AND VICTIMS 2 (2000) https://doi.org/10.1891/0886-6708.15.2.161.
2 *See* Hirschel & Buzawa, *supra* note 1; Mears, *supra* note 1; Riger et al., *supra* note 1.
3 *See* Hirschel & Buzawa, *supra* note 1; Mears, *supra* note 1; Riger et al., *supra* note 1.
4 *See* Mears, *supra* note 1.
5 *See* Hirschel & Buzawa, *supra* note 1; Mears, *supra* note 1; Riger et al., *supra* note 1.
6 *See* Mears, *supra* note 1; EVAN STARK, COERCIVE CONTROL: HOW MEN ENTRAP WOMEN IN PERSONAL LIFE (2007).
7 Mears, *supra* note 1 at 129; *accord* STARK, *supra* note 6.
8 *See* Mears, *supra* note 1.
9 *See Id.*
10 *Id.* at 129–30. This explanation is for definitional purposes only. To reiterate, in this book, "domestic violence," "domestic abuse," "family violence," and "intimate partner violence" are used interchangeably unless otherwise indicated.
11 *See* Hirschel & Buzawa, *supra* note 1; Mears, *supra* note 1; Riger et al., *supra* note 1; STARK, *supra* note 6; Deborah Tuerkheimer, *Recognizing and Remedying the Harm of Battering: A Call to Criminalize Domestic Violence*, 94 THE JOURNAL OF CRIMINAL LAW & CRIMINOLOGY 959 (2004).
12 *See* Michael P. Johnson, *Langhinrichsen-Rolling's Confirmation of the Feminist Analysis of Intimate Partner Violence: Comment on "Controversies Involving Gender and Intimate Partner Violence in the United States,"* 62 SEX ROLES 212 (2010) https://doi.org/10.1007/s11199-009-9697-2; Claire Wright, *Torture at Home: Borrowing from the Torture Convention to Define Domestic Violence*, 24 HASTINGS WOMEN'S L. J. 457 (2013).

13 *See* Mary Ann Dutton & Lisa A. Goodman, *Coercion in Intimate Partner Violence: Toward a New Conceptualization*, 52 SEX ROLES 743 (2005) https://doi.org/10.1007/s11199-005-4196-6; STARK, *supra* note 6.
14 *See* Tom Lininger, *The Sound of Silence: Holding Batterers Accountable for Silencing Their Victims*, 87 TEXAS LAW REVIEW 857 (2009); Aysan Sev'er, *Recent or Imminent Separation and Intimate Violence Against Women: A Conceptual Overview and Some Canadian Examples*, 3 VIOLENCE AGAINST WOMEN 566 (1997) https://doi.org/10.1177/1077801297003006002.
15 G.A. Res. 48/104, Declaration on the Elimination of Violence against Women, at 3 (Feb. 23, 1994).
16 *See* Ciara Nugent, *"Abuse is a Pattern:" Why These Nations Took the Lead in Criminalizing Controlling Behavior in Relationships*, TIME (June 21, 2019).
17 Natalie Nanasi, *The Trump Administration Quietly Changed the Definition of Domestic Violence and We Have No Idea What For*, SLATE ¶ 2 (Jan. 21, 2019); *accord* Nugent, *supra* note 16.
18 Office on Violence Against Women, *Domestic Violence*, U.S. DOJ ¶ 1 https://www.justice.gov/ovw/domestic-violence (last visited June 5, 2023).
19 *Id.*
20 *See* Courtney K. Cross, *Coercive Control and the Limits of Criminal Law*, 56 U. OF CALIFORNIA, DAVIS 195 (2022); Melanie Kalmanson, *Filling the Gap of Domestic Violence Protection" Returning Human Rights to U.S. Victims*, 43 FLA. ST. U. L. REV. 1359 (2107); Lininger, *supra* note 14.
21 *See* JODY RAPHAEL, SAVING BERNICE: BATTERED WOMEN, WELFARE, AND POVERTY (2000); STARK, *supra* note 6.
22 NANCY BERNS, FRAMING THE VICTIM: DOMESTIC VIOLENCE MEDIA AND SOCIAL PROBLEMS 133 (2004).
23 LENORE E. WALKER, THE BATTERED WOMAN 55 (1979).
24 *See Id.*
25 *See Id.*
26 *See Understanding the Power and Control Wheel*, DOMESTIC ABUSE INTERVENTION PROGRAMS, https://www.theduluthmodel.org/wheels/faqs-about-the-wheels/ (last visited June 5, 2023).
27 *See Id.*
28 *See Id.*
29 *See Power and Control Wheel*, DOMESTIC ABUSE INTERVENTION PROGRAMS, https://www.theduluthmodel.org/wp-content/uploads/2017/03/PowerandControl.pdf; *Understanding the Power and Control Wheel*, *supra* note 26.
30 *See Understanding the Power and Control Wheel*, *supra* note 26.
31 *See* Kathy Jones, *The Maze of Coercive Control: The Power & Control Wheel "Grows Up,"* MOTHER JUSTICE NETWORK, https://motherjusticenetwork.org/maze/ (last visited June 5, 2023).
32 *Id.* at ¶ 3.
33 *See Id.*
34 *Id.* at ¶ 15.
35 *See* WALTER S. DEKESEREDY & MARTIN D. SCHWARTZ, DANGEROUS EXITS: ESCAPING ABUSIVE RELATIONSHIPS IN RURAL AMERICA (2009); STARK, *supra* note 6.
36 *See* BERNS, *supra* note 22; STARK, *supra* note 6.
37 *See* Cheryl Hanna, *The Paradox of Progress: Translating Evan Stark's Coercive Control Into Legal Doctrine for Abused Women*, 15 VIOLENCE AGAINST WOMEN 1458 (2009) https://doi.org/10.1177%2F1077801209347091; STARK, *supra* note 6.

38 *See* Gretchen Arnold, *A Battered Women's Movement Perspective of Coercive Control*, 15 VIOLENCE AGAINST WOMEN 1432 (2009) https://doi.org/10.1177/1077801209346836; Hanna, *supra* note 37.
39 *See* Tuerkheimer, *supra* note 11.
40 *See* Lininger, *supra* note 14.
41 *See* Hanna, *supra* note 37; Donna J. King, *Naming the Judicial Terrorist: An Exposé of an Abuser's Successful Use of a Judicial Proceeding for Continued Domestic Violence*, 1 TENN. JOURNAL OF RACE, GENDER, & SOCIAL JUSTICE 153 (2012); STARK, *supra* note 6.
42 *See* Hanna, *supra* note 37; King, *supra* note 41; STARK, *supra* note 6.
43 *See* Molly Dragiewicz, *A Left Realist Approach to Antifeminist Fathers' Rights Groups*, 54 CRIME LAW SOC. CHANGE 197 (2010) https://doi.org/10.1007/s10611-010-9253-6.
44 *See* Evan Stark, *Re-Presenting Women Battering: From Battered Woman Syndrome to Coercive Control*, 58 ALB. L. REV. 973 (1995); STARK, *supra* note 6; Evan Stark, *Rethinking Coercive Control*, 15 VIOLENCE AGAINST WOMEN 1509 (2009) https://doi.org/10.1177/1077801209347452.
45 *See* Kristin L. Anderson, *Gendering Coercive Control*, 15 VIOLENCE AGAINST WOMEN 1444 (2009) https://doi.org/10.1177/1077801209346837; Arnold, *supra* note 38; Hanna, *supra* note 37; Kathryn Libal & Serena Parekh, *Reframing Violence Against Women as a Human Rights Violation: Evan Stark's Coercive Control*, 15 Violence Against Women 1477 (2009) https://doi.org/10.1177/1077801209346958.
46 *See* Stark, *supra* note 44, *Re-Presenting*; STARK, *supra* note 6; Stark, *supra* note 44, *Rethinking*.
47 *See* Stark, *supra* note 44, *Re-Presenting*; STARK, *supra* note 6; Stark, *supra* note 44, *Rethinking*.
48 *See* Nugent, *supra* note 16.
49 Tuerkheimer, *supra* note 11 at 961.
50 *See Id.*
51 *See Id.*
52 *See* STARK, *supra* note 6; Tuerkheimer, *supra* note 11.
53 *See* Hanna, *supra* note 37.
54 *See Id.*
55 *See Id.*
56 *See Id.*
57 *See Id.*
58 *See Id. See also* STARK, *supra* note 6.
59 *See* Hanna, *supra* note 37. *See also* STARK, *supra* note 6.
60 *See* Hanna, *supra* note 37.
61 *See Id.*
62 *See Id.*
63 *See Id.*
64 *See Id.*
65 *See Id. See also* STARK, *supra* note 6.
66 *See* Kalmanson, *supra* note 20.
67 *See* Joanna Birenbaum & Isabel Grant, *Taking Threats Seriously: Section 264.1 and Threats as a Form of Domestic Violence*, 59 CRIMINAL LAW QUARTERLY 1 (2013); NATIONAL INSTITUTE OF JUSTICE, U.S. DEPARTMENT OF JUSTICE, QUESTIONS AND ANSWERS IN LETHAL AND NON-LETHAL VIOLENCE: PROCEEDINGS OF THE SECOND ANNUAL WORKSHOP OF THE HOMICIDE RESEARCH WORKING GROUP (1992).

68 *See* DeKeseredy & Schwartz, *supra* note 35; Molly Dragiewicz, Equality with a Vengeance: Men's Rights Groups, Battered Women, and Antifeminist Backlash (2011); Johnson, *supra* note 12; Jennifer Langhinrichsen-Rohling, *Controversies Involving Gender and Intimate Partner Violence in the United States*, 62 Sex Roles 179 (2010) https://link.springer.com/article/10.1007/s11199-009-9628-2.
69 *See* Joan B. Kelly & Michael P. Johnson, *Differentiation Among Types of Intimate Partner Violence: Research Update and Implications for Interventions*, 46 Family Court Review 476 (2008) https://doi.org/10.1111/j.1744-1617.2008.00215.x.
70 *See* Dragiewicz, *supra* note 68.
71 *See Id.*
72 *See Id.*
73 *See* Berns, *supra* note 22.
74 *See* Garland Waller, *The Yuck Factor, the Oprah Factor, and the "Stickiness" Factor: Why the Mainstream Media Has Failed to Expose the Custody Court Scandal, in* Domestic Violence, Abuse, and Child Custody: Legal Strategies and Policy Issues (Mo Therese Hannah & Barry Goldstein eds., 2010).
75 *See Id.*
76 *See* Dutton & Goodman, *supra* note 13.
77 *See Id.*; Johnson, *supra* note 12; Kelly & Johnson, *supra* note 69; Langhinrichsen-Rohling, *supra* note 68.
78 *See* Dutton & Goodman, *supra* note 13.
79 *See Id.*; Johnson, *supra* note 12; Kelly & Johnson, *supra* note 69; Langhinrichsen-Rohling, *supra* note 68.
80 *See* Johnson, *supra* note 12. The terminology of "violence perpetration" is very important to the overall conclusion that situational couple violence is gender symmetrical due to the fact that both men and women have been measured "on a ridiculously narrow definition of symmetry in terms of incidence/prevalence." In studies that determine gender symmetry, men and women have acknowledged having engaged in at least one act of violence based on the survey used, no matter the outcome of that violence. However, studies using agency samples, i.e., those stemming from law enforcement, courts, hospitals, and shelters, result in gender asymmetry. (Johnson, *supra* note 12.)
81 *See* Dutton & Goodman, *supra* note 13.
82 *See* Kelly & Johnson, *supra* note 69.
83 *Id.* at 484.
84 *Id.*
85 *See Id.*

2 Not All Intimate Partner Violence Is Created Equal

To work toward providing improved protections for all intimate partner violence (IPV) victims, this empirical research study contributes to the understanding of how devastating and deadly coercive control can be in an intimate partner relationship. It presents first-hand knowledge and insight into the experiences of the IPV victim, including those who experience the non-violent tactics of coercive control without physical violence prior to the killing.

> Traditionally, police and prosecutors do not consider a crime "serious until there is a felony, a dead body, or blood and guts." Domestic violence, however, often defies such stereotyping. Sophisticated abusers can inflict incredible violence without leaving any physical marks and yet the vast majority of domestic violence cases end up being categorized as misdemeanors. It is a tragic mistake to assume these cases are therefore insignificant.[1]

Although Gwinn and O'Dell (1992) were referring to misdemeanor domestic violence (DV) crimes that do not leave physical marks and law enforcement did not consider as significant, their statement above is a foreshadowing for intimate partner homicide (IPH) victims who were victims of coercive control where no physical violence was present.[2] Indeed, law enforcement resources are generally spent on major crimes such as homicides.[3] Domestic disputes are considered run-of-the-mill type calls for law enforcement officers, which do not fall under major crimes for responding officers.[4] But, as Gwinn and O'Dell explain, DV defies the stereotyping of typical crimes and should be considered as major crimes; thus, it is important to remember that a seemingly run-of-the-mill DV type call can turn tragic at any moment.[5] In fact, it is quite possible for a domestic dispute call to turn deadly for the IPV victim as they are dialing 911, while law enforcement is en route to the location of the 911 call, or while the offender of an IPH engages law enforcement.[6]

DOI: 10.4324/9781003097488-4

Coercive Control's Impact on the Intimate Partner Violence Victim

Coercive control is the most destructive and widespread form of IPV in the United States, as well as throughout the world.[7] It relies on society's gender imbalances and subordination of its victim for its ongoing success.[8] Without structured gender inequalities throughout society, coercive control would not be as effective in today's patriarchal world.[9] Yet, many of its victims *do not realize they are victims* because coercive control does not require physical violence for its effectiveness.[10] This lack of awareness of being a victim of IPV generally stems from the belief that one must be subjected to physical violence in order to qualify as an IPV victim. Its victims live in a virtual prison that is often not apparent to them or other close family and friends. Coercive control's non-violent tactics, imposed by the IPV abuser against the victim, are primarily comprised of intimidation, isolation, humiliation, and power and control.[11] For those who do recognize they may be one of its victims, they understand they are living in a world where these intangible forms of abuse are generally misunderstood by those who love them. Indeed, living in a world whereby they must meet their abuser's every demand to avoid negative consequences may not be apparent to their closest friends and family, creating an invisible barrier that only the victim understands which isolates them even more. Although these repercussions are typically not physical in nature, when the non-violent tactics of coercive control are extremely effective, the alternative to physical violence experienced by the victim is often described as worse than any physical harm imagined.[12]

Intimidation

Intimidation often presents in the form of threats to do physical harm to the IPV victim, their loved ones, or their pets.[13] However, this non-violent coercive control theme can manifest in the form of threats of suicide by the IPV abuser. The abuser does not have to act upon these threats for them to successfully invoke constant fear in the victim for the purpose of torturing them and maintaining their compliance with the abuser's agenda.[14] As detailed below, other non-violent forms of intimidation include animal abuse, harassment, surveillance, threats against the IPV victim, threats against the IPV victim's family and friends, and brandishing weapons.[15]

Animal Abuse

Animal abuse, a subtheme of intimidation, is a tactic of coercive control used against the IPV victim that is non-violent toward the victim but may involve violence toward the targeted animal(s) or may result in the death of the animal(s); thus, it is not wholly without violence when utilized. The concept that this tactic of coercive control is non-violent is because the IPV victim does not directly experience any physical violence to her person; however, this does not decrease this tactics effectiveness.[16] Indeed, there is a clear link between animal cruelty and IPV.[17] Women IPV victims are at significant risk of being threatened with the physical harm or death of their animal, which may prevent them from leaving an abusive intimate relationship for fear of what may come to their beloved animal.[18] As a result, abusers understand they can utilize an animal to manipulate their victim, as well as any child(ren), into remaining in the home by creating fear in them of the safety of their animal.[19]

Harassment

As a subtheme of intimidation, harassment, similar to its definition in stalking laws, describes behavior by the IPV offender, such as continuously contacting the IPV victim or doing something the victim has asked them to stop doing.[20] Examples of harassing behavior by the abuser include unwanted, excessive texting and/or phone calling to the victim. However, unlike the legal definition of stalking as employed by most jurisdictions, harassment within the context of coercive control utilized in this study applies to both current and former intimate partners and does not require the element of substantial emotional distress.[21] But it is quite possible that the IPV victim, who is experiencing harassment within the context of coercive control, will meet the legal requirement of "substantial emotional distress" as well.[22]

Surveillance

Surveillance is a very effective non-violent coercive control tactic intended to strip the IPV victim of all sense of privacy and independence. It functions similarly to harassment in that it operates as an element of most stalking laws because the IPV abuser maintains unwanted information about the victim by following them, videotaping them, accessing their technology, listening to their conversations, etc. Often, IPV victims describe their abusers attaching GPS devices on their vehicles to maintain constant information about where they are at all time of the day and night. One example includes an IPV abuser talking on the phone with his victim while she was at dinner with a friend; but at the same time, he drove by the restaurant to verify she was where she said she was and with whom she said she was with. Because of these tactics, the victim feels the abuser's omnipresence. As a result, although he might be travelling out of the country, his established presence over her is felt no matter how far away he may be from her. His intimidation tactics, through the subtheme of surveillance, have worked to ensure that he maintains her compliance when he is away.

Threats

Threats, as a non-violent coercive control tactic, may take on various complexities and work together with several other themes or subthemes as described throughout this book. For example, the theme of intimidation, in general, may arise in the form of the IPV abuser threatening to kill themself; however, when they threaten to kill the IPV victim, as well as themself, then the subtheme of threats is implicated. But the subtheme of threats does not have to include the threat to kill the IPV victim. Indeed, any threat that includes acts or words by the abuser intended to cause immense fear of imminent danger for the IPV victim is associated with this subtheme. Additionally, if the threat describes acts or words by the abuser that are meant to evoke incredible fear in the IPV victim that something terrible will happen in the future, the subtheme of threats has been deployed. For this subtheme, it is important to understand that it is the acts or words of the abuser that are the focus rather than the reaction of the victim to the abuser's behavior.

Threatens Friends and Family

Similar to the subtheme of threats, threatens friends and family is a non-violent coercive control tactic; but it is unique in that the IPV abuser utilizes the victim's friends and family as their targets for abuse rather than the victim. As with threats, it is the acts or words of the abuser that are the focus rather than the people the abuser's behavior is directed toward. However, often the goal of this non-violent tactic is to alienate the IPV victim's closest support system so that they will have less resources in which to leave their abuser if such an attempt is contemplated. This subtheme describes acts or words the abuser deploys toward the IPV victim's friends and family that are intended to evoke immense fear in the IPV victim that there is imminent danger of something terrible happening to their loved ones. Indeed, the abuser might realize that, at some point, the IPV victim may give up and stopped fighting for their own safety and well-being; but it might also be apparent to the abuser that threatening the victim's loved ones is enough escalation of the threats to, once again, regain compliance from the victim.

Weapons

The IPV abuser's brandishing of weapons is incredibly persuasive as a non-violent coercive control tactic. When the weapon is used to threaten the IPV victim and is not used to physically harm them, this tactic is considered non-violent. However, once the weapon is used to cause physical harm to the victim, this non-violent tactic morphs into a violent act; and the tactic of physical violence is implicated.[23] As a result, the subtheme of weapons, under the non-violent theme of intimidation, is a complex tactic that cannot be viewed completely separately from the other tactics of coercive control as described in this study. Likewise, when the abuser claims to possess a weapon or threatens to purchase a weapon, his non-violent acts and words are quite effective for causing compliance from the victim who is already in enormous fear of their abuser.

Isolation

The theme of isolation is a tactic whereby the abuser prevents a victim from having access to support systems such as family and friends because such access may help them prevent the abuse or assist them in leaving the abusive relationship.[24] For some, isolation means moving across the country, or to another country, away from her friends and family.[25] An example of this tactic is when the IPV abuser isolates the mail-order bride.[26] Some men marry women who cannot speak English or have a very limited understanding of the language.[27] Additionally, when suddenly entering a new country, the culture may be completely unfamiliar, so the woman's entire atmosphere is foreign.[28] Thus, she relies solely on the man for support and guidance.[29] For other IPV victims, they may have their family and friends stay to visit, only to be isolated from them through the abuser's conversational techniques and unwillingness to interact with their family and friends. This repetitive behavior during each visit becomes so humiliating, they stop inviting their family and friends to their home. Because they are so embarrassed and humiliated by the abuser's behavior, they stop associating with their friends and discontinue visits with their family. Although the theme of humiliation may be implicated as well, the effect on the IPV victim are feelings of loneliness and seclusion; thus, the theme of isolation is accomplished.

Economic Control

Economic control, deployed as a subtheme of isolation, is also a very effective non-violent form of coercive control.[30] Many male abusers prevent or forbid women from working or going to school for fear that their victims will achieve financial independence and leave the abusive relationship.[31] Other non-violent tactics that are used include interfering with the IPV victim's work or school activities, such as calling them at work to threaten them, calling their boss to attempt to get them fired, threatening their safety through their employer, and appearing at their place of employment or school.[32] When the abuser is able to accomplish his goals, the victim often quits their job or drops out of school.[33] As a result, the IPV victim is not able to continue to work toward any type of economic independence. The inability to establish additional school and work history is, similarly, devastating for the victim. This is because, if the IPV victim leaves their abuser, the lack of schooling or work references decreases their ability to compete for higher paying jobs to adequately support themself and their children. It is because of this cycle of abuse that many IPV victims become dependent on the system and live in poverty. Indeed, it is estimated that IPV costs the U.S. economy upwards of $12.6 billion annually.[34]

False Imprisonment

Isolation, in the form of false imprisonment, whether for a very short time or a relatively longer time, can be very disconcerting for the IPV victim. This non-violent subtheme is quite effective in maintaining control over the victim because their physical person is confined in a particular space by the abuser. Indeed, although this tactic does not require having to meet the legal definition of false imprisonment or kidnapping, the abuser must hold the IPV victim against their will or without their knowing consent.[35]

Financial Control

Isolation's subtheme of financial control, although similar to economic control, functions differently in that the abuser directly controls certain aspects of the IPV victim's financial resources, such as money, shelter, transportation, medical expenses, etc. To invoke financial control over an IPV victim, abusers often regulate all forms of access to financial resources, including the victim's own wages.[36] Unlike economic control, the abuser may allow the victim to work; however, he will not allow her to have any access to the funds produced from their efforts. This may occur through the demand of their paycheck being handed over directly to the abuser on payday or through direct deposit into a checking account that the abuser controls. This type of financial control over the victim's wages prevents the IPV victim from having any type of independence because lack of access to the fruits of one's labor can be quite subjugating.[37] Indeed, if the victim had access to their own money, it might give rise to other forms of independence and autonomy the abuser wants to suppress.[38] Certainly, a victim's ability to leave an abusive relationship is often dependent upon their financial independence.[39] As DeKeseredy and Schwartz (2009) explain, these types of coercive control victims feel trapped in a volatile relationship, regardless of whether any physical violence is present.[40]

Isolation and intimidation are forms of coercive control that compare to the torture experienced by prisoners of war.[41] However, these tactics may be just as, or even more, detrimental to an IPV victim than they are to a prisoner of war because they are deployed by the intimate partner of the victim. As a result, these tactics will most likely have a greater psychological impact than for prisoners of war, who are generally tortured by an unknown person representing an unknown belligerent power. In each case, isolation can lead to the victim becoming more dependent on their abuser for survival, which includes basic necessities, such as food, healthcare, shelter, etc., as well as their emotional needs.[42] Isolation destroys a victim's capacity for "selfhood, social authority, and personal identity."[43]

Humiliation

The theme of humiliation is a non-violent tactic of coercive control that is more powerful than anyone who has never been abused by someone using it could realize. It strips an IPV victim of their self-worth and identity.[44] Over time, the IPV victim who is humiliated due to coercive control begins to "buy into" the degradation and name calling that the abuser constantly barrages them with to the point that they begin to internalize the humiliation. Indeed, constantly telling an IPV victim that they are "stupid" will ultimately cause them to believe that they *actually* are stupid, especially when they are isolated from any other friends or family who might tell them otherwise. And even if they are exposed to other people, such as loved ones, it becomes very difficult to fend off the demons inside that the continued humiliation creates. Likewise, consistently being told that they are an "ugly whore" will eventually cause an IPV victim to feel little to no self-worth, as would the words "fat pig." Often, when taken to its extreme, an abuser will humiliate an IPV victim by degrading them and calling them names in public.

Degradation

Degradation, a subtheme of humiliation, operates within the same space as humiliation to strip the IPV victim of any sense of well-being and self-worth. This non-violent tactic describes a range of behaviors by the IPV abuser that shows disrespect or contempt for the IPV victim, whether in public or private. Examples include the abuser screaming obscenities or cursing repeatedly at the victim in public to ensure that people can hear what is being said. This non-violent tactic is effective to ensure that the victim is mortified with the abuser's behavior so that they will comply with their demands. It also operates to isolate the victim because some people may view them as a pariah even though it is the abuser's behavior that caused the incident.

Name Calling

Similar to degradation, name calling is a subtheme of humiliation in which the abuser hurls humiliating and/or degrading names at the IPV victim either in public or in private. Names such as "bitch," "whore," and "cunt," are just a few examples of the types of vitriolic and invective words the abuser may use toward the victim to ensure that this non-violent coercive control tactic is as effective as possible. In some cases, the abuser may not ever call the victim by their actual name. The abuser may only use certain vitriolic and invective terms to refer to the victim no matter who is around, whether in public or in private. This tactic, taken to its extreme, causes the victim to not only lose their self-worth, but to lose their self-identity as well.

Power and Control

The non-violent tactic of power and control has a very broad application when deployed within the context of coercive control. There are many varying behaviors an IPV offender can take to invoke authority and regulation over their victim. Generally, these acts are meant to obtain and maintain compliance from them; however, it can be one of the most insidious tactics because victims may not recognize its subtle forms as abuse. For example, an abuser will often tell the IPV victim what to do or how to think on a regular and ongoing basis. Comments such as "As long as you think the way I think and do what I say, everything will be ok" are indicative of the non-violent tactic of power and control. Indeed, this theme is one in which the victim can feel the abuser's omnipresence no matter where they are in physical relation to each other.

Child Abuse and Violent Acts toward Family and Friends

Other non-violent tactics of power and control include the subthemes of child abuse and violent acts toward the IPV victim's family and friends. Although child maltreatment and/or neglect may include physical violence, sexual abuse, or psychological abuse against the child, in the context of the non-violent tactics of coercive control, it does not take on the form of physical violence toward the IPV victim. Psychological abuse of the child may come when the abuser attempts to utilize the child against the IPV victim during an argument between the abuser and the victim.[45] However, child abuse is unique in that the child is also affected when exposed to the abuser's acts against the IPV victim; thus, physical violence against the IPV victim does play a role in child abuse when the child is exposed to the physical violence between the abuser and the IPV victim, meaning child abuse takes place at the point of exposure to the violence.[46] This same consideration applies to violent acts toward the IPV victim's family and friends. Because the violent act is not directed toward the IPV victim, this coercive control tactic is considered non-violent; however, it has a tremendous effect on the victim in the form of power and control over the victim. Indeed, the abuser understands that the victim will do whatever they can to ensure that their children, as well as their loved ones, are protected.

Taking Children from the Intimate Partner Violence Victim

Another power and control tactic that is utilized quite effectively is when the abuser either takes the children from the IPV victim or threatens to take the children from them. Many victims will risk their lives for their children, and their abusers know this to be true. As a result, the threat of having their children taken away from them, made by the abuser, whether the abuser is capable of follow through or not, is often enough to maintain compliance from the victim for a substantial length of time, especially if the children are very young. Thus, the subtheme of taking children from the IPV victim is a powerful non-violent coercive control tactic.

Deprivation of Necessities

The subtheme of deprivation of necessities works to maintain power and control over the IPV victim because the abuser controls life's everyday resources needed to survive. Tactics include, but are not limited to, withholding food, clothing, and medicine from the victim to obtain their compliance.[47] Such deprivation of necessities causes the IPV victim to become so dependent upon the abuser that they must comply to their demands or go without these basic needs. Other examples of deprivation of necessities include such extremes as not allowing the victim to toilet alone or to shower in solitude, causing the victim to feel as though the abuser is omnipotent. For those who have not experienced this non-violent tactic of coercive control, these daily activities are taken for granted; but for the IPV victim who is familiar with these tactics, they are anything but mundane, underappreciated activities. Once implemented, the victim must rely upon their abuser for their daily needs and are stripped of their autonomy and personal liberty.

Psychologically Controlling

The subtheme of psychologically controlling by the abuser over the IPV victim, which is accomplished through acts whereby non-violent tactics help to maintain a form of mental control over the victim, is an effective means of invoking power and control. Within the vernacular of academia, personnel who work with IPV victims, and those who experience this form of abuse, the effect of *psychological abuse* on the victim is used to describe a cornucopia of behaviors implemented by the abuser.[48] However, the subtheme of psychologically controlling, as identified in this book as a specific non-violent tactic of coercive control, is recognized more narrowly in its implementation between the intimate partners than the general conception of psychological abuse. This is because the many coercive control tactics, which may be categorized under the umbrella of psychological abuse, are identified as separate subthemes in this study, causing psychologically controlling to have a more precise application.

The theme of power and control, invoked through the subtheme of psychologically controlling, may be most well recognized through the cycle of violence, introduced in Chapter 1 and exemplified in Chapter 6, in which the intimate partners in the relationship engage in a cycle of physical violence, apologies, forgiveness, and a honeymoon period.[49] When the honeymoon period ends, a phase of tension building begins, which leads to the next physical act of violence.[50] Often, the abuser will physically abuse the IPV victim, only to immediately tell them that they love them. For a victim of coercive control, who has been stripped of self-worth and is deprived of any type of emotional support from family and friends through other ongoing tactics, craving love from their abuser is natural. Thus, even though the beating happened, it is difficult to withstand the apologies, the promises that it will never happen again, and the fact that the abuser offers their declarations of love. As a result, the cycle of abuse is allowed to continue.

Although the physical abuse is violent, the psychological control, stemming from the physical violence, manifests in the form of mental control over the victim, which is non-violent. Additionally, it is not necessary for the physical abuse to occur in order to invoke psychological control over the victim. The complete cycle of abuse includes physical violence; but with coercive control, it is not necessary for physical violence to enter the cycle for the coercive control abuser to maintain their mental control over the victim. It is possible that the abuser may use threats, destroy the home or the victim's personal property, etc., which are behaviors and acts that may cause the abuser to apologize. Thus, the cycle of the behavior initiating the apology, forgiveness, honeymoon, and tension building occurs without physical violence ensuing between the intimate partners. Nevertheless, the subtheme of psychologically controlling has been invoked.

For the IPV victim who can withstand the apologies and declarations of love, meaning they begin to recognize the cycle of violence themself, it is still difficult to break the cycle, especially when attempting to leave the abuser. The cycle of violence has no set time frame for when it repeats. It may begin to repeat once a year but can shorten dramatically to every couple of months or weeks. If allowed to manifest, this form of psychological control can be repeated as often as every day or every hour.[51] However, this pattern of psychological control does not necessarily follow a definitive, linear rule of timing as to whether the phases move forward without taking backward turns.[52] IPV victims must understand this cycle of abuse and attempt to recognize where the danger lies, as abusers may become more erratic and unpredictable the shorter the cycle becomes.[53] Indeed, it is during these decreased time frames that the victim should understand the heightened risk and seek help from outside sources.[54]

Verbal Abuse

Similar to psychological abuse, verbal abuse is an often-cited form of IPV that generally refers to a plethora of behaviors by the abuser against the victim. But even victims refer to this form of abuse without providing specific details regarding the abuse they experience beyond describing it as "verbal abuse."[55] However, the subtheme of verbal abuse, as explained through the theme of power and control in this study, describes specific verbal acts of vitriol and invective that are spewed by the abuser toward the IPV victim, including cussing at them. Still, this subtheme is differentiated from the subthemes of degradation and name calling because the IPV victim might not have provided more specific details as to their experience of verbal abuse other than to say that they were victims of verbal abuse. As a result, the subthemes of degradation and name calling were not implicated in such instances. Thus, this non-verbal tactic is considered verbal abuse, *per se*, i.e., "of, in, or by itself; standing alone without reference to additional facts."[56]

Household, Clothes, and Personal Belongings Destroyed

Household, clothes, and personal belongings destroyed is a subtheme of power and control that describes acts and behaviors by the IPV abuser that may or may not be specifically directed toward the victim. Examples of behaviors not intentionally directed toward the victim include the abuser destroying the home by punching holes in the wall or other means; breaking or burning the household furniture; smashing electronic equipment; damaging vehicles; etc. Although non-violent toward the IPV victim, these destructive coercive control tactics have a tremendous effect on them no matter how they are directed. This is because the abuser may destroy items the victim cares deeply about or does so in a way that is threatening to their own personal selfhood. For example, destroying personal effects, such as personal photographs, yearbooks, and family heirlooms, is a tactic that causes the IPV victim to feel as though her abuser is attempting to eliminate any trace of her personal existence. Indeed, when all of one's clothes and personal belongings are burned in a pile in the backyard, the realization of the emptiness is overwhelming. In combination with other non-violent coercive control tactics, the victim's ability to withstand the devastation, grief, and mourning one goes through from losing themself to the destruction of their life's personal effects and cherished mementos, including those of their children's keepsakes at the hands of their abuser, can be debilitating.

Fearful of the Future

The theme of fearful of the future helps to explain the IPV victim's expression of fear or dread of something happening in the future due to the abuser's actions. Because the themes and subthemes throughout this study are derivatives from the analyses of petitions for injunctions for protection from DV filed by persons seeking protection from a court of law from their abusers, it seems obvious that authors of the petitions would state within their narratives that they are afraid of their abuser. Indeed, pursuant to Florida statute, being "a victim of domestic violence" or having reasonable belief of "imminent danger of becoming a victim of domestic violence" is a very important aspect of the case for the court to take into consideration.[57] Many IPV victims expressed fear in relation to the actions their abusers might take in the future, especially as it pertained to their own personal safety with threats of killing the victim being cited often.

Fear of Children's Safety

Similar to the theme of fearful of the future, the subtheme of fear of children's safety describes the IPV victim's fear that the abuser will harm the children and/or stepchildren of, or those in common with, the abuser and the IPV victim. Often, the fear for the children's safety was expressed in combination with the fear expressed for the IPV victim's own safety. It is within these statements that the victim may also explain their reasons for staying within the abusive relationship as that of a protective parent. Indeed, the conundrum of remaining in an abusive relationship for the safety of the children versus leaving the relationship for the same reason is a very difficult dilemma to face. Understanding that it is not safe to stay, only to possibly make matters less safe when you leave, is one of the most impossible choices to make, especially when you have children depending on you for their safety and survival.

Pregnant

Pregnant is a subtheme of fearful of the future for those IPV victims who explained to the court that they were pregnant during the time of the incident they indicated in their petition for injunction. The purpose of informing the court about the pregnancy was because the IPV victim was concerned about the health of the fetus due to the actions of the abuser.

Resistance to Abuse

The theme of resistance to abuse describes non-violent acts taken by the IPV victim, which may have been acknowledged by the victim to be against their own best interests, that were specified as overt actions against the abuser's tactics of abuse. Examples of such actions taken by the victim include removing themselves from a physical altercation with the abuser; contacting law enforcement to report the abuser; filing the instant petition for injunction; separating from the abuser; etc. Because IPV victims are often viewed as helpless or abusive toward the IPV offender, it is important to stress that this theme is a non-violent theme, as the victims worked to resolve their abusive situations within the confines of the judicial system, with law enforcement, or with the abuser themselves prior to having to file the petition for injunction. Often, victims are blamed for being as responsible for the abuse as the abuser; but that misconception does not withstand this theme's data.

Helping Abuser

The subtheme of helping abuser describes when the IPV victim chose to assist their abuser with his/her needs all-the-while describing abusive acts and/or coercive control tactics within the same petition for injunction narrative. The subtheme is indicative of the internal struggle IPV victims have when they are attempting to leave their abuser, as well as trying to remain permanently separated from their abuser once they have left.

Separated or Estranged

Separated or estranged, as a subtheme of resistance to abuse, explains that the IPV victim and abuser are no longer living together or are living together but in different quarters of the marital home at the time the petition for injunction was written. Many cases might have had scant information regarding the living arrangements of the couple subject to the petition for injunction; however, only those cases with information that could be confirmed as to their separation or estrangement status were considered for this subtheme. Because this subtheme is under the theme of resistance to abuse, any case coded under it is one in which the IPV victim was considered working toward some type of independence from the abuser.

Abuser Mental Illness

The theme abuser mental illness indicates the abuser has a history of or tendency toward a wide range of conditions that affect mood, thinking, and behavior, i.e., mental disorder or is dealing with some type of mental disorder. While not taken as absolute diagnoses for the purposes of professional assessment, this theme involved coding of many IPV victim's amateur diagnoses of their spouses' mental health issues or a declaration of their spouses' mental health diagnoses from professionals. Although mental illness and abuse are two separate occurrences, it is important to recognize that mental illness and abuse can coincide.[58] As a result, this theme considers mental illness in the context of abusive behavior.

Drinking Alcohol

The subtheme of drinking alcohol indicates the abuser drinks alcohol in excess or to the point that the IPV victim believed it necessary to raise this fact in the petition for injunction. While alcohol consumption or alcoholism alone are not a cause for IPV, they can help to make the abuse more intense.[59] Indeed, it is possible for alcohol to trigger IPV in a violent person.[60] However, removing alcohol from an intimate partner relationship where violence or coercive control is present does not necessarily mean that the abuse will cease.[61]

Drug Use

Drug use, as a subtheme of abuser mental illness, indicates the abuser uses illegal drugs or prescription drugs other than as prescribed. While substance use coercion may be common in IPV relationships, whereby the abuser invokes control upon the IPV victim using illicit drugs, this subtheme does not consider these types of cases.[62] Instead, the narratives that discuss drug use in this study were coded as such when the IPV victim stated the abuser used drugs that were illicit or not prescribed for such purposes.

Paranoia

Paranoia, as a subtheme of abuser mental illness, describes "1. mental illness characterized by systematized delusions of persecution or grandeur usually without hallucinations; 2. A tendency on the part of an individual or group toward excessive or irrational suspiciousness and distrustfulness of others" that manifests in statements or acts by the abuser, such as threats to kill themselves or accusing the IPV victim of seeing another person.[63] Many of the petitions for injunction were replete with accusations of the abusers toward the victims regarding their supposed infidelity. Such "severe possessiveness of the victim and intense jealousy are precursors to potentially lethal abuse" as this study and others have shown.[64]

Physical Violence

The theme of physical violence encapsulates those acts the IPV victim described in the petition for injunction that were committed by the abuser against them which were violent in nature. Some of these acts might have been what one could consider a simple touching; however, many of these acts are quite atrocious. In all, the physical acts of violence are generally described in combination with the other non-violent coercive control tactics. As a result, the interplay of coercive control tactics and the continuum of abuse is evident from the petitions that were filed.

Nonfatal Strangulation

As a subtheme of physical violence, nonfatal strangulation explains acts by the abuser the IPV victim described in their petition for injunction in which the normal breathing or blood flow to the brain was obstructed. Nonfatal strangulation is common in IPV relationships, with sixty-eight percent of abused women surviving this type of physical abuse and averaging over five attempts per survivor.[65] But these injuries are difficult to detect because many of the cases do not display visible injuries of the strangulation itself.[66] Its long-term outcomes are associated with the IPV victim's physical and mental health, but another major concern is the fact that prior nonfatal strangulation is a known predictor for lethality.[67] Indeed, the estimated risk of homicide for an IPV victim who has previously been strangled is seven and a half times higher compared to those who have not experienced strangulation.[68]

Rape and Sexual Abuse

Rape and sexual abuse is a subtheme of physical violence that describes acts in which the abuser forced sexual acts and other types of unwanted sexual violence upon or against the IPV victim. This subtheme did not have to meet the legal definition of rape or sexual abuse to qualify for the subtheme's criteria but focused on the forced or coerced sexual interaction described in the petition. Although sexual interaction between intimate partners is considered a private matter not to be discussed through public means, the IPV victims who wrote about their experiences in their petitions for injunction were quite forthright in the details they provided for the court to consider.

Notes

1 Casey G. Gwinn & Anne O'Dell, *Stopping the Violence: The Role of the Police Officer and the Prosecutor*, 8 (1992), https://www.academia.edu/9781000/Stopping_the_Violence_The_Role_of_the_Police_Officer_and_the_Prosecutor.
2 See Id.
3 See Id.
4 See Id.
5 See Id.
6 See Id.
7 See, e.g., Kristy Candela, *Protecting the Invisible Victim: Incorporating Coercive Control in Domestic Violence Statutes*, 54 FAMILY COURT REVIEW 112 (2016); Donna J. King, *Naming the Judicial Terrorist: An Exposé of an Abuser's Successful Use of a Judicial Proceeding for Continued Domestic Violence*, 153 TENN. JOURNAL OF RACE, GENDER, & SOCIAL JUSTICE 153 (2012); EVAN STARK, COERCIVE CONTROL: HOW MEN ENTRAP WOMEN IN PERSONAL LIFE (2007).
8 See King, *supra* note 7; Andy Myhill, *Measuring Coercive Control: What Can We Learn from National Population Surveys?*, 21 VIOLENCE AGAINST WOMEN 355 (2015) https://doi.org/10.1177/1077801214568032; STARK, *supra* note 7;

Sylvia Walby & Jude Towers, *Untangling the Concept of Coercive Control: Theorizing Domestic Violent Crime*, 18 CRIMINOLOGY & CRIMINAL JUSTICE 7 (2018) https://doi.org/10.1177/1748895817743541.

9 *See* King, *supra* note 7; Myhill, *supra* note 8; STARK, *supra* note 7; Walby & Towers, *supra* note 8.
10 *See, e.g.*, Candela, *supra* note 7; King, *supra* note 7; STARK, *supra* note 7.
11 *See infra* Chapter 5, Intimidation, Isolation. *See infra* Chapter 6, Humiliation, and Power and Control. *See, e.g.*, Gretchen Arnold, *A Battered Women's Movement Perspective of Coercive Control*, 15 VIOLENCE AGAINST WOMEN 1432 (2009) https://doi.org/10.1177/1077801209346836; Charlotte Barlow & Sandra Walklate, *Gender, Risk Assessment and Coercive Control: Contradictions in Terms?*, 61 BRIT. J. CRIMINOL. 887 (2021) https://doi.org/10.1093/bjc/azaa104; STARK, *supra* note 7.
12 *See* Candela, *supra* note 7; STARK, *supra* note 7.
13 *See* King, *supra* note 7; STARK, *supra* note 7.
14 *See* Diane Balkin et al., *Animal Cruelty Issues: What Juvenile and Family Court Judges Need to Know*, NATIONAL COUNCIL OF JUVENILE AND FAMILY COURT JUDGES (2019); STARK, *supra* note 7.
15 *See infra* Chapter 2, Animal Abuse, Harassment, Surveillance, Threats, Threatens Friends and Family, Weapons.
16 *See* STARK, *supra* note 7.
17 *See* Balkin et al., *supra* note 14.
18 *See Id*.
19 *See Id*.
20 *See* FLA. STAT. § 784.048(1)(a) (2022) (defining "Harass" as "engag[ing] in a course of conduct directed at a specific person which causes substantial emotional distress to that person and serves no legitimate purpose" FLA. STAT. § 784.048(1)(a) (2022)); *See also* Ashford-Cooper v. Ruff, 230 So.3d 1283 (Fla. App. 2017) (explaining that FLA. STAT. § 784.048(1)(a) requires sufficient evidence of substantial emotional distress).
21 Marilyn McMahon et al., *An Alternative Means of Prosecuting Non-Physical Domestic Abuse: Are Stalking Laws an Under-Utilised Resource?*, in CRIMINALISING COERCIVE CONTROL: FAMILY VIOLENCE AND THE CRIMINAL LAW (Marilyn McMahon & Paul McGorrery eds., 2020) https://link.springer.com/chapter/10.1007/978-981-15-0653-6_5.
22 *See* WASH. ADMIN. CODE § 478-121-157 (2017) (defining "substantial emotional distress" as "significant mental suffering or anguish that may, but does not necessarily, require medical or other professional treatment or counseling" WASH. ADMIN. CODE § 478-121-157 (2017)).
23 *See infra* Chapter 8, Physical Violence.
24 *See* Arnold, *supra* note 11; MOLLY DRAGIEWICZ, EQUALITY WITH A VENGEANCE: MEN'S RIGHTS GROUPS, BATTERED WOMEN, AND ANTIFEMINIST BACKLASH (2011); King, *supra* note 7.
25 *See infra* Chapter 6, Power and Control, Psychologically Controlling, Huss v. Huss; Chapter 8, Judicial Terrorism® Revisted, Frasch v. Frasch.
26 *See infra* Chapter 6, Power and Control, Psychologically Controlling, Huss v. Huss.
27 *See infra* Chapter 6 Power and Control, Psychologically Controlling, Huss v. Huss; Chapter 8, Judicial Terrorism® Revisted, Frasch v. Frasch.
28 *See infra* Chapter 6, Power and Control, Psychologically Controlling, Huss v. Huss; Chapter 8, Judicial Terrorism® Revisted, Frasch v. Frasch.

29 *See infra* Chapter 6, Power and Control, Psychologically Controlling, Huss v. Huss; Chapter 8, Judicial Terrorism® Revisted, Frasch v. Frasch.
30 *See* King, *supra* note 7; STARK, *supra* note 7.
31 *See* JODY RAPHAEL, SAVING BERNICE: BATTERED WOMEN, WELFARE, AND POVERTY (2000).
32 *See infra* Chapter 5, Isolation, Economic Control.
33 *See Domestic Violence*, NCADV, https://assets.speakcdn.com/assets/2497/domestic_violence-2020080709350855.pdf?1596828650457 (2020).
34 *See Id.*
35 *See* FLA. STAT. § 787.02(1)(a) (2022) (defining "false imprisonment" as "forcibly, by threat, or secretly confining, abducting, imprisoning, or restraining another person without lawful authority and against her or his will" FLA. STAT. § 787.02(1)(a) (2022)).
36 *See* RAPHAEL, *supra* note 31.
37 *See Id.*
38 *See Id.*
39 *See* Kara Bellew, *Silent Suffering: Uncovering and Understanding Domestic Violence in Affluent Communities*, 26 WOMEN'S RIGHTS LAW REPORTER 39 (2005); King, *supra* note 7.
40 *See* WALTER S. DEKESEREDY & MARTIN D. SCHWARTZ, DANGEROUS EXITS: ESCAPING ABUSIVE RELATIONSHIPS IN RURAL AMERICA (2009).
41 *See* King, *supra* note 7; STARK, *supra* note 7.
42 *See* King, *supra* note 7; STARK, *supra* note 7; SUSAN WEITZMAN, "NOT TO PEOPLE LIKE US:" HIDDEN ABUSE IN UPSCALE MARRIAGES (2000).
43 King, *supra* note 7 at 158; *accord* STARK, *supra* note 7.
44 *See* STARK, *supra* note 7.
45 *See* Office on Women's Health, *Effects of Domestic Violence on Children*, OASH, https://www.womenshealth.gov/relationships-and-safety/domestic-violence/effects-domestic-violence-children (last visited June 1, 2023). *See infra* Chapter 5, Intimidation, Threats, Donna Wood v. William Wood.
46 *See* Office on Women's Health, *supra* note 45.
47 *See* STARK, *supra* note 7.
48 *See* About Abuse, *Emotional and Psychological Abuse*, WOMENSLAW.ORG, https://www.womenslaw.org/about-abuse/forms-abuse/emotional-and-psychological-abuse (last visited June 1, 2023).
49 *See* Domestic Violence: It's Everybody's Business, *Step by Step Guide to Understanding the Cycle of Violence*, DOMESTICVIOLENCE.ORG, https://domesticviolence.org/cycle-of-violence/ (last visited Jan. 13, 2023). *See supra* Chapter 1, Gender and Intimate Partner Violence: Legislating against Patriarchal Violence. *See infra* Chapter 6, Power and Control, Psychologically Controlling, Huss v. Huss.
50 *See* Domestic Violence: It's Everybody's Business, *supra* note 49. *See infra* Chapter 6, Power and Control, Psychologically Controlling.
51 *See* Heather Allen, *Troubled Marriage Ends in Death*, HERALD-TRIBUNE (April 27, 2007); *See also* Domestic Violence: It's Everybody's Business, *supra* note 49. *See infra* Chapter 6, Power and Control, Psychologically Controlling.
52 *See* Domestic Violence: It's Everybody's Business, *supra* note 49.
53 *See Id.*
54 *See Id.*
55 *See infra* Chapter 6, Power and Control, Verbal Abuse.
56 *See* BLACK'S LAW DICTIONARY 566 (Bryan A. Garner et al. eds., 4th ed. 2011).

57 Fla. Stat. § 741.30(3)(h) (2022).
58 *See* Alexander, *Abuse and Mental Illness: Is There a Connection?*, National Domestic Violence Hotline, https://www.thehotline.org/resources/abuse-and-mental-illness-is-there-a-connection/ (last visited June 1, 2023).
59 *See Alcohol and Domestic Abuse*, Alcohol Rehab Guide, https://www.alcoholrehabguide.org/alcohol/crimes/domestic-abuse/ (last visited June 1, 2023).
60 *See Id.*
61 *See Id.*
62 *See* Echo A. Rivera et al., *The Relationship Between Intimate Partner Violence and Substance Use: An Applied Research Paper*, National Center on Domestic Violence, Trauma & Mental Health, http://www.nationalcenterdvtraumamh.org/wp-content/uploads/2014/09/IPV-SAB-Final202.29.1620NO20LOGO-1.pdf (2015).
63 Dictionary, *Paranoia*, Merriam-Webster.com, https://www.merriam-webster.com/dictionary/paranoia (last visited March 5, 2023).
64 *Lethality Indicators: Possessiveness Over Victim or Severe/Morbid Jealousy*, http://georgiafatalityreview.com/lethality-indicators/possessiveness-over-victim-or-severe-morbid-jealousy/ (last visited June 1, 2023).
65 *See* Amy Reckdenwald et al., *Prosecutorial Response to Nonfatal Strangulation in Domestic Violence Cases*, 35 Violence and Victims 160 (2020) https://connect.springerpub.com/content/sgrvv/35/2/160.
66 *See* Martyna Dendlin & Lorraine Sheridan, *Nonfatal Strangulation in a Sample of Domestically Violent Stalkers: The Importance of Recognizing Coercively Controlling Behaviors*, 46 Crim. Just. & Behavior 1528 (2019) https://doi.org/10.1177/0093854819843973.
67 *See* Reckdenwald et al., *supra* note 65.
68 *See Id.*

3 Assessing the Risk
Understanding an Intimate Partner Violence Victim's Risk of Death

The Risk of Leaving: She Knows He's a Threat, but Does Anyone Else?

"Why didn't she just leave?" is a common question often asked by those who do not understand coercive control's power and control tactics.[1] It is very difficult for a victim to leave an intimate partner relationship where coercive control exists, especially if they have children because access to their own mental, physical and tangible resources are, most likely, depleted.[2] Davies et al. (2009) assert that society erroneously believes the solution for a victim of intimate partner violence (IPV) is to simply leave the abusive relationship.[3] There is a societal failure to understand that: (1) women do not willingly or knowingly enter into abusive relationships; (2) when women recognize they are in an abusive relationship, it is very difficult to determine what to do about it; and (3) women face extraordinarily difficult challenges when attempting to permanently leave their abuser because one who invokes coercive control does not simply let go of such levels of power and control enjoyed in the abusive relationship, which vanishes when the victim is outside of his physical space.[4] Indeed, he will view her audacity to invoke such autonomy as unacceptable, causing him to become angry and willing to rise to levels of physical violence that may not have been previously experienced in the relationship.[5]

Society views the victim's unwillingness to leave their abuser as a sign of weakness rather than considering that they understand their peril and are attempting to prevent an escalation of violence, either to save their life or the life of their children, by deciding to stay with their abuser.[6] In fact, leaving their abuser is a calculated risk between maintaining physical proximity with them and knowing that the violence will most likely escalate once they leave.[7] Indeed, the coercive control, i.e., the victim's oppressive living conditions, must become so unbearable while in the physical presence of the abuser that it becomes obvious to the victim that leaving, and risking possible death, is the better option than staying. Because of this societal misconception that the victim's reluctance to leave their abuser is veiled in their

DOI: 10.4324/9781003097488-5

weakness rather than viewing it as a sign of strength, society's inclination is to blame the victim.[8] Sev'er (1997) explains that this societal misconception stems from the fact that many people believe that marriage provides men with a license to employ violence to keep women under their control;[9] however, many IPV victims are not married to their abusers and are free from physical abuse until the time they separate from their abuser. Some victims, who *had not experienced physical violence prior to leaving their abuser*, are physically assaulted for the first time once separation takes place.[10] Although the term "separation assault" was introduced to raise awareness of the problem, most people do not realize that physical violence usually begins, increases, or becomes deadly once a victim leaves their abuser.[11]

Aldridge and Browne (2003) explain that the point in time an IPV victim leaves the relationship is the deadliest because abusers often feel the most emotional and vulnerable.[12] Thus, victims of IPV find making the decision to leave extraordinarily difficult.[13] To explain the causes of continued IPV and the severity of the risk of lethality when the victim leaves their abuser, it is important to emphasize the fact that many abusers become obsessed with their former intimate partner because they no longer have access to them.[14] The mere circumstance of a victim having left the abusive relationship often makes their situation more dangerous than remaining with their abuser due to their lack of power and control over them.[15]

Another consideration for the increased violence at the time of separation is the victim's reduced ability to engage in self-guardianship. Although some IPV victims live in a constant state of *hyper*arousal due to their stress level and possible post-traumatic stress, others may feel more comfortable and at ease in their new surroundings, without their abusers' presence.[16] Thus, some victims are more vulnerable because they let their guards down. Others, although still in a state of *hyper*arousal, are no longer able to read their abusers' every move because they are no longer in their physical presence and cannot anticipate what they will do next. Therefore, they are inherently more vulnerable to attacks as well. Certainly, many IPV victims, who understand that leaving will make them more vulnerable to violence from their abuser, when considering their options prior to leaving an abusive relationship, will leave their only after they accept the possibility of death over continuing to live in their unbearable, abusive intimate partner relationship.[17]

The Role of Intimate Partner Homicide-Suicide in Intimate Partner Homicide

The concept of the termination of an intimate partner relationship resulting in a homicide of one of the persons involved in that intimate relationship may be difficult for some who have never been involved in an abusive relationship to understand. To take it a step further, when that intimate relationship terminates in an intimate partner homicide-suicide (IPHS), most people find this exceedingly problematic to comprehend. Likewise, the complete end to a family when the intimate relationship ends, with the killing of the spouse, children, and/or other family members by the "family annihilator," who also takes their own life, is unbearable for the community at large.[18]

It is estimated that between 1000 and 1500 murder-suicide deaths occur each year in the United States, and about 65% of these deaths were the result of an IPHS.[19] It is difficult to determine the risk factors for an abuser who may commit an IPHS because there is no "one size fits all" profile for this type of killer.[20] Salari and Sillito (2016) suggest that lethality risk factors are not as predictive for IPHS, making it more difficult for community and criminal justice responses because these killings tend to take place more as a reaction to relationship situational circumstances.[21] In fact, most IPHSs occur in the home, specifically in the bedroom more than any other room of the house.[22] Children are often exposed to, if not victims of, IPHSs as well, making them orphans when both parents are killed in an IPHS.[23] Undeniably, IPHS is distinct from homicide or suicide alone. And to be clear, with IPV, homicide is the best way for an abuser to maintain ultimate control over their victim.

Richards et al. (2014) explain that, of all forms of homicide-suicide, IPHS is the most common.[24] They emphasize the interwoven risk factors of domestic violence (DV) and homicide while pointing out the fact that suicide reporting guidelines inadequately instruct on DV considerations.[25] This is considerably dangerous for the IPV victim, especially when depression and mental illness are considered as two risk factors found for IPV and suicide.[26] Because of this connection between IPV and suicide risks, Richards et al. (2014) emphasize the fact that the media should report on the history of any collective problems rather than simplifying the event or suggesting it came "out of the blue."[27] Indeed, according to Morton et al. (1998), these types of homicides, i.e., IPHSs "are rarely sudden, isolated occurrences. They are typically the culmination of long-standing turmoil and conflict including threats, physical abuse, and victim attempts to leave the relationship."[28]

Although there are very few studies that include statistics for the percentage of intimate partner homicides (IPHs) that result in IPHSs, Velopulos et al. (2019) found that 46.5% of the male offenders in an IPH, when the victim is a female, attempted suicide and were successful with their attempts 35% of the time.[29] However, Vatnar et al. (2019) explain that, in Norway and Sweden, nearly one fourth of IPHs resulted in an IPHS, somewhat lower than what they state is the United States' estimate of 27% to 32%.[30] Velopulos et al. (2019) assert that the 35% successful IPHS percentage is astonishing and worthy of further investigation as it pertains to IPV and suicidality.[31]

The Disillusionment of the Protections of an Injunction for Protection against Domestic Violence: Why and When Are They Important to Intimate Partner Violence Victims?

It is often said that an injunction for protection against DV is "just a piece of paper" and does nothing to protect the person holding one when it comes to *actual* protection from abuse.[32] But some IPV victims are, generally, willing to jump through all the legal hoops it takes to obtain such a civil protective order because one is usually enforced through the criminal judicial system, meaning possible jail time if the abuser violates the order.[33] A civil protective order may provide relief to the IPV victim and their children in addition to protection from physical violence, which may include exclusive use and possession of the home during the pendency of the temporary or final injunction. Also, relief from the non-violent tactics of coercive control can come when a temporary or final injunction is entered because it is more difficult to invoke these tactics from afar but is certainly not impossible.[34]

The process to obtain a final injunction can be overwhelming and cumbersome, especially for anyone who is not familiar with the legal process, i.e., the typical IPV victim. Most U.S. states have similar statutes and processes, and many of them have non-profit and community-based organizations that include women's shelters to help IPV victims with their legal filings for little to no cost.[35] Some local and county organizations offer victim advocate support services to assist IPV victims with their cases, especially if they must go to a hearing by themselves. These advocates do not provide legal services, but they are familiar with the legal processes and paper filings. This allows them to support the IPV victim throughout the entire legal process. Of course, the ideal situation is to have the IPV victim hire a licensed attorney to represent them from the beginning of the process of filing the initial petition for injunction against the abuser; but, many IPV victims do not have the financial resources to hire an attorney to assist them with this process.

To obtain a final injunction against an abusive intimate partner, a petition for injunction must be sworn to and filed by the IPV victim, which is then reviewed *ex parte* by the court.[36] At that point, the petition for injunction is either denied with no further hearing, temporarily granted with a temporary injunction while a hearing is set for the final injunction, or denied with a hearing set for the final injunction. The subsequent hearing is usually set within a ten-day to two-week time frame.[37] Because the initial petition for injunction is heard *ex parte*, it is incumbent upon the court to hold the hearing, with notice to the respondent, i.e., the alleged abuser as soon as possible so that the responding party may have their due process.[38]

There is a debate among researchers about the effectiveness of temporary injunctions and final injunctions in stopping abuse and preventing the lethality of IPV victims.[39] Indeed, these protections are state specific; and many IPV victims, who do not realize they have been or are being abused, due to the lack of physical injury they receive from their abuser, often fail to appreciate the fact that they may be eligible for assistance from law enforcement or protection from the court, depending upon their state's protections.[40] Each of the individual states throughout the United States have statutes providing for temporary injunctions and final injunctions for IPV victims who experience "battery, assault, bodily injury, threat of bodily injury, or placing a person in fear of physical injury."[41]

The absence of non-violent tactics in these laws makes it difficult for IPV victims, who are abused exclusively through non-violent tactics, to obtain temporary injunctions and final injunctions because they are rarely able to produce evidence of any physical bodily harm through the filing of a petition for injunction or during an evidentiary hearing. Without evidence of the physical forms of IPV enumerated in the statutes governing when the court may issue temporary injunctions and final injunctions, the IPV victim who experiences ongoing non-violent abuse must employ self-guardianship to preserve their safety and well-being because they cannot rely on law enforcement or the court. Alternatively, many victims of IPV, who feel they have no other option, look to the family court system for their personal safety and well-being, especially within the context of a divorce proceeding because they are too afraid to seek help by filing a petition for injunction or have been denied a petition for injunction in the past.[42]

Litigation Abuse or Judicial Terrorism®?

Often, the IPV victim finds themselves involved in litigation with their abuser.[43] Whether before a criminal or civil court, the process can be very difficult for the IPV victim as they can feel revictimized by the legal system, as well as by their abuser.[44] Nevertheless, it is necessary to file certain cases with the court to secure legal rights, including obtaining a temporary injunction or final injunction.[45] In many cases, the IPV victim and the abuser may file multiple injunctions for protection, especially when coercive control is present in the intimate relationship. One of the reasons for this is because the DV protection system is "one incident" focused rather than able to handle a couple's cumulative file, forcing the court to treat each violent incident as a separate court action.

Often, litigation with their abuser can cause the IPV victim to feel isolated from friends and family, especially when the litigation takes on the form of coercive control through a judicial proceeding. This is because the non-violent tactics of coercive control can be deployed through litigation rather effortlessly.[46] And this form of abuse through the judicial system is perfectly legal and impossible to control. Indeed, isolation of the IPV victim can occur through the criminal justice system and family law courts when the abuser and others blame the IPV victim by challenging their innocence, as well as their role within the violent intimate relationship, attributing their behavior as contributing to, or being responsible for, the violence.[47] In fact, victims are often viewed as masochistic and, therefore, just as responsible for their victimization as the abuser, or for at least encouraging the abuse.[48] But it can be difficult for a victim to disengage from litigation with their abuser, especially within a civil court proceeding, which goes unrecognized and misunderstood by those who view the litigation from the sidelines.

Abusers recognize that the judicial system is an effective vehicle for economic control. It allows abusers to legally create and prolong divorce litigation, which often generates exorbitant legal fees for the victim, further causing hardship to the victim, their children, and the entire family, as well as furthering the abuser's ongoing control over the victim and often, by proxy, their loved ones.[49] Likewise, abusers may use child support payments, or the lack thereof, to maintain control over their victim's financial independence and personal autonomy.[50] If the victim is employed, her job is an optimal target for the abuser, who may attempt to sabotage her job by hailing her into court continuously, be it for legitimate or frivolous claims.[51] As a result, experts recognize that legislation addressing these issues is necessary to combat coercive control tactics inside and outside the courtroom.[52]

The U.S. judicial system is one in which a litigant may institute a judicial proceeding against another person for any reason, whether legitimate or not. It is up to the opposing party to argue against the lawsuit that has been filed against them before it is either dismissed or eventually won in their favor or lost against them. In the meantime, when litigation is instituted between an IPV abuser and their victim, it is possible for much damage to occur to both parties, especially when the litigation is frivolous. Because family law courts have great discretion, causes of action between intimate partners are typically given great deferential treatment as to due process; thus, the potential for frivolous actions being allowed forward in family law courts is high. As a result, the tactics of isolation, intimidation, harassment, and power and control are able to be invoked against the IPV victim through litigation in a family law case. Indeed, it is very intimidating to constantly be haled into court, to have to regularly testify in court or in a deposition, or to have to respond to court papers whether represented or not.

A constant barrage of court filings and notices of hearings can feel like harassment, especially when the IPV victim must manage more than one lawsuit with their abuser. In fact, simply having to face the abuser, who they garnered enough strength to leave, only to have to regularly see in open court, operates as a form of harassment. Additionally, the abuser, through absolute privilege, can utilize the legal proceeding to create legal papers to publish anything they want about their victim.[53] Court documents contain allegations that must be proven in court; thus, the abuser is able to allege frivolous claims against their victim in court papers because the allegations do not have to be proven until they go to court. This is especially true when the abuser is a *pro se* litigant and is not under the guidance of a licensed attorney who might be more willing to keep the court papers less invective and full of vitriol.[54]

The effect of having the papers filed is enough to accomplish the goal of the harassment. The abuser can also call the victim names in court documents, which are published through the clerk of court, whether the documents are ever heard before the judge or not. For the victim, seeing derogatory allegations that are not factual, as well as reading their abuser calling them names in court documents, is a very efficient and effective non-violent form of harassment that can have devastating effects.[55] Nevertheless, these tactics are perfectly legal because they are within the confines of a judicial proceeding. If the abuser were committing similar, repetitive acts outside of court, it could be considered a form of stalking.

What is more, court papers and orders from one case between the abuser and IPV victim may be utilized in other cases between the parties. If the abuser obtains a favorable order from the court, they can use that order to institute a new lawsuit against the victim. However, the order they file to establish the new lawsuit may be out of context. Indeed, the abuser might not have *actually* won any litigation against the victim. The order may be a non-final order, and the abuser may file it in a different jurisdiction for frivolous or harassment purposes to create additional litigation against the victim. To do so may cause the victim to have to hire additional attorneys, take off more work, spend more time away from their children, and expend more energy they already do not have. This functions as the power and control the abuser can institute over the victim from wherever they are, no matter the time of day or night because now, the victim has left then, but they are omnipresent through the judicial system.

The judicial system was the one place the IPV victim thought they could turn to for help; but instead, it has become their worst nightmare.[56] They thought it would protect them and assist them through the process of their separation and litigation toward the finality they need with their abuser. After all, society expects them to leave their abusive intimate partner relationship, right? The victim garnered the strength to leave the abuser, to remove themself from the onslaught of the coercive control tactics; however, the judicial system allows the abuser to access the victim for continued abuse from which there is no escape. It causes one to ask the question, is this *simply* "litigation abuse" committed by the abuser because of the inherent judicial system's rules and regulations that allows them to continue to terrorize their victim through a judicial proceeding?[57]

Providing a label that expresses the true nature of terror that the non-violent tactics of coercive control deployed through a judicial proceeding evokes in its victim is a political act intended to bring awareness to the issue.[58]

Names and definitions help to draw attention to otherwise unnoticed or ignored social problems.[59] Although litigation abuse might adequately explain some of the processes that occur when an abuser utilizes the judicial system to further a coercive control agenda, it does not adequately describe the cumulative effect the tactics have on its victim nor does it effectively explain those cases in which the abuser engages the victim in litigation for many, many years, or even decades.[60] Indeed, "judicial terrorism®," the unique dynamic created by an abuser between a victim of DV and the court because of the abuser's use of the U.S. judicial system for continued DV long after separation and divorce, is a label that helps to encapsulate the enormous amount of fear and despair the abuser is able to create within the victim by utilizing the U.S. judicial system as the abuser's weapon of mass destruction.[61]

Gender Bias in the Courts

Many studies and task forces examining gender bias in the courts have been completed over the past several decades, finding that "gender bias is pervasive and has serious consequences."[62] To understand this form of bias, it is first important to understand the definition of gender bias as defined by the National Judicial Education Program to Promote Equality for Women and Men in the Courts because it can often be misunderstood.[63] "Gender bias refers to attitudes and behaviors based on sex stereotypes, the perceived relative worth of women and men and myths and misconceptions about their economic and social positions."[64] The role of gender and its implicit hierarchal structure between men and women within the judicial system not only affects the personnel working within and among it every day but the members of society who are exposed to the rule of law and its judicial orders.[65] Indeed, the law itself is based on a patriarchal precedent of social and cultural norms that bind women and men to a legal jurisprudence developed almost exclusively by white men with privilege. Today, this inherently male dominated legal system seeks to disempower women and reinforce male supremacy.

One of the forms of disempowerment of women in the judicial system is the constant questioning of her credibility.[66] While challenged with judicial proceedings against their abuser, many victims of IPV are still under enormous stress of the trauma from the abuse they face(d) from the same person they now must confront in court. Often, this trauma related stress can cause the IPV victim to appear agitated or dissociated with their surroundings, making them seem less credible than the non-traumatized litigant.[67] When these outward manifestations of trauma occur, the non-trauma informed court or attorney, most likely, will not take the IPV victim's abuse and trauma symptomology into account.[68] Thus, when a petition for injunction is heard without any visible evidence of recent physical violence and the victim presents agitated or dissociated, the court may be inclined to view their claims of abuse as non-credible, effectively empowering the abuser to continue their abuse unabated.[69]

Litigation and Coercive Control: Not Every Petition for Injunction for Protection against Domestic Violence Is the Same

Agnew-Brune et al. (2017) explain that 37% of all violent crimes against women are classified as IPV.[70] Due to such repeated exposure to violence from their intimate partner, victims of IPV apply for temporary injunctions and final injunctions throughout the country on a regular basis to prevent their partner from intimidating, threatening, harassing, assaulting, or contacting the person filing for the court order for protection from DV.[71] It is up to the judge to determine the severity of the case and to base it on the statute's language as to whether the temporary injunction or final injunction may be granted. Judges have great discretion in denying or granting temporary injunctions and/or final injunctions and are mandated to make objective decisions without inserting their personal beliefs into the decision-making process.[72] However, Agnew-Brune et al. (2017) explain that judges' perceptions of what severity of violence that is required to cross the line for the issuance of a temporary injunction and/or final injunction may be very different.[73] They explain that, in the absence of physical evidence of injuries, such as visible bruising and lacerations, judges rely on their own personal definitions of what should be "enough" to issue the temporary injunction and/or final injunction.[74]

One judge in the Agnew-Brune et al. (2017) study explained that they use intuition to determine whether a temporary injunction or final injunction should be granted.[75] Specifically, they explained that they observe the IPV victim's demeanor, rather the alleged abuser's behavior in court.[76] Judges look to the reactions of the victims in court to see if they are afraid or in fear of what has or is taking place to determine whether they believe the fear of physical violence is high enough to cross the threshold for the granting of a temporary injunction or final injunction.[77] An appearance by the victim of normalcy, i.e., such as not seeming tearful enough, caused some judges to feel as though the victim was not in enough fear to warrant the issuance of an order for protection.[78] Indeed, judges went as far as to accuse victims who appeared in court and happened to smile as having faked their abuse or playing games with the court system.[79]

The Agnew-Brune et al. (2017) study did not indicate that any of the judges stated they paid attention to the abusers' demeanor in court to determine how they interacted with court personnel or the victim.[80] Often, body language can indicate a person's social interactions and skills, especially regarding how they are perceived by others and whether they are manipulating and controlling. Instead, regarding the abusers, the judges in the study focused on their anticipated regret for (1) erroneously issuing the protecting order due to the havoc it would reap in the lives of the innocently accused and (2) worrying about not issuing the protective order for fear that they would allow the DV to escalate if one was not issued.[81] Yet, different from the influences of the victims' presentations in court, the judges did not let these fears of regret impact their decisions on the bench.[82]

Notes

1 Donna J. King, *Naming the Judicial Terrorist: An Exposé of an Abuser's Successful Use of a Judicial Proceeding for Continued Domestic Violence*, 1 TENN. JOURNAL OF RACE, GENDER, & SOCIAL JUSTICE 153, 170 (2012); WALTER S. DEKESEREDY & MARTIN D. SCHWARTZ, DANGEROUS EXITS: ESCAPING ABUSIVE RELATIONSHIPS IN RURAL AMERICA (2009); MOLLY DRAGIEWICZ, EQUALITY WITH A VENGEANCE: MEN'S RIGHTS GROUPS, BATTERED WOMEN, AND ANTIFEMINIST BACKLASH (2011); EVAN STARK, COERCIVE CONTROL: HOW MEN ENTRAP WOMEN IN PERSONAL LIFE (2007).
2 *See* DEKESEREDY & SCHWARTZ, *supra* note 1.
3 *See* Lorraine Davies et al., *Gender Inequality and Patterns of Abuse Post Leaving*, 24 J. FAM. VIOL. 27 (2009) https://doi.org/10.1007/s10896-008-9204-5.
4 *See* Davies et al., *supra* note 3; R. Emerson Dobash et al., *Lethal and Nonlethal Violence Against an Intimate Female Partner: Comparing Male Murderers to Nonlethal Abusers*, 13 VIOLENCE AGAINST WOMEN 329 (2007) https://doi.org/10.1177%2F1077801207299204; Aysan Sev'er, *Recent or Imminent Separation and Intimate Violence Against Women: A Conceptual Overview and Some Canadian Examples*, 3 VIOLENCE AGAINST WOMEN 566 (1997).
5 *See* Dobash et al., *supra* note 4; Sev'er, *supra* note 4.
6 *See* Mary Ann Dutton & Lisa A. Goodman, *Coercion in Intimate Partner Violence: Toward a New Conceptualization*, 52 SEX ROLES 743 (2005) https://doi.org/10.1007/s11199-005-4196-6.
7 *See* STARK, *supra* note 1.
8 *See* Davies et al., *supra* note 3.
9 *See* Sev'er, *supra* note 4.
10 *See* Dobash et al., *supra* note 4; Sev'er, *supra* note 4.
11 *See* Davies et al., *supra* note 3; DEKESEREDY & SCHWARTZ, *supra* note 1; Dobash et al., *supra* note 4; JODY RAPHAEL, SAVING BERNICE: BATTERED WOMEN, WELFARE, AND POVERTY (2000).
12 *See* Mari L. Aldridge & Kevin D. Browne, *Perpetrators of Spousal Homicide: A Review*, 4 TRAUMA, VIOLENCE, & ABUSE 265 (2003) https://journals.sagepub.com/doi/10.1177/1524838003004003005.
13 *See* RAPHAEL, *supra* note 11; SUSAN WEITZMAN, "NOT TO PEOPLE LIKE US:" HIDDEN ABUSE IN UPSCALE MARRIAGES (2000).
14 *See* Aldridge & Browne, *supra* note 12; Dobash et al., *supra* note 4; Desmond Ellis, *Male Abuse of a Married or Cohabiting Female Partner: The Application of Sociological Theory to Research Findings*, 4 VIOLENCE AND VICTIMS 235 (1989).
15 *See* Dobash et al., *supra* note 4; Sev'er, *supra* note 4.
16 *See* Jerrell Dayton King & Donna J. King, *A Call for Limiting Absolute Privilege: How Victims of Domestic Violence, Suffering with Post-Traumatic Stress Disorder, Are Discriminated Against by the U.S. Judicial System*, 6 DEPAUL JOURNAL OF WOMEN, GENDER AND THE LAW 1 (2017).

17 *See* Laurie M. Graham et al., *The Danger Assessment: An Instrument for the Prevention of Intimate Partner Homicide*, in HANDBOOK OF INTERPERSONAL VIOLENCE ACROSS THE LIFESPAN (R. Geffner at al. eds., 2019) https://doi.org/10.1007/978-3-319-62122-7_145-1; RAPHAEL, *supra* note 11.
18 Sonia Salari & Carrie LeFevre Sillito, *Intimate Partner Homicide-Suicide: Perpetrator Primary Intent Across Young, Middle, and Elder Adult Age Categories*, 26 AGGRESSION AND VIOLENT BEHAVIOR 26, 27 (2016) https://doi.org/10.1016/j.avb.2015.11.004; *accord* Emma Morton et al., *Partner Homicide-Suicide Involving Female Homicide Victims: A Population-Based Study in North Carolina, 1988–1992*, 13 VIOLENCE AND VICTIMS 91 (1998). *See infra* Chapter 8, The Family Annihilator.
19 *See American Roulette: Murder-Suicide in the United States*, VIOLENCE POLICY CENTER (2020) https://vpc.org/studies/amroul2020.pdf.
20 *See* Salari & Sillito, *supra* note 18.
21 *See Id.*
22 *See American Roulette: Murder-Suicide in the United States*, *supra* note 19.
23 *See Id.*
24 *See* Tara N. Richards et al., *Reporting Femicide-Suicide in the News: The Current Utilization of Suicide Reporting Guidelines and Recommendations for the Future*, 29 J. FAM. VIOL. 453 (2014) https://doi.org/10.1007/s10896-014-9590-9.
25 *See Id.*
26 *See Id.*
27 *Id.* at 455.
28 Morton et al., *supra* note 18 at 13.
29 *See* Catherine G. Velopulos et al., *Comparison of Male and Female Victims of Intimate Partner Homicide and Bidirectionality: An Analysis of the National Violent Death Reporting System*, 87 J. TRAUMA ACUTE CARE SURG. 331 (2019) https://doi.org/10.1097/TA.0000000000002276; Shilan Caman et al., *Trends in Rates and Characteristics of Intimate Partner Homicides Between 1990 and 2013*, 49 J. OF CRIMINAL JUSTICE 14 (2017) https://doi.org/10.1016/j.jcrimjus.2017.01.002.
30 *See* Solveig K. B. Vatnar et al., *A Comparison of Intimate Partner Homicide With Intimate Partner Homicide-Suicide: Evidence From a Norwegian National 22-Year Cohort*, 36 JOURNAL OF INTERPERSONAL VIOLENCE 1 (2019) https://doi.org/10.1177/0886260519849656.
31 *See* Velopulos et al., *supra* note 29. *See infra* Chapter 11, Future Directions for Research.
32 *See* TK Logan & Robert Walker, *Civil Protective Order Effectiveness: Justice of Just a Piece of Paper?*, 25 VIOLENCE AND VICTIMS 332, 342 (2010) https://doi.org/10.1891/0886-6708.25.3.332; *accord* Brynn E. Sheehan et al., *Intimate Partner Homicide: New Insights for Understanding Lethality and Risks*, 21 VIOLENCE AGAINST WOMEN 269 (2015) https://doi.org/10.1177/1077801214564687.
33 *See* TK Logan et al., *Protective Orders: Questions and Conundrums*, 7 TRAUMA, VIOLENCE, & ABUSE 175 (2006) https://doi.org/10.1177/1524838006288930.
34 *See supra* Chapter 2. *See infra* Part II.
35 *See* Logan & Walker, *supra* note 32.
36 *See* Logan et al., *supra* note 33.
37 This timing is generally driven by the court's docket, but the two-week time frame is the standard by which most courts try to adhere.
38 It is important to keep in mind that, if the temporary injunction is granted at the *ex parte* stage, the alleged abuser loses their rights without notice or a hearing,

i.e., without due process. It is because of this that it is so important to ensure the level of abuse alleged meets the criteria to issue the temporary injunction and to make sure that the scheduled hearing on the final injunction is held as soon as possible after service of the temporary injunction to the alleged abuser.

39 *See* Logan & Walker, *supra* note 32.
40 *See* Melanie Kalmanson, *Filling the Gap of Domestic Violence Protection" Returning Human Rights to U.S. Victims*, 43 FLA. ST. U. L. REV. 1359 (2107); Donna J. King et al., Coercive Control Legislation: Legislating Against Non-Violent Forms of Domestic Violence (June 6, 2023) (unpublished manuscript) (on file with author); Lois Schwaeber, *Recognizing Domestic Violence: How to Know It When You See It and How to Provide Appropriate Representation*, in DOMESTIC VIOLENCE, ABUSE, AND CHILD CUSTODY: LEGAL STRATEGIES AND POLICY ISSUES (Mo Therese Hannah & Barry Goldstein eds., 2010); STARK, *supra* note 1.
41 Margaret E. Johnson, *Redefining Harm, Reimagining Remedies and Reclaiming Domestic Violence Law*, 42 U.C. DAVIS L. REV. 1107, 1131 (2009); *accord* Logan & Walker, *supra* note 32. The terminology utilized for the issuance of the order for protection against domestic violence is, sometimes, locally determinative.
42 *See* Kara Bellew, *Silent Suffering: Uncovering and Understanding Domestic Violence in Affluent Communities*, 26 WOMEN'S RIGHTS LAW REPORTER 39 (2005).
43 *See Id.*; King, *supra* note 1; Nilgün Özçakar et al., *Domestic Violence Survivors and Their Experiences During Legal Process*, 40 J. OF FORENSIC AND LEGAL MEDICINE 1 (2016) https://doi.org/10.1016/j.jflm.2016.01.023.
44 *See* Bellew, *supra* note 42; King, *supra* note 1; Özçakar et al., *supra* note 43.
45 *See* Cara J. Person et al., *"I Don't Know That I've Ever Felt Like I Got the Full Story": A Qualitative Study of Courtroom Interactions Between Judges and Litigants in Domestic Violence Protective Order Cases*, 24 VIOLENCE AGAINST WOMEN 1 (2018) https://doi.org/10.1177/1077801217738582.
46 *See* King, *supra* note 1.
47 *See infra* Chapter 3, Litigation and Coercive Control: Not Every Petition for Injunction for Protection against Domestic Violence is the Same. *See also* NANCY BERNS, FRAMING THE VICTIM: DOMESTIC VIOLENCE MEDIA AND SOCIAL PROBLEMS (2004).
48 *See* BERNS, *supra* note 47.
49 *See* King, *supra* note 1; WEITZMAN, *supra* note 13.
50 *See* JOCELYN ELISE CROWLEY, THE POLITICS OF CHILD SUPPORT IN AMERICA (2003); Kalmanson, *supra* note 40.
51 *See* King, *supra* note 1.
52 *See* Cheryl Hanna, *The Paradox of Progress: Translating Evan Stark's Coercive Control Into Legal Doctrine for Abused Women*, 15 VIOLENCE AGAINST WOMEN 1458 (2009) https://doi.org/10.1177%2F1077801209347091; STARK, *supra* note 1; Deborah Tuerkheimer, *Recognizing and Remedying the Harm of Battering: A Call to Criminalize Domestic Violence*, 94 THE JOURNAL OF CRIMINAL LAW & CRIMINOLOGY 959 (2004).
53 *See* King & King, *supra* note 16.
54 *See* Northern District of Florida, *Filing Without an Attorney*, U.S. DISTRICT COURT https://www.flnd.uscourts.gov/filing-without-attorney#:~:text=%22Pro%20se%22%20is%20Latin%20for,attorney%20is%20considered%20pro%20se (last visited June 7, 2023) (explaining that "'Pro se' is Latin for 'in one's own behalf.'").
55 *See* King & King, *supra* note 16.
56 *See Id.*

57 *See Litigation Abuse*, WOMENSLAW.ORG (March 24, 2022) https://www.womenslaw.org/about-abuse/forms-abuse/litigation-abuse; *Abusive Litigation: When Your Abuser Exploits the Legal System*, LEGAL VOICE (2021) https://www.legalvoice.org/abusive-litigation. *See also* King & King, *supra* note 16.
58 *See* King, *supra* note 1; King & King, *supra* note 16; STARK, *supra* note 1. *See also Litigation Abuse, supra* note 57.
59 *See* King, *supra* note 1; STARK, *supra* note 1.
60 *See* King, *supra* note 1; King & King, *supra* note 16; STARK, *supra* note 1. *See also Litigation Abuse, supra* note 57.
61 *See Judicial Terrorism*®, VICTIMS' SAFE HARBOR FOUNDATION, INC., http://victimssafeharbor.org/ (last visited Feb. 18, 2023). *See also* King, *supra* note 1.
62 Molly Dragiewicz, *Gender Bias in the Courts: Implications for Battered Mothers and Their Children, in* DOMESTIC VIOLENCE, ABUSE, AND CHILD CUSTODY: LEGAL STRATEGIES AND POLICY ISSUES 5-7 (Mo Therese Hannah & Barry Goldstein eds., 2010); *accord* Judith McConnell & Kathleen F. Sikora, *Gender Bias and the Institutionalization of Change: Lessons from the California Experience*, 39 JUDGES J. 13 (2000); Lynn Hecht Schafran & Norma Juliet Wikler, *Gender Fairness in the Courts: Action in the New Millennium*, NATIONAL JUDICIAL EDUCATION PROGRAM (2001); Lynn Hecht Schafran & Norma Juliet Wikler, *Operating a Task Force on Gender Bias in the Courts: A Manual for Action*, THE FOUNDATION FOR WOMEN JUDGES (1986).
63 *See* Schafran & Wikler, *supra* note 62.
64 *Id.* at 2 n.1. The terms "gender" and "sex" are often used interchangeably; however, sex refers to the female or male category as biologically assigned at birth. Gender refers to the social construct of femininity and masculinity as applied to the sexes (*See* Dragiewicz, *supra* note 62).
65 *See* Dragiewicz, *supra* note 62; King, *supra* note 1; King & King, *supra* note 16.
66 *See* Dragiewicz, *supra* note 62; King & King, *supra* note 16.
67 *See* King & King, *supra* note 16. Dissociation is a coping mechanism that manifests in a trauma victim when confronted with a trauma inducing situation that causes the need for the victim to escape from their immediate surroundings (*See* C.J. Eubanks Fleming & Patricia A. Resick, *Predicting Three Types of Dissociation in Female Survivors of Intimate Partner Violence*, 17 J. OF TRAUMA & DISSOCIATION 267 (2016) https://doi.org/10.1080/15299732.2015.1079807).
68 *See* King & King, *supra* note 16.
69 *See Id.*
70 *See* Christine Agnew-Brune et al., *Domestic Violence Protective Orders: A Qualitative Examination of Judge's Decision-Making Processes*, 32 J. OF INTERPERSONAL VIOLENCE 1921 (2017) https://doi.org/10.1177/0886260515590126.
71 *See Id.*
72 *See Id.*
73 *See Id.*
74 *See Id.*
75 *See Id.*
76 *See Id.*
77 *See Id.*
78 *See Id.*
79 *See Id.*
80 *See Id.*
81 *See Id.*
82 *See Id.*

4 Understanding Intimate Partner Homicide Victims from Their Own Data

The focus of this mixed-methods study was to determine whether coercive control, exclusive of a prior reporting of physical violence to law enforcement or the court before an intimate partner homicide (IPH), presents a significant risk of death. Through inductive and deductive reasoning, this study tests Black's (2010) Theory of the Behavior of Law against the empirical research regarding whether the victim of an IPH sought the assistance of law enforcement or the court at various times during the heterosexual spousal relationship prior to the IPH.[1] Additionally, the term "coercive control" was contextualized and operationalized from the secondary data collected relevant to petitions for injunction filed between heterosexual spouses who are the subjects of the IPHs for this study.

This study looked at certain variables, such as intimate partner homicide-suicide (IPHS), record of petition for injunction, and weapons used, and compared frequencies among the variables.[2] These data provide insight into the frequencies of the cases studied that had prior reporting of physical violence and those that did not have prior reporting of physical violence before the IPH. It assumes that the IPH involved physical violence between the intimate partner violence (IPV) victim and the offender, so the violence at the time of the killing was not considered IPV for prior physical violence to the IPH for the purposes of this study. The data were organized, coded, and analyzed following the qualitative and quantitative methods described below. Additionally, a detailed description of the data collection process and resulting conceptualization and operationalization of coercive control, as described below, is vital to this study.

Methodology for Data Collection: Sourcing Public Records

Deliverables for this study, including the conceptualization and operationalization of coercive control, were sourced from data for January 1, 2006, through June 30, 2016, that were collected from the Uniform Crime Report-Supplemental Homicide Report (UCR-SHR), various law enforcement agencies throughout the state of Florida, and multiple Florida county clerks of court.[3] Heterosexual married couples were chosen for this study because IPHs are known for being expressive, i.e., the main reason the killing occurs is because the offender's motive was to intentionally hurt the victim and because coercive control is more prevalent in heterosexual relationships.[4]

The Florida Department of Law Enforcement Uniform Crime Report-Supplemental Homicide Report Data

To initiate the collection of data, this study utilized email for all the Florida Department of Law Enforcement (FDLE) public records requests to the official FDLE Office of General Counsel email at publicrecords@fdle.state.fl.us.[5] Specifically, requests were made for all UCR-SHR data "that are coded for all homicides involving spouses, no matter the circumstance code, where one spouse is the victim and the other is the offender … for all Florida counties."[6] For the period of January 1, 2006, to June 30, 2016, the overall total of reported IPH cases provided by the FDLE was 665. However, the FDLE does not filter its UCR-SHR public records requests to provide only the cases requested; thus, all public records from all law enforcement agencies involved in the UCR-SHR were contacted to ensure external and internal validity of this study. In other words, the FDLE's UCR-SHR data, on its face, cannot be taken as an exact measure for Florida heterosexual spousal IPHs.[7]

One of the reasons for the fact that the UCR-SHR data cannot be taken at face value, as Campbell et al. (2007) explain, is because the UCR-SHR data misclassifies intimate partners, mostly because they do not have a category to account for ex-boyfriend/girlfriend.[8] Thus, for this study, the data provided by the FDLE's UCR-SHR were cross-referenced against the incident report for each IPH from the reporting law enforcement agency to ensure accuracy. More importantly, this cross-referencing was completed to confirm that each homicide on the UCR-SHR data were, in fact, a heterosexual spousal IPH, especially because it was possible that some cases that were reported may be other types of IPH cases.[9] Additionally, the data collected from law enforcement in the second phase of this study, as well as the data collected from the county courthouses, further helped to cross-reference against the UCR-SHR data for any IPH cases that may not have qualified within this study's criteria.

Of the 665 cases originally provided by the FDLE's UCR-SHR, forty-seven (47) cases were excluded from this study for the reasons listed immediately below, bringing the total number of cases to 618. As discussed above, when cross-referencing the UCR-SHR with the data collected from law enforcement as well as the county courthouses, it became evident that cases on the UCR-SHR data did not qualify within this study's criteria for the following reasons:

- The IPH victim and offender were not married = seventeen (17) cases
- The heterosexual spouses were involved in a drunk driving/vehicular homicide rather than an IPH = nine (9) cases
- The homicide victim(s) was/(were) killed by an unknown assailant = ten (10) cases
- The case is not an IPH between heterosexual spouses = three (3) cases
- Both spouses committed suicide = one (1) case
- Both spouses were victims of a crime (not necessarily a homicide) = two (2) cases
- The wrong case number and year of incident was provided; the case is outside the criteria of the study = one (1) case
- Missing person report; not an IPH = one (1) case
- Homicide victim was family member of suspect, not spouse of suspect = one (1) case
- The case was not a homicide between the heterosexual spouses; it was a simple battery = one (1) case
- The case was not an IPH; it was an accidental drug overdose = one (1) case

Florida Local Law Enforcement Agencies

The UCR-SHR provides information to link each IPH to their respective reporting law enforcement agency to obtain the names of the IPH victim and offender by tracking the Agency Report Number. This information was necessary for further qualitative data collection. For this study, each agency was provided a public records request of the UCR-SHR excerpt pertaining to its Agency Report Number(s) and case(s) so that the incident report(s) for the homicide(s) was/were provided. Once the first round of incident report(s) from each law enforcement agency were logged, coded, and analyzed, a second public records request was sent to each local law enforcement agency within the county where the IPH occurred. The difference with the second public records request was that it contained the name of the IPH victim and offender, as opposed to the anonymous Agency Report Number that was provided on the UCR-SHR data. The purpose of the second public records request was to collect all incident reports within the Florida county where the IPH occurred to account for all possible prior physical violence reports that may have been made to local law enforcement agencies before the killing. Thus, it was possible to log the prior reporting of physical violence between the IPH victim and offender that might have taken place at any time during their relationship prior to the killing by obtaining these data.

There were 163 law enforcement agencies that were contacted during the data collection process for the 665 cases for the first reports as described above. Of the 163 law enforcement agencies, 139 responded to the first request for records. Twenty-four (24) law enforcement agencies did not respond to the first request for records, which generally stemmed from a lack of response after multiple attempts to contact the public records department and/or contact persons for the identified law enforcement agencies.

For the first round of public records requests, lack of availability of records from various law enforcement agencies, based on either their unresponsiveness to requests for public records or their public records rules, such as the unavailability of public records while criminal trials and appeals were still in progress, prevented 125 cases from being included in this study. This brought the total number of cases from the 618 after the UCR-SHR phase of data collection to 493, allowing for generalizability at this level of the study. The breakdown of reasons as to why cases were excluded during the first round of public records requests from law enforcement agencies is as follows:

- Law enforcement agencies' unresponsiveness to requests for public records for this study = sixty-seven (67) cases
- Law enforcement agencies' policy of not releasing records while litigation regarding the suspect in the case is still taking place = twenty-seven (27) cases
- The name of either the IPH victim and/or offender provided by law enforcement agencies was legally redacted under F.S. Chapter 119 for various reasons, such as the IPH victim or offender was a police officer (some reasons for redaction were undisclosed by law enforcement) = five (5) cases
- The name of either the IPH victim and/or offender provided by law enforcement agencies was unknown for various reasons, such as the IPH report was handwritten and illegible; and additional requests to obtain the names were unsuccessful = seventeen (17) cases
- The name of either the IPH victim and/or offender provided by law enforcement agencies was missing from the first request of IPH reports, and additional requests to obtain the names were unsuccessful = six (6) cases
- Law enforcement agencies destroyed the IPH reports, as a matter of standard agency procedure, requested through the public records request = two (2) cases
- The name of the victim and offender provided by the law enforcement agency was labeled as "unknown;" and the case was not an IPH = one (1) case

Of the 139 law enforcement agencies that responded to the first request for records, 119 responded to the second request for records. Thus, twenty

(20) agencies were non-responsive at the second request phase of the law enforcement agency data collection portion of the study, affecting sixty (60) cases in the study.[10] In other words, sixty (60) IPH cases do not have the prior physical violence data from law enforcement for analysis. Reasons for lack of response at the second request phase were similar to those at the first request phase, even though relationships with public records departments were built during the first phase of data collection. Other reasons for lack of inclusion of second phase data include excessive costs to obtain the records, as well as the extensive time needed by some agencies to complete the public records requests which fell outside the time frame of this study.

The Florida County Courthouse

The final source of public access for data collection was the county courthouse. Today, most, if not all, county courthouses in Florida have on-line access to their public records dockets. As a result, for this study, it was possible to research each of the 493 cases for which the name of the IPH victim and offender were obtained, as described above, making it possible to research the court records on-line between them. Specifically, petitions for injunctions for protection against domestic violence (DV) filed between the IPH victim and offender, whether filed by the IPH victim or against the victim, were searched for using the relevant county's on-line court access vehicle to determine whether the couple had any prior petitions for injunction filed between them.[11] The county courthouse search was limited to the county in which the IPH occurred. Each name, i.e., the IPH victim and offender, was searched separately in the clerk of court's on-line system to ensure that all possible cases were found through the on-line system. Only petitions for injunction cases that matched both parties were included in this study. Eight cases' petitions for injunction documents, identified through the on-line search process as described above, were destroyed as a matter of the clerk of courts' administrative procedures. For purposes of the county courthouse data source, 100 petitions for injunction, spanning sixty-two (62) cases were collected. However, because it is possible to do additional on-line docket research into the complete history of the petitions for injunction cases, 108 petitions for injunction from the same sixty-two (62) cases were able to be used for analysis in the qualitative phase of this study but not for content analysis.[12]

These petitions for injunction data are critical for the qualitative methods phase of this study, as well as the quantitative methods phase. Once the identification of each petition for injunction was made, the public records request to the relevant clerk of court was made to obtain the petition for injunction if they were not readily available through on-line services.

Generally, the clerk of courts local rules allowed them to respond via their on-line systems; however, some responded via mail, e-mail, or only in person. At times, clerks of court were particularly resistant to providing the requested documents, citing privacy issues relevant to the parties in the cases. When this arose, additional correspondence was required to explain the nature of the study and to remind the clerk of Florida's Sunshine Law, including Florida Statute, Chapter 119, which allowed for access to the public records that were being requested.[13] This correspondence was effective and produced the desired effect of receiving the requested documents from the resistant clerk of court.

Petitions for injunction contain attested-to narratives, written by the person in the IPV relationship who is asking the court for protection. These provided insight into the history of the forms of IPV that would have been experienced by the person seeking protection prior to the IPH. Any such records are inherently rich in details because it is incumbent upon the person seeking protection from the court to provide detailed information for the court to determine whether to provide a temporary injunction, as explained in Chapter 3, The Disillusionment of the Protections of an Injunction for Protection: Why and When are They Important to IPV Victims?[14] Indeed, the petitions for injunction are first-hand accounts, provided by the IPH victims and/or their offenders, prior to the killing, making this study the first of its kind to obtain these data for analysis.

Aldridge and Browne (2003) explain that the key witness to the IPH, i.e., the murder victim is unavailable when collecting data; and researchers have attempted to do their best to piece together the personal aspects of the intimate partner relationship prior to the killing.[15] However, police records, medical examiner reports, coroner reports, covictims' interviews, newspaper collections, social media, witnesses' interviews, etc., do not have the same intimate details as the IPH victim, who is seeking the court's protection from their abuser. Aldridge and Browne (2003) explain that all the various sources of data, other than the IPH victim, may have varying agendas when collecting data or providing information.[16] Conversely, the IPV victim, attesting to their petition for injunction narrative to the court, should be viewed as having one agenda, i.e., seeking protection from the court due to a perceived threat of violence from their abuser.

A Comparison of Intimate Partner Homicide Studies

To develop lethality risk factors most accurately for IPV victims, it is necessary to access the best data available. Recently, researchers have begun to look to covictims as "the source of firsthand and intimate knowledge regarding the relationship between the victim and the perpetrator."[17] However, for the multitude of reasons already discussed above and for those discussed below, obtaining data from the IPH victim prior to the killing provides credible facts about the relationship that cannot otherwise be obtained. For this reason, prior studies on IPH must be compared to this study because the persons the researcher looks to for the data collection and how the research is conducted, i.e., the methodology of the study, ultimately plays a central role in the outcome of the results. In other words, it is possible that the study or its primary or secondary data may erroneously focus on prior physical violence alone; thus, the results may be skewed with an overall focus on physical violence predating the killing due to the methodology of the study. But recent studies on coercive control have endeavored to improve their methodologies to overcome these obstacles.[18]

In 1992, Dr. Jacquelyn C. Campbell stated that about two thirds of IPH victims were physically abused before they were killed.[19] This statement was provided in support of the initial lethality risk assessment tool that was being presented to the National Institute of Justice at the time and has been heavily relied upon ever since.[20] In addition to Dr. Campbell's risk assessment, the entire report provided during the "Proceeding of the First Annual Workshop of the Homicide Research Working Group" on "Questions and Answers in Lethal and Non-Lethal Violence," included Dr. Richard Block's and Dr. Carolyn Rebecca Block's detailed report on how they collected data for their "Chicago Homicide Dataset [that, at the time,] contain[ed] over 200 variables ... and almost 20,000 cases."[21] These data were derived from the Chicago police department and included all homicide cases known to them occurring between 1965 and 1990.[22] Police investigation files were the data source for the study, which lead to a focused study on IPH published in 1995.[23]

Block and Christakos (1995) utilized "the largest, most detailed data set on violence available in the United States" at the time of their IPH study, which spanned over 22,000 homicides.[24] Of the 22,000 cases, 2556 homicides utilized for their study were the result of an IPH.[25] Block and Christakos (1995) make it very clear when explaining their data and methodology that "[t]he Chicago Homicide Dataset contains information from the *police* point of view – all cases that police investigation determined to be homicides – regardless of the eventual outcome of prosecution."[26] Indeed, they ensured that the reader understands the offender's designation in the case was not taken to prosecution, i.e., the police determined culpability. However, what is also important to understand is that the data set was developed from a third-party's viewpoint of the case, meaning the IPH victim did not participate or have a voice in the development of the data set. The results of the study are very detailed and useful; yet Block and Christakos (1995) explain that IPH prevention is unresolved because it requires longitudinal analysis of IPV cases to their eventual outcome, lethal or nonlethal.[27]

Moracco et al. (1998) study of femicide in North Carolina between 1991 and 1993 utilizes two unique, but complimentary, data sources to create a data set that is generalizable and detailed.[28] First, they accessed the data from the statewide medical examiner system which is mandated in North Carolina to investigate all unnatural causes of death.[29] Second, they conducted telephone interviews of the law enforcement officers who completed the IPH investigations.[30] In the course of a fifteen to twenty minute interview, targeted questions centered on any prior history of DV, information about the IPH offender, circumstances surrounding the killing, information about the intimate partner relationship (if any), and the legal status or outcome of the case.[31] For this study, Moracco et al. (1998) defined the term "domestic violence" as "a set of physically violent and/or threatening behaviors perpetrated against an intimate partner."[32] An example scenario offered by Moracco et al. (1998) is as follows:

> We asked the law enforcement officers whether specific behaviors (e.g., the perpetrator physically assaulted the victim, the perpetrator threatened the victim's family) had occurred prior to, but not during the femicide. If any of these behaviors occurred, or if a history of domestic violence was noted anywhere in the medical examiner file (including the narrative section of the Report of the Medical Examiner Investigation and/or enclosed newspaper clippings), we classified the case as having a history of domestic violence.[33]

Thus, details of any other form of domestic abuse or coercive control, including questions thereof, were not included or considered.

Campbell et al. (2003) published their case-control study that utilizes proxies as data sources for the IPH victims' relationship with the abuser information.[34] This study analyzes 307 cases with at least 2 proxy informants who are familiar with the details of the intimate relationship between the killer and the IPH victim prior to the killing.[35] However, 19.2% of the 307 cases were eliminated because the proxy reported no prior abuse by the femicide perpetrator, essentially requiring that all proxy cases had prior abuse to qualify for the study.[36] Additionally, the 343 control cases were randomly identified intimate partners who had to meet the criteria of "abused," which meant "physically assaulted or threatened with a weapon by a current or former intimate partner during the past 2 years."[37] Thus, this study limits the data's ability to express any notion of domestic abuse other than physical violence or the threat thereof.

Dobash et al. (2009) named their study "The Murder in Britain Study," and it incorporated three different data sets.[38]

> The study included three distinct sources of data: (a) two extant Homicide Indexes containing, annual reports of all known homicides within Britain (approximately 700-800 in England/Wales and about 100 in Scotland); (b) an original data set including quantitative and

qualitative data gathered from the case files of a sample of 866 men and women convicted of murder; and (c) another original data set of qualitative data based on 200 in-depth interviews with men and women currently serving life in prison for murder.[39]

For their article "'Out of the Blue': Men Who Murder an Intimate Partner," which is the focus of this comparison, Dobash et al. (2009) analyzed 104 cases of men who were convicted of IPH.[40] Their data are incredibly detailed and span the lifetime of the killer, with life circumstances and details of the murder adding to the holistic framework.[41] Indeed, "the police, forensic experts, solicitors, trial judges, psychiatrists/psychologists, medical staff, social workers, probation officers, school teachers, family members, witnesses, and the offender" all contributed to the rich data collected for this study, which are available because of the offender being in prison in the United Kingdom for the IPH.[42]

The processes the United Kingdom developed for the IPH offender evaluation for prison release is extraordinarily extensive, and the study's access to these data is invaluable.[43] However, much of the data are specific to the offender and does not provide any information regarding the IPV victim's point of view about the intimate relationship.[44] In addition, and most importantly to this study's focus, Dobash et al. (2009) specifically acknowledge that IPH research in the United States is "*primarily limited to cases with a history of previous violence to the victim*" [emphasis added].[45] This type of limitation, especially for an entire class of cases, such as those studied in the United States, potentially narrowed the results of a huge swath of IPH studies. Indeed, limiting data collection to cases with a history of previous physical violence to the victim might have very well eliminated potential IPH victim identification for decades.

In their exploratory IPH study, Sheehan et al. (2015) explain that accessing covictims as a source of data for information regarding the IPH victim is a neglected area of study.[46] They explain that, although IPV advocates, medical examiner reports, and police records provide some information regarding the intimate partner relationship, obtaining access to family members and close friends increases the level of understanding of the intimate relationship to improve development of IPH risk factors.[47] As a result, the Sheehan et al. (2015) study, which consists of fourteen (14) covictims representing nine (9) incidents, sixteen (16) deaths, and nine (9) IPH victims, is instructive.[48] However, their study is not generalizable; and the covictims were interviewed approximately six (6) years after each IPH.[49]

Sheehan et al. (2015) explained their methodology in detail to determine that, although a specific topic of conversation was "the covictims' perspective on level of dangerousness[,]" the study was not specifically focused on prior physical violence.[50] Indeed, the method of free-flowing, conversation-like interviews conducted for this qualitative study allowed for the covictims to provide the information they had about the intimate partnership without interruption.[51] Thus, this exploratory study's results, although not generalizable, were quite interesting in terms of prior physical violence because, according to the covictims, all nine (9) IPH cases had a history of DV.[52] In fact, the covictims provided details as to the types of prior reporting the IPH victims had done in their attempts to seek protection from their abusers leading up to the killings, i.e., law enforcement, IPV advocate, and health-care professional.[53]

Although the studies discussed above are exceptional, methodologically each tends to lend itself to the inevitable conclusion that physical violence between intimates is a precursor to IPH. The Sheehan et al. (2015) study seems the most promising for data collection from those as close to the IPH victim in determining prior reporting of physical violence without the potential for bias; however, additional data for generalization is needed.[54] Indeed, this type of data may be difficult to collect due to covictims' reluctance to participate, as is the citizenry's reluctance to mobilize the law when they witness IPV.

Theorizing Intimate Partner Violence and Intimate Partner Homicide

There are many theoretical approaches to homicide and violence within the family, macro- and micro-social orientation respectively.[55] To provide a predominant theoretical framework for IPH, where the determinates consider the non-violent aspects, as well as the physically violent exchanges between the victim and offender, it is often necessary to consider a theoretically synthesized approach.[56] However, for this study, Black's Theory of the Behavior of Law provides the best theoretical perspective because it considers the IPV victim's decision to mobilize the law, either criminal or civil, for self-protection prior to the killing.[57]

Due to the finality between parties to an abusive intimate relationship when an IPH occurs, including less restrictive legal concerns for privacy, IPH cases may be the most enlightening as to: (1) the totality of the content needed in lethality assessments for living victims; (2) common signs provided by the IPV victim and/or the abuser which may provide useful information for the need to expedite legal intervention than is generally applicable by today's standards; and (3) the need for more collaboration and coordination between the criminal and civil court systems as well as various authorities among all jurisdictions involved in any IPV case.[58] The results of this study may help to better identify an abusive intimate relationship as high-risk for lethality and provide a more in-depth understanding of the risk factors that affect the interactions between an abuser, the IPV victim, and the legal system, i.e., the behavior of law.

Black's Theory of the Behavior of Law

Black's (1973, 2010) work provides various propositions and explanations about why and how people utilize the law and when they determine to mobilize it for their own benefit.[59] This "mobilization of law" takes shape in many forms, from an emergency when the initial call to 911 is made to the filing of a civil lawsuit, whether an actual crime was ever committed because it is "the process by which a legal system acquires its cases."[60] Black (2010) considers many societal characteristics to explain his theory about how certain groups of people may or may not behave in relation to the law.[61] According to Black (2010), for an offense against a victim of a private crime, such as IPV, to result in the arrest and subsequent prosecution of the IPV offender, it is necessary for someone, meaning the IPV victim, to mobilize the law.[62] Thus, Black (2010) asserts that people of different social classes, races, educational levels, and income levels determine when or how to mobilize the law based on several different societal propositions.[63] These propositions form the basis of his theory, "the behavior of law."[64]

Black (2010) provides the foundation for his Theory of the Behavior of Law through six propositions of social interaction that help to explain why prior physical violence may not be as critical a factor in the risk assessment for an IPH.[65] Black's (2010) six propositions are as follows: (1) stratification, (2) morphology, (3) culture, (4) organization, (5) social control, and (6) anarchy.[66] These propositions work together to serve as an overarching theory for when, why, and how people within certain social settings will mobilize the law.[67] Yet, Black (2010) states that "law is inactive among intimates."[68] His theory on the mobilization of law between intimate partners espouses the notion that those in close proximity to each other, such as intimate partners, will not mobilize the law, regardless of whether violence is present.[69] He explains that U.S. law takes legal actions between intimates less seriously.[70] Hence, a person who is at the greatest risk of becoming a victim of an IPH, i.e., an abused intimate partner, or the abuser themselves may not become involved in the system or be subjected to a lethality risk assessment because the victim will not mobilize the law on their own behalf, knowing the system will not take them seriously.[71] Additionally, IPV victims, who do enter the system, may not necessarily disclose the intimate details of their spousal relationships to another person whether they are a loved one or more distantly associated.[72] These details are often necessary for advocates and authorities to determine that mobilization of the law is necessary to protect the victims' personal safety.[73] Therefore, Black (2010) concludes that "intimacy provides immunity from law."[74]

According to Payne and Triplett (2009), special attention has been given in the arena of IPV research to: (1) its cycle of violence, (2) the intergenerational transmission of violence, and (3) the reaction of various government agencies that could help to break the cycle of violence between an IPV victim and their offender if they choose.[75] Payne and Triplett (2009) explain that much research attention has been paid to "front line workers dealing with domestic violence," including the police and the courts.[76] Their study is victim centered; and they explain that not all IPV victims come to the attention of law enforcement or the courts, as the simplistic police and judicial response inadequately meets the special needs of most IPV victims.[77] Most of the programs assessed by Payne and Triplett (2009) place the responsibility on the victim and those people whose main goal or job it is to help or advocate for the victim, as does Black's Theory of Law.[78]

Although Payne and Triplett (2009) recognize that many IPV cases do not enter the system because the police are never called (lack of mobility of the law), their study does not actually assess IPV victims' reasons for their lack of the mobilization of the law.[79] Certainly, such a myriad of reasons an IPV victim may choose to remain unknown to law enforcement, as well as the criminal and civil judicial system, is complex and confounding. However, it is possible to explain this phenomenon through Black's (1970) account of the citizenry's option to invoke the power of law enforcement.[80] Black (1970) asserts that the legal "system responds only to those who call upon it while it ignores illegality that citizens choose to ignore."[81] An IPV victim who is constantly physically abused may not mobilize the law in her own defense, i.e., for fear of retaliation from her abuser, whereas another may attempt to mobilize the law to protect herself but does not have the law on her side because she has not been physically abused. Neither result is effective in protecting the IPV victim, but it does help to explain why some victims are left to their own self-guardianship.

Avakame et al. (1999) produced a study based on Black's (1973) Theory of the Behavior of Law, which focused on IPV and calls to the police as well as law enforcement authorities' reactions to the calls.[82] It is a socioeconomic focused study.[83] Avakame et al. (1999) explain that certain components of Black's (1973) Theory of the Behavior of Law asserts that intimates, especially married and employed people, are more likely to mobilize the law and utilize it aggressively, especially using the court system.[84] Therefore, married, upper-middle class socioeconomic groups are more likely to call the police and effectuate an arrest.[85] However, this assertion is in direct contradiction with Bellew (2005), where she explains that married, affluent women who are victims of IPV are less likely to call the police for help.[86]

Bellew's Explanation of the Intimate Partner Violence Socioeconomic Divide

Bellew (2005) explains that married, affluent women are more likely to utilize divorce attorneys for escape from an abusive intimate relationship rather than contacting any law enforcement authorities or contacting IPV shelters for help, even when they fear for their own physical safety.[87] She suggests that the women she studied remained as far away from the criminal justice system as possible, resulting in a complete lack of mobilization of the criminal law system.[88] Thus, Bellew's assertions support a mobilization of the civil law system as opposed to the criminal law system regarding the various demographic groups of IPV victims she studied.

The contradiction between Bellew's (2005) assertions and Black's (1973) theory is expected because IPV is a very complex and misunderstood crime.[89] The multifaceted dynamic of IPV is compounded by the fact that there is a lack of available data regarding many stages of IPV prior to the mobilization of the law and an IPH.[90] This lack of data is especially due to a lack of IPV victim reporting. Although well-known and respected surveys are conducted that do not involve police reporting, such as the National Crime Victimization Survey [hereinafter *NCVS*] and the National Family Violence Surveys [hereinafter *NFVS*], they still rely on the victims' truthfulness, perception of the seriousness of the crime, and ability to speak freely without fear of repercussions from their abusers.[91] Walker (1994) and Johnson (2010) assert that IPV victims and offenders may be reluctant to provide information regarding their experiences and that the phrasing of questions during a survey are critical to the survey's success and accuracy.[92]

Bellew (2005) explains that IPV victim surveys do not include those victims who were killed by their intimate partner and those who chose to deal with their situation in a different form of law mobilization than penal law, such as through the process of a divorce which occurs in the civil law system.[93] Yet, by utilizing the NCVS, the Avakame et al. (1999) study produced some interesting results in relation to Black's (2010) Theory of the Behavior of Law.[94] The Avakame et al. (1999) results suggest that the race of the IPV offender/victim, the age of the IPV offender/victim, and the gender of the IPV offender/victim each affect the probability of the mobilization of the law when IPV is involved, including when people call the police as well as when the police decide to make an arrest.[95] It is well recognized that gender plays a large role in the outcome of a conflict, especially between intimate partners, with females being more likely to be killed by their spouse or an estranged partner.[96] Thus, it is important that the law is mobilized by someone who is aware of the IPV occurrence, even when the IPV victim is not able to do so themselves.

Theoretical Implications from the Avakame et al. (1999) Study

The first step the system takes in determining to mobilize the law is at the point of responding to a 911 call. If the police, while using their discretion, do not make an arrest, then the remaining *criminal law* processes are devoid of their ability to determine whether to mobilize the law [emphasis added].

Some of the Avakame et al. (1999) results supported Black's (1973) theory, but other results do not.[97] Thus, the results of the Avakame et al. (1999) study were mixed in relation to the support of Black's (1973) theory.[98] Avakame et al. (1999) found that many factors, outside of the structural variables of Black's (1973) theory, account for the different ways in which IPV victims, offenders, and authorities mobilize the law.[99] In reconciling why this might be the case, Avakame et al. (1999) explained that, today, IPV is handled differently than when Black first published his theoretical book in 1976, including new mandatory arrest policies which affect the reported data.[100] Nevertheless, they concluded that Black's (1973) theory is supported by several factors including the race of the IPV offender/victim, the age of the IPV offender/victim, and the relationship between the IPV victim and offender: (1) the older the IPV victim, the more likely the law will be mobilized; (2) if the IPV offender is a minority, the more likely the law will be mobilized against them; and (3) the further apart the relationship between the IPV victim and the offender, the more likely the law will be mobilized.[101] In addition, Block and Christakos (1995) studied many of the same factors when they reviewed Chicago's homicide data between the 1960s and 1990s.[102] They found that age, gender, race, and the type of weapon used were all relevant to the outcome of an IPH.[103]

Notes

1 *See generally* DONALD BLACK, THE BEHAVIOR OF LAW: SPECIAL EDITION (2010).
2 This variables list is not all inclusive. *See infra* Chapter 9.
3 Researchers utilize the process of conceptualization to define a concept for the purposes of their study because some researchers may conceptualize a concept differently than others. Once conceptualization takes place, the concept is able to be specified as to how it will be measured; thus, operationalization has taken place. *See Chapter 5 Conceptualization, Operationalization, and Measurement*, THE UNIVERSITY OF UTAH (2021) https://content.csbs.utah.edu/~fan/fcs3200/slides/chapter05.pdf.
4 *See* Carolyn Rebecca Block & Antigone Christakos, *Intimate Partner Homicide in Chicago Over 29 Years*, 41 CRIME & DELINQUENCY 496 (1995); Joan B. Kelly & Michael P. Johnson, *Differentiation Among Types of Intimate Partner Violence: Research Update and Implications for Interventions*, 46 FAMILY COURT REVIEW 476 (2008) https://doi.org/10.1111/j.1744-1617.2008.00215.x.
5 *See FDLE's Guide to Public Records Requests*, FLORIDA DEPARTMENT OF LAW ENFORCEMENT (2019) http://www.fdle.state.fl.us/Open-Government/Documents/FDLEGuidetoPublicRecords.aspx (last visited June 2, 2023).
6 E-mail from Donna J. King, Doctoral Student, Department of Sociology, University of Central Florida, to FDLE (Jan. 31, 2017, 12:52 EST) (on file with author).
7 *See* Jacquelyn C. Campbell et al., *Intimate Partner Homicide: Review and Implications of Research and Policy*, 8 TRAUMA, VIOLENCE, & ABUSE 246 (2007) https://doi.org/10.1177/1524838007303505.
8 *See Id.*
9 *See Id.*

10 There were times that third requests for public records were necessary to obtain all the documents from a particular agency; however, this was agency specific as each agency had their own set of protocols.
11 It is important to note that since the time the data collection for this study was completed, Florida changed its policy on public access to court records for certain cases, including those pertaining to injunctions for protection against domestic violence. As a result, the same type of access that was available to the court files at the time of data collection when this study was completed is no longer available for all Florida county courthouses.
12 By utilizing the 108 petitions for injunction, 4 additional cases were included in the analysis for a total of 66 cases.
13 Florida's Government-in-the-Sunshine Law, enacted in 1967, supports the public's right to access most governmental and governmental agency records. *See* Attorney General, *Open Government – The "Sunshine" Law*, STATE OF FLORIDA, https://www.myfloridalegal.com/open-government/the-quotsunshinequot-law (last visited June 2, 2023).
14 *See supra* Chapter 3, The Disillusionment of the Protections of an Injunction for Protection against Domestic Violence: Why and When are They Important to Intimate Partner Violence Victims?
15 *See* Mari L. Aldridge & Kevin D. Browne, *Perpetrators of Spousal Homicide: A Review*, 4 TRAUMA, VIOLENCE, & ABUSE 265 (2003) https://doi.org/10.1177/1524838003004003005.
16 *See Id.*
17 Brynn E. Sheehan et al., *Intimate Partner Homicide: New Insights for Understanding Lethality and Risks*, 21 VIOLENCE AGAINST WOMEN 269, 270 (2015) https://doi.org/10.1177/1077801214564687. Sheehan et al. (2015) defines a *covictim* as family members and close friends who have lost loved ones to a homicide. Researchers also utilize the term "proxy" to describe someone they consider knowledgeable about the victim's relationship with the perpetrator but who does not have direct information about the IPH. (*See Id.*).
18 *See* Charlotte Barlow & Sandra Walklate, *Gender, Risk Assessment and Coercive Control: Contradictions in Terms?*, 61 BRIT. J. CRIMINOL. 887 (2021) https://doi.org/10.1093/bjc/azaa104; Andy Myhill & Katrin Hohl, *The "Golden Thread": Coercive Control and Risk Assessment for Domestic Violence*, 34 J. OF INTERPERSONAL VIOLENCE 4477 (2016) https://doi.org/10.1177/0886260516675464.
19 *See* NATIONAL INSTITUTE OF JUSTICE, U.S. DEPARTMENT OF JUSTICE, QUESTIONS AND ANSWERS IN LETHAL AND NON-LETHAL VIOLENCE: PROCEEDINGS OF THE SECOND ANNUAL WORKSHOP OF THE HOMICIDE RESEARCH WORKING GROUP (1992).
20 *See Id.* In 1992, the risk assessment tool was termed "Danger Assessment Instrument." (*Id.* at 31).
21 *See Id.*
22 *Id.* at 1, 98.
23 *See Id.*; Block & Christakos, *supra* note 4.
24 Block & Christakos, *supra* note 4 at 497.
25 *See Id.*
26 *Id.* at 497.
27 *See Id.*
28 *See* Kathryn E. Moracco et al., *Femicide in North Carolina, 1991–1993: A Statewide Study of Patterns and Precursors*, 2 HOMICIDE STUDIES 422 (1998) https://doi.org/10.1177/1088767998002004005.

29 See Id.
30 See Id.
31 See Id.
32 Id. at 427.
33 Id.
34 See Jacquelyn C. Campbell et al., *Risk Factors for Femicide in Abusive Relationships: Results from a Multisite Case Control Study*, 93 AMERICAN JOURNAL OF PUBLIC HEALTH 1089 (2003) http://dx.doi.org/10.2105/AJPH.93.7.1089.
35 See Id.
36 See Id.
37 See Id. at 1089.
38 R. Emerson Dobash et al., *"Out of the Blue;" Men Who Murder an Intimate Partner*, 4 FEMINIST CRIMINOLOGY 194, 194, 204 (2009) http://dx.doi.org/10.1177/1557085109332668.
39 Id. at 195.
40 Id. at 194.
41 See Id.
42 Id. at 205; *accord* R. EMERSON DOBASH & RUSSELL P. DOBASH, WHEN MEN MURDER WOMEN (2015) https://doi.org/10.1093/acprof:oso/9780199914784.001.0001.
43 See Dobash et al., *supra* note 38 at 205; DOBASH & DOBASH, *supra* note 42.
44 See Dobash et al., *supra* note 38 at 205; DOBASH & DOBASH, *supra* note 42.
45 Dobash et al., *supra* note 38 at 202.
46 See Sheehan et al., *supra* note 17.
47 See Id.
48 See Id. The study originally identified fifty-nine (59) covictims from thirty-nine (39) IPH cases. (*See Id.*)
49 See Id. Mean length of time since the homicide. (*See Id.*)
50 Id. at 274.
51 See Id.
52 See Id.
53 See Id.
54 See generally Id.
55 See Robert Nash Parker & Allison M. Toth, *Family, Intimacy, and Homicide: A Macro-Social Approach*, 5 VIOLENCE AND VICTIMS 195 (1990).
56 See Id.; Daniel P. Mears, *Research and Interventions to Reduce Domestic Violence Revictimization*, 4 TRAUMA, VIOLENCE & ABUSE 127 (2003) https://doi.org/10.1177%2F1524838002250764.
57 See generally BLACK, *supra* note 1.
58 See NATIONAL INSTITUTE OF JUSTICE, *supra* note 19; Moracco et al., *supra* note 28; LENORE E. A. WALKER, ABUSED WOMEN AND SURVIVOR THERAPY: A PRACTICAL GUIDE FOR THE PSYCHOTHERAPIST (1994).
59 See generally Donald J. Black, *The Mobilization of Law*, 2 THE JOURNAL OF LEGAL STUDIES 125 (1973) https://doi.org/10.1086/467494; BLACK, *supra* note 1.
60 Black, *supra* note 59 at 126. See also BLACK, *supra* note 1.
61 See generally BLACK, *supra* note 1.
62 See Id.
63 See Id.
64 Id. at 4.
65 See Id.

66 See Id. A simplified explanation of Black's (2010) six propositions is as follows:
1. Stratification explains inequality of wealth, and the litigant's ability to access the courts, i.e., access to justice;
2. Morphology explains "the patterns of social life," and the litigant's "quantity and style of law" (Id. at 37–38);
3. Culture explains "the symbolic aspect of social life, including expressions of what is true, good, and beautiful," as well as historical jurisprudence (Id. at 61);
4. Organization explains "the capacity for collective action ... patterns of revolt ... [and] the success of social movements"; thus, law varies based on "the organization of law itself" (Id. at 85–86);
5. Social control explains normative behavior and that behavior which is considered deviant; thus, law is social control;
6. Anarchy explains a society without law; thus, the relationship between law and anarchy is inverse. (See Id.).

67 See Edem F. Avakame et al., *"Did You Call the Police? What Did They Do?": An Empirical Assessment of Black's Theory of Mobilization of Law*, 16 JUST. Q. 765 (1999) https://doi.org/10.1080/07418829900094361; BLACK, *supra* note 1.
68 BLACK, *supra* note 1 at 41.
69 See Id.
70 See Id.
71 See Id.
72 See Id.
73 See Id.
74 Id. at 42.
75 See Brian K. Payne & Ruth Triplett, *Assessing the Domestic Violence Training Needs of Benefits Workers*, 24 JOURNAL OF FAMILY VIOLENCE 243 (2009) https://doi.org/10.1007/s10896-009-9225-8.
76 Id. at 243.
77 See Id.
78 See Id.; BLACK, *supra* note 1.
79 See Payne & Triplett, *supra* note 75.
80 See Donald J. Black, *Production of Crime Rates*, 35 AMERICAN SOCIOLOGICAL REVIEW 733 (1970) https://doi.org/10.2307/2093948.
81 Id. at 739.
82 See Avakame et al., *supra* note 67. See also Black, *supra* note 59.
83 See Avakame et al., *supra* note 67.
84 See Id. See also Black, *supra* note 59.
85 See Avakame et al., *supra* note 67.
86 See Kara Bellew, *Silent Suffering: Uncovering and Understanding Domestic Violence in Affluent Communities*, 26 WOMEN'S RIGHTS LAW REPORTER 39 (2005).
87 See Id.
88 See Id.
89 See Id.; Black, *supra* note 59.
90 See Avakame et al., *supra* note 67; Moracco et al., *supra* note 28.
91 See Avakame et al., *supra* note 67; Moracco et al., *supra* note 28; Michael P. Johnson, *Langhinrichsen-Rolling's Confirmation of the Feminist Analysis of Intimate Partner Violence: Comment on "Controversies Involving Gender and Intimate Partner Violence in the United States,"* 62 SEX ROLES 212 (2010) https://doi.org/10.1007/s11199-009-9697-2; WALKER, *supra* note 58.

92 *See* WALKER, *supra* note 58.
93 *See* Bellew, *supra* note 86.
94 *See* Avakame et al., *supra* note 67. *See also* BLACK, *supra* note 1.
95 *See* Avakame et al., *supra* note 67.
96 *See* Block & Christakos, *supra* note 4.
97 *See* Avakame et al., *supra* note 67. *See also* Black, *supra* note 59.
98 *See* Avakame et al., *supra* note 67. *See also* Black, *supra* note 59.
99 *See* Avakame et al., *supra* note 67. *See also* Black, *supra* note 59.
100 *See* Avakame et al., *supra* note 67.
101 *See Id. See also* Black, *supra* note 59.
102 *See* Block & Christakos, *supra* note 4.
103 *See Id.*

Part II
Voices of Intimate Partner Homicide Victims

This part reflects the voices of those lost to intimate partner homicide (IPH). The 100 petitions for injunction collected for this study provide first-hand accounts of the intimate partner relationships analyzed for this study, particularly from the point of view of the IPH victim. As the petition for injunction data were analyzed and themes began to emerge, phrases were coded within NVivo 12 Pro, allowing for the free-flowing generation of new themes, subthemes, and codes. As discussed previously in Chapter 4, the total overall number of cases for this study is 493; and there were sixty-two (62) cases with petition for injunction documents for analysis. It is important to note that, as previously discussed, some cases had more than one petition for injunction; thus, the number of petitions for injunction, i.e., 100, and the number of cases with petitions for injunction, i.e., sixty-two (62), are different. The following cases introduce the reader to a glimmer of the lives of the IPH victims and offenders who provided the data for the content analysis portion of this study.

5 The Torture of Coercive Control

From the context of the data collected, this study conceptualizes and defines "coercive control" as an ongoing pattern of behavior by an abuser that includes, but is not limited to, intimidation, isolation, humiliation, physical violence, and power and control, which is utilized against a victim of intimate partner violence (IPV) to invoke constant fear, even when the victim is able to resist abusive tactics, that may culminate into future physical injury or death. Within this definition, the themes of the qualitative phase of the study begin to appear. Together, twenty-seven subthemes, generating eight main themes, were derived from the petition for injunction data.[1] However, as a collective, these themes do share similar qualities; thus, when reviewing the cases throughout this book, it is important to remind oneself that, alt hough the context of coercive control's themes and subthemes are presented to highlight each theme and subtheme, they do not necessarily function as though they are mutually exclusive.

The order of the presentation of the themes and subthemes is intentional for its overall organization, as well as the substantive presentation of the data (Table 5.1). The themes of *intimidation*, *isolation*, *humiliation*, *power and control*, and *fearful of the future* refer to the characteristics that the IPV victim is experiencing as a result of the abuser's actions. *Resistance to abuse* is a theme that describes an action taken by the IPV victim in response to the abuse or actions taken by the abuser. *Abuser mental illness*, although a theme that describes an attribute of the abuser, includes subthemes that are actions taken by the abuser and includes some behavior directed toward the IPV victim. The final theme presented, *physical violence*, is another characteristic that the IPV victim experiences because of the abuser's action; however, it is separated in its presentation in this study because it was utilized as a dependent variable in the quantitative analysis.

The qualitative methods phase of this study utilized secondary data collected from 100 petitions for injunction from various Florida clerks of court that were filed at the trial court level.[2] The content analysis performed on these data analyzed the nature of the IPV relationships between

DOI: 10.4324/9781003097488-8

Table 5.1 Coercive Control Themes and Subthemes

Theme	Subtheme
Result of Abuse	
Intimidation	
	Animal Abuse
	Harassment
	Surveillance
	Threats
	Threatens Family and Friends
	Weapons
Isolation	
	Economic Control
	False Imprisonment
	Financial Control
Humiliation	
	Degradation
	Name Calling
Power and Control	
	Child Abuse
	Violent Acts toward Family and Friends
	Taking Children from Victim
	Deprivation of Necessities
	Psychologically Controlling
	Verbal Abuse
	Household, Clothes, and Personal Belongings Destroyed
Fearful of the Future	
	Fear for Children's Safety
	Pregnant
Response to Abuse	
Resistance to Abuse	
	Helping Abuser
	Separated or Estranged
Attribute of the Abuser	
Abuser Mental Illness	
	Drinking Alcohol
	Drug Use
	Paranoia
Result of Abuse	
Physical Violence	
	Nonfatal Strangulation
	Rape and Sexual Abuse

Note: Physical violence was used as a dependent variable in quantitative analysis.

heterosexual spouses living in Florida that resulted in sixty-two (62) intimate partner homicides (IPHs) occurring between January 1, 2006, and June 30, 2016, with the dates of the petitions for injunction spanning from August 1993 to December 2015. The data were analyzed for the identification of coercive control tactics, including physical violence, utilized by the IPV offender spouse as attested to by the IPV victim spouse in the petition for injunction prior to the killing. It is important to note that, in some cases, the petition for injunction may have been filed by the IPH offender rather than the IPH victim. In fact, several cases include petitions for injunction in which the IPH victim and offender filed multiple petitions for injunction against each other before the killing took place.

NVivo 12 Pro assisted in organizing, coding, and analyzing the 100 petitions for injunction so that the conceptualization and operationalization of the emotions and tactics of coercive control were able to be defined.[3] The processes of conceptualization and operationalization were necessary so that strictly defined variables for coercive control could be empirically and quantitatively measured; these measures were utilized in the quantitative phase of this study. As previously discussed in the Introduction to this book,[4] one of the most important questions asked by this study and for which the petition for injunction data were collected is: "What role the non-violent tactics of coercive control play in IPV compared to physical violence prior to the IPH?"

Content analysis involves a systematic method for identifying, organizing, and indexing units of meaning to explore overarching themes, patterns, and main ideas that emerge from the data.[5] Each of the one hundred (100) petitions for injunction documents were uploaded into a NVivo 12 Pro database as a PDF document. The narrative portion of the petition for injunction was typed into a Microsoft® Word document because NVivo 12 Pro was not able to read the text of the PDF. Thus, each Microsoft® Word document representing the one hundred (100) petitions for injunction narratives were uploaded into the same NVivo 12 Pro database as well. The Microsoft® Word documents, representing the one hundred (100) petitions for injunction narratives, were coded; the one hundred (100) petitions for injunction documents in PDF format were used for reference if needed.

The Domestic Abuse Intervention Program's Power and Control Wheel and The Maze of Coercive Control: The (New!) Recreated Power & Control Wheel[6] provided guidance as to the types of coercive control behaviors that the content analysis coding should substantiate, as did the literature reviewed in this study. To be very clear about the questions asked in this phase of this study and the data coded to answer these questions, the center of The Domestic Abuse Intervention Program's Power and Control Wheel focuses on the terms "Power" and "Control."[7] Based on most current U.S. state statutes, for behavior to be considered actionable IPV, the offender must become physically violent with the victim or threaten such acts, i.e., behavior that ignores the central and internal parts of the wheel as it passes from its physical violence outer rim toward the controlling persistence of its spokes and center wheel. Indeed, all the pie shaped sections that contain concepts and examples of the non-violent acts of coercive control are treated as though they do not exist if focusing on physical violence alone. This study focuses on evidence of all these types of abuses, many of which have been traditionally ignored and unregulated. Also, valuable information regarding the use of various non-violent coercive control tactics used for abuse may be gleaned from the Jones et al. (2010) study.[8]

The first level of coding was guided by the literature reviewed for this study and the most understood tactics of coercive control, i.e., intimidation, isolation, power and control, and physical violence. However, within the data, many subsets of these forms of coercive control began to emerge from the data, as did other themes. As additional themes and subthemes emerged and the need for more codes arose, second and third level coding took place to ensure that all cases were properly coded. This process continued until all cases were completely coded and all necessary codes were inputted. To this point, some themes and subthemes were outside the scope of the four main tactics of coercive control. In fact, some codes provide for the coercive control victim, although being victimized, attempting to find her agency as a citizen, often becoming resistant to her abuse and her abuser.[9]

Before discussing the results of this phase of the study, it is important to recognize the language barriers inherent in the petitions for injunction submitted by the IPV victims to the court for requests for protection that were utilized for the qualitative data analysis. Not only are these language barriers evident from those who experience English as a second language, but many narratives are written by people who might have achieved less than a high school education. Especially when they are not represented by an attorney, these individuals may struggle with either handwriting or typing the narrative that is often required of them by the court to be responsive for filing their petition for injunction documentation.

Also, even for those who are well educated, it is important to understand that many IPV victims, when experiencing the extreme stressors and anxieties of abuse, i.e., trauma, are not always the most articulate communicators of their abusive experiences. Additionally, a person who is living "in survival mode," because they are dealing with these stressors, will, often, write in such a way that comes across as incoherent and difficult to read even though they do not realize it comes across as such. And even if they do realize their petition for injunction narratives may not be written as they might like, it is the best they can do under the high-stress conditions they find themselves in at the time they are filing for protection from IPV, which is a difficult decision to make in the first place. As a result, some of the IPV victims' first-hand accounts from the petitions for injunction may seem out of sorts, including spelling and punctuation errors; however, their form should be considered normal to the reader, as it is viewed as common in the IPV community, for all the reasons described above.

Intimidation

"Intimidation" is a theme that describes acts by the abuser that are meant to create fear in the IPV victim in general, such as threatening suicide or making the IPV victim afraid, including creating fear for their safety, by using certain behaviors and gestures. In total, 1.6% of the 493 cases and 12.6% of the sixty-two (62) cases, as well as 10.0% of the 100 petitions for injunction analyzed in this phase, resulted in an intimidation coding. "[T]hreats of suicide to himself" is an example of the non-violent tactic of intimidation that Christine Dunn told the trial court about in her petition for injunction, when requesting protection from her husband on October 12, 2007.[10] Another victim, Glenda Santiago Nuñez, explained the same type of threats, when she wrote that her estranged husband's "final words before leaving my home were that he would kill me and himself if we could not be together."[11] This type of intimidation indicates that the abuser is attempting to coerce the victim into compliance, especially by terrorizing them enough to keep them from creating a new life for themself away from the abuser or beginning a new romantic relationship.

Torres v. Torres

After fifteen years of marriage and having five young boys together, on August 24, 2009, Marta Torres told the court that her husband "was taking the gun to [her] and clicking it like he wanted to shoot the gun. Then after that, he told [her] that he wanted to kill himself."[12] Elliot Torres had held the gun to Marta's head for approximately eight hours while making threats to kill her and himself.[13] When Marta told this to her employer after it had first happened, the company notified the local Police Department on her behalf.[14] Elliot was Baker Acted, Florida's law that allows for involuntary examination for the need to provide care or treatment to a person, who, among other criteria, "poses a real and present threat of substantial harm to his or her well-being[,]" and had his gun confiscated.[15] During most of their marriage, the couple lived in south Florida; however, Marta relocated with the boys to live with a friend in central Florida to hide from Elliot and escape the abuse.[16]

Marta endured very abusive behavior from Elliot that included physical violence, as well as other forms of non-violent coercive control tactics such as painting all the windows in their house.[17] According to a witness to the homicide, Elliot's reasoning for painting the windows was "to prevent anyone from looking in and/or out of the residence."[18] To monitor Marta and the boys' movements, Elliot installed cameras within their home.[19]

The day before Marta asked the court to protect her, she went to the Police Department in the new locale about her fears of her husband harming her and that he had learned where she was living.[20] She wanted the police report on file, just in case something was to happen to her.[21] She obtained the temporary injunction from the court, and Elliot was served with its notice in south Florida.[22] However, during the hearing for the final injunction on September 3, 2009, the court dropped the injunction action for reasons that still are unclear.[23] Later that month, in a phone call with Marta, Elliot asked her if she was dating anyone, to which she explained she had a boyfriend.[24] The next day, on September 29, 2009, Elliot confronted Marta at her place of work where he got her outside and opened fire.[25] Marta ran away from him and began to scream "Don't kill me" as he continued to fire.[26] She had four gunshot wounds and was killed on the scene.[27] Elliot died at the scene by a self-inflicted gunshot wound to the head.[28] As a result, the case was exceptionally cleared because Elliot could not be prosecuted.[29]

Dhani v. Dhani

In 2001, 2007, and 2008, Kalowti Dhani filed three petitions for injunction against her ex-husband, Khemraj Dhani, in which she described in two of the three petitions how he threatened to kill himself.[30] She was successful in obtaining a final injunction for her 2001 request for protection, which remained in force until February 8, 2002.[31] In April 2007 and September 2008, he told her that he was going to kill Kalowti, their daughter, and himself. In her April 2007 petition for injunction, Kalowti detailed Khemraj's threats to the court by writing "[W]hen I went back home I seen a few pieces of string hanging from the ceiling fan in the living room. My daughter told me when I came [home] that he showed it to her and told her that he was going to hang himself."[32] Although the reference to the few pieces of string and being able to hang oneself from string does not comport,[33] it does not minimize the references to the offender wanting to kill the family and himself. Nevertheless, Kalowti was not successful in obtaining any type of protection from the court based on her 2007 request.[34]

Similar threats by Khemraj resurfaced in September 2008 when Kalowti reported to the court that he threated to kill her and the entire family.[35] On September 26, 2008, in her narrative to the court, she explained how afraid she was that he would hurt her.[36] She supported her request for an injunction for protection by explaining that Khemraj described in details how he was going to kill her, and that the police were trying to find him to Baker Act him.³⁷ She successfully obtained a temporary injunction on the same day she filed her petition.³⁸

Kalowti was awarded a final injunction on October 8, 2008.³⁹ Additionally, Khemraj was ordered to surrender his firearms or provide an affidavit of no firearms.⁴⁰ However, on December 20, 2008, while the final injunction was still in force, Khemraj entered Kalowti's home, where she was living with her daughter, and began shooting.⁴¹ Kalowti was killed by Khemraj shooting her several times in the head.⁴² The couple's pregnant daughter, who was home at the time of the attack, escaped through the bathroom window just before Khemraj tried to kill her.⁴³ Khemraj also critically wounded Kalowti's ex-husband from a previous marriage, who was in the home helping her as a friend.⁴⁴ He died several days later from five gunshot wounds.⁴⁵

Animal Abuse

"Animal abuse" is a subtheme of intimidation and, for the purposes of this study, describes acts the abuser has committed or threatens to commit that are, or would be, harmful, neglectful, or of a physically or sexually abusive nature toward animals that are loved by the IPV victim. One reason for such efficacy in this area for abusers is because pets have become so important within socio-demographic and socio-economic landscape.⁴⁶ Indeed, pets, i.e., family members play a central role within the fabric of American lives.⁴⁷ As a result, abusers understand that targeting the IPV victim's pet is a very effective means to target the emotions of their victim. The threat of removing or killing the victim's dog is an effective form of intimidation to obtain compliance from the victim. In this study, 0.4% of the 493 cases and 3.1% of the sixty-two (62) cases, as well as 2.0% of the 100 petitions for injunction analyzed in this phase, resulted in an animal abuse coding. In one case, Nancy Olms explained to the trial court in her petition for injunction in December 2009 that her estranged husband "threatened to come to [her] apartment and take [her] dogs away from [her]."⁴⁸ The second case is detailed below.

Cloaninger v. Colley

Among other non-violent tactics of coercive control and acts of violence Amanda Cloaninger described in her petition for injunction dated July 13, 2015, she explained how, on June 11, 2015, her husband, James Colley, threatened to kill her dog.⁴⁹ She was initially provided protection from the court through a temporary injunction on the same day she filed her petition, "precluding him from having any contact with [her] including going to her home and her place of employment."⁵⁰ James was served with the injunction on July 20, 2015.⁵¹

On July 29, 2015, James filed for divorce against Amanda.[52] On that same day, he appeared before the injunction judge to answer for certain acts he committed in violation of the injunction that included texting Amanda, entering her home while she was at work, and driving through her work parking lot looking for her car.[53] Because of this violation, on July 29, 2015, the injunction judge issued an order continuing the temporary injunction for Amanda.[54] Additionally, on July 29, 2015, the local Sheriff's Office arrested James for violation of the temporary injunction.[55] As a result, a misdemeanor case for "violation of injunction for protection against domestic violence" ensued against James.[56] At his first appearance on July 30, 2015, James was ordered to have "no contact [with Amanda] with the exception of & subject to those terms ordered under [the injunction case]."[57] On August 10, 2015, the injunction court granted a final injunction to Amanda.[58]

On August 27, 2015, at 4:00 am, with the final injunction still in place, James ransacked Amanda's home when he learned that Amanda was not at home.[59] Amanda got home about 9:00 am to learn what James had done to her home.[60] She contacted her boyfriend, who called the nonemergency police line to report the damage.[61] An officer arrived at Amanda's home around 9:55 a.m.[62] However, Amanda decided not to file formal charges against James because she wanted to speak to her mother and attorney first.[63] As a result, the officer left her home.[64] Two of Amanda's friends and her boyfriend arrived minutes afterwards.[65]

That morning, at the same time Amanda was dealing with the damage to her house, James was attending a hearing for his criminal misdemeanor case related to his violation of the injunction for protection the State of Florida had against him.[66] At court, because his demeanor was good, the trial judge let him plead no contest to the charges he was facing and placed him on unsupervised probation.[67]

Immediately after court, James apparently collected ammunition for guns he either already had in his vehicle or obtained at his sister's home and drove toward Amanda's house.[68] There, he began shooting at the house, giving warning to all four occupants that he was heading toward them.[69] Amanda's boyfriend successfully escaped through the garage; however, Amanda and her two friends retreated to the master bedroom area.[70] Once there, the women were trapped and would have to beg James for their lives.[71] Amanda hid in the bathroom, and her two friends barricaded themselves in a closet.[72] Amanda and one of her friends each called 911 from their cellphones.[73]

James found Amanda first.[74] James' focus was on Amanda's boyfriend.[75] That is who James was looking for and demanding from Amanda to turn over to him.[76] Amanda explained that she did not know where he was and begged for James to put the gun down.[77] Then, he turned his attention to the closet.[78] When he tried to open the closet door, one of Amanda's friends who was hiding in it put her foot on the door to hold it shut.[79] At that point, Amanda begged James to leave her friends alone.[80] She explained that her boyfriend was not in the closet.[81] James went back to the bathroom and shot Amanda but did not kill her.[82] Then, he went back to the closet.[83] When he was unable to open the closet door again, he shot through the closet door.[84] One of Amanda's friends was shot in the arm, but barely.[85] This caused her to let go of the door, so she ran out of the closet.[86] At that point, James entered the closet and found the second friend, who was crouched down, hiding.[87] He shot and killed her.[88] Then, he went back to the bathroom to find Amanda.[89] He shot her three more times, until his first gun was out of bullets.[90] He dropped that gun and continued to shoot Amanda five more times using a second gun.[91]

James left Amanda's house, went back to his sister's home, dumped his cell phone, and fled Florida.[92] Police arrested him in at a traffic stop hours later in Virginia.[93] He was charged with two counts of first-degree murder, two counts of attempted first-degree murder, and other related charges.[94] At trial, the State was able to prove its case against James with the help of Amanda's boyfriend and friend who survived the ordeal, as well as with cell phone and video records documenting James' actions leading up to the shootings.[95] The medical examiner testified as to the victims' wounds, including whether the victims who died were aware of what was happening.[96] Indeed, the chief medical examiner testified that Amanda had several defensive wounds and that "She was aware. She had a – a knowledge of what's happening and – through the entire shooting process."[97] However, Amanda's friend's gunshot wounds were immediately lethal.[98] The jury unanimously found James guilty of all counts of first-degree murder and attempted first-degree murder.[99] Also, "the jury unanimously recommended that the trial court impose a death sentence for each murder."[100] On direct appeal to the Florida Supreme Court, the Court affirmed the trial court's convictions and sentences.[101]

Harassment

"Harassment" is a subtheme of intimidation that describes the abuser continuously contacting the IPV victim or doing something the victim has asked the abuser to stop doing. In this study, 3.4% of the 493 cases and 26.9% of the sixty-two (62) cases, as well as 21.0% of the 100 petitions for injunction analyzed in this phase, resulted in a harassment coding. Most of the phrases and concepts focused on either the IPV victim or offender stating in their petition for injunction that they were being harassed. Many cases involve language about excessive texting and phone calls, such as when Alyssa Hogan-McCarthren explained to the court that her husband left "32 messages,"[102] or when Nancy Olms wrote that Frank Olms had "called my cell phone continuously ... the repeated calls to me started again every 2 minutes on the phone & my nextel radio."[103] However, this subtheme escalates in its lethality risk assessment once viewed in context with other harassment phrases that introduce physical acts or threats thereof to the harassment subtheme framework. Indeed, many petitions for injunction discuss the IPV offender following them or being in the IPV victim's house when they should not have been there, potentially even when it is violation of an existing order temporary or final injunction.

Jodi Wood v. William Wood

It is not uncommon for an abuser to file multiple reports with law enforcement to harass a victim. As an example, on October 28, 2009, Jodi Wood explained that her ex-husband "filed a report with Sherriff's Dept .... They called me but did not come out. Then at 1 am that same evening they came out and said he called ... They spoke with [] me then left. They stated he had been calling nonstop."[104] The court entered the temporary injunction that same day and provided a final injunction after an evidentiary hearing that was in effect until November 6, 2010.[105] Jodi had previously filed for an injunction on August 15, 2009, as well, claiming, among other coercive control tactics, that her husband "has verbally called and texts repeatedly harrassing [sic] and say things that are crude each day."[106] She was awarded a temporary injunction for this petition but did not receive a final injunction.[107]

On August 1, 2010, while the final injunction from Jodi's October 28, 2009, petition was still in force, William Wood arrived with a gun at the home Jodi shared with the couple's children and went after Jodi.[108] Even though their daughter was trying to get between them to protect her mother, William chased Jodi into the garage.[109] It was there that he shot and killed Jodi and himself.[110] Their daughter and other two children were not physically harmed, as they ran out of the house and into the woods until police arrived.[111]

Harassment can escalate to such heights that the victim's bodily integrity becomes endangered, which is why it is often utilized as a component of stalking laws.[112] Fabiano Romero's case is indicative of one in which many tactics of coercive control interact together, but multiple system failures prevent the IPV victim from obtaining protection from their abuser.[113] Although this case is detailed below in the theme of isolation, it is instructive for several other themes and subthemes, including, but not limited to, harassment, surveillance, humiliation, power and control, child abuse, and physical violence because Fabiana was very detailed in her narrative to the court.[114] When Fabiana described to the court in her petition for injunction the harassment she experienced from her husband, Jesus, in September 2008 after an argument they had, she began by explaining that he called her constantly.[115] She explained that he called her to ask why she took a different route to work.[116] She continued to explain that "Sometimes he follows me in his car doing bumper to bumper to scare me."[117] In another passage, she explained, "Some nights when I am sleeping, he kicks me constantly just to start a fight; this happens at all times during the night."[118] As a result, although theoretically the subtheme of harassment may seem non-violent (a behavior that appears to have become so commonplace in today's America), in practice, it has the potential to threaten one's personal safety and must be taken seriously.

Surveillance

"Surveillance" is a subtheme of intimidation that describes acts by the abuser intended to maintain constant information about what the IPV victim is doing and with whom they are doing it. In this study, 2.8% of the 493 cases and 22.2% of the sixty-two (62) cases, as well as 15.0% of the 100 petitions for injunction analyzed in this phase, resulted in a surveillance coding. As with harassment, most of the phrases and concepts within the surveillance coding focused on either the IPH victim or offender. Within this node, the word "followed" is used most, tending to show that IPV abusers utilize this form of surveillance most often. Other surveillance tactics that emerged from the data describe the abusers going through the IPV victims' phone, purse, house, and truck. However, some abusers, who were the killers in the IPH offense, escalated their surveillance tactics beyond the ordinary searching of one's personal belongings.

Daley v. Benevides

Surveillance is an extremely difficult non-violent tactic of coercive control to live with because the IPV victim is stripped of her sense of privacy. In one petition for injunction alone, Amy Daley explained that she had learned from her husband that "people are listening to my phone calls," "that I am being followed," that "[h]e has gotten into my email," and "that he could break into my home and the police could not do anything about it."[119] The court awarded her a temporary injunction on April 3, 2007, which required both parties to appear before the court on April 13, 2007, to testify regarding the matter.[120] No final injunction was issued, and the case was dismissed on April 13, 2007.[121]

Although Amy had experienced domestic violence (DV) on January 20, 2007, for which her husband, David Benevides, was arrested, she did not appear at the hearing for the final injunction.[122] As a result, an Order of Dismissal of the injunction proceeding was entered on April 16, 2007.[123] It is unclear why Amy did not attend the injunction hearing.[124]

Eleven days later, on April 27, 2007, David entered Amy's house while she was not home.[125] Neighbors were aware of the violence between the couple and tried to warn her not approach the house as she came home because they knew he had been around the house that evening; however, Amy disregarded the warnings when she told them, "Don't worry. I'll talk to him."[126] David shot her minutes before she was able to enter the home.[127] He shot himself immediately thereafter.[128]

In another case, Natasha Whyte-Dell reported surveillance tactics to the court when she wrote, "He put up [a] video camera up in the house without my knowledge."[129] Similarly, Fabiana Romero explained "Lastly, I do not have any privacy because he installed a system on all phones so he can tape/record and listen into every call. He uses that against me saying he will always know where we are. He has followed us on many occasions."[130] Fabiana also wrote in another petition for injunction that, "He let me know that he knew exactly where I am because he installed a GPS device to follow me everywhere."[131]

She continued:

> He is recording all of our fights and saying he will be using that in court to protect himself; he is using a video camera to record in the house; I once found out he was recording us while we were together when I saw the video in his computer; I felt devastated.[132]

Indeed, surveillance is a very effective intimidation tactic as it strips IPV victims of their sense of privacy and security. It also lets the victim know that their abuser is an omnipresent force in their life, causing them to lose their sense of autonomy. This helps to explain why Fabiana wrote to the court that she felt devastated to learn that her husband had not only recorded their fights and her movements in the house but their most private moments as well.

Threats

"Threats," a subtheme of intimidation, describes acts or words by the abuser toward the IPV victim that are meant to evoke immense fear of imminent danger or worry of something to occur in the future. In this study, 8.9% of the 493 cases and 69.8% of the sixty-two (62) cases, as well as 75.0% of the 100 petitions for injunction analyzed in this phase, resulted in a threats coding. The most common word within this code is "kill," with the most common phrase or usage being "[he] threated [sic] to kill me"[133] or some variation thereof.[134] Often, the threat to kill is preceded by the explanation, "he said if I leave" and continues with "he will kill himself or kill me[,]" meaning the offender utilizes threats of death to prevent the IPV victim from leaving the relationship and to bring them back into compliance.[135] As stated previously and demonstrated below, coercive control tactic themes and subthemes are not mutually exclusive because they may emerge and be utilized in various contexts. For example, the abuser who threatens to kill the IPV victim and himself exemplifies the subtheme of threats but, also, incorporates the subtheme of abuser mental illness, as will be explained further in Chapter 7.

Donna Wood v. William Wood

Throughout Donna Wood's post-separation relationship with her husband, William, she filed three different petitions for injunction, spanning over six years.[136] In her October 10, 2002, narrative, Donna described how William threatened her life in front of their son.[137] She explained how William "said she'll just run to her attorney as soon as I let her out of here, so I have to go ahead [and kill her] now. She's not going to change her mind [about filing for divorce]."[138] She continued to describe how William explained to their son how the only way he would calm down was "if you can get her to say she won't go through with this divorce."[139] Donna explained that her son "began getting [her] to promise that [she] would not file any more papers in the divorce & would not go talk to [her] attorney. [She] just said yes to get him to stop."[140] She was awarded a temporary injunction for this petition, but it was dismissed after a full evidentiary hearing.[141]

Although William was threatening Donna with physical violence during this detailed event, the theme of power and control and its subtheme of child abuse are also evident, as more extensively discussed in their respective sections. Because William utilized threats of physical violence against Donna to obtain his desired result of getting her to agree that she would not go through with filing for divorce, he effectively utilized the tactic of power and control over her. Additionally, William incorporating the help of his son to effectuate this power and control over Donna, brings in the subtheme of child abuse.

On November 28, 2005, Donna wrote another petition for injunction stating that William:

> began threatening me as well (as he has done many times in the past), that when my second son [] leaves for college, he is going to kill me .... He said he can't do it now as long as my (our) son is still in the house, but he will make sure it happens when he leaves and then afterwards he said he will kill himself.[142]

Again, this is an example of multiple subthemes with threats playing a predominate role and abuser mental illness because of William's threat of killing himself. For this petition, Donna was awarded a temporary and final injunction; however, the final injunction was dismissed after Donna filed a motion to dismiss it just days after the final judgment was entered.[143]

Two years later, on December 17, 2007, Donna wrote in another petition for injunction that William threatened to kill her many times and that he stabbed at his own arm with the threat that he would tell police she did it.[144] Again, Donna was awarded a temporary injunction, but it was dismissed after the hearing on the case.[145] In 2009, once their son was old enough to be in college, William killed her in an intimate partner homicide-suicide (IPHS).[146] As he promised, he shot her to death in her own home; and then, apparently, went out on the water with his boat where he took his own life.[147] His body was found the next day in a canal near where he lived.[148]

In some of the petitions for injunction, the IPV victims are very detailed in their descriptions of the threats to kill them that their abusers make, especially in the manner of the death threats. Heather Rimmer explained that her husband threatened to kill her by "snapping" her neck and told her "that he was sick enough to do it."[149] Although, ultimately, her husband did not kill her by the method Heather wrote about in her petition for injunction, her fear of his threat being serious was much warranted, as are the fears of so many other countless IPV victims who look to the judicial system for protection.

Kalowti Dhani, discussed in detail above in Intimidation, asked the court for protection from her ex-husband several times when she filed her petitions for injunction describing that "he was plotting to kill me" when he explained to their daughter that "he was going to tie [Kalowti] up, and burn [her] in the car."[150] Kalowti continued to explained to the court, "I'm scared because over the years he had threatened me, but this time he described it in details all he is going to do to me, I'm afraid he will snap and hurt me."[151] As detailed above, Kalowti was killed in an IPHS three months after she wrote these statements.[152]

Davis v. Davis

On December 29, 2009, Louise Davis told the court that her husband, Gregory Davis, on December 25, 2009, "threated [sic] to kill me and I tried to live [sic] the house."[153] She continued to explain that Gregory had a 20-gauge shotgun while he was making these threats.[154] At the time Louise wrote her petition for injunction, Gregory was in jail because he was arrested and charged with aggravated battery and use with a deadly weapon due to this incident.[155] Louise's temporary injunction was granted, but the final injunction was not. On January 12, 2010, Gregory was charged with aggravated battery (deadly weapon bodily harm) for the same Christmas day incident.[156] On September 10, 2010, Gregory pled no contest to the charges, agreeing that the State of Florida could prove a prima facie case against him.[157] The court did not allow for jail credit served; and, on October 8, 2010, sentenced him to a term of six (6) months in the County jail, as well as a period of six (6) months' probation upon release from jail.[158]

On July 15, 2011, Gregory and Louise were found dead in their home with gunshots wounds inflicted by Gregory as an IPHS.[159] Another victim survived the incident with gunshot wounds as well.[160] It was unclear as to the impetus of the shooting at the time it was committed.[161]

Thomas v. Thomas

During the early morning hours of June 30, 2006, sheriff's deputies responded to calls that an individual was unconscious and bleeding severely.[162] Tonya Thomas had been shot by her estranged husband Damon Thomas multiple times in the head, chest, and arm.[163] Her parents found her in her car after having been shot and brought her into the living room to try to render first aid.[164] She was rushed to the hospital where she later died from her injuries.[165]

On March 27, 2006, three months prior to her death, Tonya filed a petition for injunction explaining to the court that she was "afraid of [Damon] because he has threaten [sic] my life on several occasions, and he has a very bad temper."[166] On March 31, 2006, Tonya received a temporary injunction against Damon.[167] And, on April 13, 2006, she received a final injunction against Damon that was to last for a year; therefore, the final injunction was in place at the time Damon killed her.[168]

Damon was arrested for violating the final injunction Tonya had against Damon on June 30, 2006.[169] On July 1, 2006, a complaint for first degree murder was filed against Damon and that case was consolidated with the violation of the final injunction case for prosecution.[170] After a jury trial in 2007, he was adjudicated guilty on three counts.[171] The first count was for first degree murder, a capital offense.[172] The other two were first degree misdemeanor offenses for violation of the final injunctions.[173] He was sentenced to life in prison.[174]

Threatens Friends and Family

"Threatens friends and family" is a subtheme of intimidation that describes acts or words by the abuser toward the IPV victim's friends and/or family that are meant to evoke immense fear in the IPV victim that there is imminent danger of something terrible happening to their friends or family. In this study, 2.8% of the 493 cases and 22.2% of the sixty-two

(62) cases, as well as 14.0% of the 100 petitions for injunction analyzed in this phase, resulted in a threatens friends and family coding. Unlike the threats to the IPV victim in general, there is no pattern to the threatens friends and family code; however, "kill" is still the most common word among this code. Many of these incidents bear a resemblance to the other non-violent tactics of intimidation, only utilizing the victim's friends and family to deploy this tactic. Often, the abuser brings the IPV victim's closest people and support system into the fray to challenge her will and to attempt to reduce the number of people who may be willing to assist her in resisting the abuse. Indeed, she may have given up on caring about her own safety and well-being; but threatening others in her life escalates the severity level of the threats.

Warren v. Warren

In explaining how her husband, Ronnie Warren, threatened her friend, Tonya Warren wrote to the court on April 14, 2009, that he:

> Threatened me and my friend verbally ... He left the house in my truck looking for the friend he thought I was with before coming home stating he would beat him to a pulp if he found him. He has called this person multiple times and threatened his life.[175]

Ronnie and Tonya were separated and planning to divorce.[176] And on April 17, 2009, the court issued a temporary injunction to protect Tonya from Ronnie, including a provision of no use or possession of firearms or ammunition, that was to last until a hearing the court scheduled for April 28, 2009.[177] However, through his licensed attorney, Ronnie filed a motion to continue the April 28, 2009, hearing, arguing, among other things, that "[s]ince the entry of the [temporary injunction], [Tonya] has been in the presence of [Ronnie], on more than one occasion, and she has not appeared to be afraid of [him]."[178] Because of his motion to continue, at the hearing on April 28, 2009, the court did not hear evidence regarding Tonya's injunction for protection; rather, it rescheduled the injunction hearing for June 2, 2009, and provided an extension of the temporary injunction until that time.[179]

Less than a month later, on May 12, 2009, while the temporary injunction order was still in place, which prevented Ronnie from using or possessing firearms or ammunition, he shot Tonya twice in front of their nine (9) year old son at a bait-and-tackle shop and then turned the gun on himself.[180] Tonya initially survived the shooting, but Ronnie died immediately.[181] Tonya was pronounce dead at the hospital after emergency life saving measures were determined to be unsuccessful.[182]

Garvin-Williams v. Williams

Yolanda Garvin-Williams wrote how her husband, Jeremiah Williams "went on saying how he would start killing my family members to make me suffer."[183] She was granted the temporary injunction; however, when she did not appear for the permanent injunction hearing, the court dismissed her injunction proceedings.[184] One month later, Jeremiah shot Yolanda to death outside her place of employment, a local hospital.[185] After the killing, the family told reporters that Jeremiah had abused her throughout their nine-year marriage; and this study revealed calls to police throughout that time as well.[186] Yolanda had also filed a petition for injunction in October 2000, stating that Jeremiah "hit me several times he's also threatened to kill me several times" for which she was awarded a temporary injunction but did not receive a final injunction.[187]

Local police stated to reporters that a recent statement from Yolanda prior to the killing had "nothing in [it] that would even hint at the level of violence that took place."[188] Truly, it is because of this tone deafness regarding the non-violent tactics of coercive control and their potential for lethality, as well as the fact that threats of physical violence that occur over an extended period of time that help to show the continuum of abuse that is coercive control without an immediate precursor of physical violence, that this study was conducted. The professionals within the judicial system, law enforcement, policy makers, and those who work to advocate for IPV victims, who are not as well educated on the non-violent tactics of coercive control, need to understand that physical violence, or the threat thereof, is not the only indicator of imminent harm to an IPV victim. By providing empirical data, this study seeks to prove that it is possible to have an immediate risk of *death* even when there is no present, imminent threat of physical violence or threat thereof. Indeed, it is vital for law enforcement, policy makers, professionals within the judicial system who work with IPV victims and abusers, advocates, and medical personnel to work together to understand the key components of the statements provided within a petition for injunction so that better care may be provided for all individuals involved.

Weapons

"Weapons," a subtheme of intimidation, describes the abuser's possession of weapons, threat to use a weapon against the IPV victims or intent to purchase a weapon. In this study, 2.4% of the 493 cases and 19% of the sixty-two (62) cases, as well as 12.0% of the 100 petitions for injunction analyzed in this phase, resulted in a weapons coding. The most coded weapon is "gun," with "knife" as the second most coded weapon. Many of the cases included in weapons involve the abuser insinuating a use of the weapon against the IPV victim rather than overtly doing so. For example, Yana Huss wrote,

"He pretended that he [sic] reaching for the gun."[189] Other cases were more direct with the abuser making overt actions to ensure the weapon was shown to the IPV victim. For example, Demetria Bennett stated that "he was pointing a silver gun at me."[190] Natasha Whyte-Dell wrote about her husband chasing her with a knife.[191] When an abuser brandishes a weapon to intimidate an IPV victim, it can be a very persuasive tactic because it often evokes the desired effect, including compliance with the abuser's wishes.

Curry v. Curry

On December 16, 2011, Christopher Curry filed a petition for injunction asking the trial court to protect him from his wife, Michelle, because she "broke window of car and throwed brick's [sic] at me."[192] He received a temporary injunction the same day he filed his petition for injunction as well.[193] Michelle was ordered to "surrender any firearms and ammunition to the County Sheriff's Department until further order of the court."[194] Christopher was not provided a final injunction.

Prior to Christopher's petition for injunction in 2011, Michelle filed her own petition for injunction on September 1, 2006, alleging that Christopher verbally threatened her and physically harmed her by telling the trial court that he "pulled on my arm where I do have bruises."[195] On September 1, 2006, Michelle was granted a temporary injunction against Christopher; and, like Michelle, he was ordered to surrender all firearms and ammunition to the County Sheriff's Department.[196] And, similar to Christopher, Michelle was not provided a final injunction.

On January 9, 2012, Michelle filed a Petition for Dissolution of Marriage [hereinafter *DOM*], and proof of service to Christopher was filed on January 13, 2012.[197] However, she filed a Notice of Voluntary Dismissal on January 23, 2012.[198] Then, again, on April 22, 2013, Michelle filed another Petition for DOM, and proof of service to Christopher was filed on April 24, 2013.[199] Although the court docket shows that a Motion for Default was filed and a Default was entered on June 12, 2013, Christopher and Michelle continued to have an on-again, off-again relationship.[200] Michelle explained to her best friend, who Christopher forbid Michelle from seeing, that he was abusive and controlling.[201] During the summer of 2013, Michelle moved into her own apartment and began to date another person.[202] However, eventually, Christopher convinced Michelle to move back in with him at some point in the late fall of 2013.[203]

Michelle and Christopher fought the weekend of November 16 and 17, 2013, which did become physically violent at times.[204] According to Christopher's ex-wife, he was an alcoholic, who became more abusive when he drank, and smoked marijuana and crack cocaine, as well as abused Xanax.[205] He had a habit of hitting his ex-wife, as well as other women in his life, in the head so "[t]hat way it won't show."[206]

Michelle's best friend received several texts from Michelle throughout the weekend of November 16 and 17, 2013, causing her to believe Michelle was planning to leave Christopher by the end of the weekend.[207] One of Michelle's last texts, sent at 12:35 pm on November 17, 2013, read "Still here ... no fatalities ... yet."[208] The final text was sent four minutes later and simply said "Tomorrow night."[209] Her friend took this to mean that Michelle was planning to leave Christopher on November 18, 2013.[210]

Michelle had different plans. During the evening of November 17, 2013, she retrieved a gun from inside the home she shared with Christopher and began shooting at him.[211] The first shot missed, allowing him to move toward her; however, the next shot hit him in the arm.[212] As he continued to move further toward her, she shot him again, hitting him in the chest with a fatal wound.[213] Immediately after, Michelle attempted to shoot herself in the head but missed.[214] On her second attempt, she was successful, dropping to the floor where she stood.[215] The Medical Examiner's report revealed that both Michelle and Christopher had alcohol in their system.[216] Further results showed that Michelle's body had bruising at varying stages of healing, which indicates she sustained the injuries at different times.[217]

Reddick v. Jackson

On February 9, 2007, Erica Jackson received a temporary injunction protecting her from her, then, live-in boyfriend, Christopher Reddick.[218] In her petition for injunction filed the same day, she explained to the court that Christopher "rammed the back of my car with a truck in which our 1 year old son was inside" and "pulled a knife and cut me and threated [sic] my life."[219] On February 21, 2007, the court entered an amended temporary injunction on behalf of Erica when the hearing for the final injunction did not go forward.[220] On March 5, 2007, Erica received a final injunction that remained in effect until March 5, 2008.[221]

For the next seven years, volatile and abusive would characterize the nature of the relationship between Erica and Christopher.[222] The morning of January 18, 2015, they got into an argument that turned into a physical altercation.[223] As a result, Erica, in self-defense, stabbed Christopher, causing fatal wounds to his chest with a kitchen knife.[224] Erica was not charged due to the lack of evidence of an intent to kill Christopher, so the case was Administratively cleared as justifiable homicide.[225]

Isolation

"Isolation" is a theme that describes acts by the abuser that cause the IPV victim to feel alone or secluded. In this study, 3.4% of the 493 cases and 26.9% of the sixty-two (62) cases, as well as 22.0% of the 100 petitions for injunction analyzed in this phase, resulted in an isolation coding. Common phrases in isolation describe the abuser preventing the IPV victim from having access to the phone, as a result, "phone" is the most coded word within this theme.[226]

Romero v. Romero

Another common phrase in isolation is the abuser preventing the IPV victim from having access to family and friends. Fabiana Romero applied for several petitions for injunction regarding her husband, Jesus Romero, between January 2008 and December 2010.[227] She wrote in her January 2008 petition for injunction:

> [H]e took away my cell phone, he doesn't let me use '1' minute to talk with nobody, he said the phone is just to talk with him and the kids. Nobody can visit me .... I do not have any family here in U.S. [sic], just my kids. He took my cell phone and the car that belongs to both of us.[228]

The court dismissed this case.[229] Later, in September 2008 and after fifteen years of marriage, which produced four children, she wrote:

> [H]e does not let me talk to anybody on the phone; nobody can come to our house and even my own family that came all the way from Venezuela to visit us could not stay with us .... One time when I was going to work he laid in front of my car so I could not leave.[230]

Although she provided additional information relevant to other coercive control tactics discussed in other themes and subthemes, on September 29, 2008, the court twice denied Fabiana's request for protection.[231] In the court's first order, it ruled that Fabiana had failed to explain any "current acts of violence. Needs a clear statement times dates places & acts of violence" and directed her to "file for a dissolution of marriage for relief" from the abuse she had described in her petition.[232] The second order stated that she failed to show "clear acts of violence with specificity times dates & places."[233]

On December 22, 2010, Fabiana, again, applied to the court for protection from her husband; and, on December 23, 2010, she filed for divorce.[234] In her 2010 petition for injunction, she told the court, "I have been wanting to leave the house for months and he always prevents it .... I have no family here. I have nowhere to go."[235] She received a final injunction that was to remain in effect until July 6, 2011.[236] On February 2, 2011, Fabiana filed an affidavit claiming that Jesus violated the final injunction.[237] On February 9, 2011, the court scheduled a hearing regarding

Fabiana's affidavit to be heard on March 18, 2011.[238] However, on February 10, 2011, Jesus filed a motion claiming that Fabiana's allegations in her affidavit were not true.[239] On February 18, 2011, Jesus's motion was also set to be heard on March 18, 2011, at the same time Fabiana's affidavit was to be heard.[240]

In a similar action on December 22, 2010, Jesus filed for protection from Fabiana when he explained to the court in his petition for injunction that "she hit me on the head and face with her hands, causing me to bleed on the forehead."[241] He continued to explain that this was not the first time that she had hit him.[242] Similar to Fabiana, he received a final injunction that was to remain in effect until July 6, 2011.[243] However, the court granted Jesus exclusive use of the marital home, allowing Fabiana some time to retrieve some of her personal items but that she must be accompanied by a law enforcement officer when she does so.[244] The final injunction read that if Fabiana went to the marital home to retrieve her personal belongings or at any other time, without a police officer, it would be a violation of the final injunction against her, which is standard language for final injunctions in Florida.[245]

On January 7, 2011, Jesus filed an affidavit stating that Fabiana violated the terms of the final injunction against her because she called him about going to the marital home to drop off their kids and to pick up some clothes.[246] Jesus made it clear in his affidavit that he explained to Fabiana that she was not allowed in the home without a police officer but that she went to the home anyway.[247] On January 12, 2011, the court scheduled Jesus' affidavit for hearing to be heard on February 25, 2011.[248] On February 25, 2011, the court granted Jesus' request to hold Fabiana in contempt of court for violating the final injunction.[249] She was ordered to pay Jesus' attorney's fees for having had to bring the action against her.[250]

The morning of March 16, 2011, at the apartment complex where she lived, Fabiana got up and took her children to school around 8:30 am.[251] At some point after she returned, a witness saw Jesus confronting her and hitting her in her car with an unknown object.[252] Fabiana was struggling and screaming for help.[253] She managed to get out of the car and run to a nearby apartment to attempt to get help, but Jesus shot her in the head before anyone could save her.[254] He immediately shot himself in the head, killing both of them.[255]

This tragic story helps to explain that an abuser understands that isolating their IPV victim causes her to become more vulnerable, disenfranchised, and incapable of having resources to leave them and the abuse. Isolation is a very powerful, misunderstood, non-violent tactic of coercive control that can prevent IPV victims from seeking help, even when they know and understand the extent of the danger they live with every day.

Alvarez v. Alvarez

On July 28, 2007, Jennifer Alvarez was working on a report for school; so, she did not want to go on a trip to the park with her husband, Christopher, and their children.[256] The fact that she wanted to stay home to work on her schooling made him mad, so he broke her computer keyboard.[257] When Christopher became more violent, Jennifer attempted to leave with their children; but he would not let them leave.[258] She tried to call 911; but he got the phone from her and broke it.[259]

Jennifer reported all of this information, including additional details related to the physical violence she and her children endured that day, to the police and to the court.[260] As part of her petition for injunction, while requesting temporary exclusive use and possession of the marital home, Jennifer explained that she had no other "safe place to live because I have not been allowed to have friends so I have nowhere else to go."[261] She was provided a temporary and final injunction by the court for protection against Christopher, although it appears as though they were allowed to have contact relating to their children.[262] The final injunction was ordered to remain in force until August 10, 2008.[263]

On September 28, 2007, Jennifer filed for DOM and provided the final injunction that was issued on July 28, 2007, which was recognized by the clerk of court as an ongoing standing order.[264] However, even though the final injunction was in place requiring Jennifer and Christopher not to have contact with each other, they went to dinner the same evening she filed for divorce.[265] Once they got to the marital home, they got into an argument that made Jennifer scared; so she used pepper spray on Christopher.[266] As a result, Jennifer and Christopher were both arrested for violation of the DV injunction and other related charges; however, the state attorney dismissed/abandoned all charges against both of them prior to trial.[267] Still, the contested divorce between Christopher and Jennifer ensued throughout the remainder of 2007.[268]

During the late hours of January 9, 2008, a body was found in an unlit area next to a canal and a busy highway.[269] It was determined through several unique tattoos and fingerprints that the body was that of Jennifer Alvarez, who had been reported by a friend as missing since the new year.[270] This friend was integral in the extensive investigation that took place by the Sheriff's department to determine who killed Jennifer.[271] Jennifer also had a serious online boyfriend that Christopher knew about who she would chat with most nights, including the New Year's Eve she went missing.[272] In fact, the online boyfriend witnesses, through the webcam, arguing between Jennifer and Christopher, as well as threats made by Christopher to Jennifer about physical violence against her.[273] He also reported to 911 on January 1, 2008, after he could not reach Jennifer any further on December 31, 2007, that he saw "a male hand grabbing Jennifer (via web-camera) prior to their online communications ending."[274]

Throughout the investigation into Jennifer's death, there were no details or any information released to the public regarding the cause of her death; thus, only the killer(s) or someone informed by the killer(s) would have had such knowledge before the case was closed.[275] When Christopher was informed by Sheriff's deputies that Jennifer had been found dead, he did not ask how she died or where she was found.[276] He eventually explained to investigators that he killed Jennifer but tried to claim it was self-defense.[277] He described an altercation between Jennifer and himself on December 31, 2007, in which she threatened him with a knife.[278] According to Christopher, before he was able to disarm her, she cut him on his hand and the back of his leg.[279] However, the cut on the back of his leg was actually a scar that could not have healed quickly enough for it to be a recent wound.[280]

Nevertheless, according to Christopher, although he did disarm her, in response to Jennifer's attack, "he choked her and stabbed her with the [same] knife."[281] Then, he wrapped her body in a blanket and dumped her body by the canal where it was found days later.[282] On January 11, 2008, Christopher was arrested for the first degree murder of Jennifer, which was caused by two stab wounds; the second of which was fatal.[283] He was prosecuted on information for second degree murder.[284] On April 20, 2009, Christopher plead no contest to the charge of second degree murder for Jennifer's death.[285] He was adjudicated guilty and sentenced to twenty years seven months in prison.[286]

Economic Control

"Economic control," a subtheme of isolation, describes the abuser preventing the victim from going to work or school, as well as interfering with the IPV victim's work or school activities. In this study, 2.0% of the 493 cases and 15.8% of the sixty-two (62) cases, as well as 10.0% of the 100 petitions for injunction analyzed in this phase, resulted in an economic control coding. The most common words in this subtheme are "job" and "work." Coded phrases explain how the abuser prevented the IPV victim from going to work. For example, two different IPV victims detail, "I don't even have a vehicle to go to work;"[287] and "One time when I was going to work, he laid in front of my car, so I could not leave."[288] Additionally, even if the IPV victim got to work, many coded phrases explain how the abuser inserted himself into the IPV victims' daily work environment. For example, several different IPV victims explain, "Calling me on the job with threats;"[289] "He's came [sic] on my job. Speaking with my Don, to try and cause myself and a coworker to lose our jobs;"[290] and "he has been calling my employer and treatning [sic] to kill me."[291]

Hogan-McCarthren v. McCarthren

When Alyssa Antoinette Hogan-McCarthren filed for protection from her husband, Terrance, with the court on February 7, 2012, she stated "Since the separation he has come to the school that I work at twice. The first time to pick me up because he was holding the vehicle. The second he came to the back by passing the office banging on my portable door."[292] Here, Alyssa was the IPV victim filing for the protection against DV; and the court temporarily granted that protection on the same day as Alyssa's request until a final hearing could be held on February 21, 2012.[293] However, on February 21, 2012, the court entered an order extending the temporary injunction and setting the final hearing for March 13, 2012.[294] The order extending the temporary injunction stated that it was:

> upon Petitioner's action for an extension of injunction for protection and it appearing to the Court as follows: **Ex parte.** The claims in the petition for extension of injunction for protection make it appear to the Court that there is an immediate and present danger of domestic, repeat or dating violence, as required under section 741.30 or section 784.046, Florida Statutes.[295]

Nevertheless, at the March 13, 2012, hearing, the court dismissed the injunction proceedings because Alyssa failed to appear at the hearing.[296]

It was not until November 21, 2014, two and one-half years after Alyssa filed for her injunction for protection, that any reported violence occurred, which was in the form of an IPH between the couple.[297] In fact, Alyssa killed Terrance when she stabbed him with a knife during an altercation in their family residence.[298] She was arrested and charged with second-degree murder.[299] At the time of the incident, the couple's 9-year-old daughter was home, as well as Terrance's 18-year-old son from a previous relationship.[300] Their daughter witnessed the event and told investigators that Terrance was the aggressor.[301] The son, who had knife wounds to his arm from his attempts to intervene, had a conflicting account from the daughter and blamed Alyssa.[302] Alyssa's account of the events that night details an angry and alcohol influenced Terrence who wanted her out of the house but countered that demand with his physical blocking of the exit.[303]

At trial, Alyssa invoked self-defense based on a "stand your ground defense," which her attorney explained is more difficult for success when the defendant is a woman because they are not expected to defend themselves.[304] However, in Alyssa's case, this defense strategy worked; and she was found not guilty on October 21, 2016.[305] She regained custody of her children, started her own business, and planned to become an advocated for DV.[306]

Economic control affects many facets of the IPV victim's life, including being able to perform at work or school to her fullest capacity. When one is constantly bombarded with threats at work, it is difficult to concentrate on the task at hand. When one is prevented from going to work, it is difficult to become independent and maintain a sense of autonomy from their abuser. Indeed, this is the goal of isolation through economic control. It is a very effective tactic of non-violent coercive control.

False Imprisonment

"False imprisonment," in this study, is a subtheme of isolation that describes the abuser confining or restraining the IPV victim against their will. In this study, 2.0% of the 493 cases and 15.8% of the sixty-two (62) cases, as well as 11.0% of the 100 petitions for injunction analyzed in this phase, resulted in a false imprisonment coding. The two most coded words for false imprisonment are "let" and "leave," respectively. The most common phrases for this subtheme are exemplified by the following: "would not let me leave;"[307] "he got in front of the door and wouldn't let me go;"[308] "He wouldn't let me leave the room;"[309] and "Held us there in my house wouldn't let us use phone or door."[310]

As previously discussed in the subtheme threatens friends and family, Tonya Warren detailed to the court that she was a victim of false imprisonment when she explained that her husband, Ronnie, "refused to let me leave the house ... and took my truck keys."[311] She continued her narrative by describing that months earlier "[he] sat on me for two hours saying he would see me dead before he let me leave."[312] Tonya was killed less than a month later before Ronnie took his own life.[313]

Although false imprisonment may seem as though it is about the length of time the abuser holds the IPV victim, this is not necessarily the case. Whether false imprisonment occurs once or several times, it can seem very isolating to the IPV victim, which can have the euphoric effect of power and control for the abuser. False imprisonment is about how the IPV victim feels and whether they did not want to be held in that situation.[314]

Rimmer v. Rimmer

Heather Rimmer, who was previously discussed in threats, explained to the Court on August 7, 2008, that "he wouldn't let me out of the bathroom .... He didn't let me out of the bathroom for a [sic] hour and a half."[315] She was granted a temporary injunction on August 7, 2008, but she dropped it on August 20, 2008.[316] Friends explained that Heather wanted to keep her daughters with their father, so she returned to the family home after ending the injunction proceedings in an attempt "to work it out for the sake of the children."[317]

During an argument on August 23, 2008, Heather and her husband argued about the fact that she wanted him to leave the home; but he did not want to leave.[318] At some point, he retreated to their bedroom and returned with a 9 mm handgun.[319] Just five days after Heather dropped her temporary injunction against him, she was shot and killed by her husband in front of their two young daughters, ages 7 and 12.[320] Then, he shot and killed himself.[321]

Martin v. Martin

During the early hours of July 5, 2009, Shannon Martin was helping friends clean up after a Fourth of July cook out when her estranged husband, Carl, drove up and tackled her to the ground.[322] He proceeded to beat her, picked her up, and threw her into his truck.[323] After he ripped her bathing suit top off, he beat her again; and told her he would kill her by strangling her if she tried to get out of the truck.[324] When she tried to get out of the truck, he grabbed her hair and would not let her get out.[325] Once he got into the truck, he continued to beat her for the next 10 miles until they reached the marital home.[326] He forced her into their house, and "would not let [her] leave the house when [she] kept asking him to."[327] She was finally able to "quietly" call her father to pick her up without Carl realizing it.[328] When her father arrived, Carl allowed her to leave because he thought it was the police who had come to their home.[329] With Carl following her, Shannon had to climb over the approximately 8-foot to 10-foot-high patio wall to get to her father.[330] Carl realized it was not the police, threatened them, and would not let them leave by standing in the way of her father's opened car door.[331] After a few minutes of them arguing, Carl finally let them leave.[332] Once Shannon was safe, she called the police to report the incident.[333] Charges were filed against Carl for false imprisonment and domestic battery.[334]

On July 6, 2009, Shannon filed a petition for injunction explaining to the trial court the events, as detailed above, which occurred during the early morning hours of July 5, 2009.[335] She was awarded a temporary injunction; however, Carl was not ever served with that injunction.[336] Evidently, authorities had an inaccurate address for Carl in which to serve him.[337]

On August 15, 2009, while the temporary injunction was still in place but unserved on Carl, Shannon requested assistance from sheriff's deputies to obtain personal possessions from the marital home.[338] She was allowed to do so based on the temporary injunction.[339] Once in the home, the sheriff's deputy found an arsenal of weapons in Carl's gun cabinet, including five handguns and seven long guns.[340] Four additional guns were found in other areas of the home, as well as ammunition for all the guns was found throughout the home.[341] The fact that these guns were located inside the home where Carl was living is significant because the temporary injunction ordered Carl "to turn over all firearms and ammunition to law enforcement personnel."[342] However, Shannon told sheriff's deputies that he still had two handguns that were unaccounted for and for which he had concealed weapons carry permit.[343] The sheriff's deputy confiscated the guns, ammunition, and other paraphernalia found in the home.[344] Shannon did not want to remain in the home for fear of her own personal safety.[345]

By the morning of September 16, 2009, Carl had been served with the temporary injunction and the hearing for the final injunction was scheduled for the next day.[346] Shannon had surrounded herself with roommates, and she and Carl were working on trying to mediate a divorce.[347] Shortly after 7:00 am, Shannon left her home and was immediately confronted by Carl, who began shooting at her.[348] One of Shannon's roommates heard multiple gunshots; and then, heard her scream "No!"[349] Once they went outside, they only saw Shannon's purse on the driveway; but they heard Shannon running down the street screaming "No! No! No!"[350] By that point, Shannon had been shot at least once.[351] She was attempting to seek help from anyone along a very sparsely populated road full of vacant lots.[352]

By the time Shannon reached neighbors who were home, they could hear her screaming "Help, help, help, somebody help me."[353] These neighbors had already heard the shots Carl had fired at Shannon, which they described as "at least six shots in rapid succession."[354] The neighbor could see the silhouette of Shannon at his front door while she was beating on it.[355] He could tell there was blood all over the door.[356] By the time he got his gun, Shannon was still at the door; but he saw another person in his driveway.[357] As he got closer to the door, he was hit with glass from the right window of his front door.[358] Shots were being fired into his house at the same time Shannon was at his front door begging to be let into his house.[359] When the gunfire stopped, he opened the door and saw Shannon covered in blood.[360] She was "leaning on the wall ... sliding down to the ground."[361]

Once the neighbor seemed to identify the person who had been in his driveway who seemed to him to be the one doing the shooting, he yelled at him "what the fuck."[362] At that moment, the man raised his weapon at the neighbor.[363] As a result, the neighbor shot three times at the man, apparently missing him each time.[364] The man walked around the corner and disappeared into the woods.[365] Collectively, neighbors worked to try to save Shannon's life before the Med unit arrived; but it was too late.[366] She suffered six gunshot wounds, two of which were fatal.[367]

After the neighbor confronted him, Carl took his own life in the woods by a self-inflicted gunshot to the head.[368] The gun Carl used to kill Shannon and take his own life was apparently one of the handguns that was not found in the home on August 15, 2009.[369] It was one of the guns Shannon told authorities Carl still had in his possession the day the Sherrif's deputy removed the guns from their home.[370] During Carl's autopsy, a letter in his wallet was found that read "Dear Lord, Please forgive me. IT HAD TO BE DONE SHANNON, We never were divorced we die together [Shannon's parents] YOU LOSE!!! I love you Nancy (my Dog)."[371] The reference to Shannon's parents was because they supported her throughout her order with Carl without question.[372] Her parents later explained that she feared for her life the first time she filed a complaint against Carl for his abusive behavior.[373] She told her mother, "I just signed my death warrant."[374]

Financial Control

"Financial control," a subtheme of isolation, describes the abuser's ability to control certain aspects of the IPV victim's financial resources, such as money, shelter, car, etc. In this study, 2.2% of the 493 cases and 17.4% of the sixty-two (62) cases, as well as 13.0% of the 100 petitions for injunction analyzed in this phase, resulted in a financial control coding. "Money" is the most common word coded in the subtheme of financial control coding. In this subtheme, phrases range from payments about houses to cars, as well as electric bills. IPV victims also asserted that their abusers were not providing money for food, medical expenses, and other necessities. As stated above, tactics of coercive control are not mutually exclusive. This subtheme is an example of one that is characteristic of other subthemes, such as deprivation of necessities.

Jackson v. Jackson

Meloney Jackson stated that her husband "makes me beg for money to go to my doctors & get my meds."[375] She was not awarded a temporary injunction for her petition. In fact, in this case, Meloney became the IPH offender when she shot and killed her husband, Kevin, on March 3, 2008.[376] She was arrested on March 3, 2008, for first-degree murder but, at the scene of the crime, provided Sheriff's deputies with a claim of self-defense.[377] One theory Meloney provided to authorities was that Kevin was "trying to kill her, and that he changed his mind and turned the gun on himself."[378] However, this theory was not plausible because Kevin had multiple gunshot wounds.[379] Sheriff's deputies conducted a detailed investigation, which included information from Meloney and Kevin's thirteen-year-old daughter, who was home at the time of the killing.[380] On July 20, 2009, Meloney was sentenced to life without the possibility of parole after having been convicted of first-degree murder.[381]

In other cases, Natasha Whyte-Dell, as previously mentioned in surveillance and weapons, wrote, "He has not pay [sic] any bill toward the house for water, food, FPL etc."[382] And, Adam Frasch, the IPH offender, wrote six months before killing his wife, Samira, that, "She has taken assets, took my personal items, clothes and guns etc. out of house and safes, & bank account."[383] Often, financial resources prevent the victim from accessing critical basic necessities; however, these resources can stop the victim from implementing a realistic escape plan from their abuser, making it even more isolating for the victim as well.

Notes

1 The Codebook – Coercive Control Themes and Subthemes, developed as a part of this study, is available for review in the Appendix.
2 *See supra* Chapter 4, Methodology for Data Collection: Sourcing Public Records, The Florida County Courthouse. For further clarification, any time the court is mentioned in this book, unless otherwise discussed, it is a reference to the trial court as opposed to any other level of the judiciary.
3 NVivo 12 Pro is a qualitative and mixed-methods data analysis social sciences software package.
4 *See supra* Introduction.
5 *See* Tara N. Richards et al., *Reporting Femicide-Suicide in the News: The Current Utilization of Suicide Reporting Guidelines and Recommendations for the Future*, 29 J. OF FAMILY VIOLENCE 453 (2014) https://doi.org/10.1007/s10896-014-9590-9; Sonia Salari & Carrie LeFevre Sillito, *Intimate Partner Homicide-Suicide: Perpetrator Primary Intent Across Young, Middle, and Elder Adult Age Categories*, 26 AGGRESSION AND VIOLENT BEHAVIOR 26 (2016) https://doi.org/10.1016/j.avb.2015.11.004.
6 *See supra* Chapter 1, Gender and Intimate Partner Violence: Legislating against Patriarchal Violence.
7 *See supra* Chapter 1, Gender and Intimate Partner Violence: Legislating against Patriarchal Violence.
8 *See* Alison Snow Jones et al., *Complex Behavioral Patterns and Trajectories of Domestic Violence Offenders*, 25 VIOLENCE AND VICTIMS 3 (2010) https://doi.org/10.1891/0886-6708.25.1.3.
9 *See* EVAN STARK, COERCIVE CONTROL: HOW MEN ENTRAP WOMEN IN PERSONAL LIFE (2007).
10 Dunn v. Dunn, 07-002347DR, 2 (2007) (Pet. for Inj. for Prot. Against Dom. Viol.).
11 Santiago Nuñez v. Nuñez, 2007-DR-014851, 3–4 (2007) (Pet. for Inj. for Prot. Against Dom. Viol.).
12 Torres v. Torres, 2009-3837-DR-FJ, 3 (2009) (Pet. for Inj. for Prot. Against Dom. Viol.).
13 C. E. Walsh & Miguel A Gauthier, 200900165132 at 6.
14 *Id.* at 7.
15 FLA. STAT. § 394.463(1)(2)(b)(1) (2023); *accord* Walsh & Gauthier, *supra* note 13 at 6.
16 Walsh & Gauthier, *supra* note 13 at 6.
17 *Id.* at 6–7.

18 *Id.* at 7.
19 *Id.*
20 *Id.* at 8.
21 *Id.* at 6, 8.
22 *Id.* at 9.
23 *Id.*
24 *Id.* at 8.
25 *Id.* at 2–3, 8.
26 *Id.* at 2.
27 *Id.* at 3.
28 *Id.* at 11.
29 *Id.*
30 Dhani v. Dhani, 53-2007DR-003091, 3 (2007) (Pet. for Inj. for Prot. Against Dom. Viol.); Dhani v. Dhani, 53-2008DR-007905, 2 (2008) (Pet. for Inj. for Prot. Against Dom. Viol.); Dhani v. Dhani, 53-2001DR-0001758 (2001) (This petition for injunction was not able to be collected due to the clerk of court's administrative destruction of the case file. The details of the docket for this case may be found at https://pro.polkcountyclerk.net/PRO (last visited Nov. 29, 2022)).
31 Dhani, 53-2001DR-0001758 (2001) (Pet. for Inj. for Prot. Against Dom. Viol.) (This petition for injunction was not able to be collected due to the clerk of court's administrative destruction of the case file. The details of the docket for this case may be found at https://pro.polkcountyclerk.net/PRO (last visited Nov. 29, 2022)).
32 Dhani, 53-2007DR-003091, 3 (2007) (Pet. for Inj. for Prot. Against Dom. Viol.).
33 It is possible that a language barrier caused the misinterpretation.
34 Dhani, 53-2007DR-003091.
35 Dhani, 53-2008DR-007905, 2.
36 *Id.*
37 *Id.* at 2–3.
38 *See Id.*
39 *See Id.*
40 *See Id.*
41 *See* Matthew Cromartie, 2008-232389 at 1; *All Die in Triangular Love Affair in Florida*, Kaieteur News (Dec. 29, 2008).
42 *See All Die in Triangular Love Affair in Florida*, *supra* note 41.
43 *See Id.*; *Survivor in Florida Murder/Suicide Tells Her Story*, Stabroek News (Jan. 26, 2009).
44 *See* Cromartie, *supra* note 41 at 1; *All Die in Triangular Love Affair in Florida*, *supra* note 41.
45 *See All Die in Triangular Love Affair in Florida*, *supra* note 41.
46 *See* Nicole Owens, The Interspecies Family: Attitudes and Narratives (2015) (Ph.D. dissertation, University of Central Florida) (STARS).
47 *See Id.*
48 Olms v. Olms, 2009-DR-21006, 5 (2009) (Pet. for Inj. for Prot. Against Dom. Viol.).
49 Cloaninger v. Colley, DR15-1136, 5 (2015) (Pet. for Inj. for Prot. Against Dom. Viol.).
50 State of Florida v. James Terry Colley Jr, 15001586MMMA, 3 (2015) (Charging Affidavit/Arrest Report).
51 *See Id.*

52 Colley v. Cloaninger, DR15-1263 (2015) https://apps.stjohnsclerk.com/Benchmark/CourtCase.aspx/Details/839487?digest=4W7s6WjIX%2FG1i6IGOFKLew (last visited Nov. 29, 2022).
53 State of Florida v. James Terry Colley Jr, 15001586MMMA, 1, 3 (2015) (Charging Affidavit/Arrest Report).
54 Cloaninger v. Colley, DR15-1136 (2015) https://apps.stjohnsclerk.com/Benchmark/CourtCase.aspx/Details/837666?digest=Hk1e6hpRU1LFAOxotxLiOQ (last visited Nov. 29, 2022).
55 James Terry Colley Jr, 15001586MMMA at 6.
56 State of Florida v. James Terry Colley Jr, 15001586MMMA (2015) https://apps.stjohnsclerk.com/Benchmark/CourtCase.aspx/Details/839677?digest=VwdoswX1U%2B2%2Fqhx9GFrLfg (last visited Nov. 29, 2022).
57 State of Florida v. James Terry Colley Jr, 15001586MMMA, 1 (2015) (First Appearance Form).
58 Colley v. State of Florida, 310 So. 3d 2, 1 (Fla. 2020).
59 *Id.* at 2.
60 *Id.*
61 *Id.*
62 *Id.*
63 *Id.* at 2–3.
64 *Id.* at 3.
65 *Id.*
66 State of Florida v. James Terry Colley Jr, 15001586MMMA (2015) (Judgment/Sentence).
67 Colley, 310 So. 3d at 3; Colley Jr, 15001586MMMA at 5.
68 Colley, 310 So. 3d at 3.
69 *Id.* at 4.
70 *Id.*
71 *Id.*
72 *Id.*
73 *Id.*
74 *Id.*
75 *Id.*
76 *Id.*
77 *Id.* at 4–5.
78 *Id.* at 5.
79 *Id.*
80 *Id.*
81 *Id.*
82 *Id.*
83 *Id.*
84 *Id.*
85 *Id.*
86 *Id.*
87 *Id.*
88 *Id.*
89 *Id.*
90 *Id.*
91 *Id.*
92 *Id.*
93 *Id.*
94 *Id.*

95 *Id.* at 6.
96 *Id.*
97 *Id.*
98 *Id.* at 6–7.
99 *Id.* at 7.
100 *Id.* at 13.
101 *Id.* at 1, 31.
102 Hogan-McCarthren v. McCarthren, 2012-DR-001236-O, 3 (2012) (Pet. for Inj. for Prot. Against Dom. Viol.).
103 Olms v. Olms, 2009-DR-21006, 4 (2009) (Pet. for Inj. for Prot. Against Dom. Viol.).
104 Wood v. Wood, 09-569 DV, 11 (2009) (Temp. Inj. for Prot. Against Dom. Viol. With Minor Child(ren)).
105 *Id.* at 1–7; Brian Rix, 201000036539 at 2.
106 Wood v. Wood, 09-429 DV, 11 (2009) (Temp. Inj. for Prot. Against Dom. Viol. With Minor Child(ren)).
107 *Id.*
108 Rix, *supra* note 105 at 2; David Sterphone, *Murder/Suicide Update*, Columbia County Sheriff's Office (August 4, 2010), https://columbiasheriff.org/2010/08/04/murdersuicide-update/.
109 Rix, *supra* note 105 at 2; Sterphone, *supra* note 108.
110 Rix, *supra* note 105 at 2; Sterphone, *supra* note 108.
111 Rix, *supra* note 105 at 2; Sterphone, *supra* note 108.
112 *See* FLA. STAT. § 784.048(1)(a) (2022) (defining "Harass" as "engag[ing] in a course of conduct directed at a specific person which causes substantial emotional distress to that person and serves no legitimate purpose); *See also* Ashford-Cooper v. Ruff, 230 So.3d 1283 (Fla. App. 2017) (explaining that FLA. STAT. § 784.048(1)(a) requires sufficient evidence of substantial emotional distress).
113 Romero v. Romero, 2008-DR-0000778-O (2008) (Pet. for Inj. for Prot. Against Dom. Viol.); Romero v. Romero, 2008-DR-0015103-O (2008) (Pet. for Inj. for Prot. Against Dom. Viol.); Romero v. Romero, 2010-DR-021349-O (2010) (Pet. for Inj. for Prot. Against Dom. Viol.).
114 Romero v. Romero, 2008-DR-0015103-O, 3–5 (2008) (Pet. for Inj. for Prot. Against Dom. Viol.). It is common for IPV victims to experience and to report about multiple forms of non-violent coercive control within the relationship at the same time; thus, the same case may appear throughout this study in multiple themes and sub-themes.
115 *Id.* at 3.
116 *Id.*
117 *Id.* at 4.
118 *Id.*
119 Daley v. Benevides, 53-2007DR-003064-0000-00, 3 (2007) (Pet. for Inj. for Prot. Against Dom. Viol.).
120 Daley v. Benevides, 53-2007DR-003064-0000-00, 1 (2007) (Temp. Inj. for Prot. Against Dom. Viol. Without Children).
121 Daley v. Benevides, 53-2007DR-003064-0000-00 (2007) https://pro.polkcountyclerk.net/PRO (last visited Nov. 30, 2022).
122 Jonathan McKinney, 2007-015025 at 7; Daley v. Benevides, 53-2007DR-003064-0000-00, 1 (2007) (Order of Dismissal).
123 Benevides, 53-2007DR-003064-0000-00 at 1.

124 Benevides, 53-2007DR-003064-0000-00 at 1; The Ledger, *Murdered Wife had Warnings*, NEWS CHIEF (April 29, 2007).
125 The Ledger, *supra* note 124.
126 *Id.* at ¶ 4.
127 Heather King, 2007-086086 at 1; The Ledger, *supra* note 124.
128 King, *supra* note 127 at 1; The Ledger, *supra* note 124.
129 Whyte v. Dell, 2008DR003807, 3 (2008) (Pet. for Inj. for Prot. Against Dom. Viol.).
130 Romero v. Romero, 2010-DR-021349-O, 6 (2010) (Pet. for Inj. for Prot. Against Dom. Viol.).
131 Romero v. Romero, 2008-DR-0015103-O, 3 (2008) (Pet. for Inj. for Prot. Against Dom. Viol.).
132 *Id.* at 4.
133 Davis v. Davis, 67-09-DV-159, 4 (2009) (Pet. for Inj. for Prot. Against Dom. Viol.).
134 Bailey v. Bailey, 632006DR194, 3 (2006) (Pet. for Inj. for Prot. Against Dom. Viol.); Wallace-Taylor v. Taylor, 2013DR009926, 4 (2013) (Pet. for Inj. for Prot. Against Dom. Viol.).
135 Romero, 2010-DR-021349-O at 4.
136 Wood v. Wood, 02-12705-FD-9 (2002) (Pet. for Inj. for Prot. Against Dom. Viol.); Wood v. Wood, 05-14620-FD-9 (2005) (Pet. for Inj. for Prot. Against Dom. Viol.); Wood v. Wood, 07-14215-FD-009 (2007) (Pet. for Inj. for Prot. Against Dom. Viol.).
137 Wood, 02-12705-FD-9 at 3–5.
138 *Id.* at 4.
139 *Id.*
140 *Id.*
141 Wood v. Wood, 02-12705-FD-9 (2002) https://ccmspa.pinellascounty.org/PublicAccess/CaseDetail.aspx?CaseID=132865 (last visited Nov. 30, 2022).
142 Wood v. Wood, 05-14620-FD-9, 3–4 (2005) (Pet. for Inj. for Prot. Against Dom. Viol.).
143 Wood v. Wood, 05-14620-FD-9 (2005) https://ccmspa.pinellascounty.org/PublicAccess/CaseDetail.aspx?CaseID=273872 (last visited on Nov. 30, 2022).
144 Wood v. Wood, 07-14215-FD-009, 3–4 (2007) (Pet. for Inj. for Prot. Against Dom. Viol.).
145 Wood v. Wood, 07-14215-FD-009 (2007) https://ccmspa.pinellascounty.org/PublicAccess/CaseDetail.aspx?CaseID=378961 (last visited on Nov. 30, 2022).
146 Daniel Godsall, 2009-037042 at 12–13; Jamal Thalji, *Where are the Dogs after Two Lives are Taken?*, TAMPA BAY TIMES (July 1, 2009).
147 Godsall, *supra* note 146 at 12–13; Kameel Stanley, *Body Found in Tierra Verde Canal Leads to Another Body in Snell Isle Home (FL)*, DENOMSHI'S MURDER-SUICIDE BLOG (May 23, 2009, 1:38 PM) https://denomshi.wordpress.com/2009/05/23/body-found-in-tierra-verde-canal-leads-to-another-body-in-snell-isle-home-fl/.
148 Godsall, *supra* note 146 at 12–13; Stanley, *supra* note 147.
149 Rimmer v. Rimmer, 53-2008DR-006441-0000-00, 2 (2008) (Pet. for Inj. for Prot. Against Dom. Viol.).
150 Dhani v. Dhani, 53-2008DR-007905, 2 (2008) (Pet. for Inj. for Prot. Against Dom. Viol.). *See supra* Chapter 5, Intimidation.
151 Dhani, 53-2008DR-007905 at 2.
152 *See* Cromartie, *supra* note 41 at 1.

153 Davis v. Davis, 67-09-DV-159, 4 (2009) (Pet. for Inj. for Prot. Against Dom. Viol.).
154 *Id.*
155 *Id.* at 3; Charles Williams, WCSO09ARR001421 at 1.
156 State of Florida v. Davis, 09-00363CF, 1 (2010) (Charging Affidavit).
157 State of Florida v. Davis, 09-00363CF, 1–2 (2010) (Plea, Waiver and Consent).
158 State of Florida v. Davis, 09-00363CF, 1 (2010) (Order of Probation).
159 Levi Yohn, WCSO00OFF001054 at 1–3.
160 *Id.*
161 *Id.*
162 Travis Leslie, 06-58881 at 2.
163 *Id.* at 8–9.
164 *Id.* at 2.
165 *Id.* at 10.
166 Thomas v. Thomas, DR06-4781, 3 (2006) (Pet. for Inj. for Prot. Against Dom. Viol.).
167 Thomas v. Thomas, DR06-4781 (2006) https://myeclerk.myorangeclerk.com/ (last visited Dec. 5, 2022).
168 *Id.*; Leslie, *supra* note 162 at 7.
169 Leslie, *supra* note 162 at 10.
170 State of Florida v. Thomas, 2006CF009126 (2006) https://myeclerk.myorangeclerk.com/ (last visited Dec. 5, 2022).
171 *Id.*
172 *Id.*
173 *Id.*
174 *Id.*
175 Warren v. Warren, 2009DR776, 2–3 (2009) (Pet. for Inj. for Prot. Against Dom. Viol.).
176 D. H. Borst, 09-05-375 at 10; Warren v. Warren, 2009DR776, 2 (2009) (Motion to Continue).
177 Warren v. Warren, 2009DR776, 1–5 (2009) (Temp. Inj. for Prot. Against Dom. Viol. with Minor Child(ren)).
178 Warren v. Warren, 2009DR776, 2 (2009) (Motion to Continue).
179 Warren v. Warren, 2009DR776, 1 (2009) (Order Extending Inj. for Prot. Against Dom. Viol.).
180 Borst, *supra* note 176 at 9–10; Anthony Colarossi & Stephen Hudak, *Woman Killed by Husband Feared his Violent Threats*, ORLANDO SENTINEL (May 14, 2009).
181 Borst, *supra* note 176 at 14.
182 *Id.*
183 Garwin-Williams v. Williams, 05-2009-DR-033286-XXXX-XX, 3 (2009) (Pet. for Inj. for Prot. Against Dom. Viol.).
184 Garwin-Williams v. Williams, 05-2009-DR-033286-XXXX-XX, 3 (2009) (Order of Dismissal of Temp. Inj. for Prot. Against Dom. Viol.); *Husband Charged in Fatal Florida Hospital Shooting*, EMS WORLD (June 7, 2009).
185 Scott Andrews, 09-38446 at 2–3; *Husband Charged in Fatal Florida Hospital Shooting, supra* note 184.
186 *Husband Charged in Fatal Florida Hospital Shooting, supra* note 184. Although it appears that the nature of the complaints to the Titusville Police Department were physical battery domestic violence reports, details of the reports are not available due to the administrative destruction of the reports.

187 Garvin v. Williams, 052000DR13334XXXXX, 3 (2000) (Pet. for Inj. for Prot. Against Dom. Viol.); Garvin v. Williams, 052000DR13334XXXXX (2000) https://vmatrix1.brevardclerk.us/beca/all_results.cfm?x=4BB88F8C738788-AC99BFD224CC0A2DDB7BDFE7BF9D13E70EFC00EDD8DFCBC76526 FA6ABF&CFID=26982323&CFTOKEN=1caf342e0076d70c-12FEA001-5056-B465-1FB3FCB6272E59AC (last visited Dec. 1, 2022).
188 *Husband Charged in Fatal Florida Hospital Shooting, supra* note 184.
189 Huss v. Huss, 07-234 DV, 3 (2007) (Pet. for Inj. for Prot. Against Dom. Viol.).
190 Bennett v. Harp, 2008-DR-0003342-O, 3 (2008) (Pet. for Inj. for Prot. Against Dom. Viol.).
191 Whyte-Dell v. Dell, 2010DR006153, 4 (2010) (Pet. for Inj. for Prot. Against Dom. Viol.).
192 Curry v. Curry, 11-493 DV, 11 (2011) (Temp. Inj. for Prot. Against Dom. Viol. without Minor Child(ren) ***Extended to January 3, 2012***).
193 *Id.* at 2–6.
194 *Id.* at 4.
195 Curry v. Curry, 06-488 DV, 10 (2006) (Temp. Inj. for Prot. Against Dom. Viol. without Minor Child(ren)).
196 *Id.* at 1–7.
197 Curry v. Curry, 122012DR000011DRAXMX (2012) https://www.civitek florida.com/ocrs/app/caseinformation.xhtml?query=HQY_pELQrJE7i5 EElurxj092qlEfuqS2_D_Mi9qGRlY&from=partyCaseSummary (last visited Dec. 1, 2022).
198 *Id.*
199 *Id.*
200 Charles Vaughan, CCSO13OFF006816 at 4–5; Curry, 122013DR000446 DRAXMX.
201 Vaughan, *supra* note 200 at 5.
202 *Id.*
203 *Id.*
204 *Id.* at 4.
205 *Id.* at 5.
206 *Id.* at 4–5.
207 *Id.* at 5.
208 *Id.*
209 *Id.*
210 *Id.*
211 *Id.* at 4.
212 *Id.*
213 *Id.*
214 *Id.*
215 *Id.*
216 *Id.*
217 *Id.*
218 Jackson v. Reddick, 07-DR-002525, 1 (2007) (Pet. for Inj. for Prot. Against Dom. Viol.); Jackson v. Reddick, 07-DR-002525, 1 (2007) (Temp. Inj. for Prot. Against Dom. Viol. with Minor Child(ren).
219 Jackson v. Reddick, 07-DR-002525, 2–3 (2007) (Pet. for Inj. for Prot. Against Dom. Viol.).

220 *See generally* Jackson v. Reddick, 07-DR-002525 (2007) (Amended Temp. Inj. for Prot. Against Dom. Viol. with Minor Child(ren)).
221 Jackson v. Reddick, 07-DR-002525, 1 (2007) (F. Judg. of Inj. for Prot. Against Dom. Viol. with Minor Child(ren) (after Notice)).
222 *See* Alvin Cruz, 2015-33903 at 1, 7–8, 10.
223 *Id.* at 5.
224 *Id.* at 5, 12.
225 *Id.* at 10, 12.
226 Grindrod v. Grindrod, 12-000494DR A, 3 (2012) (Pet. for Inj. for Prot. Against Dom. Viol.).
227 Romero v. Romero, 2008-DR-0000778-O (2008) (Pet. for Inj. for Prot. Against Dom. Viol.); Romero v. Romero, 2008-DR-0015103-O (2008) (Pet. for Inj. for Prot. Against Dom. Viol.); Romero v. Romero, 2010-DR-021349-O (2010) (Pet. for Inj. for Prot. Against Dom. Viol.).
228 Romero, 2008-DR-0000778-O at 4–5.
229 Romero, 2008-DR-0015103-O at 2.
230 *Id.* at 4–5.
231 Romero v. Romero, 2008-DR-0015103-O (2008) (Order Denying Pet. for Inj. for Prot. Against Dom. Viol.); Romero v. Romero, 2008-DR-0015103-O (2008) (Order Denying *Supp*. Pet. for Inj. for Prot. Against Dom. Viol.). *See supra* Chapter 5, Intimidation, Harassment, Surveillance. *See infra* Chapter 6, Humiliation, Power and Control, Child Abuse.
232 Romero v. Romero, 2008-DR-0015103-O, 1 (2008) (Order Denying Pet. for Inj. for Prot. Against Dom. Viol.).
233 Romero v. Romero, 2008-DR-0015103-O, 1 (2008) (Order Denying *Supp*. Pet. for Inj. for Prot. Against Dom. Viol.).
234 Romero v. Romero, 2010-DR-021349-O (2010) (Pet. for Inj. for Prot. Against Dom. Viol.); Romero v. Romero, 10-21390 (2010) (Pet. for Diss. of Marriage with Dep. Or Minor Child(ren)).
235 Romero, 2010-DR-021349-O at 4–5.
236 Romero v. Romero, 2010-DR-021349-O, 1–8 (2010) (F. Judg. of Inj. for Prot. Against Dom. Viol. with Minor Child(ren) (after Notice)).
237 Romero v. Romero, 2010-DR-021349-O (2010) (Pet. by Aff. for Order to Show Cause for a Viol. of F. Judg. of Inj. for Prot. Against Dom. Viol.).
238 Romero v. Romero, 2010-DR-021349-O (2010) (Nt. of Hearing).
239 Romero v. Romero, 2010-DR-021349-O (2010) (Motion).
240 Romero v. Romero, 2010-DR-021349-O (2010) (Nt. of Hearing).
241 Romero v. Romero, 2010-DR-021373-O, 5 (2010) (Pet. for Inj. for Prot. Against Dom. Viol.).
242 *Id.* at 5–6.
243 Romero v. Romero, 2010-DR-021373-O, 1 (2010) (F. Judg. of Inj. for Prot. Against Dom. Viol. with Minor Child(ren) (after Notice)).
244 Romero v. Romero, 2010-DR-021373-O, 1 (2010) (Court Minutes); Romero v. Romero, 2010-DR-021373-O, 4 (2010) (F. Judg. of Inj. for Prot. Against Dom. Viol. with Minor Child(ren) (after Notice)).
245 Romero v. Romero, 2010-DR-021373-O, 4 (2010) (F. Judg. of Inj. for Prot. Against Dom. Viol. with Minor Child(ren) (after Notice)).
246 Romero v. Romero, 2010-DR-021373-O, 1–2 (2010) (Pet. by Aff. for Order to Show Cause for a Viol. of F. Judg. of Inj. for Prot. Against Dom. Viol.).
247 *Id.* at 2.
248 Romero v. Romero, 2010-DR-021373-O (2010) (Nt. of Hearing).

249 Romero v. Romero, 2010-DR-021373-O (2010) (Order).
250 Id.
251 Miguel Rosario, 11-22426 at 6.
252 Id.
253 Id.
254 Id.
255 Id.
256 Alvarez v. Alvarez, 562007DR002140, 3 (2007) (Pet. for Inj. for Prot. Against Dom. Viol.).
257 See Id.
258 See Id.
259 See Id.
260 See Id.
261 See Id. at 4.
262 See Alvarez v. Alvarez, 2007DR002140 (2007) https://courtcasesearch.stlucieclerk.com/BenchmarkWebExternal/CourtCase.aspx/Details/1815826?digest=%2BISafaEEe2rD%2FZNbbb0jew (last visited Dec. 13, 2022).
263 Id.
264 Alvarez v. Alvarez, 2007DR002784 (2007) https://courtcasesearch.stlucieclerk.com/BenchmarkWebExternal/CourtCase.aspx/Details/1816470?digest=ra3vmArvHQmmZV0XTmwsDA (last visited Dec. 28, 2022).
265 State of Florida v. Alvarez, 562007CF004010A, 2 (2007) (Arrest Aff.); State of Florida v. Alvarez, 562007CF004472A, 2 (2007) (Arrest Aff.).
266 Alvarez, 562007CF004472A at 2.
267 Alvarez, 562007CF004010A at 2; Alvarez, 562007CF004472A at 2; State of Florida v. Alvarez, 562007CF004010A (2007) (No Info.); State of Florida v. Alvarez, 562007CF004472A (2007) (No Info.).
268 Alvarez v. Alvarez, 2007DR002784 (2007) https://courtcasesearch.stlucieclerk.com/BenchmarkWebExternal/CourtCase.aspx/Details/1816470?digest=ra3vmArvHQmmZV0XTmwsDA (last visited Dec. 28, 2022)
269 Russell Tucker, 08-00413 at 6.
270 Id. at 8, 18.
271 Id. at 8–25.
272 Id. at 14.
273 Id. at 13–14, 21–20.
274 Id. at 18.
275 Id. at 20.
276 Id. at 19.
277 Id. at 20.
278 Id.
279 Id.
280 See Id.
281 Id.
282 Id.
283 See generally State of Florida v. Alvarez, 562008CF000197A (2008) (Arrest Aff.).
284 State of Florida v. Alvarez, 562008CF000197A (2008) (Info.).
285 See generally State of Florida v. Alvarez, 562008CF000197A (2008) (Felony Plea Form).
286 See generally State of Florida v. Alvarez, 562008CF000197A (2008) (Judgment).

287 Nicholson v. Nicholson, 04-2667-CA, 3 (2004) (Pet. for Inj. for Prot. Against Dom. Viol.).
288 Romero v. Romero, 2008-DR-0015103-O, 4 (2008) (Pet. for Inj. for Prot. Against Dom. Viol.).
289 Tubwell v. Welch, 2010 DR 002065, 4 (2010) (Pet. for Inj. for Prot. Against Dom. Viol.).
290 Allen v. Allen, 12-15371, 3 (2012) (Pet. for Inj. for Prot. Against Dom. Viol.).
291 Strong v. Fulgham, 2008-4461-DRFJ, 4 (2008) (Pet. for Inj. for Prot. Against Dom. Viol.).
292 Hogan-Mccarthren v. Mccarthren, 2012-DR-001236-O, 4 (2012) (Pet. for Inj. for Prot. Against Dom. Viol.).
293 *Id.* at 1, 8; *See generally* Hogan-Mccarthren v. Mccarthren, 2012-DR-001236-O (2012) (Temp. Inj. for Prot. Against Dom. Viol. with Minor Child(ren)).
294 *See generally* Hogan-Mccarthren v. Mccarthren, 2012-DR-001236-O (2012) (Order Extending Inj. for Prot. Against Dom. Viol.).
295 *Id.* at 1.
296 *See generally* Hogan-Mccarthren v. Mccarthren, 2012-DR-001236-O (2012) (Order of Dismissal of Temp. Inj. for Prot. Against Dom. Viol.).
297 *See* Jeff Weiner, *Teacher's Daughter Witnessed Father's Fatal Stabbing, Records Show*, ORLANDO SENTINEL (Jan. 28, 2015).
298 *See Id.*
299 *See generally Woman Found Not Guilty of Stabbing Husband to Death has Message for Community*, COX MEDIA GROUP (Oct. 31, 2016).
300 *See generally* Weiner, *supra* note 297.
301 *See generally Id.*
302 *See generally Id.*
303 *See generally Id.*
304 *Woman Found Not Guilty of Stabbing Husband to Death has Message for Community*, *supra* note 299 ¶ 14.
305 *See generally Id.*
306 *See generally Id.*
307 Huss v. Huss, 03-485DV, 2 (2003) (Pet. for Inj. for Prot. Against Dom. Viol.); Martin v. Martin, 2009 DR 001008, 4 (2009) (Pet. for Inj. for Prot. Against Dom. Viol.).
308 Nicholson v. Nicholson, 04-2667-CA, 4 (2004) (Pet. for Inj. for Prot. Against Dom. Viol.).
309 Wood v. Wood, 05-14620FD-9, 4 (2005) (Pet. for Inj. for Prot. Against Dom. Viol.).
310 Bailey v. Bailey, 632006DR194, 3 (2006) (Pet. for Inj. for Prot. Against Dom. Viol.).
311 Warren v. Warren, 2009DR776, 2 (2009) (Pet. for Inj. for Prot. Against Dom. Viol.). *See supra* Chapter 5, Intimidation, Threatens Friends and Family.
312 Warren, 2009DR776 at 3.
313 *See supra* Chapter 5, Intimidation, Threatens Friends and Family, *Warren v. Warren*.
314 This is not to say that the legal standard for false imprisonment may be different. Here, this analysis concerns the non-violent tactic of coercive control, which is not meant to meet the higher legal standard.
315 Rimmer v. Rimmer, 53-2008DR-006441-0000-00, 2 (2008) (Pet. for Inj. for Prot. Against Dom. Viol.). *See supra* Chapter 5, Intimidation, Threats.

316 *See generally* Rimmer v. Rimmer, 53-2008DR-006441-0000-00 (2008) (Temp. Inj. for Prot. Against Dom. Viol. with Children); *See generally* Rimmer v. Rimmer, 53-2008DR-006441-0000-00 (2008) (Order of Dismissal).
317 John Chambliss, *Slain Wife Sought, Then Withdrew Injunction*, ¶ 5 THE LEDGER (Aug. 26, 2008).
318 *See generally Id.*
319 *See generally Id.*
320 *See generally* Rimmer v. Rimmer, 53-2008DR-006441-0000-00 (2008) (Order of Dismissal); *See generally* Chambliss, *supra* note 317.
321 *See* Chambliss, *supra* note 317.
322 *See* Martin v. Martin, 2009 DR 001008 (2009) (Pet. for Inj. for Prot. Against Dom. Viol.); Erlandson, 2009-00041057 at 2.
323 *See* Martin, 2009 DR 001008; Erlandson, *supra* note 322.
324 *See* Martin, 2009 DR 001008; Erlandson, *supra* note 322.
325 *See* Martin, 2009 DR 001008; Erlandson, *supra* note 322.
326 *See* Martin, 2009 DR 001008; Erlandson, *supra* note 322.
327 Martin, 2009 DR 001008 at 4; Erlandson, *supra* note 322.
328 Martin, 2009 DR 001008 at 4.
329 Erlandson, *supra* note 322.
330 *Id.*; Costello, 2009-00050821 at 2.
331 Erlandson, *supra* note 322.
332 *Id.*
333 *Id.*
334 *Id.*
335 *See generally* Martin v. Martin, 2009 DR 001008 (2009) (Pet. for Inj. for Prot. Against Dom. Viol.).
336 Costello, *supra* note 330; *Law & Disorder: Flagler Man, Wife Dead in Apparent Murder-Suicide*, ¶ 3 THE TIMES-UNION (Sept. 17, 2009).
337 *Law & Disorder: Flagler Man, Wife Dead in Apparent Murder-Suicide*, *supra* note 336 at ¶ 3.
338 Costello, *supra* note 330.
339 *Id.*
340 *Id.*
341 *Id.*
342 *Id.*
343 *Id.*
344 *Id.*
345 *Id.*
346 *See* Frank Fernandez, *Piece of paper Can't Stop Killer*, THE DAYTONA BEACH NEWS-JOURNAL (Aug. 15, 2012).
347 *See Id.*
348 Purtis, 2009-00058067 at 2; *See* Fernandez, *supra* note 346.
349 Fernandez, *supra* note 346 at ¶ 33.
350 *Id.* at ¶ 34.
351 *See generally Id.*; *See* Purtis, 2009-00058067.
352 *See generally* Fernandez, *supra* note 346; *See* Purtis, *supra* note 351.
353 Purtis, *supra* note 351 at 3; *accord* Fernandez, *supra* note 346.
354 Fernandez, *supra* note 346 at ¶ 38.
355 Purtis, *supra* note 351 at 3.
356 *Id.*
357 *Id.*

358 *Id.*
359 *Id.*
360 *Id.*
361 *Id.*
362 *Id.*
363 *Id.*
364 *Id.*
365 *Id.*
366 *Id.* at 4.
367 *Id.*
368 *Id.*
369 *Id.*
370 *Id.*
371 *Id.*
372 *See* Fernandez, *supra* note 346.
373 *See Id.*
374 Fernandez, *supra* note 346 at ¶ 53.
375 Jackson v. Jackson, 02-2007-DR-000202, 4 (2007) (Pet. for Inj. for Prot. Against Dom. Viol.).
376 *See generally* Curtis Ruise, BCSO08OFF000513.
377 *See* Id. at 3–6.
378 *Sheriff: Teen Calls 911 after Mom Shot Dad*, NEWS4JAX (March 5, 2008); *accord* Ruise, *supra* note 376 at 3.
379 *Sheriff: Teen Calls 911 after Mom Shot Dad*, *supra* note 378.
380 Ruise, *supra* note 376 at 3.
381 Kelley Lannigan, *Life without Parole for Jackson*, THE BAKER COUNTY PRESS (July 23, 2009).
382 Whyte-Dell v. Dell, 2010DR006153, 4 (2010) (Pet. for Inj. for Prot. Against Dom. Viol.).
383 Frasch v. Frasch, 13DR3955, 4 (2013) (Pet. for Inj. for Prot. Against Dom. Viol.).

6 The Insidious and Omnipresent Coercive Control

Humiliation

"Humiliation" is a theme that describes acts the abuser did to the intimate partner violence (IPV) victim to evoke feelings of mortification. In this study, 1.4% of the 493 cases and 11.1% of the sixty-two (62) cases, as well as 10.0% of the 100 petitions for injunction analyzed in this phase, resulted in a humiliation coding. Often, the abuser humiliates the IPV victim in front of others. As previously discussed, themes and subthemes share similar qualities. As IPV victims' statements explain their abusers' behavior, the theme of humiliation, as well as the more specific subthemes of degradation and name calling emerge, as exemplified below. For example, Fabiana Romero explained that she felt "he likes to provoke me by saying humiliating and degrading things."[1] She recognized that he was utilizing this non-violent coercive control tactic against her to attempt to provoke certain emotions from Fabiana. However, because she understood this behavior, she was able to communicate it to the court.

Gordon v. Gordon

On October 27, 2014, Antoinette Gordon wrote in her petition for injunction that her estranged husband, Hugh, "calls me 'bitch', 'fornicator' and a 'liar' in front of our son. I have texts of harrassments [sic] and a video when he entered the guest room threatening and cursing me."[2] In another section of her narrative, she explained that he used other acts to humiliate her, "He grabbed open my bathrobe stating, 'that I had shaved for my boyfriend.'"[3] She was awarded a temporary and final injunction based on her petition.[4] The final injunction expired on May 12, 2015.[5]

While they were going through their divorce, Antoinette and Hugh were separated but living in the same house.[6] On October 14, 2014, Hugh filed his own petition for injunction against Antoinette, accusing her of being "loud & aggressive" and "threatening [him] & provoking [him] around the home"[7]; but it was unsuccessful in obtaining him any protection from the court. And after Antoinette's final injunction from her October 27, 2014, petition for injunction expired on May 12, 2015, she filed a second petition for injunction on June 8, 2015; but by this point, the couple was living apart.[8] Hugh had come to the backyard of the marital home, unannounced and unwelcomed, where Antoinette was living.[9] He was standing in the backyard, taking pictures.[10] When Antoinette came out of the house, Hugh "just stood there staring at her with a smile on his face."[11] When she asked what he was doing there, he just stayed there in the backyard.[12] Antoinette went into the house and locked herself in the bedroom.[13] She called the authorities, but they were not able to do anything because the prior injunction for protection she had against Hugh expired in May 2015.[14] As a result, her June 2015 request to the court for protection from Hugh was denied.

On the evening of April 29, 2016, Hugh and Antoinette met at a McDonald's to exchange their young child for a custody visit.[15] Hugh shot Antoinette about two dozen times in front of their son.[16] Then, he turned the gun on himself and died from self-inflicted gunshot wounds.[17]

Degradation

"Degradation," a subtheme of humiliation, describes a range of non-violent tactics used by the abuser to disrespect or show contempt for the IPV victim, whether in public or private. In this study, 1.8% of the 493 cases and 14.2% of the sixty-two (62) cases, as well as 11.0% of the 100 petitions for injunction analyzed in this phase, resulted in a degradation coding. By its very definition, this non-violent tactic of coercive control explains that "saying humiliating and degrading things,"[18] cursing repeatedly,[19] and "constantly being disrespectful and rude"[20] over time, can be very harmful to an IPV victim's sense of well-being and self-worth. Indeed, if anyone had a friend with them when their abuser was "yelling" and "cussing" at them and telling them to leave, the words are not just derogatory but the effect on the IPV victim is also humiliating. However, yelling at the IPV victim is not the only tactic that may be utilized with degradation as there are other means to accomplish this non-violent tactic, such as causing the victim to do or say things they otherwise would not do without being forced to do by the abuser. As the tactic of degradation is utilized by the abuser, it often flows into other humiliation tactics, such as name calling. The following cases are indicative of such.

Olms v. Olms

Abusers, such as Frank Olms, understand that "screaming obscenities" in public places, such as being "loud enough for all of [their] neighbors to here [sic]," making sure they become "more vulgar & obseen [sic]," is the best way to ensure their victim is degraded.[21] Nancy Olms explained these experiences to the trial court on December 14, 2009, after her estranged husband, Frank, came to her apartment on the night of December 12, 2009.[22] In this same petition for injunction, Nancy described physical violence she experienced at the hands of Frank and that she feared for her life because "he is very unstable and has always drank obsessively."[23] She was denied any type of injunction for protection by the court against Frank for her petition.[24]

On January 2, 2007, Frank filed a petition for injunction requesting the court provide protection to him against Nancy because she was drinking frequently and becoming verbally abusive.[25] He also accused her of becoming physically abusive, especially during a time when they were in the car while Frank was driving.[26] The court provided Frank with a temporary and final injunction for his request for protection from Nancy.[27]

On August 5, 2011, after having recently moved back in together, Frank shot Nancy in the head in their back yard.[28] Frank attempted to kill himself at the scene by a self-inflicted gunshot wound but was unsuccessful.[29] When asked by police what happened, Frank stated, "I shot her because she is a bitch."[30] He further explained, "I shot her then me."[31] Frank was arrested for first degree murder; however, the prosecution tried him on information for second degree murder with a firearm.[32] Frank was found guilty and was sentenced to life in prison.[33]

Diller v. Diller

Theodore Diller filed two injunctions in 2008 and 2010 for protection against his wife, Rhonda, complaining to the court that she had "chased me through the yard cursing and spitting" at him.[34] He also described the fact that "she continually calls me filthy names."[35] In the February 2008 petition whereby he described the cursing and spitting, among other acts by Rhonda, he was provided a temporary injunction but filed a notice of voluntary dismissal shortly after she was served with the injunction.[36] However, during that same month, he filed for dissolution of marriage action (DOM); but, in May 2008, that action was quickly resolved between the couple through a joint stipulation to dismiss the case.[37]

Theodore was not provided a final injunction for the second petition for injunction he filed in January 2010.[38] On January 11, 2010, he filed for DOM for the second time, which became a very contentious divorce between the couple.[39] They began to live apart but were in separate homes very close to each other.[40] Rhonda explained to a neighbor she knew for sixteen (16) years that she had spent $60,000 in attorney's fees.[41] She also told that same neighbor, even though there is no record of Rhonda having filed for an injunction for protection, that she was "scared [Theodore] is going to kill me."[42] Even though they were divorcing and lived in separate homes, neighbors were aware of the couple regularly fighting.[43]

On the morning of February 22, 2012, Rhonda's body was found in her backyard under a blanket with a gunshot wound to the chest.[44] Theodore was found unconscious on the kitchen floor from having taken an unknown amount of prescription medication.[45] Once he regained consciousness for a moment, Theodore told first responders that he "was shooting squirrels, I mean I was shooting armadillo."[46] On February 24, 2012, he was arrested and charged with first degree murder for Rhonda's death.[47] An extensive criminal trial against Theodore took place for the following two years until the trial against him was set to begin in late June 2014.[48] However, on June 24, 2014, the court declared a mistrial because, as Theodore was being transferred from his jail cell to the courthouse for trial, he jumped headfirst from a second story flight of stairs within the jail, causing him critical injuries.[49] He died on July 5, 2014, without the trial having taken place.[50]

Name Calling

For this study, "name calling," a subtheme of humiliation, explains situations in which the abuser calls the IPV victim humiliating and/or degrading names either in public or in private. In this study, 4.6% of the 493 cases and 36.5% of the sixty-two (62) cases, as well as 23.0% of the 100 petitions for injunction analyzed in this phase, resulted in a name calling coding. "Bitch" is the most common word coded in the subtheme of name calling. Phrases such as "constantly calling me names,"[51] "cursing @ me & calling me names,"[52] and "continually calls me filthy names"[53] are indicative of the expressive language IPV victims used to explain the fact that the non-violent tactic of name calling is utilized on an ongoing basis. Phrases with specific names used in name calling, such as "bitch, ho," "cunt," "fucking bitch," "whore," and "worthless piece of shit," help to explain the vitriol and invective used in this non-violent tactic.[54] As with degradation, name calling is very effective at breaking down the IPV victim's self-worth, making it more difficult for her to believe that she is worthy of any other life than the one she is living with her abuser, often preventing her from seeking help outside the relationship.

Nicholson v. Nicholson

Besides the other tactics of coercive control Sandra Nicholson described to the Court that include economic control and false imprisonment as shown above, her May 28, 2004, petition for injunction is overflowing with examples of name calling by her estranged husband, Donald.[55] She explained to the court that Donald kept cursing at her by calling her "'bitch,' 'you cunt.' ... You fucking bitch."[56] One incident she described to the Court occurred in 2003 whereby Donald held a pillow to her face and told her to "stop yelling you bitch."[57] She was awarded a temporary injunction for her petition but filed a motion to dismiss that injunction on July 9, 2004, which was granted on July 15, 2004.[58] Additionally, she filed for divorce on May 27, 2004, but dropped that petition for DOM.[59] The first DOM case between Sandra and Donald was dismissed on October 17, 2005.[60]

A neighbor of the Nicholson's described Donald as jealous and controlling.[61] In fact, by March 2007, Sandra told her friends, family, and new divorce attorney that if she ever did not show up to work or went missing, something is definitely wrong; and it is most likely related to Donald.[62] In late March 2007, Donald threated to kill Sandra and feed her to the alligators.[63] On March 29, 2007, Sandra was reported as missing by friends and family; and Donald was arrested and charged with second-degree murder.[64] On April 1, 2007, Sandra's nude body was found in a canal, partially eaten by alligators more than a week after she went missing; but the medical examiner determined she was strangled to death.[65] Donald was sentenced to twenty-two years for second-degree murder in state prison after pleading no contest to the charges levied against him.[66]

Belcher v. Belcher

Gwendolyn and Christopher Belcher, discussing how to raise their son, did not agree, causing Christopher to become angry and to begin "calling [Gwendolyn] different types of verbal names."[67] On October 21, 2008, she explained to the court in her petition for injunction that he "continued to threaten me and use verbal abuse" and that the verbal abuse had been ongoing for two years.[68] She continued to explain that "Chris is very verbal, physical & mentally abusive."[69] Besides filing her petition for injunction for protection against Christopher, Gwendolyn also filed a police report related to this same incident; but he was not arrested.[70] Instead, he was ordered to appear to answer for a criminal misdemeanor for battery against Gwendolyn.[71] Gwendolyn was provided a temporary injunction for her petition, which was not served on Christopher; and she was not provided a final injunction because she failed to appear at the hearing for the final injunction.[72] As a result, the injunction case against Christopher was dismissed on November 3, 2008.[73]

Four years later, on September 16, 2012, Gwendolyn's family members reported her missing to the Hillsborough County Sheriff's Office.[74] On that same day, deputies found a vehicle registered to Gwendolyn and Christopher "completely burned to the ground."[75] After further investigation, deputies on the scene realized there were human remains in the back seat of the vehicle, which was located within five miles of the Belcher home.[76] A detective from the State Fire Marshal's Office found that the type of fire the vehicle suffered was indicative of one started by an accelerant.[77]

Christopher's thirteen-year-old daughter provided information to investigators during a forensic interview in which she explained that he and Gwendolyn got into an argument the night of September 15, 2012.[78] Christopher had accused her of cheating on him.[79] The argument became physical when he began to hit her in the face with an open fist while she was lying on the couch.[80] Christopher then sent his daughter to her room.[81] After, the young girl described hearing loud sounds of beating and "something banging against a table."[82] Shortly, she heard sounds of what she thought were Gwendolyn being strangled, such as Gwendolyn yelling at times, sounding muffled at times, and at other times was gasping for breath.[83] When the yelling stopped, Christopher told his daughter to go to bed; and she did not see Gwendolyn at the house the next morning when she woke up.[84]

Through dental records, the human remains found in the burnt-out vehicle were positively identified as Gwendolyn's.[85] However, the cause of death was "homicidal violence" rather than her having been burned to death; but the manner of death was "a homicide by unspecified means."[86] During the execution of a search warrant at the Belcher home, investigators found what appeared to be evidence of blood and blood spatter in several areas throughout the residence.[87] DNA profiles from the blood and blood splatter matched Gwendolyn's and a male individual.[88]

As a result of the investigation into Gwendolyn's disappearance, an arrest warrant was issued on October 25, 2012, against Christopher for second degree murder and arson of an occupied structure.[89] On July 24, 2015, a jury found him guilty on both counts.[90] He was sentenced to life, with an additional thirty years for the related arson count.[91]

Power and Control

For this study, "power and control" is a theme that describes acts of authority and regulation the abuser maintains over the IPV victim to obtain compliance from the victim. About 7.3% of the 493 cases and 57.1% of the sixty-two (62) cases, as well as 48.0% of the 100 petitions for injunction analyzed in this phase, resulted in a power and control coding. The two most coded words for the theme power and control are "car" and "phone," respectively. This is because many of the coded phrases involve the abuser preventing the IPV victim from driving the car, often described by the IPV victim as the abuser taking the car keys away, or preventing them from being able to use the phone, particularly when the IPV victim is attempting to contact the police.[92] This theme of power and control is distinguished from the theme of isolation and its subtheme of economic control because it is often tied to the IPV victim's attempt to contact authorities in the event of an emergency or is particularly related to the abuser's acts toward the victim.

For example, Sandra Nicholson, discussed previously in the name calling subtheme, described how her husband admitted to her that "he had tampered with [her] vehicle so [she] didn't have access to one. So [she] wouldn't know what he was planning to do."[93] Another example is when Yana Huss explained to the court that when she tried calling 911 after her husband, Scott, threatened to kill her and was reaching for a gun, while she "was talking with operator 911 [sic], Scott cut telephone line."[94]

Herbert v. Herbert

On April 15, 2010, Julia Herbert explained to the court how "[her] husband takes car keys and parts out of the cars so I can not leave, if there were an emergency."[95] She was provided a temporary injunction for this petition. Indeed, family and friends of Julia and Wallace "Mark" Herbert, who knew the couple for any length of time, described their relationship as "controlling."[96] Although he never witnessed any physical violence between Julia and Mark, Mark's boss explained that he was once good friends with Mark.[97] However, he began to feel that Mark was not treating Julia as he should and was controlling her.[98] Another friend of the couple, who knew them for 10 years and never saw any physical violence between them, explained that Mark would make Julia do hard physical labor, even while she was pregnant.[99] Also, he would not let her leave the house unless she was with the children.[100] Again, Julia's oldest child confirmed this type of information about the couple's relationship by "stat[ing] that she has never seen Mark physically harm Julia but he would mentally control her."[101] The couple's pastor, who knew Julia and Mark for over 10 years, echoed these comments when "He described the relationship as controlling and stated that Mark would hold things over Julia to get her to do what he wanted her to do."[102]

Also in April 2010, Julia filed for divorce, causing Mark's behavior toward Julia to deteriorate even further as time went on.[103] He began to send to Julia's mother threatening texts and signs of possible attempts to enter Julia's home began to emerge.[104] Mark told Julia that "he would kill her and kill himself if he had too [sic]."[105] His texts to Julia became more aggressive, and he called her "a 'greedy bitch'" in relation to mediation having to do with the divorce proceedings.[106]

On April 8, 2011, Mark's stepmother contacted authorities after she received a call from him, telling her that he had killed Julia and was about to kill himself.[107] Sheriff's deputies arrived at Julia's home where her young daughter was alone inside with Julia's dead body.[108] Julia was lying on the kitchen floor with a gunshot wound to her chest.[109] Upon contacting deputies, the little girl stated, "'Mommy is dead' 'Daddy shot Mommy.'"[110]

Mark was later found on the ground outside the home, deceased from a self-inflicted gunshot wound to the head.[111] Prior to killing himself but after he killed Julia, he made several phone calls.[112] The first call was to his stepmother.[113] The next call was to his boss in which he explained he killed Julia and said his goodbyes.[114] The final call was to his divorce attorney whereby he also explained he killed Julia.[115] Friends later confirmed that Julia feared for her life at the hands of her husband, just days before her death, by forwarding threatening texts to them to ensure they would have them in the event something happened to her.[116]

Other non-violent power and control coercive control tactics detailed throughout the power and control coded phrases exemplify the abuser telling the IPV victim what to do on a regular basis. However, when these demands by the abuser for compliance from the IPV victim became more invective, the general response from the victim was to either comply or refuse to comply by attempting to call for help, which the abuser often thwarted by taking the phone away from the IPV victim.

For example, Fabiana Romero, discussed previously in harassment, surveillance, and isolation, explained how her husband "took [her] phone away from [her] while [she] was talking to the 911 operator" because she was reporting that "[her] husband bit [her] hand and hit [her] with the car's front passenger door."[117] Another common concept with phones involves the abuser obtaining the IPV victim's phone to delete information from it, such as emails and photographs that pertain to the victim attempting to collect evidence against the abuser.[118]

Shook v. Shook

Melissa Shook's January 23, 2007, petition for injunction contains a comparatively short narrative, but it explains enough of how her husband, Joseph, was treating her that she obtained an evidentiary hearing to secure a final injunction against him that was ordered to last until February 5, 2008.[119] In her narrative, she explained to the court that Joseph deleted the pictures she had taken on her camera after he hit her with a belt across her hamstrings.[120] Joseph was ordered to relinquish all of his firearms and ammunition to the Sheriff's Department within 24 hours of the final injunction, and Melissa was provided "temporary exclusive use and possession of the home," as well as temporary custody of the minor children.[121] Joseph was to have supervised visitation with their daughter's godparents doing the supervising because the no contact portion of the final injunction only provided for contact between Melissa and Joseph through the godparent third party contact.[122] Melissa and Joseph signed the final injunction order acknowledging its terms and conditions, which seemingly provided for all facets of Melissa's safety.[123] In other words, in this case, the Court appeared to take all the necessary steps it had at its disposal to try to guarantee Melissa's safety and well-being.

Still, on April 11, 2007, Joseph contacted the local Sheriff's Office to complain that Melissa came by his home to pick up their children when a physical altercation between the two of them took place.[124] But Melissa's version of events, as described to the investigating officer, were very different from Joseph's.[125] Joseph explained that Melissa simply came to his residence to pick up their children.[126] Melissa explained that, because she had a restraining order against Joseph, she was supposed to pick up the children from day care.[127] According to Melissa, Joseph made it difficult for the exchange at day care to occur; so, she attempted to have him meet her at other public places, which he refused to do.[128] Eventually, Melissa went to Joseph's home to pick up the children; and the argument between them ensued, at which point Joseph "grabbed her cell phone and removed her sim card stating he would call Everyman [sic] in there until he found out who she was cheating on him with."[129] Although Joseph claimed that Melissa was responsible for the physical altercation, she explained to the investigating officer that she also tried to call 9-1-1; but Joseph pulled the wires out of the socket from the house phone to prevent her from contacting the sheriff.[130] The investigating officer determined that there "was no physical evidence or independent witness's [sic] to confirm either story."[131] As a result, Melissa and Joseph's sworn statements were "sent to the Domestic Violence unit for possible warrant considerations," but no arrests were made.[132]

On July 24, 2007, while the final injunction was still in force, Melissa was reported missing by her father when she did not return to work after dropping off her youngest son at Joseph's house.[133] He explained to the deputies that it was odd for family members or him to not speak to her on the phone for such a length of time but that he had received text messages from her phone.[134] He tried calling her phone several times, but it went to voicemail each time.[135] He also explained that the content in the text messages coming from Melissa were odd, especially because one of them stated that she "was going to go get some help, and would be gone a while."[136] Another text said, "that she was ok, and she got to the 'place,' and that she just had to get her 'mind straight.'"[137] When deputies went to Joseph's home, he told them he thought Melissa might have tried to check herself into a mental health facility; however, her stepmother explained that Melissa had not been admitted to one in the past and did not seem upset or mentally ill.[138] As a result, deputies began the process of treating Melissa's unknown location status seriously by canvassing the immediate area, having her father sign a missing person affidavit, alerting the sergeant, and calling in a Be-On-the-Look-Out (BOLO).[139]

After Melissa was found by her stepfather four blocks away from Joseph's home on July 29, 2007, Joseph was arrested for second-degree murder on August 9, 2007.[140] Melissa had been "buried in a shallow grave with her hands tied behind her back and duct tape across her mouth."[141] Investigators matched a shovel purchased by Joseph on July 18, 2007, that was found in his garage, rope used to bound Melissa's hands behind her back that was consistent with rope he purchased on July 18, 2007, and duct tape that was torn from a roll in his garage used to cover her mouth.[142] At Joseph's week-long murder trial, it was revealed that Melissa was strangled to death.[143] He was convicted of second-degree murder in December 2009 after the jury took a mere two hours to deliberate.[144] He was sentenced to life in prison without parole in January 2010.[145]

Child Abuse

"Child abuse," in this study, is a subtheme of power and control that indicates the abuser has committed acts of child maltreatment and/or neglect or has threatened to commit acts of child maltreatment and/or neglect, including physical violence, sexual abuse, or psychological abuse against the children and/or stepchildren of, or those in common with, the abuser and the IPV victim, including committing acts of IPV or coercive control by the abuser against the IPV victim in front of the children. In this study, 3.4% of the 493 cases and 26.9% of the sixty-two (62) cases, as well as 23.0% of the 100 petitions for injunction analyzed in this phase, resulted in a child abuse coding. Although some coded phrases in the subtheme of child abuse exemplify the traditional connotation of child abuse, which involves physical abuse and neglect, the commonly coded phrases for this subtheme reference the abuser conducting themselves abusively with the IPV victim in front of the children, which is also considered a form of child abuse.[146]

This is exemplified above in the case of *Wood v. Wood* in the threats subtheme, whereby William Wood threatened Donna Wood in front of their son and incorporated him in their altercation, utilizing the nonviolent tactics of threats and child abuse.[147] Further indications of this type of abuse are detailed by several comments provided by additional IPV victims in their petition for injunction narratives that describe statements by abusers, including one written by Kristen Finn when she explained that her husband, Michael, told a Polk County Florida Sheriff's Office deputy, "I will mutilate her face so my kids have to look at it every day."[148] Other child abuse phrases were coded that met the more traditional sense of child abuse, in which the abuser directly harms the children, detailing the abuser from a much more disturbing and violent viewpoint.

Caso v. Caso

Deborah Caso explained the concepts of indirect and direct child abuse to the Court in two different narratives.[149] On December 6, 2004, she wrote that their children witnessed her husband "hitting [her] in the side of the head and began choking [her]" and they "yelled for him to stop."[150] She was awarded a temporary injunction on the same day she filed her petition and received a final injunction on December 22, 2004.[151] An order of supervised visitation was issued on December 22, 2004, as well.[152] Deborah's first case against her husband was dismissed on April 28, 2005.[153]

When she filed for her second injunction for protection on June 12, 2007, Deborah explained that the situation with her husband's treatment of the children had gotten much worse and more direct, "Father jumped up started hitting son .... Husband punched step daughter [sic] in right side of head. Daughter pushed him back. He came back and started hitting son and daughter."[154] An order for a temporary injunction was issued the same day Deborah filed her petition.[155] However, on August 9, 2007, the case was dismissed at the hearing for the final injunction when Deborah did not appear in court to have her petition heard.[156]

Less than a month later, on September 2, 2007, while Deborah was working as a waitress at Denny's Restaurant, her husband entered the restaurant where she worked.[157] He immediately pulled out a pocketknife and stabbed her to death, while multiple witnesses watched in horror.[158] Although witnesses attempted to follow him, he successfully fled the scene.[159] He lived on the run until he was caught on U.S. soil at the Mexican border near Hidalgo, Texas.[160] He was charged with first-degree murder but plead no contest to second-degree murder with a weapon and received 30 years in prison.[161]

Marshall-Burkhart v. Marshall

Dale Marshall-Burkhart explained to the Court on August 28, 1997, that her husband, John, among other violent acts, "hit, slapped and kicked" their son.[162] She also described how "He has slapped all the children in the face before, though not often, and is often verbally abusive to them."[163] She was initially denied a temporary injunction for her petition on August 28, 1997.[164] She filed for divorce on September 8, 1997, asking the judge to protect her and their children from John.[165] On September 10, 1997, the injunction case and divorce case were consolidated.[166] On October 7, 1997, Dale was issued a temporary injunction against John that lasted until November 3, 1997.[167] After a hearing on temporary relief in the divorce proceedings on November 3, 1997, an order was issued by the trial court on December 4, 1997.[168] Remarkably, within the order from the temporary hearing, a final injunction, with no expiration date, was issued against John, making it a permanent injunction in favor of Dale.[169]

Although John was ordered to pay over $2000 per month in child support, he refused to do so while he traveled all over the world, leaving Dale to raise and support their five children.[170] However, in 2003, Dale married again; and the new couple decided to go after the back child support Dale was owed, as well as half the rights in a commercial building in London she purchased with John during the marriage.[171] She was successful in obtaining over a $1 million judgment that might have become the motive in the shooting death of Dale and her new husband.[172] On the morning of May 6, 2010, John confronted Dale and her husband at their home and shot them both on the street outside.[173] Dale was in her SUV trying to escape, and her husband was on foot.[174] Then, John turned the gun on himself.[175]

Melissa Shook, previously discussed in the theme of power and control, wrote in her petition for injunction three months before she was killed, that her husband "slapped [her] across [her] face in front of kids 3, 2 year old – Then always told me I was stupid told the kids mommy was stupid I lied, I stoled [sic] etc."[176] She continued to explain that he "started hitting kids w/a belt for any and everything they did wrong along with slapping them."[177]

In *Huss v. Huss*, a case discussed previously in weapons, false imprisonment, and power and control, Scott Huss, who became the intimate partner homicide (IPH) offender, detailed for the court how Yana Huss's behavior changed when he wrote, "Her radically abusive, accusing, and degrading comments to [his] son has made [his son] so afraid that he does not want to be at our home."[178] However, one month before she was killed, Yana wrote in one of her petitions for injunction that Scott, "choked [her son], and pulled his ear, and push [sic] him with his hand at his throat. He leaved [sic] multiple bruises on his body."[179] She continued in her narrative to discuss Scott's treatment of their little baby girl by describing that he slapped her too hard when the baby was sitting in her chair crying, "He hit her little hands hard because she dropped some Cheerios on the floor."[180] These episodes of child abuse are indicative of the violence abusers are willing to inflict on IPV victims' children, even when they are their own.

Another non-violent example of child abuse includes Fabiana Romero telling the court that her husband "tells the kids I am a bitch because I am always smiling to everyone."[181] In that same petition for injunction, she went on to explain to the court that she wanted to start a new life but that she felt trapped.[182] She explained that she had four children and that her older children were very worried about her.[183] She stated that they were "very affected by this constant abuse."[184] She told the court her children deserved better.[185] Indeed, the children of these IPH cases, who survived the killings, deserve much better than the system has provided them to this point. Increased protection for their abused parent and themselves must be of the highest priority for the United States and the global community. It is possible to improve lethality risk assessments for the abused parents of these children to better protect both the IPV victim and their children.[186]

Violent Acts toward Family and Friends

"Violent acts towards family and friends" is a subtheme of power and control that describes violence by the abuser toward family and friends of the IPV victim. In this study, 0.4% of the 493 cases and 3.1% of the sixty-two (62) cases, as well as 2.0% of the 100 petitions for injunction analyzed in this phase, resulted in a "violent acts towards family and friends" coding. There were two (2) petitions for injunction out of the 100 analyzed that were given a violent acts toward family and friends coding, and both were a single victim/single offender IPH. The first petition for injunction was filed by the offender of the IPH, Christy Peacock, who stated that her husband yelled and cussed at her mom and "raised his hand up like he was gonna [sic] hit her [mom]."[187] This case is detailed in Chapter 7 in the "drug use" subtheme. The second petition for injunction case for "violent acts towards family and friends" is detailed below.

Mattaini v. Lennon

Nilda Mattaini explained to the Court on October 5, 2004, that her husband "slashed the tires of [her] brother's car" after he and her brother had gotten into a disagreement.[188] She was issued a temporary injunction against her husband on October 6, 2004, with a hearing set for October 14, 2004, that also included an allegation of repeat violence against her husband.[189] Nevertheless, Nilda's injunction case was dismissed because she did not appear at the hearing on October 14, 2004.[190]

One and a half years later, on February 8, 2006, in response to a welfare check at Nilda and her husband's home, authorities found them both lying in bed deceased.[191] The investigation revealed that Nilda was killed by strangulation/asphyxia, and her husband "committed suicide by means of self inflicted multiple sharp stab wounds from a kitchen knife."[192]

Taking Children from Victim

"Taking children from victim," a subtheme of power and control, explains situations in which the abuser either did take the children from the IPV victim or threatened to take the children from the victim. In this study, 1.2% of the 493 cases and 9.5% of the sixty-two (62) cases, as well as 7.0% of the 100 petitions for injunction analyzed in this phase, resulted in a taking children from victim coding. Abusers are known to threaten to "take" IPV victims' children from them, especially when couples are in the process of separation.[193] For example, Amanda Cloaninger, who also wrote about tactics of animal abuse as explained above, detailed to the Court about her estranged husband:

> He has taken my children twice as a means to keep them away from me .... He told me if I tried to get them he would stay on the run with them so I cannot locate them ever. He still has them and will not let me see them.[194]

As detailed below in the subtheme of household, clothes and personal belongings destroyed, Amanda's husband utilized many coercive control tactics against her.[195] However, often, the children from the relationship between the IPV victim and the abuser become an unfortunate tool for manipulation both inside and outside of the judicial system where coercive control tactics can be easily utilized quite effectively for continued abuse even after separation.[196]

Sandra Nicholson, discussed in economic control, false imprisonment, and name calling, wrote in her petition for injunction in 2004 that she had no idea where her estranged husband had taken her children.[197] She explained that, when she got home from work, all the children's clothing and medication were gone.[198] She continued, "The children's favorite stuffed animals they sleep with were gone .... I don't know where [the children] are at. I had no idea that he was taking them."[199] She described how he would not tell her where he went with the children, even though she asked to see them, "he said he doesn't know when I'll get to see them."[200] She continued to explain to the court that, from her point of view, he was supposed to take the children to daycare; but, instead, ran away with the kids.[201] In her petition for injunction, she respectfully requested the custody of her children.[202] Sandra and her husband had five (5) children at the time of her death in the spring of 2007.[203]

Strong v. Fulgham

In another case that was fueled by child custody issues, the IPH victim and the offender both wrote that the other either threatened to or did take the children out of state in an effort to keep the children from the other parent.[204] On September 3, 2008, and September 17, 2008, Joshua Fulgham and Heather Strong each filed petitions for injunction, respectively.[205] In his narrative, Joshua accused Heather of "[making] the statement to a couple of people and myself she was going to take the kids and run to Mississippi. She has already took [sic] them from me and went there 3 times before."[206] Joshua was successful in obtaining a temporary injunction that gave him temporary custody of their children with Heather having no visitation rights until a scheduled hearing on September 17, 2008.[207] Joshua did not receive a final injunction against Heather.[208] In her application for temporary injunction against Joshua, Heather accused him of "[stating] that he was taking my kids to the state of Mississippi."[209] Heather received a temporary injunction, but she was not successful in obtaining a final injunction against Joshua either.[210]

Florida Department of Children and Families [hereinafter *DCF*] had been involved in investigating Joshua and Heather since February 2004, due to an abusive incident whereby Joshua and Heather argued over money; and he covered her mouth with his hand, preventing her from breathing.[211] At that time, DCF explained they could remove the child from the home to protect the child; however, before DCF could file a petition for dependency or provide voluntary services, the family moved with no forwarding address.[212] The next contact DCF had with the family was on September 3, 2008, when they began investigating the allegations Heather and Joshua had in their respective petitions for injunction against each other.[213] As part of this investigation, DCF also included the relationships between Joshua, Heather, Joshua's girlfriend at the time, Emilia Carr, and Heather's boyfriend at the time, Benjamin McCollum.[214] This new investigation went on until the end of October 2008, seemingly ending by DCF providing Heather with voluntary services.[215]

Heather broke up with Benjamin in December 2008 to get back together with Joshua to try to make their family work.[216] Heather and Joshua were married on December 26, 2008; but by January 11, 2009, she filed another petition for injunction against him that included her explaining she had been threatened by Joshua's mother to go to the State Attorney's Office to drop charges against him stemming from him having pulled a gun on Heather.[217] She received a temporary injunction for this petition, but a final injunction was not issued. Heather was also threatened at knife point by Emilia in a desperate attempt by Emilia to get Joshua out of jail due to charges related to him having pulled the gun on Heather.[218] And, indeed, on February 6, 2009, the State Attorney's Office dropped the charges against Joshua based on the grounds that "The victim, Heather Fulgham, requested the SAO drop the case."[219] And still, Joshua and Heather continued to have issues over the custody of their children.[220]

On February 24, 2009, Heather's sister, Misty Strong, reported her missing to the Marion County Sheriff's Office in Ocala, Florida.[221] Misty explained that she was in Mississippi but that she and Heather maintained daily contact by phone or email.[222] The last time she heard from Heather was on February 15, 2009.[223] Misty also explained that Joshua and Heather were separated now.[224] Through further investigation, deputies learned that Heather received a call on February 15, 2009, at work from Joshua, which made her very upset.[225] In fact, the manager at Heather's work explained that she was in fear of Heather's life due to Joshua's continual harassment and his threatening to harm to Heather.[226] Joshua's mother told investigators that she had not heard from Heather prior to February 15, 2009, and saw Joshua at her residence with their children.[227] She said she had no idea why he had the children.[228]

Although she was still missing, on March 18, 2009, investigators were alerted to the fact that Heather's debit card was used on March 3, 2009, at a local grocery store's ATM to withdraw $42.00.[229] Evidence provided from the assistant manager at the store, including a video from the ATM transaction, helped investigators identify Joshua as the individual who utilized Heather's debit card to withdraw the money on March 3, 2009.[230] Investigators also had other information related to the use of Heather's debit card but had a more difficult time tying its usage directly to Joshua.[231] Additionally, on March 18, 2009, while investigating the case, deputies became aware of the fact that Heather's debit card was in use at a different grocery store.[232] It was also learned later that day that the person using the debit card was Joshua, for which he was "arrested for the organized fraud, fraudulent use of the credit card and petit theft."[233] Deputies interviewed Joshua and Emilia Carr shortly thereafter.[234] Both of their interviews lead investigators to understand that, with the assistance of Joshua's mother and sister, he had a letter typed for Heather to sign giving full custody of their children to Joshua.[235] The main investigator tasked with locating Heather's children learned that, on March 13, 2009, one of the children had just been placed at a new elementary school and was signed in by Joshua's mother, using the letter she typed for him for Heather to sign.[236] Emilia was listed as an emergency contact on the school's paperwork, linking her to Joshua shortly after Heather disappeared.[237]

During the interview with investigators at the Sheriff's Office on March 18, 2009, Joshua admitted to knowing where Heather's body was located.[238] After he showed investigators where Heather's body was buried, on March 19, 2009, a search warrant was obtained; and a makeshift gravesite was found in the back of the residence shared by Emilia and her mother.[239] Once removed from the grave, Heather was found "in what appeared to be a rolling suitcase ... [with] a blue blanket over the head and face of the body."[240] The next day, Joshua's fingerprint was matched to a piece of duct tape recovered from the immediate area where Heather was killed.[241] On March 21, 2009, Joshua admitted to planning, with Emilia, to kill Heather by luring her to Emilia's mother's property and into a storage trailer where they both attacked her.[242] They successfully overpowered her, hit her over the head with a flashlight, bound her to a computer chair, attempted to break her neck, and killed her by placing a garbage bag over her head while constricting the air flow with duct tape and holding her nose and mouth shut.[243] Heather's body was placed under a table in the kitchen for two days, partially hidden in a large suitcase with wheels with the other part covered by a blanket, until Joshua and Emilia were able to return to bury her body in the suitcase in a shallow grave behind the storage trailer.[244]

At trial, facts from the case emerged that showed Heather was so terrified once she realized what was taking place in the storage trailer that she attempted to flee, breaking a window to escape, all-the-while urinating on herself before she was attacked with a flashlight, allowing them to more easily overpower her to bound her to a chair.[245] Throughout the attack that led to her murder, "Heather pleaded and begged for her life, stating that she was 'claustrophobic.'"[246] She continued to plead, crying, and asking "Josh, why?"[247] He responded "because you keep trying to take my kids."[248] He made her sign the letter his mother prepared earlier that day, giving him custody of their children.[249] Once she was immobilized with duct tape on her hands and feet, Emilia attempted, unsuccessfully, to break her neck twice.[250] Then they used a plastic garbage bag around her neck, secured by duct tape, and "continued to suffocate her."[251] Facts at trial proved that "[f]or approximately five minutes she is conscious, aware of her surroundings, aware that she will not get away, and aware that she is going to die."[252] Joshua described how "he heard Heather making gurgling sounds and she gave a final jerk and he knew she was dead."[253]

A probable cause affidavit was issued on March 24, 2009, alleging facts supporting the arrest of Joshua, as defendant, and Emilia, as co-defendant, for the kidnapping and first-degree murder of Heather.[254] They were both indicted in April 2009 and were tried separately, with the state seeking the death penalty for each defendant.[255] On February 22, 2011, Emilia was sentenced to death for Heather's first-degree murder by a jury vote of seven to five and received a concurrent life sentence for her kidnapping.[256] At the time of her sentencing, she became the second women to sit on Florida's death row and the youngest women in the United States on death row.[257]

On February 23, 2011, Emilia appealed her conviction and death penalty punishment, which was affirmed by the Florida Supreme Court on February 5, 2015.[258] However, on July 5, 2017, because Emilia challenged her death sentence through post-conviction motions after her conviction and sentencing was affirmed on appeal, her death penalty punishment was waived by the state of Florida during the post-conviction process.[259] The court granted Emilia a new penalty phase hearing due to the U.S. Supreme Court decision in *Hurst v. Florida*, as well as the Florida Supreme Court decision in *Hurst v. State*, which changed Florida's capital sentencing scheme, essentially requiring a unanimous jury vote for the imposition of death and applying that requirement retroactively to many cases such as Carr's.[260] As a result, Emilia was resentenced to life in prison for Heather's murder.[261]

In April 2012, Joshua was found guilty but was sentenced to life in prison at the trial level.[262] He appealed the conviction and sentence from the trial court to Florida' Fifth District Court of Appeal; however, Joshua's conviction and life sentence was affirmed on January 28, 2014.[263]

Deprivation of Necessities

"Deprivation of necessities" is a subtheme of power and control that explains non-violent tactics the abuser uses to deprive the IPV victim of necessities such as food, medicine, showering, toileting, etc. In total, 1.0% of the 493 cases and 7.9% of the sixty-two (62) cases, as well as 5.0% of the 100 petitions for injunction analyzed in this phase, resulted in a deprivation of necessities coding. Deprivation of necessities is a less recognized form of non-violent coercive control that evokes power and control over the IPV victim, causing them to feel as though the abuser is omnipotent. Indeed, when the abuser does not allow the IPV victim to complete everyday tasks, such as showering or toileting without being watched, stood over, or forced to have their abuser participate, this deprives the victim of certain personal necessities and qualities of life, including autonomy, that those who have not experienced this form of abuse take for granted. The non-violent coercive control tactic of power and control is the force in the IPV victim's life where a private shower and toileting opportunity are anything but ordinary. As a result, the IPV victim must continue to look to their abuser for the necessities they need for daily survival.

When an IPV victim is dependent on her abuser for medical necessities, her daily life becomes a matter of life or death depending upon the seriousness of the medical issues. This theme arose throughout the coding of deprivation of necessities as the IPV victims detailed their offenders having deprived them of the medical treatment they required. For example, Julia Herbert, detailed in power and control above, explained to the court in October 2008 that she was very sick and in need of medical attention that her husband would not allow when she wrote "specialist & primary care dr [sic] said go to emergency room ... husband would not let me .... Dr's said I needed to start treatment, husband denied me .... Dr's at Shands High Risk Clinic said I needed treatment husband said no."[264] This statement from Julia helps to explain the deprivation of necessities her husband utilized against her as a non-violent tactic of coercive control, which placed her bodily integrity in jeopardy.

Hawkins v. Hawkins

Some of the IPV victims, such as Yvette Hawkins, were dependent on their abusers for daily care; so, when they were abandoned, as their narratives explain, they were without food or water for days at a time – "Due to him leaving me w/o food or water from Aug 15 – 24, 08, we began to argue as I felt he would do so again."[265] Yvette had health issues that prevented her from being able to care for herself, leaving her dependent on her husband, Louis, who was abusive and neglectful of Yvette.[266] On September 11, 2008, Yvette was awarded a temporary injunction, the day after she filed her petition.[267] She was issued a final injunction by the trial court on September 25, 2008.[268]

However, on May 21, 2010, Yvette, too, became the IPH offender when she shot Louis multiple times at point blank range.[269] Yvette was arrested for second degree murder on August 3, 2010, and plead guilty to manslaughter on August 16, 2012.[270] The terms of her plea agreement sentenced her to thirty-six (36) months in prison followed by twenty-four (24) months of community control, to be followed by probation of ten (10) years.[271] Yet, in the same Judgment/Order, the Court stayed and withheld her prison sentence and placed her on immediate community control to be completed under the supervision of the Department of Corrections for the twenty-four (24) month period.[272] On May 5, 2022, less than twelve (12) years after she killed Louis, Yvette was released from probation.[273]

In combination with other non-violent tactics, such as isolation, deprivation of necessities can be all the more effective. When Sandra Nicholson, discussed throughout this book, wrote about her car and heater being tampered with by her husband, she also described how her refrigerator had been turned off, causing her food to spoil.[274] She explained that she had to throw her food away.[275]

When deployed separately and over an extensive period, the types of non-violent coercive control tactics described by Sandra may not seem shocking enough to effectuate power and control over a person that might rise to the level of IPV. To the contrary, constant, slow, and methodical implementation of coercive control tactics, especially that of power and control, causes even the seemingly slightest intentional affront to one's daily routine and necessities to remind the victim of the abuser's omnipresence.

Psychologically Controlling

"Psychologically controlling," in this study, is a subtheme of power and control that explains acts by the abuser whereby non-violent tactics are used for maintaining a form of mental control over the IPV victim. In this study, 2.8% of the 493 cases and 22.2% of the sixty-two (62) cases, as well as 17.0% of the 100 petitions for injunction analyzed in this phase, resulted in a psychologically controlling coding. Most abusers are very good at psychologically controlling their IPV victim, and this can be one of the most effective tactics of non-violent coercive control. One of the most common patterns of psychologically controlling behaviors is for the abuser to apologize and tell the IPV victim he loves her after the physical violence has taken place.

IPV victim, Yana Huss, discussed throughout this book, wrote on June 23, 2003, that her husband, Scott, beat and raped her, then "The next morning Scott said he was sorry that it happened and that he loved me."[276] Less than a year later on February 18, 2004, Yana stated that she was harmed by her husband again, "Some days Scott cry and tell that he so sorry, and that he really a very good kind person."[277] These statements exemplify the cycle of domestic violence (DV) in which the abuser beats his victim, then apologizes; the victim forgives her abuser, after which there is a honeymoon period. But then, another beating occurs once the tension rebuilds. Indeed, this cycle is a difficult one to break, even for the victims who recognize it and do not necessarily believe the apologies, as Sandra Nicholson wrote, "he kept saying I'm sorry but I didn't believe him."[278] The cycle of violence may be repeated as often as every hour, every day, or in Yana Huss' case, as she reported here, it began with several months in between, then it cycled longer, and then it shortened again.[279]

It is important to remember that every case is different, and there is no set rule or pattern to the cycle of DV in relation to timing or whether the process moves forward without taking a few backward turns.[280] After the serious battering incident occurs and the apologies are offered by the abuser, and might be accepted by the victim, the honeymoon period begins.[281] Again, the length of this phase varies, making it difficult for the victim to understand where the couple is in the cycle.[282] A victim's best defense against further serious harm is to understand how the cycle works and to look for its signs. A shorter honeymoon phase means the victim must be on high alert more often than a longer honeymoon phase; however, it is the "not knowing" that is the most difficult part of the cycle of violence for a victim to manage as it progresses.[283] When the honeymoon period begins to fade, the tension building phase begins to build, with the abuser becoming more erratic and unpredictable.[284] It is during this tension building phase that the victim may begin to understand that danger lies ahead and, at this stage, might seek help from outside resources, if possible, in anticipation of any potential physical violence.[285]

Huss v. Huss

Yana and Scott Huss were stuck in the cycle of violence for many years, essentially beginning immediately after their wedding on February 7, 2003.[286] They met in March 2002 through a mail-order bride service, and Scott spent almost a year traveling between the United States and Russia before they were married.[287] On June 11, 2003, Scott filed a petition for injunction claiming that Yana was verbally and emotionally abusive to his son and that she was threatening to leave for Russia.[288] He also explained that she hit him in the chest several times.[289] He was provided a temporary injunction for his petition.

On June 23, 2003, Yana filed a petition for injunction making several claims against Scott, some of which have previously been detailed, and which includes an April 6, 2003, local article about Scott having told Yana that he would "shoot her and feed her to the alligators."[290] The threat by Scott is further supported by a probable cause affidavit against him filed on April 5, 2003, in an aggravated assault with a deadly weapon case.[291] However, inexplicably, this case was apparently not prosecuted, four (4) of Scott's guns were returned to him, and his bond was released back to him.[292] Nevertheless, Yana was awarded a final injunction for her June 23, 2003, petition for injunction on the same day, which Scott violated the very same day as well.[293] Even still, this case against Scott for violating the injunction for protection Yana had against him did not go to trial; and Scott did not enter a plea either.[294] Instead, the court, on its own motion, entered an order that, in effect, closed the action against Scott for the allegation of having violated the injunction for protection Yana had against him.[295]

By February 18, 2004, Yana filed another petition for injunction against Scott, claiming he committed child abuse against her son, alleging he deleted pictures of the injuries from the child abuse off her camera, and explaining the extent of the abuse she and her son endure daily.[296] She was awarded a temporary and final injunction for this petition; but by March 16, 2004, Scott violated the injunction by contacting Yana.[297] Once again, Scott was not fully prosecuted for the allegations against him because state prosecutors entered a Notice of Nolle Prosequi, essentially abandoning the case against him on April 29, 2004.[298]

On April 23, 2006, Yana filed her next petition for injunction alleging child abuse against the young daughter that Scott and Yana shared.[299] This petition coincides with a probable cause affidavit issued against Scott on April 22, 2006, which included the allegations of child abuse.[300] As a result, an Order of No Contact against Scott was filed in this criminal case on April 23, 2006, that included Yana and their daughter.[301]

Due to a report by Yana and a probable cause affidavit dated April 22, 2006, a separate criminal felony case was opened on April 23, 2006, against Scott for child abuse allegations.[302] However, this case did not remain open long.[303] After little prosecutorial activity, the case was dropped/abandoned on June 14, 2006, due to "Insuff[icient] Evidence to Prove Beyond Reasonable Doubt."[304] However, the misdemeanor case opened against Scott related to Yana continued longer than the criminal felony child abuse case.[305] Although she was court ordered to do so, Yana did not appear as a witness for trial in this case; so, the court issued an order to show cause against her for criminal contempt.[306] Additionally, the state issued another Nolle Prosequi, abandoning the case against Scott.[307]

Yana's last petition for injunction was filed on March 26, 2007, when she explained to the Court that Scott abused both of her children and that he made overt threats against her life, including cutting the telephone line when she tried to call 911 after he reached for a gun.[308] She was awarded a temporary and final injunction for this petition.[309] However, Scott had difficulty abiding by the terms of the injunction.[310] Indeed, he continued to contact Yana even after the final injunction was in place.[311] At this point, sheriff's deputies begin to check in on Yana regularly at her residence due to their concerns for her safety.[312] They continued to make such regular checks on her for the following three weeks.[313]

The final petition for injunction filed between the couple, which was denied, was Scott's; when, on April 19, 2007, he explained to the Court that "She wanted me to come over. I hung up on her. She called again and said she would not call police and she wanted to talk and 'settle this stuff.' Every other time we reconciled and she did the same thing."[314] However, police and arrest reports tell a different story because on March 30, 2007, Yana filed a police report complaining that Scott sent her "numerous instant messages attempting to get her to speak to him."[315]

The significance of this contact through instant messaging was that Yana had the final injunction in place from her March 26, 2007, petition against Scott, so she called the police for assistance regarding his violation of that order.[316] Again, on April 13, 2007, she filed another police report about the fact that Scott had violated the injunction against DV; only this time, he was in her home.[317] Scott called Yana many times during the day, asking to come over.[318] He told police that "she invited me over."[319] Around 9:30 p.m. that night, she let her dogs outside and found him standing in the house when she came back in.[320] She explained to the police that she had no idea how he was able to enter the house because she did not allow him in.[321] Scott had also contacted Yana's son prior to his entry into the home, against the terms of the final injunction, by peering through one of the windows.[322] She explained to the police that Scott regularly violates injunctions but that she does not know of any other way to try to keep him away.[323] Scott was arrested and a court case ensued.[324] Nevertheless, Scott was free on bond during the pendency of the case.[325]

On April 25, 2007, at 1:00 p.m., Scott was arraigned for his violation of the final injunction Yana was awarded against him for the petition for injunction she filed on March 26, 2007; however, he waived his personal appearance at this hearing.[326] The injunction was still in force on April 25, 2007, when Yana's son was dropped off, covered in blood, at a relative's home at 4:20 p.m., 175 miles north from the Huss home.[327] The boy had some paperwork with him that included a will and documentation giving the relative where he was dropped custody of the boy.[328] Local authorities were contacted and interviewed the boy, who told them that he witnessed his stepdad, Scott Huss, kill his mother, Yana Huss.[329] He explained that she had been stabbed in the chest.[330] Based on this information, authorities where the Huss' lived were contacted to do a well check on Yana at her residence.[331] Upon arrival, they discovered bloody footprints and her body lying face down in a pool of blood.[332]

Scott was found at a bus station in Tallahassee, much further north from where he dropped off his stepson in central Florida and was charged with manslaughter.[333] Once at trial, he faced second-degree murder charges for Yana's death.[334] He argued that she was killed by the Russian mafia, and prosecutors argued that he stabbed her and then "slashed her throat so violently that he nearly decapitated her."[335] When sentencing Scott to life, the judge said it was "a horrendous act" and that it "was not a quick killing."[336] Since the time of his sentencing, Scott has unsuccessfully appealed his case, including multiple motions for post-conviction relief.[337]

Verbal Abuse

For this study, "verbal abuse," a subtheme of power and control, describes verbal acts of vitriol and invective spewed by the abuser toward the IPV victim, including verbal abuse, *per se*, i.e., "of, in, or by itself; standing alone without reference to additional facts."[338] In this study, 2.8% of the 493 cases and 22.2% of the sixty-two (62) cases, as well as 18.0% of the 100 petitions for injunction analyzed in this phase, resulted in a verbal abuse coding. All verbal abuse cases were coded as such because the IPV victim stated they were a victim of verbal abuse due to the "verbal abuse" they were experiencing, including cussing, causing the allegations of verbal abuse to be considered verbal abuse, *per se*.[339] This subtheme is differentiated from the subthemes of degradation and name calling because the IPV victim may not have provided more specific details of the verbal abuse they experienced to rise to the level of degradation or name calling.

Goraya v. Goraya

From the beginning of their arranged marriage in India on July 14. 2002, Rupinder Goraya experienced DV at the hands of her husband, Kultar.[340] In December 2006, the couple moved with their two-year-old son, who had special needs, to the United States on a visa Rupinder obtained as an exchange student for a nursing program.[341] Once in the United States, Rupinder began to build a life for herself with a good job as a nurse.[342] In fact, she was working to save enough money to bring her parents to the United States as well.[343]

By the spring of 2007, Rupinder filed for an injunction for protection against Kultar, in part, because of his "verbal abuse."[344] On May 18, 2007, she explained to the court how she tried to fight back by telling Kultar "Don't do abuse I will call to police if you hurts [sic] me physical" but that just caused him to become more violent and grab her by the neck.[345] Rupinder told one of her fellow nurses "that she nearly lost consciousness" during the incident and believed, if she had not gotten away from Kultar, he would have killed her.[346] On May 16, 2007, Kultar was arrested; and a criminal misdemeanor case was opened against him for battery related to the same incident Rupinder reported in her request for an injunction.[347] The fact that he was charged with battery due to the DV caused him to be very angry.[348] Rupinder was provided a temporary injunction on May 18, 2007, that lasted until a motion to dismiss was filed on July 6, 2007.[349] The case was seemingly resolved sometime toward the end of July 2007 without the injunction against Kultar continuing further although police reports seem to contradict this time frame, indicating she might have had the injunction's protection from Kultar until the fall of 2007.[350]

In mid-September 2007, Rupinder had major abdominal surgery for stomach cancer from which she needed to recover at home; however, after about two weeks, friends and family stopped hearing from her which was unusual.[351] She also did not attend her post-surgical appointments or refill her prescriptions even though one of her neighbors reported to the police that "she had checked on her several times because [Rupinder] seemed so sick."[352] Rupinder's cousin reported having spoken to her on September 30, 2007.[353] On October 1, 2007, the signature for a charge to Rupinder's credit card for her son's pediatrician appeared to match her driver's license.[354]

On October 2, 2007, both Rupinder and Kultar had cell phone activity.[355] Rupinder tried calling Kultar twice, at 9:53 a.m. and 10:32 a.m.[356] She also had a call that began at 2:05 p.m.; however, it ended abruptly with the call being disconnected and the person who was speaking to her never heard from her again.[357] Kultar's phone records match the 10:32 a.m. call; but once Rupinder was missing, he made no attempt to contact her.[358] Also, his phone had no activity with incoming or outgoing calls on October 2, 2007, between 2:19 p.m. and 6:23 p.m.[359]

On October 19, 2007, Rupinder was reported to the police "as a missing person with suspicious circumstances" by one of her co-workers.[360] Details in the police report include the fact that neighbors often heard the couple fighting loudly while their son was crying on the balcony of their apartment.[361] The police report regarding her missing person status explained Rupinder and Kultar's life together as one in turmoil even though Rupinder was very dedicated to her job and family.[362] Nevertheless, Kultar explained to those who asked about her that she simply left, possibly for Orlando or New York to begin a new job in nursing.[363] But her U.S.

employment and proof of nurse training documentation was left at the apartment she and Kultar shared.³⁶⁴

On October 15, 2007, Kultar flew to India with the couple's young son and stayed with Rupinder's family, explaining that her job was transferred to California.³⁶⁵ However, her family became suspicious when they saw him with many of her personal effects, such as her bras, panties, makeup, and wedding ring that he hid at a neighbor's house.³⁶⁶ Kultar and his son returned to the United States on November 14, 2007, and he was immediately questioned by the police during a non-custodial interview.³⁶⁷ During this interview, he spoke about his belief that Rupinder had just left and included the fact that she had taken all of her belongings with her even though he had taken so many of her personal effects to India and hid them.³⁶⁸ Throughout the investigation, police learned of veiled, or even overt, threats Kultar made to friends and acquaintances that tied to his killing Rupinder.³⁶⁹ He made many statements such as "Google my name and see what I'm all about" and "I will make you disappear."³⁷⁰ He became more emboldened as time went on and told people "I can make you disappear like my wife" and "I had to choke her. I had to kill her."³⁷¹

On November 28, 2014, more than seven years after she was reported missing, a warrant to arrest Kultar for second degree murder was issued, which stated he choked Rupinder to death on or about October 2, 2007.³⁷² Although her body has not been found, he was officially charged with her murder on January 3, 2015.³⁷³ On February 8, 2016, after a trial on the count of second degree murder, he was found guilty and sentenced to life in prison.³⁷⁴

Household, Clothes, and Personal Belongings Destroyed

"Household, clothes and personal belongings destroyed" is a subtheme of power and control that describes the abuser destroying property including the home, household furnishings and the IPV victim's personal belongings. In this study, 3.4% of the 493 cases and 26.9% of the sixty-two (62) cases, as well as 22.0% of the 100 petitions for injunction analyzed in this phase, resulted in a household, clothes and personal belongings destroyed coding. IPV victims explain that their abusers "constantly destroy[] [their] property," "poured gasoline all over furniture," broke dishes and furniture, damaged their car, punched holes in the wall, smashed laptops, etc.³⁷⁵ The petition for injunction below details the type of destruction of personal property that courts, advocates, shelters, attorneys, etc., should ask about to elicit information from IPV victims to confirm such behavior has not occurred:

> I came home after a weekend away with friends and when I walked into my closet all my clothes had been removed, as well as, all of my

clothing in all dressers. I looked everywhere in the home to see if they were packed and found nothing. I then walked to the backyard and found a scorched circle about 5ft x 5ft in diameter. I sifted through the ashes and found several pieces of my clothing, under wires from my bras, and chargers. The clothes amounted to appx. 4K dollars.[376]

Amanda Cloaninger, detailed in the animal abuser subtheme, was killed less than two (2) months after writing this narrative, even though she had a final injunction in place against her estranged husband.[377]

Green v. Green

On July 31, 2012, Marquita Green filed for an injunction for protection from her husband, Clinton, explaining to the court, among other acts, that he "broke up the bedroom lamps & other what knots."[378] She continued in her petition to describe Clinton as a very angry man who acted out by destroying household items and by being violent toward her.[379] She was provided a temporary injunction for her petition on July 31, 2012, and a final injunction on August 15, 2012.[380]

This was not the first petition for injunction Marquita had filed against Clinton in 2012.[381] On May 14, 2012, she filed a petition that had similar allegations to her July 2012 petition, again explaining that Clinton broke dishes and damaged the car, as well as dragging her around the house and choking her.[382] She detailed that she had suffered from his violence for five years, which seemed to be since the beginning of their marriage in February 2007.[383] It is unclear as to the outcome of this case.

Clinton filed two of his own petitions for injunction against Marquita.[384] The first was filed on May 14, 2012, as well.[385] He accused Marquita of leaving the house and walking to the gas station.[386] He stated that she left the door open.[387] He followed her to the gas station and saw her meet her girlfriend.[388] He explained that he had to leave for his safety because he was concerned about false allegations.[389] He completed his petition explaining that Marquita threatens him with insinuations of a gun.[390] It is unclear as to the outcome of this case as well.

The second petition for injunction Clinton filed was on August 1, 2012, just one day after Marquita's second petition in 2012.[391] In this petition, he accused her of threatening him and physically harming him.[392] Also, he states that Marquita broke the items in the home and blamed it on him.[393] Again, it is unclear as to the outcome of this case.

On August 14, 2012, Marquita filed for DOM, which Clinton was served with on August 16, 2012.[394] But on August 24, 2012, Sheriff's deputies received a call about a suspicious incident "involving a vehicle that had several bullet holes in the driver's side of the vehicle."[395] Marquita and

Clinton's neighbors reported a white vehicle that was partly in the road and partly in their driveway, and the engine was still running.[396] Clinton shot Marquita multiple times while she was in the driver's seat.[397] She died in the car.[398] Deputies found Clinton in a rocking chair under the carport dead from a self-inflicted gunshot wound to his head.[399] He committed suicide after he killed Marquita.[400]

Tinsley v. Tinsley

Nancy and Oscar Tinsley were originally married in 1972 but were divorced somewhere around 1985; however, they remarried in 1988.[401] It was not until March 16, 1998, that Nancy filed her petition for injunction asking the court for protection from Oscar because he "damaged furniture, broke a bottle against the floor, when angry."[402] She was awarded a temporary and final injunction for the incident she described.[403]

On February 14, 2014, Nancy and Oscar's adult son called the Sheriff's department regarding an argument that had taken place between his parents.[404] He reported that he heard them arguing and then heard a loud banging noise.[405] When he went into their bedroom to investigate, he found Oscar grabbing Nancy by her clothing and pushing her up against the wall.[406] He separated them from each other and called the Sheriff's department.[407] When the deputy interviewed Nancy, she explained that she and Oscar where arguing about issues related to their daughter when he hit her on her chest.[408] When she tried to get him to back off by pushing him back, "he rushed her grabbing her clothing around her neck."[409] The deputy observed red marks on Nancy around her neck and at her chest area.[410] Nancy was advised of a victims shelter for a safe place to go and provided other services; however, she "refused to write a statement and did not want [Oscar] to be arrested."[411] Oscar was arrested for the incident, and a criminal misdemeanor case was opened against him.[412] However, Oscar was placed on probation without a trial or determination of guilt by the judge in the case.[413] He was released from probation on May 1, 2014.[414]

Just two months later, on July 9, 2014, the same adult son who broke up the argument between Nancy and Oscar in February 2014 reported to the Sheriff that he found them dead in their home.[415] After trying to reach Nancy for an hour and a half during the morning, he decided to check on her.[416] Apparently, Oscar's violence toward Nancy had escalated over the previous few days since he kicked their son out of the home.[417] When their son arrived at their house around noon, he found them lying on the floor in their living room.[418] After an investigation, deputies determined that Oscar shot and killed Nancy before dying by shooting himself in the torso.[419] During the investigation, their son explained to deputies that Oscar had always been physically abusive to Nancy but that "most of the abuse between his mother and father went unreported to police."[420]

Notes

1. Romero v. Romero, 2008-DR-0015103-O, 4 (2008) (Pet. for Inj. for Prot. Against Dom. Viol.).
2. Gordon v. Gordon, 14-735-DV, 7 (2014) (Pet. for Inj. for Prot. Against Dom. Viol.).
3. Gordon, 14-735-DV at 4.
4. Nicholas Reid, 1504-009764 at 1–2.
5. Osvaldo Mesa, 1506-003538 at 2.
6. See generally Gordon v. Gordon, 14-691-DV (2014) (Pet. for Inj. for Prot. Against Dom. Viol.).
7. Gordon, 14-691-DV at 4.
8. See generally Gordon v. Gordon, 15-418-DV (2015) (Pet. for Inj. for Prot. Against Dom. Viol.).
9. See Id.
10. Id. at 3.
11. Id.
12. Id.
13. Id.
14. Id.
15. Officials: Victim in Port Charlotte Murder-Suicide was North Port HS Teacher, ¶ 1 WINK News (May 1, 2016).
16. Elio Diaz, 1604-014067 at 3; Officials: Victim in Port Charlotte Murder-Suicide was North Port HS Teacher, supra note 15 at ¶ 3.
17. Officials: Victim in Port Charlotte Murder-Suicide was North Port HS Teacher, supra note 15 at ¶ 2.
18. Romero v. Romero, 2008-DR-0015103-O, 4 (2008) (Pet. for Inj. for Prot. Against Dom. Viol.).
19. See Wood v. Wood, 02-1205FD-9, 3 (2002) (Pet. for Inj. for Prot. Against Dom. Viol.).
20. Wood v. Wood, 05-14620FD-9, 5 (2005) (Pet. for Inj. for Prot. Against Dom. Viol.).
21. See Olms v. Olms, 2009DR21006SC, 4 (2009) (Pet. for Inj. for Prot. Against Dom. Viol.).
22. See generally Id.
23. Id. at 5.
24. See Olms v. Olms, 2009DR21006SC (2009) https://secure.sarasotaclerk.com/CaseInfo.aspx (last visited Dec. 28, 2022).
25. See generally Olms v. Olms, 2007DR000005SC (2007) (Pet. for Inj. for Prot. Against Dom. Viol.).
26. Id. at 3.
27. See Olms v. Olms, 2007DR000005SC (2007) https://secure.sarasotaclerk.com/CaseInfo.aspx (last visited Dec. 28, 2022).
28. See David Miller, 201100058034 at 2, 6; See generally State of Florida v. Olms, 2011CF010399NC (2011) (Amended Probable Cause Aff.).
29. See Miller, supra note 28, 6; See generally Olms, 2011CF010399NC.
30. Miller, supra note 28 at 6; accord Olms, 2011CF010399NC at 2.

31 Miller, *supra* note 28 at 6; *accord* Olms, 2011CF010399NC at 2.
32 *See* Olms, 2011CF010399NC at 2; State of Florida v. Olms, 2011CF010399NC, 1 (2011) (Info.).
33 *See generally* State of Florida v. Olms, 2011CF010399NC, 1 (2011) (Sentence and Special Provisions).
34 Diller v. Diller, 512008DR863ES, 3 (2008) (Pet. for Inj. for Prot. Against Dom. Viol.); *accord* Diller v. Diller, 512010DR00078ES (2010) (Pet. for Inj. for Prot. Against Dom. Viol.).
35 Diller, 512010DR00078ES at 4.
36 Diller v. Diller, 512008DR863ES (2008) (Pet. for Inj. for Prot. Against Dom. Viol.) https://www.civitekflorida.com/ocrs/app/caseinformation.xhtml?query=m9ycXurMtkiPqS1bHHeDR8NZmLODyP0b8hPji9upmp0&from=partyCaseSummary (last visited Dec. 29, 2022).
37 Diller v. Diller, 512008DR000973DRAXES (2008) (Dissolution of Marriage) https://www.civitekflorida.com/ocrs/app/caseinformation.xhtml?query=m9ycXurMtkjrHmBwFi2-ZDegNPonSxpz8hPji9upmp0&from=partyCaseSummary (last visited Dec. 29, 2022).
38 Diller v. Diller, 512010DR00078ES, 4 (2010) (Pet. for Inj. for Prot. Against Dom. Viol.) https://www.civitekflorida.com/ocrs/app/caseinformation.xhtml?query=m9ycXurMtkhVnvgQVE_xCRveTwW1TyVU8hPji9upmp0&from=partyCaseSummary (last visited Dec. 29, 2022).
39 *See* Diller v. Diller, 512010DR000111DRAXES (2010) (Dissolution of Marriage) https://www.civitekflorida.com/ocrs/app/caseinformation.xhtml?query=m9ycXurMtkjifijSA1boqTkO3K7Ye4iU8hPji9upmp0&from=partyCaseSummary (last visited Dec. 29, 2022); Hope Dauphin, 12-010011 at 5.
40 *See* Diller v. Diller, 512010DR00078ES, 1 (2010) (Pet. for Inj. for Prot. Against Dom. Viol.); Hope Dauphin, 12-010011 at 5.
41 Dauphin, *supra* note 40 at 6.
42 *See Id.*; *accord* Diller, Rhonda S, https://www.civitekflorida.com/ocrs/app/partyCaseSummary.xhtml (last visited June 9, 2023).
43 Dauphin, *supra* note 40 at 5–6.
44 *Id.* at 1, 5.
45 *Id.* at 5–6.
46 *Id.* at 6.
47 *Id.* at 11.
48 State of Florida v. Diller, 512012CF001453CFAXWS (2012) (Murder First Degree Premeditated) https://www.civitekflorida.com/ocrs/app/caseinformation.xhtml?query=UM2zLa5rU64MBl9qPzh3vr8XoRCwSd7e6CYWR9u_BMg&from=partyCaseSummary (last visited Jan. 3, 2023); *Mistrial Declared after Pasco0 Man on Trial for Wife's Murder Attempts Suicide in Jail*, BAY NEWS 9 (June 26, 2014).
49 Diller, 512012CF001453CFAXWS; *Mistrial Declared after Pasco Man on Trial for Wife's Murder Attempts Suicide in Jail*, *supra* note 48.
50 State of Florida v. Diller, CRC12-01453CFAWS-03 (2014) (Abatement of Action to the Clerk of the Above-Style Court).
51 Wood v. Wood, 05-14620FD-9, 5 (2005) (Pet. for Inj. for Prot. Against Dom. Viol.).
52 Green v. Green, 16-2012-DR-001583-DVXX-MA, 4 (2012) (Pet. for Inj. for Prot. Against Dom. Viol.).
53 Diller v. Diller, 51-2010 DR-00078ES, 4 (2010) (Pet. for Inj. for Prot. Against Dom. Viol.).

54 Hogan-Mccarthren v. Mccarthren, 2012-DR-001236-O, 3 (2012) (Pet. for Inj. for Prot. Against Dom. Viol.); Nicholson v. Nicholson, 04-2667-CA, 5 (2004) (Pet. for Inj. for Prot. Against Dom. Viol.); Olms v. Olms, 2009-DR-21006-SC, 4 (2009) (Pet. for Inj. for Prot. Against Dom. Viol.).
55 *See generally* Nicholson, 04-2667-CA. *See supra* Chapter 5, Isolation, Economic Control, False Imprisonment.
56 Nicholson, 04-2667-CA at 5.
57 Nicholson, 04-2667-CA at 6.
58 Nicholson v. Nicholson, 04-2667-CA (2004) (Pet. for Inj. for Prot. Against Dom. Viol.) https://cms.collierclerk.com/CMSWeb/#!/casedetails (last visited Dec. 29, 2022).
59 Nicholson v. Nicholson, 04-2667-CA, 4 (2004) (Pet. for Inj. for Prot. Against Dom. Viol.).
60 Nicholson v. Nicholson, 2004-DR-002697 (2004) (Diss. of Marriage) https://cms.collierclerk.com/CMSWeb/#!/casedetails (last visited Jan. 3, 2023).
61 Ryan Mills, *Neighbors Said Slain Woman Feared for Her Safety*, Naples Daily News (April 4, 2007).
62 *See Id.* at 7; Aisling Swift, *Family Tends to Children as Man Serves 22 Years for Feeding Wife to Alligators*, Naples Daily News (Sept. 20, 2008).
63 *See* Mills, *supra* note 61; Swift, *supra* note 62.
64 Mills, *supra* note 61 at 7–8.
65 Swift, *supra* note 62.
66 *Id.*
67 Belcher v. Belcher, 08-DR-17155, 2 (2008) (Pet. for Inj. for Prot. Against Dom. Viol.).
68 *Id.*
69 *Id.*
70 *See generally* Bryan Lugo, 08-633887.
71 *Id.* at 14.
72 *See* Belcher v. Belcher, 08-DR-17155 (2008) (Order of Dismissal of Temp. Inj. for Prot. Against Dom. Viol. without Child(ren)); *See also* Belcher v. Belcher, 08-DR-17155 (2008) https://hover.hillsclerk.com/html/case/caseSummary.html (last visited Jan. 17, 2023).
73 Belcher v. Belcher, 08-DR-17155 (2008) (Order of Dismissal of Temp. Inj. for Prot. Against Dom. Viol. without Child(ren)).
74 State of Florida v. Belcher, 2012 CF 15461, 1 (2014) (Amended Mt. for Pretrial Detention).
75 *Id.* at 3–4.
76 *Id.* at 3.
77 *Id.*
78 *Id.*
79 *Id.*
80 *Id.* at 3–4.
81 *Id.* at 4.
82 *Id.*
83 *Id.*
84 *Id.*
85 *Id.* at 5. *See also* State of Florida v. Belcher, 2012 CF 15461, 4 (2012) (Criminal Report Aff./Notice to Appear).
86 State of Florida v. Belcher, 2012 CF 15461, 5 (2014) (Amended Mt. for Pretrial Detention). *See also* State of Florida v. Belcher, 2012 CF 15461, 4 (2012) (Criminal Report Aff./Notice to Appear).

87 See State of Florida v. Belcher, 2012 CF 15461, 4 (2012) (Criminal Report Aff./Notice to Appear).
88 See Id. at 5.
89 See State of Florida v. Belcher, 2012 CF 15461 (2012) (Arrest Warrant).
90 State of Florida v. Belcher, 2012 CF 15461 (2014) (Verdict Form).
91 See generally State of Florida v. Belcher, 2012 CF 15461 (2015) (Rule 3.992(a) Criminal Punishment Code Scoresheet). See also Man Who Killed Wife, Burned Body Gets Life Sentence, WFTV9, ¶ 1 (July 30, 2015).
92 Fulgham v. Fulgham, 2009-0136-DR-FJ, 4 (2009) (Pet. for Inj. for Prot. Against Dom. Viol.); Wilkerson v. Wilkerson, 02-2007-DR-080, 3 (2007) (Pet. for Inj. for Prot. Against Dom. Viol.).
93 Nicholson v. Nicholson, 04-2667-CA, 3 (2004) (Pet. for Inj. for Prot. Against Dom. Viol.).
94 Huss v. Huss, 07-234-DV, 3 (2007) (Pet. for Inj. for Prot. Against Dom. Viol.).
95 Herbert v. Herbert, 10-DR-965, 5 (2010) (Pet. for Inj. for Prot. Against Dom. Viol.).
96 Policastro, 2011-014161 at 15, 19.
97 Id. at 15.
98 Id.
99 Id. at 19.
100 Id.
101 Id. at 23.
102 Id. at 24.
103 Id. at 23.
104 Id.
105 Id.
106 Id.
107 Id. at 13.
108 Id. at 4.
109 Id. at 4, 21.
110 Id. at 4.
111 Id. at 6.
112 Id. at 13–17.
113 Id.
114 Id.
115 Id.
116 Matt Galnor, Friends, Family Tell of Fighting, Threats Before Clay Murder-Suicide, THE FLORIDA TIMES-UNION (April 9, 2011).
117 Romero v. Romero, 2008-DR-0015103-O, 4 (2008) (Pet. for Inj. for Prot. Against Dom. Viol.).
118 See Brown v. Brown, 15-DR-4900, 4–7 (2015) (Pet. for Inj. for Prot. Against Dom. Viol.); Huss v. Huss, 04000115DV, 3 (2004) (Pet. for Inj. for Prot. Against Dom. Viol.).
119 See generally Shook v. Shook, 07-000187DR U (2007) (Pet. for Inj. for Prot. Against Dom. Viol.); Shook v. Shook, 07-000187DR U, 1 (2007) (F. Jud. Of Inj. for Prot. Against Dom. Viol. with Minor Child(ren) (after Notice)).
120 Shook v. Shook, 07-000187DR U, 2 (2007) (Pet. for Inj. for Prot. Against Dom. Viol.).
121 Shook v. Shook, 07-000187DR U, 3–5 (2007) (F. Jud. Of Inj. for Prot. Against Dom. Viol. with Minor Child(ren) (after Notice)).
122 Id. at 5.
123 See generally Id.

124 James Wright, 07-140933 at 2.
125 *Id.* at 2–3.
126 *Id.* at 2.
127 *Id.*
128 *Id.* at 2–3.
129 *Id.* at 2.
130 *Id.* at 2–3.
131 *Id.* at 3.
132 *Id.*
133 Benjamin Woodburn, 07-284861 at 2.
134 *Id.*
135 *Id.*
136 *Id.*
137 *Id.*
138 *Id.* at 2–3.
139 *Id.* at 3; BOLO in law enforcement is an acronym for Be-On-the-Look-Out.
140 State of Florida v. Shook, 07CF19071, 4 (2007) (Record of First Appearance-Probable Cause Aff.).
141 *Id.*
142 *Id.* at 4–5.
143 Steven Beardsley, *Joseph Shook Sentenced to Life in Prison for Killing Estero Mother of Three*, NAPLES DAILY NEWS (Jan. 22, 2010).
144 *Id.*
145 *Id.*
146 *See* Susan Schechter & Jeffrey Edleson, *Effective Intervention in Domestic Violence and Child Maltreatment Cases: Guidelines for Policy and Practice*, NATIONAL COUNCIL OF JUVENILE AND FAMILY COURT JUDGES, at 11 (1999) (providing a definition for child maltreatment); *Child Witnesses to Domestic Violence*, U.S. DEPARTMENT OF HEALTH AND HUMAN SERVICES, CHILDREN'S BUREAU (2021) (explaining that in several states, "committing domestic violence in the presence of a child is a separate crime that may be charged separately or in addition to the act of violence [against the adult] *Id.* at 2); *In re the Parental Responsibilities Concerning A.F. v. Cressey*, No. 2019CA1537, at 16 (Colo. Ct. App. Dec. 3, 2020) (explaining that "[c]hild abuse may involve the unreasonable placement of the child in a situation that poses a threat of injury to the child's life or health" when discussing a physical altercation between the parents in which the child was present but physically unharmed).
147 *See supra* Chapter 5, Intimidation, Threats.
148 *See* Finn v. Finn, 53-2013DR-010012-0000-00, 4 (2013) (Pet. for Inj. for Prot. Against Dom. Viol.).
149 *See generally* Caso v. Caso, 04-20670 (2004) (Pet. for Inj. for Prot. Against Dom. Viol.); Caso v. Caso, 2007-DR-9187 (2007) (Pet. for Inj. for Prot. Against Dom. Viol.).
150 Caso, 04-20670 at 3.
151 Caso v. Caso, 04-20670 (2004) https://myeclerk.myorangeclerk.com/CaseDetails?caseId=943123&caseIdEnc=652r%2FYZCXHkgbTGo8ynM0MGC8MX7RObaA85UD%2Feubo92oBTo7eg7TPW59XTwnrPRv43xforCnzo4jE9UDF45BKnJGQetXKQO5f2kh6AjfLw%3D (last visited Jan. 6, 2023).
152 *Id.*
153 *Id.*
154 Caso, 2007-DR-9187 at 3.

155 Caso v. Caso, 2007-DR-9187 (2007) https://myeclerk.myorangeclerk.com/ CaseDetails?caseId=1256123&caseIdEnc=DCKHLfLPRNo1qALpt6JCizfjL dSTXURLTPoyarF8mvkPKz2UKsknWwwxQ2mNxrHRlWHfVTbe3jx%2F bvFG79VhE7UDsIF0leQARcvvdMDgJYc%3D (last visited Jan. 6, 2023).
156 Caso v. Caso, 2007-DR-9187 (2007) (Order of Dismissal of Temp. Inj. for Prot. Against Dom. Viol.).
157 Chris Barrette, 07-87650 at 3.
158 *Id.* at 3, 5–6; Sarah Lundy, *Husband is given 30 Years in Death of Denny's Waitress*, ORLANDO SENTINEL (Nov. 14, 2008).
159 Barrette, *supra* note 157 at 3, 5–6.
160 *See Id.* at 3, 5–6; Lundy, *supra* note 158.
161 Lundy, *supra* note 158.
162 Marshall v. Marshall, 97-3133-DR-06, 2 (1997) (Pet. for Inj. for Prot. Against Dom. Viol.).
163 *Id.* at 3.
164 Marshall v. Marshall, 97-3133-DR-06 (1997) https://courtrecords.seminoleclerk.org (last visited on Jan. 6, 2023).
165 *Id.*; Rene Stutzman, *Lake Mary Shooting: Questions Remain; Funerals Thursday*, ORLANDO SUNDAY (May 13, 2010).
166 Marshall v. Marshall, 97-3133-DR-06 (1997) https://courtrecords.seminole clerk.org (last visited on Jan. 6, 2023); Marshall v. Marshall, 1997DR003247 (1997) https://courtrecords.seminoleclerk.org (last visited on Jan. 6, 2023).
167 Marshall, 97-3133-DR-06.
168 Marshall, 1997DR003247.
169 *See* Marshall, 97-3133-DR-06.
170 Stutzman, *supra* note 165.
171 *Id.*
172 *Id.*
173 Kevin Peterson, 201001260625 at 19; Stutzman, *supra* note 165.
174 Kevin Peterson, *supra* note 173; Stutzman, *supra* note 165.
175 Kevin Peterson, *supra* note 173; Stutzman, *supra* note 165.
176 *See* Shook v. Shook, 07-000187DR U, 2 (2007) (Pet. for Inj. for Prot. Against Dom. Viol.).
177 *Id.* at 2.
178 Huss v. Huss, 03-451DV, 3 (2003) (Pet. for Inj. for Prot. Against Dom. Viol.). *See supra* Chapter 5, Intimidation, Weapons, Isolation, False Imprisonment; Chapter 6, Power and Control.
179 Huss v. Huss, 07-234DV, 2 (2007) (Pet. for Inj. for Prot. Against Dom. Viol.).
180 *Id.* at 3.
181 Romero v. Romero, 2008-DR-0015103-O, 4 (2008) (Pet. for Inj. for Prot. Against Dom. Viol.).
182 *Id.*
183 *Id.* at 4–5.
184 *Id.* at 5.
185 *Id.*
186 *See infra* Chapter 10, Reimagining Intimate Partner Violence Lethality Risk Assessments.
187 Peacock v. Peacock, 11-281-DR, 6 (2011) (Pet. for Inj. for Prot. Against Dom. Viol.).
188 Mattaini v. Lennon, 04-4789-CA, 3 (2004) (Pet. for Inj. for Prot. Against Dom. Viol.).

189 Mattaini v. Lennon, 2004-DR-004789 (2004) https://cms.collierclerk.com/CMSWeb/#!/casedetails (last visited Jan. 10, 2023).
190 Id.
191 William Fedak, 06-00519 at 3–4.
192 Id. at 9.
193 *See generally* DOMESTIC VIOLENCE, ABUSE, AND CHILD CUSTODY: LEGAL STRATEGIES AND POLICY ISSUES (Mo Therese Hannah & Barry Goldstein eds., 2010). *See also* Donna J. King, *Naming the Judicial Terrorist: An Exposé of an Abuser's Successful Use of a Judicial Proceeding for Continued Domestic Violence*, 1 TENN. JOURNAL OF RACE, GENDER, & SOCIAL JUSTICE 153 (2012).
194 *See* Cloaninger v. Colley, DR15-1136, 4 (2015) (Pet. for Inj. for Prot. Against Dom. Viol.).
195 *See Id.* at 4–5.
196 *See* King, *supra* note 193.
197 *See* Nicholson v. Nicholson, 04-2667-CA, 3 (2004) (Pet. for Inj. for Prot. Against Dom. Viol.). *See supra* Chapter 5, Isolation, Economic Control, False Imprisonment; Chapter 6, Humiliation, Name Calling.
198 Nicholson, 04-2667-CA at 3.
199 Id.
200 Id.
201 Id.
202 Id.
203 Swift, *supra* note 62.
204 *See* Fulgham v. Strong, 2008-4262-DRFJ, 3 (2008) (Pet. for Inj. for Prot. Against Dom. Viol.); Strong v. Fulgham, 2008-4461-DRFJ, 3 (2008) (Pet. for Inj. for Prot. Against Dom. Viol.).
205 *See* Fulgham, 2008-4262-DRFJ at 7; Strong, 2008-4461-DRFJ at 8.
206 Fulgham, 2008-4262-DRFJ at 3.
207 *See* State of Florida v. Fulgham, 422009CF001253CFAXXX, 17 (2008) (Misc.-See Text Descrip. Report from DCF Re: Heather Strong).
208 *See Id.*
209 Strong, 2008-4461-DRFJ at 3.
210 *See* Fulgham, 422009CF001253CFAXXX at 11–12; Fulgham v. Fulgham, 2009-0136-DR-FJ, 2 (2009) (Pet. for Inj. for Prot. Against Dom. Viol.).
211 *See* Fulgham, 422009CF001253CFAXXX at 42–45.
212 *See Id.* at 29–39, 43, 45.
213 *See Id.* at 23–27.
214 *See Id.* at 20, 27.
215 *See Id.* at 1–6.
216 Beth Billings, 09007442 at 63.
217 *See* Fulgham v. Fulgham, 2009-0136-DR-FJ, 2–4, 8 (2009) (Pet. for Inj. for Prot. Against Dom. Viol.).
218 *See* Carr v. State of Florida, 156 So. 3d 1052, 6 (Fla. 2015).
219 State of Florida v. Fulgham, 2009-CF-000064-A-Z, 1 (2009) (Announcement of No Information).
220 *See* Billings, *supra* note 216 at 15, 17, 63, 71, 83, 90; Carr, 156 So. 3d at 3.
221 Billings, *supra* note 216 at 3–4.
222 Id.
223 Id.
224 Id. at 4.

225 *Id.*
226 *Id.* at 9–10.
227 *Id.* at 10.
228 *Id.*
229 *Id.* at 12.
230 *Id.* at 12–13.
231 *Id.* at 12, 16.
232 *Id.* at 16.
233 *Id.* at 85.
234 *Id.* at 84–85.
235 *Id.* at 85, 87.
236 *Id.* at 44.
237 Carr v. State of Florida, 156 So. 3d 1052, 13–16 (Fla. 2015).
238 Billings, *supra* note 216 at 85–86; State of Florida v. Fulgham, 09-1253-CFA2, 2 (2009) (Arrest Aff./First Appearance Form).
239 Billings, *supra* note 216 at 88; Fulgham, 09-1253-CFA2 at 2; Carr, 156 So. 3d at 4.
240 Billings, *supra* note 216 at 19.
241 *Id.* at 88; Fulgham, 09-1253-CFA2 at 2.
242 Billings, *supra* note 216 at 90; Fulgham, 09-1253-CFA2 at 2.
243 Billings, *supra* note 216 at 90, 93; Fulgham, 09-1253-CFA2 at 2; Carr, 156 So. 3d at 3–4, 32–33.
244 Billings, *supra* note 216 at 90–91; Fulgham, 09-1253-CFA2 at 2; Carr, 156 So. 3d at 4, 32–33.
245 Billings, *supra* note 216 at 90–91; Fulgham, 09-1253-CFA2 at 2; Carr, 156 So. 3d at 2–3.
246 Billings, *supra* note 216 at 91; *accord* Carr, 156 So. 3d at 3.
247 Carr, 156 So. 3d at 3; *accord* Billings, *supra* note 216 at 91.
248 Carr, 156 So. 3d at 3.
249 *Id.* at 3.
250 *Id.* at 3; Billings, *supra* note 216 at 90; Fulgham, 09-1253-CFA2 at 2.
251 Billings, *supra* note 216 at 91; *accord* Carr, 156 So. 3d at 4.
252 Carr, 156 So. 3d at 32–33.
253 Billings, *supra* note 216 at 93.
254 *See generally* Fulgham, 09-1253-CFA2.
255 Carr, 156 So. 3d at 10–11; April Warren, *Lawyer for Emilia Carr, Convicted in Boardman Murder, Argues Appeal Before Fla. High Court*, THE GAINESVILLE SUN, ¶ 5 (Feb. 3, 2014); Suevon Lee, *Two Indicted in Murder of Citra Woman*, THE GAINESVILLE SUN (April 10, 2009).
256 Suevon Lee, *Death Sentence for Emilia Carr*, THE GAINESVILLE SUN (Feb. 22, 2011); Carr, 156 So. 3d at 9–10; State of Florida v. Carr, 42-2009-CF-1253-B-X, 5–6 (2017) (Order Den. Def.'s Mot. For Post-Conviction Relief After Evidentiary Hr'g).
257 Nikki Battiste et al., *'We Call It Life Row': Two of the Youngest US Women on Death Row Describe Life Behind Bars*, ABC NEWS, ¶ 2 (Feb. 24, 2015); Lee, *supra* note 256 at ¶ 1.
258 *See generally* Carr, 156 So. 3d; Carr, 42-2009-CF-1253-B-X at 6.
259 Carr, 42-2009-CF-1253-B-X at 7, 14–15.
260 *See* Carr, 42-2009-CF-1253-B-X at 7, 14–15. *See generally* Hurst v. Florida, 136 S. Ct. 616 (2016); Hurst v. State, 202 So. 3d 40 (Fla. 2016). *See also* Melanie Kalmanson, *Storm of the Decade: The Aftermath of Hurst v. Florida*

& *Why the Storm is Likely to Continue*, 74 U. MIAMI L. REV. CAVEAT 37, 47–49 (2020) (discussing the retroactivity application of Hurst v. Florida, 136 S. Ct. 616 (2016)).
261 Carr, 42-2009-CF-1253-B-X at 14–15.
262 Warren, *supra* note 255 at ¶ 7.
263 Fulgham v. State of Florida, 09-1253-CF-A (2009) (Nt. of Appeal); Fulgham v. State of Florida, 5D12-1844 (2014) https://onlinedocketsdca.flcourts.org/DCAResults/LTCases?CaseNumber=1844&CaseYear=2012&Court=5 (last visited Jan. 13, 2023). Neither Emilia's mother nor Joshua's mother were implicated in any of the crimes associated with the cases related to Heather as described herein.
264 *See* Herbert v. Herbert, 08-DR-2115, 3–4 (2008) (Pet. for Inj. for Prot. Against Dom. Viol.). *See supra* Chapter 6, Power and Control.
265 *See* Hawkins v. Hawkins, 2008-DR-052371, 3 (2008) (Pet. for Inj. for Prot. Against Dom. Viol.).
266 *Id.*
267 Hawkins v. Hawkins, 2008-DR-052371 (2008) https://vmatrix1.brevardclerk.us/beca/all_results.cfm?x=4BB88F8C738788AC99BFD224CC0A2DDB7BD7E7BF9D13E70AFD00E9DDDFCBC76526FA6ABFEBD34D16D7B733171ED4D4FE (last visited Jan. 13, 2023).
268 *Id.*
269 State of Florida v. Hawkins, 2010-CF-37041, 1 (2010) (Arrest/Notice to Appear; Probable Cause Aff./Juvenile Ref.).
270 State of Florida v. Hawkins, 2010-CF-37041, 1 (2012) (Court Minutes/Order – Plea).
271 State of Florida v. Hawkins, 2010-CF-37041, 3 (2013) (J./Order of Prob./Order of Cmty. Control).
272 *Id.* at 5.
273 *See* State of Florida v. Hawkins, 2010-CF-37041 (2022) (Order Terminating Prob.).
274 *See* Nicholson v. Nicholson, 04-2667-CA, 3 (2004) (Pet. for Inj. for Prot. Against Dom. Viol.).
275 *Id.*
276 Huss v. Huss, 03-485 DV, 2 (2003) (Pet. for Inj. for Prot. Against Dom. Viol.).
277 *Id.* at 4.
278 Nicholson, 04-2667-CA at 6.
279 *See* Heather Allen, *Troubled Marriage Ends in Death*, HERALD-TRIBUNE (April 27, 2007); *See also* Domestic Violence: It's Everybody's Business, *Step by Step Guide to Understanding the Cycle of Violence*, DOMESTICVIOLENCE.ORG, https://domesticviolence.org/cycle-of-violence/ (last visited Jan. 13, 2023).
280 *See* Domestic Violence: It's Everybody's Business, *supra* note 279.
281 *See Id.*
282 *See Id.*
283 *See Id.*
284 *See Id.*
285 *See Id.*
286 *See* Allen, *supra* note 279 at ¶ 1; *See* Huss v. Huss, 03-451 DV, 2–3, 7 (2003) (Pet. for Inj. for Prot. Against Dom. Viol.); *See* Huss v. Huss, 03-485 DV, 2 (2003) (Pet. for Inj. for Prot. Against Dom. Viol.).
287 *See* Huss, 03-451 DV at 2–3, 7; Jason Witz, *Man Gets Life for Slaying of His Wife*, HERALD-TRIBUNE, ¶ 11 (Jan. 12, 2011).

288 Huss, 03-451 DV at 1–3, 6.
289 *Id*. at 3.
290 *See* Huss v. Huss, 03-485 DV, 1–2, 12–13 (2003) (Pet. for Inj. for Prot. Against Dom. Viol.).
291 *See* State of Florida v. Huss, 2003CF000435, 1 (2003) (Probable Cause Aff.).
292 *See* State of Florida v. Huss, 2003CF000435 (2003) (Order Granting Def. Mot. To Return Property).
293 *See* Huss v. Huss, 03-485 DV (2003) (Order of Transfer).
294 *See* State of Florida v. Huss, 2003MM000874 (2003) https://courts.charlotte clerk.com/Benchmark/CourtCase.aspx/Details/21692?digest=4Q%2Fi1sahF b2COFmt3cCfBA (last visited Jan. 13, 2023).
295 *See* State of Florida v. Huss, 2003MM000874 (2003) (Order).
296 *See* Huss v. Huss, 04-115 DV, 2–3 (2004) (Pet. for Inj. for Prot. Against Dom. Viol.).
297 *See* State of Florida v. Huss, 04-367-M, 1 (2004) (Summons).
298 *See* State of Florida v. Huss, 04-367-M (2004) (Nt. of Nolle Prosequi).
299 *See* Huss v. Huss, 06-321 DV, 2–3 (2006) (Pet. for Inj. for Prot. Against Dom. Viol.).
300 *See generally* State of Florida v. Huss, 2006MM000522 (2006) (Probable Cause Aff.).
301 *See* State of Florida v. Huss, 2006MM000522 (2006) (Order of No Contact).
302 *See* State v. Huss, 2006CF000598, 1–2 (2006) (Probable Cause Aff.). *See also* State v. Huss, 2006CF000598 (2006) https://courts.charlotteclerk.com/ Benchmark/CourtCase.aspx/Details/42966?digest=R10l%2BGIq%2FLtTHh LwTyFw6w (last visited Jan. 19, 2023).
303 *See* State v. Huss, 2006CF000598 (2006) https://courts.charlotteclerk.com/ Benchmark/CourtCase.aspx/Details/42966?digest=R10l%2BGIq%2FLtTHh LwTyFw6w (last visited Jan. 19, 2023).
304 State v. Huss, 2006CF000598, 1 (2006) (Notice to the Clerk); *accord* State v. Huss, 2006CF000598 (2006) https://courts.charlotteclerk.com/Benchmark/ CourtCase.aspx/Details/42966?digest=R10l%2BGIq%2FLtTHhLwTyFw6w (last visited Jan. 19, 2023).
305 *See* State of Florida v. Huss, 2006MM000522 (2006) https://courts.charlotte clerk.com/Benchmark/CourtCase.aspx/Details/42664?digest=kjmTG%2FF3 ntpDc4h1BGQ4rw (last visited Jan. 14, 2023); *See* State of Florida v. Huss, 2006CF000598 (2006) https://courts.charlotteclerk.com/Benchmark/CourtCase. aspx/Details/42966?digest=OZL8uE%2BicWTcCkMV8B2PFQ (last visited Jan. 14, 2023).
306 *See* State of Florida v. Huss, 2006MM000522 (2006) (Court Order/Nt./ Minutes).
307 *See* State of Florida v. Huss, 2006MM000522 (2006) (County Court Sentence).
308 *See* Huss v. Huss, 07-234 DV, 2–3 (2007) (Pet. for Inj. for Prot. Against Dom. Viol.).
309 *See* State of Florida v. Huss, 2007MM000647, 1 (2007) (Probable Cause Aff.).
310 *See Id*.
311 *See Id*.
312 Allen, *supra* note 279 at ¶ 16.
313 *See Id*. at ¶ 16.
314 *See* Huss v. Huss, 07-296 DV, 3 (2007) (Pet. for Inj. for Prot. Against Dom. Viol.).
315 *See* Brian Roman, 07006504 at 1.

316 *See Id.*
317 *See* State of Florida v. Huss, 2007MM000647, 1 (2007) (Probable Cause Aff.).
318 *Id.*
319 *Id.*
320 *Id.*
321 *Id.*
322 *Id.*
323 *Id.* at 2.
324 State of Florida v. Huss, 2007MM000647, 1 (2007) (Probable Cause Aff.); *See* State of Florida v. Huss, 2007MM000647 (2007) https://courts.charlotteclerk.com/Benchmark/CourtCase.aspx/Details/50762?digest=HXrgkXTzJ1C l6SFJC31U%2Bw (last visited Jan. 17, 2023).
325 *See* State of Florida v. Huss, 2007MM000647 (2007) (Surety Appearance Bond); Allen, *supra* note 279 at ¶ 15.
326 *See* State of Florida v. Huss, 2007MM000647 (2007) (Court Order/Notice/Minutes); State of Florida v. Huss, 2007MM000647 (2007) (Def.'s Waiver of Personal Appearance at Pretrial Conferences, Hr'g and Mot. And Authorization for Continuance).
327 *See* State of Florida v. Huss, 07-000738-F, 1 (2007) (Aff.); *See* Allen, *supra* note 279 at ¶ 29.
328 Huss, 07-000738-F at 1.
329 *Id.*
330 *Id.*
331 *See Id.*
332 *Id.*
333 *See* Allen, *supra* note 279 at ¶ 7; *See* Jason Witz, *Scott Huss Testimony: Russian Mafia Killed Wife*, Herald-Tribune, ¶ 14 (Dec. 3, 2010).
334 *See* Witz, *supra* note 333 at ¶ 3.
335 *Id.* at ¶ 6.
336 Witz, *supra* note 287 at ¶ 6.
337 *See* State of Florida v. Huss, 07-000738-F (2007) https://courts.charlotteclerk.com/Benchmark/CourtCase.aspx/Details/51124?digest=GiWQvUQ7Q 3%2FYiY7bN8qUvw (last visited Jan. 17, 2023).
338 Black's Law Dictionary 566 (Bryan A. Garner et al. eds., 4th ed. 2011).
339 *See Id. See also* Goraya v. Goraya, 07-001114DR, 2 (2007) (Pet. for Inj. for Prot. Against Dom. Viol.); Marshall v. Marshall, 97-3133-DR-06, 3 (1997) (Pet. for Inj. for Prot. Against Dom. Viol.); Olms v. Olms, 07DR5SC, 3 (2007) (Pet. for Inj. for Prot. Against Dom. Viol.); Romero v. Romero, 2008-DR-000778-O, 3 (2008) (Pet. for Inj. for Prot. Against Dom. Viol.); Wood v. Wood, 2005DR014620, 4 (2005) (Pet. for Inj. for Prot. Against Dom. Viol.).
340 Ирина Хакамада, *Cold Justice S03E08 American Dream*, YouTube (Dec. 21, 2016), https://www.youtube.com/watch?v=aVNit1iJjgE; State of Florida v. Goraya, 14-CF-000497, 4 (2014) (Warrant to Arrest). *See also* Goraya, 07-001114DR at 1.
341 *See* Emily DeStefanis, 200712632 at 3–4; Хакамада, *supra* note 340.
342 Хакамада, *supra* note 340.
343 *Id.*
344 Goraya v. Goraya, 07-001114DR, 1–2 (2007) (Pet. for Inj. for Prot. Against Dom. Viol.).
345 *See Id.* at 2, 6.
346 State of Florida v. Goraya, 14-CF-000497, 12–13 (2014) (Warrant to Arrest).

347 *See generally* State of Florida v. Goraya, 2007MM022986 (2007) (Information and Notice to the Clerk). *See also* State of Florida v. Goraya, 2007MM022986 (2007) https://matrix.leeclerk.org/Case/ViewCase# (last visited Jan. 18, 2023).
348 *See* Хакамада, *supra* note 340; State of Florida v. Goraya, 2007MM022986 (2007) https://matrix.leeclerk.org/Case/ViewCase# (last visited Jan. 18, 2023).
349 *See* Goraya v. Goraya, 07-001114DR (2007) https://matrix.leeclerk.org/Case/ViewCase (last visited Jan. 18, 2023).
350 *See Id.*; DeStefanis, *supra* note 341 at 5.
351 *See* DeStefanis, *supra* note 341 4; Хакамада, *supra* note 340; State of Florida v. Goraya, 14-CF-000497, 1-2, 7 (2014) (Warrant to Arrest).
352 *See* DeStefanis, *supra* note 341 at 4–5; Goraya, 14-CF-000497 at 7.
353 Хакамада, *supra* note 340.
354 Goraya, 14-CF-000497 at 7.
355 *Id.* at 13.
356 *Id.*
357 *Id.*
358 *Id.*
359 *Id.*
360 DeStefanis, *supra* note 341 at 3.
361 *See Id.* at 5.
362 *See generally Id.*; Хакамада, *supra* note 340. *See also* Goraya, 14-CF-000497 at 19.
363 *See* Хакамада, *supra* note 340; Goraya, 14-CF-000497 at 6.
364 Goraya, 14-CF-000497 at 7.
365 *Id.* at 8.
366 *Id.*
367 *Id.*
368 *Id.* at 8, 11.
369 *Id.* at 15–19.
370 *Id.* at 15, 17.
371 *Id.* at 17, 19.
372 *See* Goraya, 14-CF-000497 at 1–2.
373 DeStefanis, *supra* note 341 at 9, 11.
374 State of Florida v. Goraya, 14-CF-000497, 1, 3 (2016) (Judgment).
375 Green v. Green, 2012-DR-001583-DVBX, 4 (2012) (Pet. for Inj. for Prot. Against Dom. Viol.); *accord, e.g.,* Diller v. Diller, 2008 DR 863, 3 (2008) (Pet. for Inj. for Prot. Against Dom. Viol.); Nicholson v. Nicholson, 04-2667-CA, 5 (2004) (Pet. for Inj. for Prot. Against Dom. Viol.).
376 Cloaninger v. Colley, DR15-1136, 4 (2015) (Pet. for Inj. for Prot. Against Dom. Viol.).
377 *See supra* Chapter 5, Intimidation, Animal Abuse.
378 Green v. Green, 2012-DR-001583-DVBX, 4 (2012) (Pet. for Inj. for Prot. Against Dom. Viol.).
379 *Id.*
380 Green v. Green, 2012-DR-001583-DVBX (2012) https://core.duvalclerk.com/CoreCms.aspx?mode=PublicAccess (last visited Jan. 19, 2023). *See also* Bourque, 2012-623765 at 15.
381 Green v. Green, 2012-DR-001583-DVXX, 4 (2012) (Pet. for Inj. for Prot. Against Dom. Viol.).
382 *Id.*

383 *Id*.; *See* Green v. Green, 2012-DR-001583-DVAX, 2 (2012) (Pet. for Inj. for Prot. Against Dom. Viol.)
384 *See* Green, 2012-DR-001583-DVAX; Green v. Green, 2012-DR-001583-DVCX (2012) (Pet. for Inj. for Prot. Against Dom. Viol.)
385 Green, 2012-DR-001583-DVAX at 1, 8.
386 *Id*. at 4.
387 *Id*.
388 *Id*.
389 *Id*.
390 *Id*.
391 *Id*. at 1, 9; Green v. Green, 2012-DR-001583-DVBX (2012) (Pet. for Inj. for Prot. Against Dom. Viol.).
392 Green, 2012-DR-001583-DVCX at 4.
393 *Id*.
394 Green v. Green. 2012-DR-005112-FMXX (2012) https://core.duvalclerk.com/CoreCms.aspx (last visited Jan. 19, 2023).
395 Bourque, *supra* note 380 at 2.
396 *See Id*. at 5, 15.
397 *Id*. at 15.
398 *Id*.
399 *Id*.
400 *Id*.
401 Tinsley v. Tinsley, 98-9313, 1 (1998) (Pet. for Inj. for Prot. Against Dom. Viol.).
402 *Id*. at 3, 6.
403 *See* Tinsley v. Tinsley, 98-9313 (1998) https://core.duvalclerk.com/CoreCms.aspx (last visited Jan. 20, 2023).
404 Tucker, 2014-104700 at 2.
405 *Id*.
406 *Id*.
407 *Id*.
408 *Id*.
409 *Id*.
410 *Id*. at 3.
411 *Id*.
412 *Id*.; State of Florida v. Tinsley, 2014-MM-2694 (2014) https://core.duvalclerk.com/CoreCms.aspx (last visited Jan. 20, 2023).
413 *See* Tinsley, 2014-MM-2694. On February 14, 2014, the court entered an order of adjudication of guild withheld, which is a special sentence under FLA. STAT. § 948.01 allowing the court, in its discretion, to order probation without a formal conviction. *Id*. (*See* FLA. STAT. § 948.01.).
414 Tinsley, 2014-MM-2694.
415 Rhatigan, 2014-469626 at 6–7. *See also* Tucker, *supra* note 404.
416 *See* Rhatigan, *supra* note 415 at 7.
417 *Id*. at 16.
418 *Id*. at 7.
419 *Id*. at 25.
420 *Id*. at 28.

7 When the Intimate Partner Violence Victim Resists the Abuse

Fearful of the Future

For this study, "fearful of the future" is a theme that indicates the intimate partner violence (IPV) victim has expressed a fear or dread of something happening in the future due to the abuser's actions. In this study, 7.0% of the 493 cases and 55.5% of the sixty-two (62) cases, as well as 42.0% of the 100 petitions for injunction analyzed in this phase of this study, resulted in a fearful of the future coding. Many of the IPV victims expressed their fear of what types of actions their abusers might take in the future, but the most prominent of all was fear for one's safety or that the abuser would kill them in the future. This was especially true because so many of the IPV victims expressed that their abusers threatened them with their lives. For example, Nancy Olms, detailed in the subtheme of degradation, wrote:

> I am very afraid for my wellbeing I don't feel safe in my own apartment for fear that he will come back to hurt or even kill me, ... I believe if allowed to continue to physically verbally [sic] & sexually abuse me he will hurt me again. I am very afraid of what is next when it comes to him, and what he will do to me.[1]

Having been denied any type of protection from the court, Nancy was killed one and one-half years later.

Mantrana v. Mora

Anay Mantrana repeatedly contacted the police about her abusive husband, Victor Mora, during their marriage.[2] The final police report she made was about a month before her death in March 2014 in which she explained she was scared of Victor and did not want him around their house anymore.[3] This sentiment is similar to prior police reports filed throughout their marriage, as many seemed to have a sense of concern relative to her fear of

Victor. But other prior police reports were factual reports of arguments that did not include as many references to Anay's fear of Victor. A March 22, 2013, report explains that Anay was "very disappointed with the Police" and told the officer "I have a 9mm gun and I guess I will have to use if I need to."[4]

Almost a year before on April 2, 2013, Anay filed a petition for injunction explaining that she "fears for safety and seeks an injunction for her protection."[5] Although fearing for safety is a common reason for filing for an injunction, many IPV victims do not specifically explain this to the court in their petitions for injunction; however, Anay specifically cited this as a reason for requesting protection from the court. She was granted a temporary injunction that was extended several times; but on June 13, 2013, she filed for a voluntary dismissal.[6] The hearing for the final injunction was cancelled, and a judgment of voluntary dismissal was entered on February 5, 2014.[7]

The evening of March 30, 2014, police responded to a call from Anay's son stating that he found Victor and her dead in their bedroom.[8] Earlier that morning, Anay's son was woken by three banging sounds; but he went back to sleep.[9] Once he woke up late morning, he left the home to get lunch, returned shortly thereafter, and began watching television.[10] After not having seen his parents all day, he spoke to his wife who suggested he check on Anay and Victor.[11] After knocking on their bedroom door and trying to go in but the door was locked, the son looked under the door.[12] He was able to see one of his parents laying on the floor.[13] Once he was in the bedroom, he found Anay and Victor both dead.[14] According to the police report, Anay was found with "a knife [sic] in her left hand and a revolver in her right hand." [15] She is considered the intimate partner homicide (IPH) offender in this case.

Fear of Children's Safety

For this study, "fear of children's safety" is a subtheme of fearful of the future that describes the IPV victim's fear of the abuser's ability to harm the children and/or stepchildren of, or those in common with, the abuser and the IPV victim. In this study, 2.8% of the 493 cases and 22.2% of the sixty-two (62) cases, as well as 16.0% of the 100 petitions for injunction analyzed in this phase, resulted in a fear for children's safety coding. Another phrase that flowed throughout the theme of fearful of the future was the notion of the IPV victim being in fear for their children's safety, as well as their own. Many of these victims explained that their motivation for remaining in the relationship was to protect their children. These phrases are differentiated from fearful of the future because they include comments about the IPV victim's children. For example, Sandra Nicholson wrote that she changed the locks to try to protect herself and her children, "I had the locks changed. He came back later & kicked the door down .... I had the locks changed because I was fearful that he would hurt me again or take the kids."[16] She went on to explain again in the same petition for injunction that she was fearful of her children's safety and remained in the relationship because of this fear:

> I was fearful that he would hurt me and take the kids. I stayed with them because I was scared .... I was scared he would suffocate me. My 2 other children were in their rooms scared .... [H]e has always threatened to take the kids and that I would never see them again.[17]

However, many petitions for injunction for this subtheme incorporate the IPV victim's dread of the future regarding their children's safety as an over-arching tone to the broader themes or subthemes provided throughout the petition for injunction, as the following case exemplifies.

Dragic v. Dragic

On September 25, 2003, Jelena Dragic filed a petition for injunction in which, among other acts of physical violence and non-violent tactics of coercive control, she described sleeping in her car for days to ensure her children's safety, as well as her own, because she feared they would be killed by her husband, Slobodan:

> We are fearful for our lives as he tries/threatens to kill us and himself. Last night we slept in the car and I have been sleeping in the car for the last 10 days, unable to go inside because of fear that he may come in during the night and kill both me and my children.[18]

Jelena was granted a temporary and final injunction for this petition.[19] The final injunction was ordered to expire on April 7, 2004; but she filed a request to dismiss on February 17, 2004, which the court granted.[20] On August 30, 2004, Slobodan engaged in a physical altercation with Jelena and his son, who intervened to ensure Jelena was able to escape additional injury.[21] In doing so, Jelena's son was punched in the face by Slobodan.[22] Slobodan was arrested for this incident, and a misdemeanor case ensued in which his bond was revoked for additional behavior that violated his pretrial release conditions, i.e., he violated the no contact order issued by the criminal court.[23] On November 2, 2004, Jelena filed another petition for injunction that included similar allegations and fears of her daughter's and her safety that were contained in her 2003 petition.[24] Jelena was awarded a temporary and final injunction for this petition as well; but like the other one in 2003, she filed to voluntarily dismiss it on December 29, 2004.[25] This is the same day Slobodan was arrested for violating the final injunction because he was living at the house with Jelena and her daughter.[26] By January 18, 2005, Jelena requested the Assistant State Attorney and the attorney representing Slobodan for the misdemeanor case to agree to modify the no contact order against him to a "no harmful contact with the victim."[27] The case against Slobodan was eventually resolved by the state of Florida as nolle prossed, i.e., dismissed in December 2005 because he "completed Domestic Battery plea & pass agreement."[28]

Essentially, there was no legal activity between Jelena and Slobodan between 2006 and 2010 that shows any signs of domestic violence (DV) or criminal allegations of violence; however, Jelena filed for dissolution of marriage on September 13, 2010.[29] However, during the morning hours of September 30, 2010, Slobodan shot Jelena twice in front of her house, causing her to fall to the ground on the driveway.[30] Slobodan immediately drove away after shooting Jelena.[31] She was airlifted to a nearby medical facility for treatment but died later.[32] Slobodan was arrested thereafter and admitted to killing Jelena.[33] He told investigators that after another argument with Jelena "he 'was finished.'"[34] He explained to the investigator that "he could not take the family problems any more."[35] So, he got a gun he purchased ten days earlier from his bedroom and shot her.[36] After the first shot, as she laid on the ground, she said to him "You are killing me!"[37] He walked over to her and shot her again in her head.[38] He was charged with first degree murder and was sentenced to life in prison without parole.[39]

Bailey v. Bailey

In the early morning hours of August 26, 2006, sheriff's deputies responded to the home of Sharon and Robert Bailey in reference to a disturbance called in by Sharon.[40] Sharon explained to the deputy that Robert was drunk, and they got into an argument.[41] When she tried to leave the home with her daughter, Robert would not let them go by blocking the door.[42] The altercation escalated to a physical interaction between them in which Robert knocked the cigarette out of Sharon's mouth and she struck him in self-defense.[43] Robert denied blocking the door and stated that Sharon struck him first, but he did admit to striking her in the mouth.[44] He was arrested for this incident because deputies believed without intervention "another incident of domestic violence on this same date" would occur.[45] In fact, this family was familiar to authorities as a police report of battery related to DV against Robert was filed on November 26, 2005, because he held his stepdaughter's head under water.[46] He was angry because she accidentally hit him in the face when he tried to wake her up.[47] He continued to choke her and threatened her life.[48] By the time Sharon arrived home,

Robert was drunk and attempted to engage in an altercation with her by breaking down the bedroom door and throwing it at her because she had tried to retreat into the bedroom to get away from him.[49] She left the home, and the police advised her to file for an injunction for protection.[50]

By the beginning of July 2006, Robert was arrested for another incident that involved battery and aggravated assault against Sharon and his stepdaughter, as well as one of his stepdaughter's friends.[51] After being at the races and drinking all day, Robert went with Sharon who was driving the girls to the friend's home.[52] The girls were in the back bed of the family's pickup truck for the short drive to the friend's home.[53] However, Robert hit Sharon several times in her face while she was driving; so, she pulled the truck over to prevent the girls from being injured from her losing control due to being hit by Robert.[54] When her daughter realized what was taking place, she went after Robert with a crowbar.[55] But Robert took the crowbar, threatened his stepdaughter with it instead, and actually attempted to hit her with it.[56] Sharon and the girls ran to a nearby residence to call the authorities.[57]

In conjunction with the police report for domestic battery dated August 26, 2006, Sharon filed for an injunction for protection later that same day.[58] In her petition for injunction, Sharon explained to the court that Robert "Stayed up all night with a gun to his mouth."[59] She continued to detail how Robert "threaten [sic] both me and child .... Threaten [sic] to take my life in front of my child .... I am afraid of my life and my child's life. He threaten [sic] to kill me in front of my child."[60] She told the court "All night wanted to kill his self [sic] if [sic] front of us."[61] She explained that Robert had been abusive for ten years.[62] She was awarded a temporary injunction for her petition.

Several years went by without any apparent reports of abuse; but on January 29, 2009, Robert's stepdaughter reported that he abused her on January 27, 2009, by forcing her to the ground and stating he was going to whip her.[63] She had visible injuries on her legs from having been forced to the floor.[64] She explained that she was very afraid of him and that he abused her mother as well.[65] However, when Sharon was contacted by deputies, she denied the veracity of her daughter's allegations against Robert.[66] When Robert spoke to authorities, he said his stepdaughter was not telling the truth; but he admitted to attempting to whip her.[67] This report was closed by a warrant affidavit, and a copy of it was forwarded to Florida Department of Children and Families (DCF).[68] Sharon's daughter planned to stay with her friend until DCF cleared the case.[69] Robert was instructed not to call the friend's home or to go there.[70] Sharon was informed by deputies that he was not allowed to be around her daughter until DCF cleared the case.[71]

By 6:53 p.m. on January 31, 2009, Sharon's daughter called the sheriff's department to report the fact that Robert called her to say that he was going to kill Sharon and himself with a shotgun.[72] She explained that she was at a friend's house and did not want to go home because she was afraid of Robert.[73] When deputies contacted Robert, he explained that he was fine and had no plans to harm himself or anyone else.[74] He further explained to deputies that "he would never harm his wife nor himself."[75] Deputies spoke to Sharon in front of Robert and she stated what her daughter said "was complete nonsense and that Robert would never harm a soul."[76]

At 12:27 a.m. on February 1, 2009, Sharon's daughter called the Sheriff's office explaining that Robert shot Sharon and tried to shoot her through the bathroom door.[77] She was able to escape to her brother's house to make the call to the Sheriff's.[78] When deputies arrived at the scene minutes later, they found Sharon and Robert dead from gunshot wounds to the head.[79] Robert killed Sharon and took his own life.[80]

Pregnant

For this study, "pregnant" is a subtheme of fearful of the future that explains that the IPV victim was pregnant at the time of the incident indicated in the petition for injunction, making the IPV victim concerned about the health of her fetus. In this study, 0.4% of the 493 cases and 3.1% of the sixty-two (62) cases, as well as 2.0% of the 100 petitions for injunction analyzed in this phase, resulted in a pregnant coding. Cases in this study coded as "pregnant" were done so because the IPV victims stated they were pregnant in the injunction for protection as a subtheme to a larger overarching theme in their narrative. As an example, Sandra Nicholson wrote, "I was pregnant with [my son] and his action scared me to death. I thought the baby would get hurt."[81] This statement indicates a fear of the future and that she is explaining her concern for her baby, i.e., her child because she is pregnant.

Wilkerson v. Wilkerson

Jennifer and Thomas Wilkerson lost custody of their children and were involved with dependency court to obtain visitation and regain custody.[82] Jennifer was working hard to follow DCF recommendations to see her children and win back custody, which included them advising her to obtain a restraining order against Thomas.[83] Thomas, on the other hand, was not working toward complying with DCF's plan.[84] On March 13, 2007, when Jennifer applied for an injunction for protection, she explained to the injunction court that Thomas comes to her house on a regular basis, refuses to leave, and does not let her call the Sheriff's office.[85] She explained that she was afraid he would hurt her to keep her from getting her children.[86] She also wrote, "I am pregnant and I'm afraid that his verbal threats and abuse will turn physical."[87] The fact that she was pregnant was an additional fact for the court to take into consideration; but she was not granted a final injunction for protection from the injunction court because no violence was indicated in her petition.[88] However, on March 22, 2007, in front of the dependency court, when asked if she had a restraining order against Thomas, Jennifer explained that the injunction court denied her petition; thus, the dependency court judge granted her a final injunction against Thomas.[89] He was served with the final injunction on March 23, 2007.[90]

Although Jennifer obtained the final injunction against Thomas and that it was a pathway for her to regain custody of her children, reports from family and friends indicate that neither of them abided by the terms of the final injunction.[91] The case worker for the children's case stated that, even though Jennifer was trying to do all that she could to comply with her case plan, Thomas was living with her in violation of the final injunction and the case plan.[92] Jennifer's mother and sister described the couple as loving each other, but her sister knew that Jennifer asked him for a divorce.[93] In fact, Jennifer began seeing another man around the same time she obtained the final injunction against Thomas.[94] According to the new man in her life, the relationship was going strong.[95] Jennifer and her new man had contact with each other every day, either in person or over the phone.[96]

Thomas' parents were charged with taking care of Jennifer and Thomas' children while they were under the jurisdiction of the dependency court.[97] He was not allowed to live with his parents because they had the couple's children, so it was unclear where Thomas was living.[98] On April 3, 2007, Thomas cut his wrists and was taken to the hospital by his mother.[99] His mother was not happy with how this incident was handled, as Thomas was released from the hospital within twenty-four hours.[100]

On April 6, 2007, Sheriff's deputies were dispatched to Jennifer's home regarding harassing phone calls Thomas was making to her.[101] She explained to deputies that Thomas had been to her home with her permission earlier in the day, but she now did not want him around and wanted him to stop calling her.[102] A co-worker of Jennifer's explained that she had overheard one of the calls from Thomas, and he was cursing at Jennifer.[103] When deputies spoke to Thomas, he acknowledged having been to Jennifer's earlier in the day with her permission.[104] Both Jennifer and Thomas agreed not to contact each other via telephone or in person.[105]

By April 9, 2007, Thomas was acting more out of character according to members of his family.[106] His sister-in-law saw him in the evening and offered him dinner at her house.[107] He declined, and she said he seemed upset because he was less talkative and did not play with her children as was normal.[108] That same night, Thomas was out "drinking and telling people that he was going to kill [Jennifer]."[109] But he said "he couldn't kill her because he loved her and she was pregnant with his child."[110]

In the morning of April 10, 2007, Jennifer contacted the clerk of court to ask why she could not have contact with Thomas.[111] By that afternoon, she was attempting to get the final injunction dismissed.[112] Additionally, she wanted a copy of the order stemming from the dependency hearing regarding her and her children.[113] The two deputy clerks who spoke to Jennifer on April 10, 2007, did not indicate that she seemed concerned for her safety; however, one indicated that she "sounded a little distraught."[114]

At about 6:00 p.m. on April 10, 2007, the new man in Jennifer's life went to her home to check on her after her phone went straight to voicemail.[115] When he knocked on the door to her home, it was ajar; so, he walked in.[116] Once inside, he found Jennifer and Thomas dead on the living room floor.[117] He ran out of the home and called the Sheriff's office.[118] Both Jennifer and Thomas died of a single gunshot wound to the head.[119] Thomas killed Jennifer and then turned the gun on himself.[120] Jennifer was about six to seven months pregnant at the time of her death.[121]

Resistance to Abuse

For this study, "resistance to abuse" is a theme that describes the IPV victim's details of acts taken by the IPV victim, which may have been acknowledged by the victim to be against their own best interests, that were specified as overt actions against the abuser's tactics of abuse, including resisting a physical altercation from the abuser; calling the police to report the abuse or the abuser; filing the instant petition for injunction against the abuser and/or detailing other petitions for injunction that had previously been filed against him; leaving or fleeing from the abuser during altercations; separating from the abuser; etc. In this study, 10.3% of the 493 cases and 80.9% of the sixty-two (62) cases, as well as 51.0% of the 100 petitions for injunction analyzed in this phase, resulted in a resistance to abuse coding. In this theme, phrases varied from each other more than in other themes, except for those in which IPV victims reported they called the police after altercations with their abusers. For example, after being choked and being told she was going to die that night by her husband, Sandy Brunson replied to him, "Oh well we all have to die sometime."[122] Then she yelled to a friend to call the police for her because she was still being held down along the highway by her abuser.[123] In another example, Sandra Nicholson wrote "I pushed away and he pushed me down and hit the floor with my knees. I called 911 & the dispatcher asked me if he was there. I said yes while on the phone [he] yelled out 'Thanks a lot you ruined everything.'"[124]

It is important to note that IPV victims are often viewed as helpless or abusive toward the IPV offender. Thus, it is significant to stress that this theme is non-violent, as the victims worked to resolve their abusive situations within the confines of the judicial system, law enforcement, or with the abuser themselves, prior to filing the petition for injunction. IPV victims are often blamed for being responsible for the abuse they experience from their abuser because they either instigate it or encourage it through their own acts; but this fallacy does not comport with this theme's data.

Rupinder Goraya, discussed in verbal abuse, wrote about her experience with her husband who was "under influence of alcohol" because he had started drinking in the afternoon and wanted to go to the store:

> I refused because I said you cann't [sic] drive under influence of alcohol. He started verbal abuse. When I said Don't do abuse I will call to police if you hurts [sic] me physical. He grabed [sic] my neck. I escaped myself and try [sic] to pick up baby. He hits glass vase on us. I escaped from hit. I tried to snatch phone and close the door but I went outside and called to [deputy] and they advice [sic] call to 911. I called and they came on spot of incident.[125]

This narrative shows the extent to which Rupinder tried to resist the abuse she was experiencing at the hands of her husband, Kultar, without being physically violent toward him. Similarly, Donna Wood, detailed in the subtheme of threats and discussed throughout this book, detailed her resistance to abuse and the repercussions it brought on her:

> I told him he better not harass my family anymore, and he began threatening me as well …. When I began to tell him that I was going to file something in court to get him out of the house completely because he has been so abusive and volatile, he came over to the bed where I was lying and he took his leg and bent it and put it on my side (I was laying on my side) and pushed down as hard as he could. I heard a crack and for a minute I couldn't breathe. I had been telling him (since he spent a night in jail from having a domestic violence incident) that if he ever laid a hand on me again, I would call the police and this time I would prosecute. Since he knew this, he blocked my way to get up and get to the phone. He held me down with his arm across my throat. He wouldn't let me leave the room. After he did, he stayed right with me to make sure I didn't call. I decided at that point to file this injunction instead.[126]

Often, the IPV victim is viewed as helpless or as abusive as the IPV offender; however, these petition for injunction narratives do not bear out either misnomer. In fact, they support the notion that IPV victims work toward regaining their autonomy and agency during their abuse. This suggests that the judiciary, authorities, policy makers, and society should take care to understand the nuances of coercive control and the IPV victim's response to it rather than viewing domestic abuse as a wholesale societal problem in general whereby the victim is as much to blame as the abuser.

Marquita Green, whose case is discussed above in the subtheme household, clothes, and personal belongings destroyed, detailed an altercation with her husband who woke her up by attacking her:

> I was laying in the bed asleep. [He] started repeatedly throwing his black bag of his belongings @ my head. I had to duck to keep from getting hit. [He] then broke up the bedroom lamps & other what knots in the bedroom. I had to dive on the floor to reach up for the phone to call 911. [He] snatched the phone out of the wall & threw it up against the wall. JSO called back & I got my son to get the phone. [He] came towards me w/his fist balled up & cursing @ me as if he was going to hit me. I got the phone in my hand & started screaming & the JSO operator heard me. I told the JSO operator that I needed help. I then ran out of the home.[127]

As detailed in Chapter 6, Marquita was killed in an intimate partner homicide-suicide (IPHS) three weeks after writing this narrative even though she had a final injunction in place against her husband.[128]

Craft-Enzor v. Enzor

On June 23, 2008, Radiah Craft-Enzor explained in her petition for injunction that after arguing with her husband, Reginald Enzor, she left the house.[129] He wanted her to come back into the house, but she refused.[130] Because she would not do as he said, he pulled at her shirt.[131] She called the police for assistance, but he was not arrested.[132] At the time of the filing of her petition for injunction, Radiah had one-month old twin boys with Reginald.[133]

Two and a half years later, on January 2, 2011, Radiah's seventeen-year-old son was woken by her screams because Reginald had her "backed into a corner of the room with her back against the wall."[134] Reginald was stabbing Radiah repeatedly.[135] Her son attempted to approach her to help, but Reginald turned toward him and said "back-up before I kill you too."[136] Both of the twins, now two years old, were in the room with Radiah.[137] The older son ran out of the house and called 911.[138] A couple minutes later, he saw Reginald fleeing the house; so, he ran back in to check on his mother who was unresponsive.[139] Radiah sustained multiple stab wounds all over her body, including several to her chest and back.[140] She also had several defensive wounds to her hands and arms.[141] She was pronounced dead at a nearby hospital a couple hours later.[142] Reginald, who was adjudicated a habitual felony offender for prior felony offenses, plead guilty to first-degree murder for killing Radiah and aggravated assault for threatening her son with a knife in exchange for a life sentence without parole.[143] He would have faced the death sentence had his case gone to trial.[144]

Music v. Music

On August 25, 2010, according to Sheriff's deputies, Bridget Music arrived at the fire station with her children because she was afraid to go home.[145] She and her husband, Jacob, got into an argument about tattoos; and it escalated into a physical altercation.[146] Jacob grabbed Bridget by the throat and threw her up against the wall.[147] While threatening her with a kitchen knife, he said "Bitch, Im [sic] gonna [sic] kill you."[148] In order to resist his abuse, Bridget answered "What about my kids?"[149] At that point, Jacob brought the knife toward her but stuck it in the wall instead.[150] He answered her by saying "What ... you dont [sic] think Im [sic] gonna [sic] kill you?"[151] He swung the knife at her again but missed her, hitting the wall a second time.[152] At this point, she was able to run out the door.[153] She picked her children up at school and drove to the fire station.[154] When questioned by deputies, Jacob included a story about Bridget throwing cooked potatoes and cabbage at him in the kitchen, which began the argument.[155] However, there was no evidence of this in the home.[156] In fact, an undisturbed pot of cabbage was on the stove and diced potatoes were in a colander in the sink.[157] Jacob was placed under arrest for domestic battery with a deadly weapon.[158]

On August 30, 2010, Bridget filed a petition for injunction regarding the incident described above.[159] She explained to the court that after Jacob grabbed her and threw her against the wall, she tried to walk to the door; but he grabbed her back.[160] He shoved her two more times into the kitchen wall because she told him she was leaving.[161] He put his forearm to her throat and held the knife to her face.[162] When she brought up her kids, she said "he said he didnt [sic] give a fuck," and went for her face with the knife again.[163] She was able to run out the door when he turned his back.[164] Bridget was awarded a temporary injunction for her petition for injunction, but the case was dismissed after she appeared at the final hearing requesting it be dismissed.[165]

During the early morning hours of June 22, 2014, the Sheriff's office received a call in reference to a vehicle that was completely engulfed in flames.[166] It became apparent to responding deputies that the vehicle was on fire due to arson.[167] The vehicle was owned by Bridget's father, who had not seen her since the morning of June 21, 2014; but Bridget always drove it.[168] Her father also explained that she never turned off her cell phone, but "it was going straight to voice mail as if it were turned off."[169] He later officially reported her missing.[170] Bridget's sister told deputies that she was sure Jacob had done something to Bridget because he was violent toward her in the past.[171] When she confronted him earlier in the day about where Bridget was, "he told her 'Bitch I'll murder you too.'"[172]

During the late-night hours of June 21, 2014, Bridget visited with friends and wanted to get high because she quit her job.[173] She met with her drug dealer and worked to get some money from her friends to pay him for what she purchased.[174] She left her house at 11:30 p.m. on June 21, 2014, to try to collect money from friends.[175] Because of this interaction Bridget had with her drug dealer and the need to collect money to pay him, Jacob told investigators that he saw Bridget on June 21, 2014, at 2:45 p.m. and gave her $230 in cash.[176] He said that was the last time he saw or heard from Bridget.[177] He explained that the drug dealer threatened to kill him and his girlfriend "just like he killed his wife" if he did not pay him $15,000 within an hour and a half.[178]

When investigators spoke to the drug dealer, he explained that he and Bridget were friends and that he would never hurt her.[179] He said that Bridget and a friend came by at 10:00 p.m. June 21, 2014, with some food, and they hung out for a while.[180] He told investigators that Bridget and her friend left his house around 11:00 p.m. that same night.[181] He received a call from Bridget at 1:31 a.m. on June 22, 2014, but he did not answer it because his phone was on vibrate.[182] The message Bridget left said "Hey call me it's Bridget, I need you call me back."[183] He never heard from her again.[184]

Meanwhile, Jacob was acting somewhat erratic and not meeting with investigators when they requested.[185] Jacob told an acquaintance of his that Bridget's decapitated body was found in a canal in a specific place even though that information was not based on fact related to the investigation.[186] Also, Jacob threatened his girlfriend that if she did not get it together, he was going to kill her.[187] Based on the comment from Jacob about the canal, deputies began to search that specific area where Bridget's body was, in fact, found.[188]

Another friend of Jacob's spoke to investigators and explained that Jacob came to his house around 2:30 a.m. on June 22, 2014, with blood on his arms.[189] He told his friend that he stabbed a guy in a nearby town.[190] His friend told him to get out of his house, so Jacob grabbed some clean clothes and left.[191] However, this friend noticed that his folding knife was missing, as was his sister's folding knife who housed Jacob's girlfriend that same night.[192] Jacob came back a little while later and asked for a ride to another town to retrieve his truck.[193] At that point, the folding knife appeared back in the place where it is normally kept; but "it looked like it had blood and hair on it."[194] At this point, Jacob's friend used tissue paper to handle the knife, wrapped it in a plastic bag, and brought it to authorities.[195] He believed that Jacob "must have had the knife and then put it back because he was the only other person in the house."[196]

Jacob was arrested and agreed to be interviewed by detectives without a lawyer present.[197] During that interview, he said "Yea, I [k]illed Bridget, but [my girlfriend] was involved."[198] He explained that his girlfriend and Bridget got into an argument, and Bridget got the best of his girlfriend.[199] So, the girlfriend pulled out a knife and stabbed Bridget in the chest.[200] He continued to explain that he was attempting to rush Bridget to a hospital or fire station, but his girlfriend got into the car without his knowledge.[201] According to Jacob, this is when Bridget's neck was cut but by his girlfriend, not him.[202] He said his girlfriend killed Bridget and put her body in the canal.[203]

Jacob denied helping his girlfriend put Bridget's body in the canal, which investigators said "[t]here is no way [his girlfriend] would be able to pick her body up and throw her in the canal and there were no drag marks on the dirt road" next to the canal where her body was found.[204] Also, during the same interview Jacob said "Did I kill Bridget, your god damn right."[205] On June 23, 2014, he was arrested for first degree murder and second degree arson.[206] A criminal case ensued; but on January 29, 2015, Jacob sent a letter to the judge on the case.[207] In his letter, Jacob explained to the judge that he hoped to bring the case to a close by changing his plea from not guilty to guilty for both counts against him.[208] He asked the judge to resolve the case as quickly as possible because of all the hurt he had caused.[209] The court held a hearing on February 13, 2015, and accepted Jacob's guilty plea.[210] He was sentenced to life without parole for killing Bridget and had to pay restitution for the arson related charges.[211]

Helping Abuser

For this study, "helping abuser" is a subtheme of resistance to abuse that is a description by the IPV victim whereby the victim helped the abuser, even though the victim also described being abused in the same narrative. In this study, 1.4% of the 493 cases and 11.1% of the sixty-two (62) cases, as well as 10.0% of the 100 petitions for injunction analyzed in this phase, resulted in a helping abuser coding. This subtheme elucidates the struggle IPV victims have with leaving their abusers, especially because the words are from petitions for injunction from IPH victims and, some, from IPH offenders. The good deeds described in them do not seem out of the ordinary until they are put into the context of the ultimate outcome of these IPH cases. And still, they are juxtaposed against the theme of resistance to abuse because the IPV victim in the case may describe having called the police but allowed the abuser to stay at the house or to come back home after being arrested.

Welch v. Welch

Just after midnight on March 16, 2006, Marilyn Tubwell called the Sheriff's office to report the fact that her ex-boyfriend of four years, Tony Welch, was stalking her.[212] She broke up with him about a week prior to the incident and was pregnant with his child.[213] Tony was calling her and making threats to her over the phone.[214] Tony was arrested for his actions with this incident.[215] Based on the deputies' DV pamphlet and information, she filed for an injunction for protection later that day.[216] In her petition for injunction, she explained that she was very afraid of Tony and that she just wanted him to leave her alone.[217] She wrote that he is very violent, has anger issues that he is not able to control, and made threats to hurt her.[218] She was provided a temporary injunction by the court, but it was dismissed on the same day as the final hearing for her failure to appear.[219]

As soon as April 1, 2006, Marilyn was calling the Sheriff's office for help again because Tony punched her in the face and bit her on her shoulder.[220] By now, she was seven months pregnant with his baby.[221] Witnesses to this incident corroborated Marilyn's account of what had taken place, and Tony was arrested for aggravated battery because he should have known that Marilyn was pregnant.[222] Nevertheless, during the pendency of his criminal felony case, the charges against Tony were not prosecuted because Marilynn requested they be dismissed.[223] She did not file for an injunction for protection related to this incident.[224]

The next reported incident that occurred between Marilyn and Tony was on July 8, 2010, when Marilyn filed a petition for injunction against Tony.[225] She explained to the court that Tony was threatening her through text messages, at her home, and at her work.[226] She also said that Tony was "jumping on me in the bathroom."[227] Even though he had moved out, he kept stopping by her home threatening her.[228] Also, he was sitting in front of her house at night and would drive by her job when she was at work.[229] She was successful in obtaining a temporary injunction against Tony, but the case was dismissed at the final hearing on July 21, 2010, because Marilyn was not present.[230] She explained in a later petition for injunction that she was not able to attend the hearing due to work.[231]

Shortly after on July 27, 2010, Marilyn and Tony engaged in an altercation at their home and were both listed on the Sheriff's report as the suspects and victims.[232] According to the report, the couple was still living together and shared two children.[233] During the early morning hours, Marilyn stated that Tony "jumped on her and threw her by her hair" because he was upset about a text on her phone.[234] The deputy did not observe any physical injuries on Marilyn, but she complained of a swollen finger.[235] Tony's version of events was somewhat similar to Marilyn's except he said Marilyn broke her own phone to prevent him from seeing her text.[236] He also said his physical aggression toward Marilyn was in self-defense, but he had no injuries either.[237] As a result, neither Marilyn or Tony were arrested because deputies could not determine which of them was the primary aggressor.[238] There is no indication that Marilyn or Tony filed for an injunction for protection related to this incident.[239]

On September 21, 2010, Marilyn filed her next petition for injunction requesting protection from Tony.[240] She explained that he was threatening her and throwing her things around the house to the point of breaking them.[241] She also described how her young son was afraid of Tony and that she was tired of being threatened.[242] She told the court that Tony stated "a restraining order means nothing to him."[243] As with the prior injunction cases between Marilyn and Tony, this case was dismissed at the final hearing on October 6, 2010.[244]

Marilyn and Tony were married on October 14, 2010.[245] A year later, on November 26, 2011, Marilyn called the Sheriff's office to report Tony for having thrown things in their home around, which subsequently escalated to him pulling some of her hair from her head.[246] Tony was arrested for this incident and the case was resolved nolle prosequi.[247] However, Marilynn filed a petition for injunction related to this incident and other issues at home on December 19, 2011.[248] She explained to the court that she wanted him to complete his court mandated counseling and case plan so that he learns how to "avoid and controll [sic] himself before committing domestic violence again."[249]

By May 30, 2013, Marilyn and Tony were estranged; however, she explained in her petition for injunction that they were "trying to get on good terms since 2011 of November."[250] When providing details as to why she was willing to help Tony, she wrote:

> I visited with him earlyier [sic] that day while kids was [sic] not home. Well my husband has been going through mental issues and only started bk [sic] conversating with because he need help threating [sic] to kill himself on several occasions as well as others. I told my husband that I didnt [sic] mind being there for him when he needed me but could never get things back like they were.[251]

However, Tony was very jealous and asked her questions about who she was talking to because he heard she was seeing someone.[252] Nevertheless, at that moment she just laughed it off.[253] But later that night, at 3:00 a.m., he entered her home and grabbed her out of bed, threatening her life.[254] He held her against the wall, telling her he was going to kill her.[255] When she told him he was hurting her, he said "Bitch I dont [sic] give a fuck" and punched her in the face.²⁵⁶ However, the Sheriff's report reads differently than Marilyn's petition for injunction related to this incident in that it explains he also "grabbed her by the throat and continued to hold her against the wall while yelling at her."²⁵⁷ The Sheriff's report also stated that he "struck her approximately eight times in the face" after which point he held a ".38 caliber handgun and pointed it at her while yelling about her wanting to see other guys."²⁵⁸ He told her "If I can't have you, no one can."²⁵⁹ When Tony was interviewed by deputies, he denied having a gun but admitted to touching Marilyn to get her out of his way when he was trying to leave the home.²⁶⁰ He was arrested for aggravated assault with a deadly weapon without intent to kill.²⁶¹ The criminal felony case against Tony was resolved nolle prosequi on both counts.²⁶²

On February 4, 2014, another incident between Marilyn and Tony occurred for which they were both considered the suspects and victims.²⁶³ Neither of them filed a petition for injunction for this altercation.²⁶⁴ The parties got into an argument over adultery accusations made by Marilyn against Tony while they were both in their vehicle.²⁶⁵ According to Marilyn, Tony punched her in the face and exited the vehicle.²⁶⁶ According to Tony, Marilyn hit him with the vehicle while he was walking on the road.²⁶⁷ However, deputies did not observe any physical injuries on either of them, which should have been the case given their respective statures and the fact that being hit by a vehicle should have cause physical injuries.²⁶⁸ As a result, no arrests were made.²⁶⁹

On May 8, 2014, Sheriff's deputies responded to a call regarding shots fired at a Motel 6.²⁷⁰ Upon arrival, they observed Tony lying on the ground in a pool of blood with Marilyn and another woman kneeling over him.²⁷¹ The other woman "had some kind of bloody cloth or towel wrapped around her right arm."²⁷² When deputies approached them, the woman exclaimed "She has the gun," indicating that Marilyn was in possession of the weapon.²⁷³ Deputies secured the gun and "handcuffed and placed [Marilyn] in [the] patrol vehicle."²⁷⁴ The autopsy report determined that Tony died from a "gunshot wound of the abdomen with the manner of death being homicide."²⁷⁵ However, the Assistant State Attorney determined the homicide was justifiable and self-defense.²⁷⁶ As a result, the case was closed as "cleared exceptional;" thus, Marilyn was not prosecuted for Tony's death.²⁷⁷

Morrow v. Morrow

On January 10, 2005, Amanda Morrow explained to the court why she helped her estranged husband, Leonard, by stating "We were driving down the road going to take the kids to the baby sitter [sic]. I had no problem helping him because he has no car."²⁷⁸ However, she went on to explain that the car ride deteriorated into a dangerous event when "He got mad because I don't want to get back with him anymore. He almost made us crash 3 times …. I dropped him off and left."[279] In her petition for injunction, she stated that they were separated since December 3, 2004, because Leonard hit her in the face with his "full fist."[280] She also described how he grabbed her by the neck and threw her up against the wall.[281] At the time she filed her petition for injunction, an ongoing dissolution of marriage action (DOM) between the parties was filed as well.[282] Amanda was awarded a temporary injunction against Leonard, but the case was dismissed at the final hearing.[283]

During the middle of the night on March 7, 2007, Sheriff's deputies responded to calls regarding a dangerous shooting at an apartment complex.[284] Residents believed a woman was inside the apartment involved and had sustained a gunshot wound.[285] Deputies found the apartment's front door ajar, so they entered to find Amanda lying on the bed face up.[286] She was shot several times in the chest and hands.[287] There was no sign of Leonard in the apartment, but he later called for help from a different location.[288] Amanda was pronounced dead at the scene.[289] Leonard was arrested for second degree murder for which he plead nolo contendere and was adjudicated guilty on May 8, 2008.[290] He was sentenced to a maximum of twenty-five (25) years in prison for killing Amanda.[291]

Separated or Estranged

For this study, "separated or estranged" is a subtheme of resistance to abuse that explains that the IPV victim and the abuser are no longer living together or are living together but in different quarters of the marital home. In this study, 5.8% of the 493 cases and 46.0% of the sixty-two (62) cases, as well as 37.0% of the 100 petitions for injunction analyzed in this phase, resulted in a separated or estranged coding. Only cases with explicit or implicit information on separation or estrangement were identified for this subtheme. This subtheme is replete with phrases explaining that the parties have "been separated,"[292] "divorce,"[293] he/she left, etc. Donna Wood wrote, "We each have a separate residence and take turns going to the marital home to care for the children."[294] Meloney Jackson wrote:

> [M]y husband has left voluntarily. The week before Christmas my husband left … he decided to move back in the first of April …. We don't sleep in the same room. We have not slept together. He has said he is there to run me off because he wants the house.[295]

Other petitions for injunction do not reflect an IPV victim stating directly that their spouse was separated or estranged; however, the context of the writing makes it clear that was the couple's current relationship status. For example, Jennifer Wilkerson wrote:

> [He] came to my home at 2:30 am .... I told him he could not be here .... I asked him four or five times to leave. I called the police. His mom came over trying to get him to leave. I'm afraid he will come back .... Police told him he could not come back.[296]

Mesac Damas wrote, "she knows that I have another girl .... She being having a boyfriend .... I try to move on."[297]

Astacio v. Astacio

On October 18, 2010, Ena Sonia Astacio detailed an event that occurred between her and her estranged husband, Jorge, on October 7, 2010.[298] She explained that the married couple of thirty-two years were separated but living in the same home.[299] She became very afraid of Jorge when he requested access to a military knife given to him as a gift.[300] As a result of her fear of Jorge, she fled the home with the intent to go to the police station.[301] Jorge followed her, so she stayed in her car in a parking lot for two hours because she was afraid to go home.[302] She informed the court that she was a victim of DV throughout the course of her marriage to Jorge and that he engages in sex with her daughter who is his stepdaughter.[303] She told the court that he "become[s] intoxicated ... and beat[s] her."[304] Because of her fear from past abuse and the most recent incident, she requested the court's protection; however, it was denied.[305]

The night of January 8, 2012, police were called regarding a shooting at the Astacio home.[306] Ena Sonia and Jorge were both found dead by one of their daughters who was inside the home with her boyfriend and a toddler at the time of the shooting.[307] The couple was involved in a verbal argument that escalated, causing Jorge to retrieve a handgun.[308] He shot Ena Sonia several times; and then, shot himself in the head.[309] Authorities explained that the couple was dealing with tragedy due to having lost two of their daughters in a violent car accident in 2009; but, specifically, stated that "[t]here's nothing at this point that shows any history of domestic violence."[310]

Wallace-Taylor v. Taylor

On September 19, 2013, Watisha Wallace-Taylor explained to the court that her estranged husband, Elton Taylor, who no longer lived with her "Threaten [sic] to blow my face off if I called his mother to tell her that he was threatening me and that I was a bitch and he hate [sic] me, he then snatched my cell phone broke it and threw it out the car while driving."[311]

When the Intimate Partner Violence Victim Resists the Abuse 183

She detailed to the court how he continued to come to her home and that he stated, "when he snaps he [sic] going to kill me first."[312] In her petition for injunction, she explained to the court that he had not lived with her had their home since an incident that occurred in July 2013 whereby he was arrested for aggravated domestic battery.[313] She was granted a temporary injunction the day she filed her petition for injunction and received a final injunction on October 2, 2013, that was to remain in effect until October 12, 2014.[314] On September 30, 2013, she filed for DOM against Elton.[315]

For several months after the entry of the final injunction, Watisha stayed at her parents' home because she was in fear of something bad happening if she stayed with Elton in their house.[316] And, in fact, on the night of October 20, 2013, Elton violated the final injunction when he forcibly entered the Wallace family home "armed with a black automatic handgun."[317] He demanded to know where Watisha was and began to look through the home by going up the stairs.[318] When he found her, he dragged her down the stairs by her shirt and took her to the back yard.[319] Meanwhile, he threatened to shoot any of the family members in the home who tried to assist Watisha who was screaming "Elton, Elton' 'What are you doing?"[320] Once outside, he shot Watisha multiple times, killing her on the scene.[321] Elton went back into the home to find the others who barricaded themselves in an upstairs bedroom.[322] He broke into the bedroom, hit them over the head with the back of the handgun several times, and pointed the gun at them.[323] At this point, he left to go back outside and shot the gun twice, attempting to kill himself.[324]

Authorities found Watisha and Elton lying side-by-side in the backyard of the home; however, Elton survived his gunshot wound.[325] He was treated for his injuries and arrested for first-degree murder, as well as several other counts including aggravated battery and false imprisonment.[326] Prosecutors argued for the death penalty due to the "shockingly evil" nature of his execution style murder of Watisha; however, after four hours of deliberation, the jury determined that a life sentence was appropriate.[327]

Abuser Mental Illness

For this study, "abuser mental illness" is a theme that indicates the abuser has a history of, or tendency toward, a wide range of conditions that affect mood, thinking, and behavior, i.e., mental disorder or is dealing with some type of mental disorder. In this study, 1.8% of the 493 cases and 14.2% of the sixty-two (62) cases, as well as 11.0% of the 100 petitions for injunction analyzed in this phase, resulted in an abuser mental illness coding. This theme involved many IPV victim's amateur diagnoses of their spouses' mental health issues or a declaration of their spouses' mental health diagnoses from professionals. Marquita Green provided an example of such a narrative when she wrote:

> [He] has an addiction to alcohol. [He] has also been diagnosis [sic] with a post traumatic stress disorder & he is suppose [sic] to take medication but he is not taking any. [He] also refuses to be under the care of a psychiatrist.[328]

In another injunction for protection, Marquita wrote that her husband was supposed to be "evaluated/diagnosis [sic] for PTSD (Post Traumatic Stress Disorder)."[329]

In her September 2008 petition for injunction, Kalowti Dhani, discussed throughout this book, referenced the Baker Act.[330] In 1998, Sandy Brunson explained that her husband stood in the middle of a highway trying to kill himself.[331] Other narratives, such as the one written by Marilyn Welch in May 2013 above, combine with the subtheme of "helping abuser" because one spouse may feel obligated or sympathetic to the other due to their mental health issues even when IPV is present.[332]

Finn v. Finn

On July 6, 2012, Sheriff's deputies responded to the home of Kristen and Michael Finn regarding an assault that took place in which Michael threw a piece of pizza at Kristen.[333] Kristen denied any physical injuries from the incident.[334] However, the deputy's report is significant because it states that Kristen and Michael advised him that Michael was diagnosed with a type of condition for which he was being medicated and that Michael "denied wanting to hurt himself or others."[335] In fact, Michael was arrested after an investigation into this incident; and his condition warranted the necessity of advising the nursing staff and the book-in sergeant at the county jail.[336] He was charged with misdemeanor domestic battery, but it was amended to disorderly conduct by the state attorney for entry of the final judgment.[337] He was found guilty and had to pay a fine.[338] The court gave him credit for time served.[339]

By November 26, 2013, Kristen and Michael were separated; and she attempted to describe to the court the extent of the immediate threat of physical harm she was in fear of due to her his erratic and menacing behavior.[340] She began her petition by explaining that Michael sent multiple threatening text messages to her within minutes of each other on November 22, 2013.[341] The first text she quoted threatened her by stating "you keep putting [me] in these places and pushing me closer to murder, that's right murder."[342] The next one said, "That's right you pushed me beyond crazy. You don't deserve to live and see your kids grow up. You deserve to be mutilated torchered [sic] for months until you finally die."[343] The next text read, "Yeah, I am now crazy Congratulations you now have to look over your shoulder. Every minute I have had to sit here, in ect. in mental hospitals your [sic] going to be torcherted [sic] you selfish bitch."[344] The final text that went directly to her stated, "Oh call the cops eventually i ll [sic] get out and you will feel the pain Im [sic] going through. Oh Richard I know your [sic] reading this ... fuck you too."[345]

Michael was arrested for these threatening texts.[346] During his arrest, he told the deputy that "when he is released from jail and the mental ward that he is going to stab [Kristen] to death."[347] He continued to tell the deputy that "he might just cut her up and disfigure the victim so that the children have to look at her disfigurement every day."[348] While Michael was at the county detox facility under an ex-parte order, he became aggravated and started to pull pictures from the wall and smashed them on the floor.[349] At least four picture frames and the glass within them were destroyed.[350] Michael was arrested at the scene for this incident, but he was released from jail on December 2, 2013.[351] On December 18, 2013, this criminal felony case was transferred to county court as a misdemeanor criminal mischief case.[352] He was found guilty for his threats against Kristen.[353]

Kristen was provided a temporary injunction for protection against Michael on November 26, 2013, the same day she filed her petition for injunction; and she received a final injunction from the trial court on December 10, 2013.[354] However, on August 22, 2014, a petition for dismissal of the final injunction was filed, which the court granted on September 9, 2014.[355] As a result, the injunction case against Michael was dismissed on September 9, 2014.[356]

On May 9, 2015, one and a half years after her petition for injunction, local Sheriff's Office Deputies were called to a DV incident at Kristen and Michael's home.[357] Kristen decided to give him another chance for the children's sake.[358] Upon arrival, deputies witnessed Kristen, with apparent stab wounds, running from Michael, and he was holding a knife.[359] As Michael was immediately placed into custody and unaware of Kristen's condition, deputies heard him state to one of his children, who also witnessed the incident, "I should have killed her."[360] As he was in the process of being transported to the Sheriff's Office, Michael continued to make spontaneous statements in the back of the patrol vehicle, "'Is my wife dead,' 'She'll live, I didn't hit any vital organs,' and 'Guess some people have to learn the hard way.'"[361] In his post-Miranda interview, Michael admitted to taking a kitchen knife, chasing Kristen across the street from their home, and stabbing her.[362]

On the 911 recording, Kristen explained that she had been battered by Michael, that he had gone out of sight; and then, she is heard saying "'Michael don't come near me,' 'Michael stay away from me,' and 'leave me alone.'"³⁶³ After that, Kristen is heard screaming continuously.³⁶⁴ The local County Sheriff explained how they heard Kristen being stabbed to death on the 911 tape, "Her last words were 'I'm dying, I'm dying.'"³⁶⁵ She suffered eleven wounds total, eight in the back, one in the chest, and two in the left arm.³⁶⁶ The Sheriff explained that Kristen's violent death was particularly "unthinkable," especially because it occurred in front of her fifteen-year-old daughter on Mother's Day weekend.³⁶⁷

Michael was charged with first degree murder for Kristen's death and held in jail without bond.³⁶⁸ Shortly thereafter, he was deemed incompetent to stand trial and was placed in a treatment facility.³⁶⁹ However, after receiving proper treatment and medication, by mid-2016, he was deemed competent to stand trial; and the case was set for trial in November 2016.³⁷⁰ Initially, prosecutors sought the death penalty, but trial was postponed again to allow for negotiations on the state's plea offer of life in prison.³⁷¹ Michael was sentenced to life in prison for Kristen's death but died from suicide while in custody at the South Florida Reception Center on January 13, 2017.³⁷²

Dunn v. Dunn

On October 1, 2007, Christine Dunn filed for DOM from her husband, Robert.³⁷³ Less than two weeks later, on October 12, 2007, she filed a petition for injunction explaining that

> Robert Dunn suffers from depression .... He sent emails to his sister of threats of suicide to himself .... And do not know how stable he is with his depression .... He said he was going to get help and then he left town. I fear for my saftey [sic] and my daughter's not knowing what kind of condition he is in. I have filled [sic] for divorce and tempory [sic] custudy [sic] of our child.³⁷⁴

Christine was not provided a temporary injunction for her petition, but the court set a hearing to have her petition heard on October 23, 2007.³⁷⁵ However, the same day of the hearing, a request for dismissal was filed, ending the case.³⁷⁶

Three months later, on January 25, 2008, Robert went to Christine's place of employment, a daycare, looking for her with a handgun.³⁷⁷ People outside of the daycare center, who saw Robert prior to his entry into the building, called 911 to report a suspicious male with a handgun.³⁷⁸ He tried to enter the front door of the building but did not have the access code, so he walked to the rear of the building.³⁷⁹ In the process, he shot the gun toward an employee's car.³⁸⁰ During this time, employees and teachers were becoming aware of the situation and were working to protect the children inside the building as best they could by locking doors and taking them to interior bathrooms.[381]

As Robert entered the building through the rear door, he was met with an employee who he pointed the gun at and told her to be still.[382] As he passed her and went down the hallway toward the classrooms, he saw a parent and asked, "her with the gun yelling, 'where is that bitch'!?"[383] The parent attempted to lead Robert out of the building, but he turned into "'Miss Christy's' classroom" and found Christine hiding with her class.[384] He fired the gun at Christine, hitting her before the parent was able to grab his arm and pull it down.[385] Once he threw the parent to the ground, he shot at Christine again; but the parent grabbed him.[386] Robert and the parent fell to the ground, and she was able to wrestle the gun away from him before he fled out the front door.[387] As he did so, police officers were arriving and took him into custody without incident even though he wanted them to shoot him.[388] Christine was pronounced dead at the scene.[389] None of the children or adults at the daycare were injured in the incident.[390]

The initial investigation revealed that the daycare center was aware of the DV issues between Christine and Robert and that "for a time, the daycare was 'locked down' daily to keep Robert away and the employees/children of the daycare safe."[391] Once investigators spoke to Dunn, who agreed to speak to them after being read his Miranda Warnings, he explained that he "snap[ped]" after being served with financial disclosures as part of the divorce process.[392] It was at this point that we purchased a gun from a pawn shop and began the process of planning to shoot Christine.[393] In the same interview, he explained "that he wanted her to feel the same pain that he was feeling and that she was not going to take his child away from him."[394] He also planned to kill himself after killing Christine.[395]

On January 25, 2008, the same day as the shooting, Robert was arrested for first degree murder and subsequently held with no bond.[396] But on February 21, 2008, the State Attorney amended the murder charge to second degree murder with a firearm and added the charge of first degree burglary while armed (structure) with a firearm.[397] On the same day, Robert filed a Written Plea of Not Guilty to these charges.[398] However, on March 13, 2008, Robert was indicted by a grand jury and formally arraigned on three counts, Count (I) first degree murder, Count (II) first degree burglary while armed (structure) with a firearm, and Count (III) child abuse.[399] On April 25, 2008, the state of Florida filed its Notice of Intent to Seek Death Penalty, which set in motion the requirement of the defendant, Robert Dunn, to provide "written notice of intent to present testimony of a mental health professional in order to establish a statutory or nonstatutory mental mitigating circumstance or circumstances" not less than twenty days before trial.[400] After which, long, costly litigation ensued that culminated in a trial, beginning in October 2012.[401]

After multiple appointments of experts at the state's expense and Robert's requests to remove his attorneys from his case, as well as medical testing for brain trauma and questions of competency to stand trial, the trial was under way with the apparent defense theory that any culpability should be removed or mitigated due to his mental health status both before and at the time of the killing.[402] However, because of the circumstances surrounding Christine's death, meaning it was during the course of a burglary, i.e., felony murder and committed in front of children, the state had the potential of sufficient aggravators to successfully obtain a death penalty sentence.[403] But by the end of the six week trial, after Robert was found guilty on all three counts, during the sentencing phase, "the defense presented 99 mitigating circumstances, and the state started with five aggravating circumstances."[404]

As part of its presentation during the sentencing phase of the trial, the defense presented three experts to testify regarding Robert's mental disorder that caused him to be Baker Acted, as well as to battle bouts of depression and manic behavior.[405] His attorney explained that Robert's medical records leading up to the killing showed that he had a "mental health breakdown" but that he was placed on the wrong medication and was turned away when he tried to seek help.[406] His attorney further explained that Robert "was misdiagnosed for years with depression, or even personality disorder, but he actually suffers from bipolar disorder."[407] The jury heard a full presentation of the mitigating circumstances regarding Robert's sentencing during four days of testimony and recommended life in prison.[408] On January 28, 2013, the court agreed with that recommendation and sentenced Robert to life in prison.[409]

Drinking Alcohol

For this study, "drinking alcohol" is a subtheme of abuser mental illness that indicates the abuser drinks alcohol in excess or to the point that the IPV victim believed it necessary to raise this fact. In this study, 3.0% of the 493 cases and 23.8% of the sixty-two (62) cases, as well as 19.0% of the 100 petitions for injunction analyzed in this phase, resulted in a drinking alcohol coding. All drinking alcohol cases in this study were coded as such because the IPV victim stated that the abuser was drinking, was addicted to alcohol, was intoxicated, or some variant thereof.[410] Often, this drinking alcohol subtheme combined with the drug use subtheme, as detailed below, because the abuser might have been combining the substances that were used at any given time.

Vargas-Brevick v. Brevick

On June 3, 2009, Francia Vargas described an incident to the court in which her fiancé, David Brevick, "was completely intoxicated (drunk)."[411]

She explained that he was threatening her and her family who were in the house, as well as falling all over the furniture.[412] She continued to detail episodes of physical violence that previously occurred in which David assaulted her, and while attempting to prevent her from screaming, he suffocated her to the point she thought she was going to die.[413] When describing another past incident of physical violence, she attributed it to the fact that "he was drinking very heavily."[414] During this incident, he broke two or three of her ribs.[415] Francia was awarded a temporary injunction against David for her petition for injunction but filed a motion to dissolve the injunction prior to the final hearing.[416]

Four years later, on May 26, 2013, David was arrested for domestic battery against Francia and her son.[417] The police report describing the incident indicated that, while David was drunk, he pushed Francia against the wall.[418] Then he slapped her son with an open fist before continuing to push Francia down against her will.[419] On October 25, 2013, the court disposed of the case because the prosecutor entered a nolle prosequi.[420]

On July 18, 2014, under Florida's Marchman Act, Francia petitioned the court to have David involuntarily treated for drug and alcohol abuse.[421] In the petition, she wrote that "[h]e abuses drugs & alcohol ie, cocaine, pain pills & alcohol to excess."[422] The court granted the petition, but she filed a motion to dismiss it three days later because she believed David left the country for rehab.[423] She told the court she felt safe and secure.[424]

However, on August 8, 2014, sheriff's deputies were dispatched in response to a call from David Brevick who stated that multiple people were inside his house and were "choking out" his wife, Francia.[425] But when the dispatcher asked for details of the intruders and descriptions of the individuals, he was not able to provide any information, including whether they had any weapons.[426] At one point during the call, he yelled out "I'm sure I'm gonna get the fucking blame, but I didn't do it."[427] When deputies arrived at the home, it was dark and secure.[428] At that time, David was still speaking to dispatch but was uncooperative.[429] Shortly after, he appeared at the front door completely naked, sweating profusely, with a cordless phone in his hand, and appeared confused.[430] However, he did tell deputies that the men who were in his house were getting away, and he wanted the deputies to stop them.[431] However, the deputies did not observe any other individuals in or around the home; so, David was secured and placed in their patrol car.[432]

Once inside the home, deputies found Francia lying on the bedroom floor, naked and unresponsive.[433] She appeared to have suffered from various trauma to her head and neck.[434] Deputies were not able to find a pulse, so they began life-saving measures that were continued when fire and rescue teams arrived.[435] She was transported to the hospital where she was placed on critical condition.[436] Meanwhile, deputies began their investigation of the home and realized that the alarm system did not activate until they arrived on the scene.[437] Upon further investigation, they determined that "the only persons present at the time [of the offense] was the defendant, the victim and her elderly mother, [], who was awakened by the responding deputies."[438]

On August 10, 2014, Francia passed away from her injuries.[439] The following day, the medical examiner performed an autopsy and determined that she had "multiple contusions on her arms, scratches and abrasions on the front and back of her neck, and a large contusion on the frontal and parietal regions of her head."[440] Other internal injuries were noted that were consistent with manual strangulation.[441] As a result, the medical examiner concluded that Francia's "cause of death was manual strangulation and the manner of death was homicide."[442] Thus, on August 11, 2014, a warrant for David's arrest for first degree murder was issued; and on September 9, 2014, he was indicted for the same.[443] But after an extensive trial, he was found guilty of second degree murder and sentenced to life in prison.[444]

White v. White

Janelle and Broze White had a tumultuous marriage with both making reports to the police and Broze filing petitions for injunction.[445] The first reported incident to the sheriff's department came from Janelle on March 13, 1999 who explained that Broze, who was a paraplegic and confined to a wheelchair, fell out of his wheelchair trying to hit her.[446] Deputies responded and the couple stated they would stay away from each other for the rest of the night.[447] Shortly after this event, deputies were called to a convenience store by Broze because Janelle was "drunk and had attacked him" and "he was in fear for his life from his wife."[448] He showed the deputy where she grabbed him around his arms and chest.[449] When the officer confronted Janelle at their residence, she was still drinking beer and was placed under arrest for domestic battery.[450] On the way to the jail, she explained to the deputy that "it was a good thing [he] stopped by there [sic] house last week because she was about to beat the holy shit out of [Broze]."[451] She also explained that she had bruised him previously.[452] Nevertheless, her domestic battery misdemeanor case was dismissed at Broze's request.[453]

On September 3, 1999, another sheriff's department reported to the local sheriff's department that Janelle was out drunk and causing problems.[454] When local deputies arrived at the White's home, Broze told them Janelle had probably gone to the corner bar; but she was not located there either.[455] Because Janelle was not found, the local sheriff's department contacted Broze to instruct him to call them if she returns and begins to cause problems.[456] Shortly thereafter, Broze called the local sheriff explaining that Janelle was back at their home and was drunk; so he got his brother to help him with leaving their house.[457]

Within two weeks, on September 17, 1999, Broze called the sheriff's office for help because Janelle had been drunk for three days.[458] He tried to barricade himself in his bedroom, but she broke down the door.[459] He rigged their truck to prevent her from driving drunk when she threatened to leave, causing her to hit him and turn his wheelchair over.[460] When deputies arrived, they found Broze sitting on the ground in their yard with his wheelchair overturned.[461] Janelle "admitted to dumping her husband out of the wheelchair."[462] She was arrested for battery, pled guilty, and was sentenced to jail for sixty days.[463] She was also placed on probation for twelve months.[464] But by November 14, 2000, Broze was still needing sheriff's deputies' assistance in dealing with Janelle's alcohol abuse.[465] He called for a deputy to escort him into his home, so he could obtain his medicine because Janelle was drunk.[466] He planned to stay at a motel and was concerned she might prevent him from doing so.[467]

On March 5, 2001, Broze filed a petition for injunction explaining that in 1999 Janelle attacked him while she was drunk.[468] He continued to explain to the court that she currently drinks and that he feels threatened when she does so to the point of him fearing for his life.[469] As he continued in his narrative, he detailed to the court about his handicap and the fact that he was limited in his means of self-protection, stating he would have to take "drastic measures" to protect himself that included having to hurt Janelle.[470] But he was denied any type of relief for his petition. Additionally, on March 5, 2001, Janelle called the local sheriff's office to speak to a deputy because she and Broze were having problems.[471] She did not want him back in their home.[472]

On May 12, 2002, Janelle called the sheriff's office regarding what she believed was a suicide attempt by Broze.[473] He took an unprescribed amount of a generic form of Xanax to "mello [sic] out and get some sleep" rather than to harm himself or to "check out permanatley [sic]."[474] Deputies and EMS ensured he was conscious until transported to the hospital.[475] He was not Baker Acted for this incident.[476]

On August 21, 2003, Janelle filed for DOM against Broze; and on September 15, 2003, Broze answered Janelle's petition for DOM, including filing a counterpetition against her.[477] However, according to official documents, the couple remained in the same home together for years after.[478] And on September 2, 2004, Broze filed a second petition for injunction explaining that Janelle "told [him] that she was going to blow [his] fucking head off" and went to another room within the home to obtain a gun to do so.[479] He continued to explain that he heard her preparing the gun, so he called 911.[480] He also described the drinking that she had done in the past, as well as the fact that she had begun drinking again recently.[481] Broze was provided a temporary injunction on September 2, 2004; however, it was dismissed after a hearing on September 3, 2004.

Six and one-half years later, on March 19, 2011, the sheriff's office was contacted by Janelle and Broze's neighbor, with whom they had a close relationship, to conduct a welfare check on the couple because she had not seen them since March 17, 2011.[482] The neighbor knew both Broze and Janelle for eleven years and, typically, had daily contact with them.[483] She was concerned because she could see their animal locked inside the home, which was not normal; and they did not keep their normal Friday evening dinner and cards date with her.[484] Over the past couple days, she attempted different ways to reach Janette and Broze but to no avail.[485] Even more alarming was a hole in the vinyl siding of what she knew to be Broze's bedroom wall.[486] She was concerned he might have had a medical emergency, considering the fact that he was wheelchair bound.[487] However, once deputies gained entrance into the home, they discovered Janelle and Broze inside the bedroom together, dead from gunshot wounds to the head.[488] Autopsy reports confirmed the fact that Janelle was shot by Broze before he shot himself.[489] There were no other indications of injury to either of them.[490]

Drug Use

For this study, "drug use" is a subtheme of abuser mental illness that indicates the abuser uses illegal drugs or prescription drugs other than as prescribed. In this study, 0.8% of the 493 cases and 6.3% of the sixty-two (62) cases, as well as 5.0% of the 100 petitions for injunction analyzed in this phase, resulted in a drug use coding. All drug use cases in this study were coded as such because the IPV victim stated that the abuser was using cocaine, smoking crack, abusing prescription drugs, or some variant thereof.[491]

Peacock v. Peacock

On June 21, 2011, Christy Peacock filed her petition for injunction explaining to the court that, her husband, Billy, left their home for "the fourth time to go smoke crack with his buddy."[492] Indeed, prior to the filing of her petition, court records show that Billy had an issue with possession of controlled substances.[493] In her petition, Christy elaborated that Billy was currently using their home to eat and sleep but, then, was leaving "to go smoke crack for a week."[494] She explained that she was concerned about the drugs being around her children and wanted Billy in rehab.[495] Within this same petition, she detailed the fact that Billy struck her arm and cussed at her.[496] She also provided information about Billy placing a choke hold on her son and squeezing his arm.[497] She was provided a temporary injunction against Billy but was not successful in obtaining a final injunction.

On July 12, 2011, Billy filed for DOM; and on August 17, 2011, Christy filed a second petition for injunction, claiming that Billy was "driving around property out of control drinking and doeing [sic] drugs in his vehicle."[498] She explained to the court again that "[e]very other week he goes off and smokes crack."[499] She also expressed frustration with the fact that she called the sheriff's office for assistance related to Billy's drug activity; and, according to her petition narrative, deputies did not "have probable cause to search or arrest him" even though they retrieved crack cocaine from him.[500] However, she also stated that she was afraid of what Billy would do to her when he gets out of jail.[501] This contradiction, i.e., Billy being in jail even though she said deputies did nothing, can be explained by a sheriff's report attached to Christy's petition for injunction, which provides details about Billy's encounter with deputies on August 16, 2011.[502] The deputy's report supports Christy's version of the facts as presented in her petition related to Billy's drug use; however, contrary to her affidavit, it explained that Billy was arrested for possession of drugs.[503] Christy was provided a temporary injunction for her petition but was not provided a final injunction.

Billy faced four counts of possession of controlled substances and paraphernalia related to the incident on August 16, 2011.[504] On October 1, 2011, he violated his bond by driving under the influence and being in possession of cocaine and narcotic equipment.[505] On April 11, 2012, he entered a plea of nolo contendere and was found guilty on all counts.[506] He served six months, ten days in the county jail after which he was placed on probation.[507] Meanwhile, a final judgment of DOM was entered on May 3, 2012.[508] However, the court docket for the DOM explains that there was ongoing post-final judgment litigation well into mid-2014 between Christy and Billy that seemed to center on child related issues, such as child support and child custody.[509] But by January 2015, the couple was back together and working on their relationship when, in the middle of the night on January 19, 2015, Christy stabbed Billy in his sleep.[510]

Billy was the first person to call 991 in which he repeated many times while struggling to breathe and maintain consciousness, "I'm about to die' and 'my girlfriend stabbed me."[511] In his second phone call to 911, Billy, continuing to have a hard time breathing and staying conscious, told the dispatcher that it was Christy who stabbed him.[512] Christy fled the scene to her neighbors but surrendered when she was found about a mile away by deputies.[513] Once she was in custody and read her Constitutional Rights, Christy made several spontaneous statements, "'I couldn't take it anymore' and 'I wanted him out of my life.'"[514] At the police station, while taking a shower to wash off all the blood from the stabbing, Christy made several more spontaneous statements about Billy and her relationship, saying that they had just moved back in together a few days ago and that she "snapped" because she could not handle the abuse anymore.[515] She also explained that "'he' was the 'devil' and he was trying to take her daughter away from her."[516]

Once in the interview room at the police station, Christy was read her Constitutional Rights again and decided she needed an attorney.[517] The interview, meaning any type of questioning from detectives, was immediately stopped; however, Christy continued to make spontaneously statements for another fifty-one minutes, thirty-two seconds while the audio/video recording continued.[518] At the beginning of the time in the interview room, Christy did not know that Billy was deceased.[519] During the time she spoke without any questioning, Christy explained that Billy had given her some sleep-aide medication to help her sleep.[520] She explained that she remembered lying in bed, dozing off, not being able to go to sleep; and when she woke up, she had a knife in her hand, while Billy was trying to get it from her.[521] She continued to make additional, spontaneous statements, "'I just snapped' .... 'I lost it, I guess'. 'I would never want to hurt him, I love him' ....'The Devil made me do what I did' .... 'I plea insanity, he drove me crazy'."[522] Throughout this time, Christy referred to Billy as the "Devil."[523] When she found out about Billy's death, she said, "'I didn't mean to do that' [and] 'That's not what I was trying to do'."[524] Based on the sheriff's observations of Christy from the audio/video recording, she was placed on suicide watch for three days once she was transported to the detention facility.[525]

After a Grand Jury convened and heard the evidence in February 2015, Christy was indicted for one count of premeditated murder on February 13, 2015.[526] Through further investigation, it was revealed that Christy and Billy were undergoing counseling and treatment for several issues, including those related to child custody battles, dating back to 1996.[527] Part of the counseling and treatment involved urinalysis testing that began in March 2014 of which Billy passed all, but Christy failed each test although neither took them weekly as scheduled.[528] Drugs in Christy's system on April 11, 2014 included THC, cocaine, morphine, oxycodone, d-amphetamine, benzodiazepines, d-methamphetamine, and codethyline.[529] Her urinalysis and blood samples after the killing came back positive for illegal narcotics as well.[530]

Throughout the murder investigation, additional information emerged about Billy and Christy's relationship, such as the fact that Christy feared Billy was molesting their young daughter.[531] She formally accused him of such in 2010; but DCF determined there was no abuse or sexual abuse.[532] Additionally, Christy attempted suicide by trying to overdose in the past.[533] Christy had eleven Jail Incident Reports between June 18, 2012, and April 24, 2015, four of which stated she was "involve[d in] verbal disputes and/or disrespect to Correction Officers."[534] After an extensive investigation, it was determined that Billy died from "'multiple stab wounds' 'to the head, face, chest, back, arms, left hand and right foot'" inflicted by Christy.[535] On May 17, 2017, a little more than two years after killing Billy, she pled guilty to the lesser charge of second degree murder and was sentenced to 35 years in state prison.[536]

Paranoia

For this study, "paranoia" is a subtheme of abuser mental illness that describes "1. mental illness characterized by systematized delusions of persecution or grandeur usually without hallucinations; 2. A tendency on the part of an individual or group toward excessive or irrational suspiciousness and distrustfulness of others" that manifests in statements or acts by the abuser, such as threats to kill themselves or accusing the IPV victim of seeing another person.[537] 3.4% of the 493 cases and 26.9% of the sixty-two (62) cases in this study, as well as 17.0% of the 100 petitions for injunction analyzed in this phase of this study resulted in a paranoia coding. As Dobash et al. (2009) explain, many abusers who commit IPH may have mental health issues, including jealousy and possessiveness, i.e., manifestations of paranoia.[538] Indeed, jealousy and possessiveness were phrases that flowed throughout the coding of this subtheme, although some of the other issues involved the abusers thinking people were after them in general. Comments from IPV victims relating to jealousy and possessiveness include accusations by the abuser that the victim was cheating on them by seeing someone else or having sex with someone else.

Common statements for this coding include phrases such as one written by Glenda Nuñez, who is detailed in the subtheme of Nonfatal Strangulation, "he became very aggressive and threatning [sic] stating that if he and I could not be together he would not allow me to be with anyone else."[539] In another case, Amanda Cloaninger, detailed in the subtheme of Animal Abuse, explained that her husband, "[o]n numerous occasions, ... told me he would cut me up or kill me if he ever found out I was cheating."[540] Still, another, Amy Daley, detailed in the subtheme of Surveillance, explained that her husband "accuses me of cheating on him."[541] And one of the most chilling accounts given by an IPH victim in this subtheme reads as follows:

> This day, [he], waited outside my apt. door around 6:30 pm when I opened the door .... He took my phone from my purse and went through my text messages. He called a friend and yelled, cursed at him and asked him to meet him. As I tried to go out the door several times he just block [sic] the way pushing me back. He pushed me on my couch, sat on my lap while he read the txt's [sic]. I told him that I was going to call the police and he said I will be dead.[542]

This narrative was written in October 2012 by Pamela Allen, who is detailed in Chapter 8 in the subtheme of Rape and Sexual Abuse.[543]

Harp v. Harp

On March 4, 2008, Demetria Bennett explained to the court that on March 2, 2008, her abuser, Cedric Harp, pointed a gun at her and threatened to kill her and her kids because he was suspicious of her cheating on him.[544] She detailed how they had been arguing because she called her sister-in-law about her brother having left his keys at work with her.[545] Demetria was trying to arrange for her brother's friend to retrieve the keys from her, but Cedric became enraged.[546] He began calling her names and "talk[ing] alot [sic]of shit."[547] That is when he pulled out the gun, pointed it at her, and threaten to kill her.[548] When her son heard her screaming, he came to check on the situation and was able to diffuse it.[549] Cedric left at that point but returned about an hour later, so Demetria called the police.[550] He was arrested and charged with aggravated assault with a deadly weapon, possession of a firearm by a convicted felon, possession of cannabis, and possession of drug paraphernalia.[551] Demetria was awarded a temporary injunction, but she failed to appear at the hearing for the final injunction.[552] As a result, the injunction case was dismissed on March 18, 2008.[553] Eventually, Cedric's criminal case was terminated via an entry of nolle prosequi by prosecutors on July 8, 2008.[554] And on September 4, 2008, Demetria and Cedric were married.[555]

On the morning of December 17, 2009, Cedric entered the local police department to report "that he had hit his wife too hard and possibly killed her."[556] He explained to the officer on duty that "he hit his wife hard and she stopped breathing."[557] With that information, officers arrived at the Harp home to find Demetria dead on the bed in master bedroom.[558] Cedric explained that they had been arguing for a while and decided to separate.[559] They were together, sexually the morning of her death; but when she began to pack her things afterwards, a physical altercation began.[560] Cedric eventually punched Demetria in the back of the head, causing her to fall to the floor.[561] He attempted to revive her but realized she stopped breathing, so he placed her on the bed.[562] Then, he drove to the police station to explain what happened.[563]

Detectives determined that the scene of the crime was consistent with Cedric's statement to police.[564] The medical examiner's report confirmed the same.[565] As a result, he was arrested and charged with second degree murder.[566] On March 4, 2011, he entered a plea of nolo contendere to manslaughter and was sentenced to six months in the county jail and five years of probation.[567] However, by August 15, 2011, Cedric violated his probation and was under arrest for aggravated battery by strangulation and grand theft of a motor vehicle.[568] This was the beginning of several post-conviction probation violations that eventually caused a resentencing order that sent him to prison for ten years for Demetria's death.[569]

When the Intimate Partner Violence Victim Resists the Abuse

Nevertheless, according to court records, his violation of probation was dismissed on June 3, 2015; and he was released from probation on December 15, 2016.[570]

Notes

1. Olms v. Olms, 2009-DR-21006, 5 (2009) (Pet. for Inj. for Prot. Against Dom. Viol.). *See supra* Chapter 6, Humiliation, Degradation.
2. *See* S. Acosta & B. Plasencia, PD1107283039 at 1; J. Gonzalez, PD120816312110 at 1–4; M. Pais, PD120923363338 at 1; Socarras, PD121005379428 at 1; E. Magarino, PD121214475435 at 1; Laveroe, PD130202043682 at 1; O. Balaez, PD130322106447 at 1–2; A. Salazar, PD130412135170 at 1; T. Solis, PD131210453864 at 1; K. Thompson, PD140102002732 at 1; S. Marshall, PD140105006524 at 1; Juliao, PD140221068175 at 1.
3. *See* Juliao, *supra* note 2. *See also* Raphael, PD140330116399 at 1.
4. Balaez, *supra* note 2 at 2.
5. Mantrana v. Mora, 13-009284-FC-04, 4 (2013) (Pet. for Inj. for Prot. Against Dom. Viol.). *See also* Juliao, *supra* note 2; Raphael, *supra* note 3.
6. Mantrana v. Mora, 13-009284-FC-04 (2013) https://www2.miamidadeclerk.gov/ocs/Search.aspx (last visited on March 12, 2023).
7. *Id.*
8. *See* Raphael, *supra* note 3 at 1–2.
9. *See Id.* at 1–2.
10. *See Id.*
11. *See Id.*
12. *See Id.*
13. *See Id.*
14. *See Id.*
15. *Id.* at 2.
16. Nicholson v. Nicholson, 04-2667-CA, 5 (2004) (Pet. for Inj. for Prot. Against Dom. Viol.).
17. *Id.* at 5–7.
18. Dragic v. Dragic, 50-2003-DR-003129-DVFA-MB, 4 (2003) (Pet. for Inj. for Prot. Against Dom. Viol.).
19. Dragic v. Dragic, 50-2003-DR-003129-DVFA-MB (2003) https://appsgp.mypalmbeachclerk.com/eCaseView/search.aspx (last visited March 13, 2023).
20. *Id.*
21. State of Florida v. Dragic, 50-2004-MM-021531-AXXX-MB, 2 (2004) (Probable Cause Aff.).
22. *Id.*
23. *See* State of Florida v. Dragic, 50-2004-MM-021531-AXXX-MB (2004) https://appsgp.mypalmbeachclerk.com/eCaseView/search.aspx (last visited March 13, 2023); State of Florida v. Dragic, 50-2004-MM-021531-AXXX-MB (2004) (Mt. to Restrict Telephone Privileges).
24. Dragic v. Dragic, 50-2004-DR-014082-XXXX-MB, 3 (2004) (Pet. for Inj. for Prot. Against Dom. Viol.).
25. Dragic v. Dragic, 50-2004-DR-014082-XXXX-MB (2004) https://appsgp.mypalmbeachclerk.com/eCaseView/search.aspx (last visited March 13, 2023).
26. State of Florida v. Dragic, 50-2004-MM-031953-AXXX-MB, 2 (2004) (Probable Cause Aff.).

27 State of Florida v. Dragic, 50-2004-MM-031953-AXXX-MB (2004) (Agreed Order to Modify Def. Plea & Pass Agreement).
28 State of Florida v. Dragic, 50-2004-MM-031953-AXXX-MB (2004) (Nolle Prosse).
29 Dragic, https://appsgp.mypalmbeachclerk.com/eCaseView/search.aspx (last visited March 13, 2023).
30 Schooley, 10131118 at 3.
31 *Id.*
32 *Id.* at 4.
33 *Id.*
34 State of Florida v. Dragic, 50-2010-CF-011372-AXXX-MB, 2 (2010) (Probable Cause Aff.).
35 *Id.* at 3.
36 *Id.* at 2–3.
37 *Id.* at 3.
38 *Id.*
39 *See Id.*; State of Florida v. Dragic, 50-2010-CF-011372-AXXX-MB (2010) https://appsgp.mypalmbeachclerk.com/eCaseView/search.aspx (last visited March 13, 2023).
40 Manning, UCSO06OFF000850 at 1.
41 *Id.*
42 *Id.*
43 *Id.*
44 *Id.*
45 *Id.* at 2.
46 Hilliard, UCSO05OFF001200 at 1.
47 *Id.*
48 *Id.*
49 *Id.*
50 *Id.*
51 *Id.* at 2.
52 *Id.* at 1–2.
53 *Id.* at 2.
54 *Id.*
55 *Id.*
56 *Id.*
57 *Id.*
58 *See generally* Bailey v. Bailey, 632006DR194 (2006) (Pet. for Inj. for Prot. Against Dom. Viol.).
59 *Id.* at 3.
60 *Id.*
61 *Id.*
62 *Id.*
63 Smith, UCSO09OFF000095 at 1.
64 *Id.*
65 *Id.*
66 *Id.*
67 *Id.*
68 *Id.*
69 *Id.* at 2.
70 *Id.*

71 Id.
72 Id. at 1.
73 Id.
74 Id.
75 Id.
76 Id.
77 Seay, UCSO09OFF000110 at 2.
78 Id.
79 Id.
80 See generally Id.
81 Nicholson v. Nicholson, 04-2667-CA, 8 (2004) (Pet. for Inj. for Prot. Against Dom. Viol.).
82 Harvey, BCSO07OFF000942 at 7–8.
83 Id. at 4, 8.
84 Id. at 4.
85 Wilkerson v. Wilkerson, 02-2007-DR-080, 3 (2007) (Pet. for Inj. for Prot. Against Dom. Viol.).
86 Id.
87 Id.
88 Harvey, *supra* note 82 at 8.
89 Id.
90 Id.
91 See generally Id.
92 Id. at 4.
93 Id. at 5.
94 Id. at 4.
95 Id.
96 Id.
97 See Id. at 7.
98 See Id.
99 See Id.
100 See Id.
101 Id. at 6.
102 Id.
103 Id. at 7.
104 Id. at 6.
105 Id.
106 See Id. at 7.
107 Id.
108 Id.
109 Id. at 5.
110 Id.
111 Id. at 8.
112 Id.
113 Id.
114 Id.
115 Id. at 4.
116 Id.
117 Id.
118 Id.
119 Id. at 5.

120 *Id.*
121 *Id.*
122 Brunson v. Brunson, 98-977 CA, 2–3 (1998) (Pet. for Inj. for Prot. Against Dom. Viol.).
123 *Id.* at 3.
124 Nicholson v. Nicholson, 04-2667-CA, 4 (2004) (Pet. for Inj. for Prot. Against Dom. Viol.).
125 Goraya v. Goraya, 07-001114DR, 2–3 (2007) (Pet. for Inj. for Prot. Against Dom. Viol.).
126 Wood v. Wood, 05-14620-FD-9, 3–5 (2005) (Pet. for Inj. for Prot. Against Dom. Viol.). *See supra* Chapter 5, Intimidation, Threats.
127 Green v. Green, 2012-DR-001583-DVBX, 4 (2012) (Pet. for Inj. for Prot. Against Dom. Viol.). *See supra* Chapter 6, Power and Control, Household, Clothes, and Personal Belongings Destroyed.
128 *See supra* Chapter 6, Power and Control, Household, Clothes, and Personal Belongings Destroyed.
129 *See* Craft-Enzor v. Enzor, 53-2008DR-005086-0000-00, 2 (2008) (Pet. for Inj. for Prot. Against Dom. Viol.).
130 *See Id.*
131 *See Id.*
132 *See Id.*
133 *See Id.* at 3–4.
134 State of Florida v. Enzor, CF11-000001, 1 (2011) (Probable Cause Aff.).
135 *Id.*
136 *Id.* at 1–2.
137 *Id.* at 2.
138 *Id.*
139 *Id.*
140 *Id.*
141 *Id.*
142 *Id.*
143 *See* State of Florida v. Enzor, CF11-000001, 8 (2012) (Commitment Checklist); Jason Geary, *Lakeland Husband Gets Life in Prison for Killing Wife*, THE LEDGER (April 24, 2012).
144 *See* Geary, *supra* note 143.
145 Goyette, 10-09017 at 3.
146 *Id.*
147 *Id.*
148 *Id.*
149 *Id.*
150 *Id.*
151 *Id.*
152 *Id.*
153 *Id.*
154 *Id.*
155 *Id.*
156 *Id.*
157 *Id.*
158 *Id.*
159 Feacher v. Music, 2010DR002996, 10 (2010) (Pet. for Inj. for Prot. Against Dom. Viol.).

160 *Id.* at 4.
161 *Id.*
162 *Id.*
163 *Id.* at 5.
164 *Id.*
165 Feacher v. Music, 2010DR002996 (2010) https://courtcasesearch.stlucieclerk.gov/BenchmarkWebExternal/CourtCase.aspx/Details/1886829?digest=b3MkOXwJs2H3pLJrPtNTKg (last visited March 19, 2023).
166 State of Florida v. Music, 562014CF001992A, 1 (2014) (Arrest Aff.).
167 *Id.*
168 *Id.*; Johnston, 14-07078 at 7.
169 Music, 562014CF001992A at 1.
170 *Id.*
171 *Id.*
172 *Id.*
173 *Id.* at 2.
174 *Id.*
175 *Id.*
176 *Id.*
177 *Id.*
178 *Id.*
179 *Id.*
180 *See Id.*
181 *Id.*
182 *Id.*
183 *Id.*
184 *Id.*
185 *See Id.*
186 *See Id.*
187 *See Id.*
188 *See Id.*
189 *Id.*
190 *Id.*
191 *Id.*
192 *Id.*
193 *Id.*
194 *Id.*
195 *Id.*
196 *Id.*
197 *Id.* at 3.
198 *Id.*
199 *Id.*
200 *Id.*
201 *Id.*
202 *Id.*
203 *Id.* at 4.
204 *See Id.* at 3–4.
205 *Id.* at 4.
206 *Id.* at 1.
207 State of Florida v. Music, 562014CF001992A, 1 (2015) (Letter to Judge).
208 *Id.*

209 *Id.*
210 State of Florida v. Music, 562014CF001992A, 1 (2015) (Judgment).
211 *See Id.*; State of Florida v. Music, 562014CF001992A (2014) https://court casesearch.stlucieclerk.gov/BenchmarkWebExternal/CourtCase.aspx/Details/21 94831?digest=QKweMV8h5iXsxdL%2FIULCiQ (last visited March 23, 2023).
212 Moretz, ECSO06OFF006725 at 3.
213 *Id.*
214 *Id.*
215 *See* Eddins, ECSO06OFF008210 at 3.
216 *See* Moretz, *supra* note 212. *See generally* Tubwell v. Welch, 06-DR-747 (2006) (Pet. for Inj. for Prot. Against Dom. Viol.).
217 *See* Tubwell, 2006-DR-000747 at 4.
218 *See Id.* at 4–5.
219 *See* Tubwell v. Welch, 2006-DR-000747 (2006). *See also* Tubwell v. Welch, 2010-DR-002065, 2 (2010) (Pet. for Inj. for Prot. Against Dom. Viol.).
220 Eddins, *supra* note 215.
221 *Id.*
222 *Id.* at 2–3.
223 *See* State of Florida v. Welch, 2006-CF-001657 (2006).
224 *See* Welch, Tony.
225 *See generally* Tubwell v. Welch, 2010-DR-002065 (2010) (Pet. for Inj. for Prot. Against Dom. Viol.).
226 *Id.* at 4.
227 *Id.*
228 *Id.*
229 *Id.*
230 Tubwell v. Welch, 2010-DR-002065 (2010). *See also* Tubwell v. Welch, 2010-DR-003085, 2 (2010) (Pet. for Inj. for Prot. Against Dom. Viol.).
231 Tubwell v. Welch, 2010-DR-003085, 2 (2010) (Pet. for Inj. for Prot. Against Dom. Viol.).
232 Swearingen, ECSO10OFF019625 at 1–2.
233 *Id.* at 3.
234 *Id.*
235 *Id.*
236 *Id.*
237 *See Id.*
238 *See Id.*
239 *See* Welch, Tony.
240 *See generally* Tubwell v. Welch, 2010-DR-003085 (2010) (Pet. for Inj. for Prot. Against Dom. Viol.).
241 *Id.* at 4.
242 *Id.*
243 *Id.*
244 Tubwell v. Welch, 2010-DR-003085 (2010).
245 Welch v. Welch, 2011-DR-004545, 1 (2011) (Pet. for Inj. for Prot. Against Dom. Viol.).
246 Jordan, ECSO11OFF034160 at 3.
247 State of Florida v. Welch, 2011-MM-027002 (2011).
248 Welch, 2011-DR-004545 at 4.
249 *Id.*

250 Tubwell v. Welch, 2013-DR-001662, 3 (2013) (Pet. for Inj. for Prot. Against Dom. Viol.).
251 *Id.*
252 *See Id.*
253 *Id.*
254 *Id.* at 3–4.
255 *Id.* at 4.
256 *Id.*
257 Nelson, ECSO13OFF015328 at 4.
258 *Id.*
259 *Id.*
260 *Id.*
261 *Id.* at 2.
262 State of Florida v. Welch, 2013-CF-002726 (2013).
263 Smallwood Jr., ECSO14OFF002738 at 1–2.
264 *See* Welch, Tony.
265 *See* Smallwood Jr., *supra* note 263 at 4.
266 *See Id.*
267 *See Id.*
268 *See Id.*
269 *See Id.*
270 Paine, ECSO14OFF011277 at 6.
271 *Id.* at 8.
272 *Id.*
273 *Id.*
274 *Id.*
275 *Id.* at 13.
276 *Id.* at 14.
277 *Id.*
278 Morrow v. Morrow, 2005DR000286, 2 (2005) (Pet. for Inj. for Prot. Against Dom. Viol.).
279 *Id.*
280 *Id.* at 3.
281 *Id.*
282 *Id.* at 5. *See also* Morrow v. Morrow, 2004DR0117370 (2004) https://pro.polkcountyclerk.net/PRO/PublicSearch/Details/XYA7KZ3nXNNnk1P27-27-0RcNR9CcO6BYk6EvKG4dHdR8Wng%3d (last visited March 24, 2023).
283 Morrow v. Morrow, 2005DR000286 (2005) https://pro.polkcountyclerk.net/PRO/PublicSearch/Details/LKzHBplWq8BUDjyLyaxwqgpA6Y0HOBL10v7qj3A3W3g%3d (last visited March 24, 2023).
284 Carver, 2007-047119 at 1.
285 *Id.*
286 *Id.*
287 *Id.*
288 *Id.* at 1–2.
289 *Id.* at 1.
290 State of Florida v. Morrow, 2007CF00180001 (2007) https://pro.polkcountyclerk.net/PRO/PublicSearch/Details/ZmIkHU0-0-TsZ3aeNbwggkI4iswP75SU4sMlnlwowfk9eo%3d (last visited March 24, 2023).
291 *Id.*

292 Astacio v. Astacio, 2010-029210-FC-04, 4 (2010) (Pet. for Inj. for Prot. Against Dom. Viol.); Mantrana v. Mora, 13-009284-FC-04, 4 (2013) (Pet. for Inj. for Prot. Against Dom. Viol.); Morrow v. Morrow, 2005DR000286, 3 (2005) (Pet. for Inj. for Prot. Against Dom. Viol.).
293 Dunn v. Dunn, 07-002347DR B, 3 (2007) (Pet. for Inj. for Prot. Against Dom. Viol.); Gordon v. Gordon, 14-735-DV, 5 (2014) (Pet. for Inj. for Prot. Against Dom. Viol.); Marshall v. Marshall, 97-3133-DR-06-G, 3 (1997) (Pet. for Inj. for Prot. Against Dom. Viol.).
294 Wood v. Wood, 05-14620-FD-9, 5 (2005) (Pet. for Inj. for Prot. Against Dom. Viol.).
295 Jackson v. Jackson, 2007-DR-000202, 4 (2007) (Pet. for Inj. for Prot. Against Dom. Viol.).
296 Wilkerson v. Wilkerson, 02-2007-DR-080, 3 (2007) (Pet. for Inj. for Prot. Against Dom. Viol.).
297 Damas v. Damas, 05-1753-DR, 3–5 (2005) (Pet. for Inj. for Prot. Against Dom. Viol.).
298 *See generally* Astacio v. Astacio, 2010-029210-FC-04 (2010) (Pet. for Inj. for Prot. Against Dom. Viol.).
299 *See Id.* at 1–2, 4.
300 *Id.* at 4.
301 *Id.*
302 *Id.*
303 *Id.*
304 *Id.*
305 *See Id. See also* Astacio v. Astacio, 2010-029210-FC-04 (2010) https://www2.miamidadeclerk.gov/ocs/Search.aspx (last visited March 24, 2023).
306 Gonzalez, PD120108010783 at 2.
307 *Id.*; Justin Finch & Brian Hamacher, *Police Investigate Murder-Suicide in Miami-Dade*, NBCMIAMI.COM (January 9, 2012).
308 Gonzalez, *supra* note 306.
309 *Id.*
310 Finch & Hamacher, *supra* note 307 at ¶ 8.
311 Wallace-Taylor v. Taylor, 50-2013-DR-009926XXXX-MB, 4 (2013) (Pet. for Inj. for Prot. Against Dom. Viol.).
312 *Id.*
313 *See Id.*; State of Florida v. Taylor, 50-2013-CF-007530-AXXX-MB (2013) (Probable Cause Aff.).
314 Wallace-Taylor v. Taylor, 50-2013-DR-009926XXXX-MB (2013) https://appsgp.mypalmbeachclerk.com/eCaseView/search.aspx (last visited March 25, 2023).
315 *Id.*
316 *See* Taylor, 50-2013-CF-011180-AXXX-MB at 2.
317 *Id.*
318 *Id.*
319 *Id.* at 2–3.
320 *Id.* at 3.
321 *Id.* at 2.
322 *Id.* at 4.
323 *See Id.*
324 *See Id. See also* Daphne Duret, *Elton Taylor Gets Life Sentence in Wife's 2013 West Palm Beach Murder*, THE PALM BEACH POST (March 14, 2018).

325 Gellin, 2013-0018014 at 3.
326 *See Id.*; State of Florida v. Taylor, 50-2013-CF-011180-AXXX-MB, 1 (2013) (Probable Cause Aff.).
327 Marc Freeman, *Man Sentenced to Life for Murdering Estranged Wife*, ¶ 6 SUN SENTINEL (March 14, 2018).
328 Green v. Green, 2012-DR-001583-DVXX, 4–5 (2012) (Pet. for Inj. for Prot. Against Dom. Viol.).
329 *Id.* at 4.
330 *See* FLA. STAT. § 394.463(1)(2)(b)(1) (2023). *See supra* Chapter 5, Intimidation. *See also* Dhani v. Dhani, 53-2008DR-007905, 3 (2008) (Pet. for Inj. for Prot. Against Dom. Viol.).
331 Brunson v. Brunson, 98-977 CA, 4 (1998) (Pet. for Inj. for Prot. Against Dom. Viol.).
332 Tubwell v. Welch, 2013-DR-001662, 3 (2013) (Pet. for Inj. for Prot. Against Dom. Viol.).
333 *See* Nason, 2012-055905 at 1.
334 *See Id.*
335 *See Id.*
336 *See Id.*
337 *See* State of Florida v. Finn, 2012-MM-007898, 1 (2012) (Information for); State of Florida v. Finn, 2012-MM-007898, 1 (2012) (Judgment).
338 *See* State of Florida v. Finn, 2012-MM-007898, 1 (2012) (Judgment).
339 *See Id.*
340 Finn v. Finn, 53-2013DR-010012-0000-00, 4–5 (2013) (Pet. for Inj. for Prot. Against Dom. Viol.); Hammersla, 130049104 at 2.
341 Finn, 53-2013DR-010012-0000-00 at 4.
342 *Id.*
343 *Id.*
344 *Id.*
345 *Id.*
346 Hammersla, *supra* note 340 at 1–2.
347 *Id.* at 2.
348 *Id.*
349 *Id.* at 4.
350 *Id.*
351 *Id.*; State of Florida v. Finn, 13CF-9597-XX (2013) (Order Granting Pretrial Release).
352 *See* State of Florida v. Finn, 13CF-9597-XX (2013) (Transfer Memo).
353 State of Florida v. Finn, 2013MM-013138 (2013) (Judgment).
354 *See* Finn v. Finn, 53-2013DR-010012-0000-00 (2013) https://pro.polkcounty clerk.net/PRO/CaseSearch/Details/TlPjDCGAKm0u1Gt8JWSshxON5id5tg I0untn0-0-t7g4n4%3d (last visited Jan. 6, 2023).
355 *Id.*
356 *Id.*
357 *See* Christopher Katsoulis, 150020706 at 2.
358 *Id.*; Jonathan Petramala, *Years of Threats Led to Stabbing of Lakeland Mother*, WTSP.COM (May 11, 2015).
359 Katsoulis, *supra* note 357.
360 *See Id.*
361 *Id.*
362 *Id.*

363 *Id.*
364 *Id.*
365 Petramala, *supra* note 358.
366 *Id.*
367 *Lakeland Man Charged with Murder in Stabbing Death of Wife*, West Orlando News, para. 7 (May 10, 2015).
368 *Id.*
369 *Michael Finn, Lakeland Man Serving Life for Murder of His Wife, Dies in State Prison*, The Ledger, para. 9 (Jan. 17, 2017).
370 *Id.*
371 *Id.* at para. 3, 9.
372 *Id.* at para. 1; Office of the Inspector General, *Criminal Investigation Investigative Assist, Case #17-00984*, Florida Department of Corrections (2017).
373 Dunn v. Dunn, 07-DR-007997 (2007) https://matrix.leeclerk.org/Case/ViewCase (last visited May 2, 2023).
374 Dunn v. Dunn, 07-DR-002347, 2–3 (2007) (Pet. for Inj. for Prot. Against Dom. Viol.).
375 Dunn v. Dunn, 07-DR-002347, 2–3 (2007) https://matrix.leeclerk.org/Case/ViewCase (last visited May 2, 2023).
376 *Id.*
377 Grau, 08-001679 at 2.
378 *Id.*
379 *Id.*
380 *Id.*
381 *Id.*
382 *Id.*
383 *Id.*
384 *Id.*
385 *Id.*
386 *Id.*
387 *Id.*
388 *Id.* at 2–3.
389 *Id.* at 3.
390 *Id.*
391 *Id.*
392 *Id.*
393 *See Id.*
394 *Id.*
395 *Id.*
396 State of Florida v. Dunn, 08-14594CF (2008) (Record of First Appearance Hearing/Order).
397 State of Florida v. Dunn, 08-14594CF (2008) (Information for).
398 State of Florida v. Dunn, 08-14594CF (2008) (Written Plea of Not Guilty).
399 State of Florida v. Dunn, 08-14594CF (2008) (Indictment for); State of Florida v. Dunn, 08-14594CF (2008) (Booking Charges).
400 State of Florida v. Dunn, 08-14594CF, 1 (2008) (Notice of Intent to Seek Death Penalty).
401 *See* State of Florida v. Dunn, 08-14594CF (2008) https://matrix.leeclerk.org/Case/ViewCase# (last visited May 3, 2023). *See also* Terry Lenamon & Reba

Kennedy, *Another Example of the Florida Indigent Defense Budget Crisis: Robert Dunn Discovery Needs*, TERRY LENAMON ON THE DEATH PENALTY: SIDEBAR WITH AN EXPERT CAPITAL LITIGATOR (October 7, 2010) https://www.deathpenaltyblog.com/another-example-of-the-florida-indigent-defense-budget-crisis-robert-dunn-discovery-needs/; Spencer Cordell, *Category Archives: Robert Dunn*, CRIMCORTS: A CRIMINAL LAW BLOG, https://crimcourts.wordpress.com/category/florida/cape-coral-southwest-florida/robert-dunn/page/2/ (last visited May 3, 2023).

402 *See* State of Florida v. Dunn, 08-14594CF (2008) https://matrix.leeclerk.org/Case/ViewCase# (last visited May 3, 2023). *See also* Lenamon & Kennedy, *supra* note 401; Cordell, *supra* note 401; *Life in Prison Recommended for Convicted Murderer*, PINE ISLAND EAGLE (December 11, 2012).

403 *See* Lenamon & Kennedy, *supra* note 401; Cordell, *supra* note 401; *Life in Prison Recommended for Convicted Murderer*, *supra* note 402.

404 *Life in Prison Recommended for Convicted Murderer*, *supra* note 402 at ¶ 13. *See also* State of Florida v. Dunn, 08-14594CF (2008) (Judgment).

405 *Life in Prison Recommended for Convicted Murderer*, *supra* note 402.

406 *Id.* at ¶ 11.

407 *Id.* at ¶ 8.

408 *See Id.*

409 Dunn, 08-14594CF.

410 *See* Goraya v. Goraya, 07-001114DR, 2 (2007) (Pet. for Inj. for Prot. Against Dom. Viol.); Green v. Green, 2012-DR-001583-DVBX, 4 (2012) (Pet. for Inj. for Prot. Against Dom. Viol.); Huss v. Huss, 03-485DV, 2 (2003) (Pet. for Inj. for Prot. Against Dom. Viol.).

411 Vargas v. Brevick, 2009-DR-029967, 12 (2009) (Pet. for Inj. for Prot. Against Dom. Viol.).

412 *Id.*

413 *Id.* at 13–14.

414 *Id.* at 14.

415 *Id.*

416 Vargas v. Brevick, 2009-DR-029967 (2009) https://vmatrix1.brevardclerk.us/beca/all_results.cfm?x=4BB88F8C738788AC99BFD224CC0A2DDB7BD6E7BF9D13E70DF60AE8DBDFCBC76526FA6ABFEBD34D16D7B733171ED4D4FE (last visited May 3, 2023).

417 State of Florida v. Brevick, 2013-MM-060950 (2013) (Arrest/Notice to Appear).

418 *Id.*

419 *Id.*

420 State of Florida v. Brevick, 2013-MM-060950 (2013) (Court Minutes/Order-Plea).

421 *See* Andrew Ford, *Rockledge Man Charged with Murder in Death of Wife*, FLORIDA TODAY (August 12, 2014). The Florida Marchman Act is a Florida Statute that was created "to help individuals who: 1) have lost the power of self-control over their substance abuse; 2) do not appreciate their own need for help and cannot make rational decisions regarding their care as a result of their substance abuse; 3) have become a danger to themselves or others." (Marchman Act Florida, *Marchman Act Overview*, https://marchmanactflorida.com/marchman-act-general/ (last visited May 3, 2023)).

422 Ford, *supra* note 421 at ¶ 2.

423 *See Id.*

424 See Id.
425 State of Florida v. Brevick, 2014-CF-37674, 1 (2014) (Affidavit for Arrest Warrant).
426 See Id.
427 Id. at 2.
428 See Id.
429 See Id.
430 See Id.
431 See Id.
432 See Id.
433 See Id.
434 See Id.
435 See Id.
436 See Id.
437 See Id.
438 Id. at 2–3.
439 See Id.
440 Id. at 3.
441 See Id.
442 Id. at 3.
443 See Id.; State of Florida v. Brevick, 2014-CF-37674 (2014) (Indictment for).
444 See State of Florida v. Brevick, 2014-CF-37674 (2014) https://vmatrix1.brevardclerk.us/beca/all_results.cfm?x=4BB88F8C738788AC99BFD224CC0A2DDB7ADBE7B88913E70CF805E9D8DFD2C76526FA6ABFEBD34D16D-7B733171ED4D4FE (last visited May 3, 2023); State of Florida v. Brevick, 2014-CF-37674 (2014) (Judgment); Chris Bonanno, *Rockledge Man Gets Life in Prison for Wife's Murder*, FLORIDA TODAY (January 6, 2015).
445 See generally 1999030294 at 1; 1999030559 at 1–2; 1999090078 at 1–2; 2000110297 at 1; 2001030115 at 1–2; 2002050346 at 1–2; White v. White, 2001-0068-CA (2001) (Pet. for Inj. for Prot. Against Dom. Viol.); White v. White, 2004-0266-CA (2004) (Pet. for Inj. for Prot. Against Dom. Viol.).
446 See 1999030294, *supra* note 445.
447 See Id.
448 1999030559, *supra* note 445 at 1.
449 See Id. at 1–2.
450 See Id.
451 Id. at 2.
452 See Id.
453 See State of Florida v. White, 1999-MM-000146 (1999) (Plea of Guilty/No Contest).
454 See 1999090078, *supra* note 445 at 2.
455 See Id.
456 See Id.
457 See Id.
458 See State of Florida v. White, 1999-MM-000474 (1999) (Plea of Guilty/No Contest).
459 See Id.
460 See Id.
461 See Id.
462 Id. at 3.
463 See Id.

464 See Id.
465 See 2000110297, *supra* note 445.
466 See Id.
467 See Id.
468 See White v. White, 2001-0068-CA, 4 (2001) (Pet. for Inj. for Prot. Against Dom. Viol.).
469 See Id.
470 See Id.
471 See 2001030115, *supra* note 445 at 2.
472 See Id.
473 See 2002050346, *supra* note 445 at 2.
474 Id.
475 See Id.
476 See Id.
477 See White v. White, 2003-DR-000264 (2003) https://www.civitekflorida.com/ocrs/app/caseinformation.xhtml?query=QQKtKaj1TejIpXjsaAwE8hMHy1KlFmLeOZR0X9NvhSo&from=partyCaseSummary (last visited May 10, 2023).
478 See White v. White, 2004-0266-CA, 1–2 (2004) (Pet. for Inj. for Prot. Against Dom. Viol.); Bryant, 2011030555 at 3.
479 White v. White, 2004-0266-CA, 4 (2004) (Pet. for Inj. for Prot. Against Dom. Viol.).
480 Id.
481 Id.
482 See Bryant, *supra* note 478.
483 See Id.
484 See Id. at 4.
485 See Id. at 3–5.
486 See Id. at 5.
487 See Id.
488 See Id. at 6.
489 See Id. at 10.
490 See Id.
491 See Dunn v. Dunn, 07-002347DR, 3 (2007) (Pet. for Inj. for Prot. Against Dom. Viol.); Hogan-Mccarthren v. Mccarthren, 2012-DR-001236, 4 (2012) (Pet. for Inj. for Prot. Against Dom. Viol.); Peacock v. Peacock, 11-281-DR, 4 (2011) (Pet. for Inj. for Prot. Against Dom. Viol.).
492 Peacock, 11-281-DR at 4.
493 See State of Florida v. Peacock, 2008CF000454 (2008) https://www.civitekflorida.com/ocrs/app/partyCaseSummary.xhtml (last visited May 11, 2023); State of Florida v. Peacock, 2008CF000468 (2008) https://www.civitekflorida.com/ocrs/app/partyCaseSummary.xhtml (last visited May 11, 2023).
494 Peacock, 11-281-DR at 7.
495 Id.
496 Id. at 4.
497 Id.
498 Id. See also Peacock v. Peacock, 2011DR000314 (2011) https://www.civitekflorida.com/ocrs/app/caseinformation.xhtml?query=j1RZCeU0j9QBmXAAcAQOkTKUBwEtfMj1JE7v4je3ygw&from=partyCaseSummary (last visited May 11, 2023).
499 Peacock v. Peacock, 11-376-DR, 4 (2011) (Pet. for Inj. for Prot. Against Dom. Viol.).

500 *Id.*
501 *Id.*
502 *See generally Id.*
503 *See generally Id.*
504 *See* State of Florida v. Peacock, 2011CF000318 (2011) (Information); State of Florida v. Peacock, 2011CF000318 (2011) (Plea of Not Guilty and Demand for Jury Trial).
505 *See* State of Florida v. Peacock, 2011CF000318 (2011) (Affidavit Violation of Bond).
506 *See* State of Florida v. Peacock, 2011CF000318 (2011) https://www.civitekflorida.com/ocrs/app/caseinformation.xhtml?query=tChums085MBSOrN2ZUFMTOs6BOUfsJHBCp7oDhHWyVk&from=partyCaseSummary (last visited May 11, 2023).
507 *See Id.*
508 *See* Peacock v. Peacock, 2011DR000314 (2011) https://www.civitekflorida.com/ocrs/app/caseinformation.xhtml?query=j1RZCeU0j9QBmXAAcAQOkTKUBwEtfMj1JE7v4je3ygw&from=partyCaseSummary (last visited May 11, 2023).
509 *See Id.*
510 *See* Hasty, WCSO15OFF000122 at 14; Sean Rossman, *Tallahassee Woman Charged with Murder in Morning Stabbing*, Tallahassee Democrat (January 20, 2015).
511 Hasty, *supra* note 510 at 23.
512 *Id.* at 24.
513 *Id.* at 15.
514 *Id.* at 17.
515 *Id.* at 16.
516 *Id.*
517 *Id.* at 18.
518 *Id.* at 18, 25.
519 *Id.* at 25.
520 *Id.*
521 *Id.*
522 *Id.* at 25–26.
523 *Id.* at 26.
524 *Id.*
525 *Id.* at 18.
526 *Id.* at 28.
527 *Id.* at 29.
528 *Id.*
529 *Id.* at 30.
530 *Id.* at 36.
531 *Id.* at 35.
532 *Id.*
533 *Id.* at 36.
534 *Id.*
535 *Id.* at 42.
536 *See generally* State of Florida v. Peacock, 15-8CF (2015) (Corrected J.).
537 Dictionary, *Paranoia*, Merriam-Webster.com, https://www.merriam-webster.com/dictionary/paranoia (last visited March 5, 2023).

538 Dobash et al., *"Out of the Blue:" Men Who Murder an Intimate Partner*, 4 FEMINIST CRIMINOLOGY 194, 199–200 (2009) https://doi.org/10.1177/1557085109332668.
539 Nunez v. Nunez, 2007DR014851, 3 (2007) (Pet. for Inj. for Prot. Against Dom. Viol.). *See infra* Chapter 8, Physical Violence, Nonfatal Strangulation.
540 Cloaninger v. Colley, DR15-1136, 5 (2015) (Pet. for Inj. for Prot. Against Dom. Viol.). *See supra* Chapter 5, Intimidation, Animal Abuse.
541 Daley v. Benevides, 53-2007DR-003064, 3 (2007) (Pet. for Inj. for Prot. Against Dom. Viol.). *See supra* Chapter 5, Intimidation, Surveillance.
542 Allen v. Allen, 12-15371, 4 (2012) (Pet. for Inj. for Prot. Against Dom. Viol.).
543 *See generally Id. See infra* Chapter 8, Physical Violence, Rape and Sexual Violence.
544 *See* Bennett v. Harp, 2008-DR-0003342, 3 (2008) (Pet. for Inj. for Prot. Against Dom. Viol.).
545 *See Id.*
546 *See Id.*
547 *Id.* at 3.
548 *See Id.*
549 *See Id.*
550 *See Id.*
551 *See* State of Florida v. Harp, 2008CF003299 (2008) https://myeclerk.myorangeclerk.com/CaseDetails?cItem=UYNmZj%2BMy3ZqA4UUhksCvPmQCSWJxlIV4cqzxOPOnFy%2Fy%2BA30bnJh0ihEOTpcXy6XWOCHAIX4M3LNXu4T3N%2BSyHQxG%2BLRaqJYDIHonSuBI0%3D (last visited May 12, 2023).
552 *See* Bennett v. Harp, 2008-DR-0003342 (2008) (Temporary Injunction for Protection against Domestic Violence without Minor Child(ren)); Bennett v. Harp, 2008-DR-0003342 (2008) (Order of Dismissal of Temporary Injunction for Protection against Domestic Violence).
553 *See* Bennett v. Harp, 2008-DR-0003342 (2008) (Order of Dismissal of Temporary Injunction for Protection against Domestic Violence).
554 *See* Harp, 2008CF003299.
555 Dept. of Health, MLW-08-0000690, STATE OF FLORIDA, MARRIAGE RECORD (September 29, 2008).
556 State of Florida v. Harp, 09-CF-18200, 3 (2009) (Charging Affidavit).
557 *Id.*
558 *See Id.*
559 *See Id.*
560 *See Id.*
561 *See Id.*
562 *See Id.*
563 *See Id.*
564 *See Id.*
565 *See Id.*
566 *See Id.*
567 State of Florida v. Harp, 09-CF-18200 (2009) (Plea(s)).
568 State of Florida v. Harp, 09-CF-18200 (2009) (Affidavit Violation of Probation).
569 *See* State of Florida v. Harp, 09-CF-18200 (2009) (Order of Disposition – Resentencing). *See also* State of Florida v. Harp, 09-CF-18200 (2009) https://

myeclerk.myorangeclerk.com/CaseDetails?cItem=2IFGTBCIXF4g%2BFJI3G3ltPB4NoSv1Kgg62pEQjVvAEjXfLa7fVrngSshm5zk5wA00EE2kV49FvEe8sqD%2Bm7FuwqPeKCJeXnuYTBpeTTu%2FtQ%3D (last visited May 12, 2023).

570 State of Florida v. Harp, 09-CF-18200 (2016) (Termination of Supervision). *See also* State of Florida v. Harp, 09-CF-18200 (2009) https://myeclerk.myorangeclerk.com/CaseDetails?cItem=2IFGTBCIXF4g%2BFJI3G3ltPB4NoSv1Kgg62pEQjVvAEjXfLa7fVrngSshm5zk5wA00EE2kV49FvEe8sqD%2Bm7FuwqPeKCJeXnuYTBpeTTu%2FtQ%3D (last visited May 12, 2023).

8 Physical Violence, the Ultimate in Power and Control?

Physical acts of violence usually accompany other non-violent coercive control tactics; however, non-violent coercive control tactics are not needed to instill paralyzing fear in its victims.[1] The complex patterns of various forms of abuse begin slowly and, generally, do not take the form of physical harm. It is because of this slow indoctrination that many intimate partner violence (IPV) victims do not recognize they have become victims of coercive control. Indeed, for many generations, society has understood IPV as physical violence alone; and it is because of this societal expectation that coercive control victims do not see themselves as such since their harm typically stems solely from the non-physically violent forms of abuse.[2]

Physical Violence

For this study, "physical violence" is a theme that describes acts of physical violence by the abuser against the IPV victim; these acts may be simple battery not resulting in the IPV victim claiming cuts or bruising, such as having their shirt pulled. 10.7% of the 493 cases and 84.1% of the 62 cases in this study, as well as 75.0% of the 100 PIFPs analyzed in this phase of this study resulted in a physical violence coding. "Hit" and "face" are the two most coded words in the theme of physical violence, respectively. Common phrases in the physical violence theme include "grabbed my arm," "pushed me," and "hit me." Often, the specifics of the acts of physical violence were provided with other non-violent coercive control tactics, detailing again that coercive control tactics are not utilized in a mutually exclusive manner.

Redd v. Redd

An example of a case in which an IPV victim provided a multitude of coercive control tactics, including physical violence, in her petition for

DOI: 10.4324/9781003097488-11

injunction was written by Patricia Redd on April 15, 2005, in which she explained to the court that her husband, David:

> pushed me into the door jam. Just as he did 3 days prior when he shoved me and into my mother to the floor. Braking [sic] my 72 yr old mothers [sic] hip ... stating F_ _ _ Both of you Bitches. Punching holes in the wall, throwing beer bottles .... Making hateful & threatening remarks. I feared for my safety & well being and the continuous destruction of my home. I've been hit, pushed down, slapped & hair pulled on more than one occasion.[3]

Here, the theme of physical violence is explained, as well as the subthemes of (1) violent acts toward family and friends; (2) name calling; (3) degradation; (4) household, clothes, and personal belongings destroyed; and (5) fearful of the future. She continued to detail how David locked her out of their home in the rain when she was six months pregnant.[4]

For years leading up to Patty filing her petition for injunction, she and David interacted with the local sheriff's office regarding disputes with each other.[5] On February 6, 2000, sheriff's deputies were called out to the Redd home regarding a physical disturbance; however, by the time they arrived, Patty and David both explained that everything was fine.[6] Neither of them provided details as to any physical violence, and David left for the evening to stay with his father.[7] The next time sheriffs were called was on June 21, 2003.[8] Patty explained that David was drunk the night before and threw her and their child out of their home.[9] She wanted information on how to file for an injunction but did not want him going to jail.[10] She also told the deputy that this was not the first time this type of incident had happened, but she was reluctant to call about it in the past and did not want to have to in the future.[11] The next report to sheriff's coincides with Patty's petition for injunction described above and was filed on April 12, 2005.[12] However, the sheriff's report does not contain the detail Patty provided in her petition for injunction.[13] In fact, the sheriff's report states that neither Patty nor David accused the other of physical violence about which they were willing to file formal complaints.[14] However, Patty stated that David shoved her; and, due to the fact that he had hit her in the past, she called the sheriff's office.[15] They both agreed not to physically interact with each other, and David left to stay with his father.[16]

Patty received a temporary injunction for her petition filed on April 15, 2005; and on April 20, 2005, David filed a report with the sheriff's office explaining that Patty contacted him in violation of the injunction.[17] He told the deputy that Patty wanted to work things out and drop the injunction, but David wanted record of the contact because he did not want to get into any trouble.[18] Patty did not obtain a final injunction, and the last record of a sheriff's report by either David or Patty against the other (although they both had other run-ins with authorities for various and sundry reasons) occurred on September 25, 2005, when Patty reported David as "her soon to be ex husband."[19] She wanted the report for filing purposes based on her attorney's advice because she was going to David's home to obtain some of her personal belongings.[20]

For almost six years, Patty and David's relationship, according to the lack of any further reports to law enforcement or the court, appears to have improved. There is also no indication that the DOM was finalized. However, a close friend of Patty's explained that, by late August 2011, she began detailing arguments between David and her in which he would "threaten[] to 'kill' her."[21] However, Patty was not concerned about these threats because she hid a gun from him.[22] But she needed to accept money from the same friend to buy groceries, so things were not good at home.[23] As for David, friends described him as depressed and would find him "laying in the 'fetal position' and crying on the front porch."[24] He was struggling dealing with the death of his mother who died decades before in a car accident.[25] He confided in his friend that he missed his mother and father.[26]

During the early noontime hour of August 25, 2011, Patty called David's friend explaining that "David is acting crazy."[27] But the call disconnected.[28] When she called back, she stated that "David just poured kool-aid on me."[29] Again, the call disconnected.[30] The friend tried calling Patty back several times but was unsuccessful in reaching her.[31] Once he was able to physically go to the Redd home, he found Patty's vehicle in the driveway with the driver's door wide open.[32] When he got to the entrance of their home, the door was partially opened; and he found both Patty and David inside, deceased.[33] It was not immediately apparent to authorities how Patty and David were killed because there were no apparent entry wounds to their bodies found at the scene although David had a handgun under his left hand where he was found.[34] However, after the autopsies were performed, it was determined that both Patty and David were shot through their mouths without exit wounds.[35] David killed Patty "by an intermediate range gun shot wound to the mouth;" and, then, "died from a self inflicted intraoral gunshot wound."[36]

Grindrod v. Grindrod

On March 19, 2012, after nine years of marriage, Michael Grindrod was arrested for domestic battery against his wife, Sarah.[37] The incident occurred because the couple was arguing about one of their children, and it became physical as the family was in Michael's truck driving home from a family outing.[38] Sarah attempted to call for help, but he threw her phone out the window of the truck.[39] As the argument escalated, he began to grab her hair and punch her in her head and face.[40] She attempted to exit the truck while it was moving and, eventually, crawled through the back window of the truck.[41] Michael's version of the story was similar, except for the fact that (1) his beard was pulled by Sarah to the point that he lost hair, (2) he did not admit to punching her but described it as pushing her instead, and (3) he explained that he got them all home despite her grabbing the steering wheel several times while he was driving 60 miles per hour.[42] The responding deputy concluded that Sarah's injuries were consistent with her statement, explaining that Michael had punched and struck her.[43] Nevertheless, the state attorney determined there was insufficient evidence to prove the case against him; so, the charges were dropped.[44]

On March 20, 2012, Sarah filed a petition for injunction regarding this incident stating that Michael "repeatidly [sic] punched me in my head, threw my phone out the window and would not let me out. At home he took all of the keys so I could not leave."[45] In the police report about the incident, Michael explained that Sarah had been drinking; so, he hid the keys.[46] But the court granted Sarah's petition, providing her with a temporary injunction the same day she filed her petition.[47] On March 27, 2012, the court entered a final injunction against Michael that lasted until September 27, 2012.[48] In its order, the court required Michael to surrender all of his firearms and ammunition to the local sheriff's department.[49] Sarah was provided temporary exclusive use and possession of the marital home.[50]

On the morning of May 11, 2012, Michael arrived at the Grindrod home and confronted Sarah and a friend while Michael and Sarah's young boys were getting ready for school.[51] Michael hit Sarah's friend with a bat, causing all three adults to run outside of the home.[52] The younger boy stayed in the house and played with the blood, but the older boy followed the adults outside.[53] He witnessed Michael shoot at Sarah's friend and, then, he saw him shoot Sarah.[54] The young boy explained that he knew Michael got hurt as well; but he did not know how, "just that there was blood dripping down his chest."[55] The sheriff's investigation concluded that there was sufficient evidence to find probable cause for Michael's arrest for the charge of first degree murder for Sarah's death; however, because he took his own life by a gunshot to the chest, the case was closed as "Exceptionally Cleared due to Death of Offender."[56]

Aguilar v. Martinez

On November 6, 2001, Martha Aguilar and Juan DeJesus obtained their final judgment dissolving their marriage.[57] Ten years later, on July 23, 2011, Martha contacted the sheriff's office regarding a domestic violence (DV) incident between Juan and her in which he punched her in the face.[58] According to the sheriff's report, Martha and Juan were living together in the same apartment at the time of the incident.[59] Prior to her being struck by Juan, they passed by each other outside; and he stated to her "Get out of my way bitch."[60] In response, Martha stated "I'm not a bitch, stupid."[61] She explained to the deputy that she typically does not stand up for herself when Juan is verbally abusive for fear of him being physically abusive, but this time was different.[62] Juan was arrested for the incident, but there are no further records of any criminal case having gone forward.[63]

On August 19, 2011, Martha filed a petition for injunction related to this same incident.[64] Her petition narrative simply read that Juan "hit me in my left eye after an argument that we had causing him to act."[65] The court did not enter a temporary injunction but scheduled the case for a final hearing on August 31, 2011.[66] However, that final hearing was rescheduled to take place on September 14, 2011; and Juan was served with the subpoena for that hearing shortly after 1:00 p.m. on September 1, 2011.[67]

That same day, between 1:14 p.m. and 1:20 p.m., Juan shot and killed Martha while they were arguing about the injunction case Martha filed against him.[68] He fled the crime scene on foot, and a two-hour search involving "K-9 units, snipers, SWAT team members and one of the sheriff's office helicopters" ensued.[69] Two elementary schools were placed on lockdowns while the search for Juan was ongoing.[70] Eventually, he was shot to death by his step-son, Martha's son, who killed him in self-defense in front of the apartment where they lived.[71]

Nonfatal Strangulation

"Nonfatal strangulation," in this study, is a subtheme of physical violence that explains the IPV victim having their normal breathing, or blood flow to the brain, obstructed during violent acts committed by the abuser against the IPV victim. In this study, 2.6% of the 493 cases and 20.6% of the 62 cases, as well as 14.0% of the 100 PIFPs analyzed in this phase, resulted in a nonfatal strangulation coding. The two most commonly coded words in the subtheme of non-fatal strangulation are "pillow" and "choke," respectively. The two most common phrases throughout the subtheme of nonfatal strangulation "he tried to choke me" and "he put the pillow over my face." Thus, choking with bare hands and suffocating with a pillow seem to be the two most common forms of nonfatal strangulation.

Santiago Nuñez v. Nuñez

On December 11, 2007, Glenda Santiago Nuñez filed a petition for injunction stating that her estranged husband, Lorenzo, threatened to kill her if they could not be together.[72] Glenda filed for DOM on June 14, 2007, and

Lorenzo wanted to discuss the status of their relationship.[73] He asked her whether she was seeing anyone else and explained to her that "he would not allow [her] to be with anyone else."[74] She continued to explain to the court in her petition that in June 2007, during an argument with Lorenzo, he admitted to stealing their son's key to her home and making a copy of it to allow himself access to her home.[75] When she tried to call for help, he broke the home phone, as well as her cell phone to prevent her from doing so.[76] He then proceeded to grab her by the neck and choke her.[77] However, she explained that "when he realized that I was out of breath he stopped what he was doing and left my home."[78] Glenda was provided a temporary injunction the same day she filed her petition; and after a final hearing, the court entered a final injunction on December 26, 2007, against Lorenzo that was to remain in effect until June 26, 2008.[79]

On January 5, 2008, while the final injunction was still in effect, Lorenzo shot and killed Glenda inside her home.[80] Then, Lorenzo took his own life by a self-inflicted gunshot wound to the head.[81] Their fourteen-year-old son found them in the home.[82]

Brunson v. Brunson

On November 3, 1998, Sandy Brunson explained to the court that her husband, Tracey:

> grab [sic] me out of a friends [sic] car and dragged me across [the highway] then threw me to the ground and started choking me ... then he bend my arm back behind my should then put his knee in my chest and begin to choke me again saying that I'm going to die tonite [sic]."[83]

As explained earlier in the subtheme of resistance to abuse, Sandy had a friend help her call the police for assistance; but Tracey also displayed behavior that was indicative of something more happening with him that might have required professional assessment.[84] According to Sandy's petition, Tracey ran out in the middle of the busy highway in front of a semi-truck in an attempt to kill himself.[85] Sandy was awarded a temporary and final injunction against Tracey for this petition.

On September 20, 2000, sheriff's deputies responded to a call in which Sandy reported that Tracey "had choked and shoved her."[86] The responding deputy observed that Sandy had visible "signs of being choked including slight discoloration around the neck."[87] When the deputy attempted to make contact with Tracey for questioning, he fled into a nearby wooded area to avoid detection.[88] He was arrested for domestic battery and resisting an officer without violence.[89] On November 21, 2000, he entered a plea of nolo contendere, and the court withheld adjudication of guilt.[90] However, Tracey was placed on probation for six months.[91]

Fifteen years passed, seemingly, without any issues between Sandy and Tracey. But on November 21, 2015, Tracey stopped by Sandy's apartment complex to visit with his son, as the couple was estranged by this point.[92] When he arrived, Sandy was outside with her children; but they all went inside her apartment, including Tracey.[93] An argument took place, and Tracey pulled out two handguns.[94] He shot Sandy before leaving the apartment and killing himself.[95] Sandy crawled out the door of the apartment and died on the scene.[96]

Pierson v. Pierson

Richard and Mary Pierson were married on September 29, 1992.[97] It was his sixth marriage and her first.[98] Less than one year later, on August 9, 1993, Mary filed a petition for injunction with 87.6% coverage range for physical violence, which reads very simply but is one of the most gruesome of the seventy-five petitions for injunction that have a physical violence coding.[99] Her petition narrative states that Richard was:

> choking me, punching & dragging across the floor. Next evening slapped me off the truck.
>
> Broke my rib. Broked [sic] my false teeth. Choke [sic] me with a lamp cord then rap [sic] wires around my fingers & tried to plug it [sic] the socket. Beat me in the head with a monkey wrench.[100]

Mary was provided with a temporary injunction the same day she filed her petition, but the case was dismissed after the final hearing because she failed to appear in court at the hearing.[101]

Court records indicate that this 1993 event was not the only time Richard was physically violent toward Mary during their marriage.[102] Multiple misdemeanor spousal battery and felony domestic battery, as well as felony domestic battery with a deadly weapon cases were filed against him between 1993 and 2013.[103] A review of these cases shows a pattern of Richard's propensity for causing the non-fatal strangulation of Mary, and her pattern of requesting prosecutors to drop the cases against him. In many of the cases, the state attorney filed a no information; so, those cases did not move forward.[104] In some of these cases, Mary filed requests not to prosecute Richard and requests to have contact with him, which might have caused the no information to be filed by prosecutors.[105]

On April 11, 2009, Richard was arrested for domestic battery for grabbing Mary by her neck.[106] On April 15, 2009, Mary filed a request not to prosecute/request for contact.[107] As a result, an Order Allowing Contact between Richard and Mary was entered on April 23, 2009, and the no information was filed on April 23, 2009, as well.[108]

On May 19, 2010, Richard was arrested for aggravated domestic battery with a deadly weapon because he used a steak knife to force Mary to have oral sex with him.[109] In doing so, he "cut[] her right arm, her breast, her abdomen, and her back."[110] He also strangled her while pinning her to the bed.[111] However, on June 7, 2010, Mary filed another request not to prosecute/request for contact; so, the no information was filed on June 17, 2010, closing the case.[112]

But when Richard attacked Mary on July 23, 2012, things were different with how prosecutors handled the case.[113] He was arrested for domestic battery for slapping Mary and pulling her hair.[114] During this incident, he promised that "he would 'be back.'"[115] Still, Mary filed a request not to prosecute/request for contact on August 1, 2012; but prosecutors filed an information in the case on August 3, 2012.[116] Richard pleaded guilty to battery and was placed on probation for one year.[117]

On the evening of September 29, 2013, with Richard just off probation and on their twenty-first wedding anniversary, neighbors heard the couple arguing, which was common.[118] They were described as a couple that "argue and fight constantly."[119] However, that night, several neighbors reported hearing Mary screaming and that it was "very loud for approximately 2 minutes, then the screaming stopped."[120] That night, another neighbor described the couple as "fighting viciously again."[121] Finally, another neighbor reported that, three weeks prior to September 29, 2013 when Richard and Mary were in another argument, "Richard was screaming that he was going to kill Mary."[122]

Shortly after 9:00 p.m. on September 29, 2013, Richard knocked on his neighbor's door and told her "I killed Mary, I know shes [sic] dead."[123] The sheriff's office was contacted; and when they arrived, Richard explained to them that he "choked her and killed her."[124] Mary was found lying on the floor in their home near the doorway.[125] She was on her back, "un-clothed with a blanket covering her from the neck down."[126] She had visible bruising on her face and scratches on her neck.[127] Richard was indicted on October 3, 2013 by a Grand Jury for first degree murder.[128] After a lengthy jury trial, he was found guilty on October 1, 2015, and sentenced to life in prison without the possibility of parole.[129]

Rape and Sexual Abuse

"Rape and sexual abuse," in this study, is a subtheme of physical violence that describes various forced sexual acts and other types of unwanted sexual violence forced on the IPV victim by the abuser. In this study, 1.6% of

Physical Violence, the Ultimate in Power and Control? 221

the 493 cases and 12.6% of the 62 cases, as well as 9.0% of the 100 PIFPs analyzed in this phase, resulted in a rape and sexual abuse coding. The two most coded words for the subtheme rape and sexual abuse are "sex" and "force," respectively; however, the phrases did not have many similar themes. The singular theme that ran through the phrases for rape and sexual abuse referred to the IPV victim resisting the abuse, which caused the abuser to force himself on her. Guerline (Dieu) Damas stated that her then boyfriend, Mesac Damas commits "assault aggravated, sexual even [when] I don't want [to] do it. He always hit me to do it."[130] However, rape and sexual abuse seem to become more intertwined with physical violence when factors such as alcohol and the IPV victim refusing to have sex with the abuser are at work, such as when Yana Huss, explained a sexually abusive event between her and her husband Scott:

> [He] had been drinking alcohol, a lot of beers and wine. We began to argue and he pushed me in my chest, causing my head to hit the wall in the bedroom. He pushed me down and forced me to have oral sex. I tried to refuse but he continued to force me by screaming threats and grabbing me by my shoulders, causing the bruises []. He kept forcing himself into my mouth, calling me bad words, and [he] then raped me violently. During this sex he hit me hard in the lower back area and lower head and forced me to have anal sex with him.[131]

Once again, multiple tactics of coercive control are detailed in this passage. The IPV offender utilized: (1) threats, (2) physical violence, and (3) name calling, to abuse his victim. In combination, these tactics are very effective as the IPV victim must overcome all of them to achieve and maintain self-worth and well-being.

Allen v. Allen

On March 18, 2012, Pamela Allen contacted the sheriff's office to report that her estranged husband, Jason, slapped her in the face and grabbed her hair; however, she reported no injuries.[132] During the investigation of the event, Jason admitted to taking Pamela's phone but did not admit to any violence against her.[133] He told the deputy that Pamela was making up stories and had not signs of injuries either.[134] As a result, the case did not go further as there was no evidence against Jason for the state attorney to pursue.[135]

On October 23, 2012, Pamela filed a petition for injunction explaining to the Court that Jason "pushed me back into the apt. where he pulled down my pants and put his fingers inside me to see if I had sex with someone else."[136] She detailed how she attempted to go out the door several times but that he kept her from doing so.[137] When she told him she was going to call the police, he told her she would be dead.[138] She further explained that she had gone to stay at various places to get away from him and his sexual abuse.[139] When she stayed with her niece, he had sex with Pamela there while Pamela was sleeping.[140] So, she moved to her mom's, and "he came there and tried to force himself on [her]."[141] The court awarded her a temporary injunction the next day, but it was dismissed on October 31, 2012, when Pamela did not appear at the hearing for the final injunction.[142]

On January 20, 2013, sheriff's deputies were called out regarding another altercation between Pamela and Jason.[143] The deputy met with both of them, and Pamela and Jason refused to cooperate with the deputy.[144] Neither one of them had called law enforcement.[145] The report stated that Pamela's ear was bleeding but that she explained her earring cut it.[146] According to the deputy, this was a plausible reason for the injury; so, nothing further was done.[147]

Later, Pamela's daughter and cousin retold an account of her husband keeping Pamela in his truck for over four hours.[148] Relatives understood that Pamela and her husband lived apart during their eight-year marriage and that their relationship was on and off again.[149] They understood the couple to have little contact with each other.[150] It is for this reason that, when Pamela and her estranged husband, Jason, were both found on April 26, 2013, "naked, lying in bed with gunshot wounds to their heads," friends and family who knew them were confused.[151] Jason shot and killed Pamela before taking his own life.[152]

Familicide and the Family Annihilator

When the intimate partner homicide (IPH) offender not only kills their intimate partner but also kills multiple family members, most commonly their children or stepchildren with the IPH victim, it is known as a familicide.[153] In addition, often, when the familicide is coupled with an intimate partner homicide-suicide (IPHS), the offender is commonly referred to as the "family annihilator."[154] Familicide is considered "a statistically rare event[;]" however, it is shocking and garners quite of bit of media attention when it happens.[155] Theoretically, there are views that support the notion that this type of killing may be motivated by the offender seeking to enact revenge upon their spouse for threatening to or actually leaving them.[156] However, it is noted that this does not completely explain why killing one's own children exacts revenge upon an estranged spouse, especially a soon-to-be murdered one.[157] Indeed, the complexity of familicide and the motivation of the family annihilator are the subject of ongoing research.[158] Still, the following cases provide insight into these types of killings and the potential motivations of the offenders and their thought processes leading up to and during the murders.

Brown v. Brown

On December 12, 2015, in her petition for injunction, Chericia Brown wrote that her managers at work were concerned about her because they knew so much about her situation with her husband, Henry, that they were texting her at home to check on her to ask if she was alright.[159] She was experiencing physical violence, threats of being killed by Henry, harassment, and other tactics of coercive control.[160] She continued to explain that Henry accused her of bringing her work into their affairs; and he wanted to know whom from her work knew about their problems.[161] In fact, it was her human resources supervisor at work who drove her to the police department to file a report about an incident that had taken place between the couple.[162] That lead to Chericia, along with their children, being able to leave Henry.[163] She was awarded a temporary and final injunction for her petition.[164] The final injunction was to remain in effect until January 8, 2017.[165] But filing for an injunction and leaving Henry was not enough to keep Chericia and their young children safe.

The night of April 17, 2016, Henry hid in the trunk of Chericia Brown's car until she got off work from Chili's when he attacked her with a knife.[166] Henry stabbed Chericia several times before dragging her into the bushes.[167] Two good Samaritans with medical backgrounds came to Chericia's aid and attempted to save her life at the scene; however, while fleeing, Henry spotted them and ran over all three people as he left Chili's.[168] Henry picked up their two small children, ages four (4) and one (1), from the babysitter and drove to the hospital where Chericia was taken.[169] There, he shot at the sheriff's deputies and security officers once he was spotted and fled once more with his children.[170] Once deputies used stop sticks to end the chase, they found Henry had killed both children and himself.[171] Chericia died from her injuries, but the two good Samaritans survived.[172]

Whyte-Dell v. Dell

On April 4, 2008, Natasha Whyte-Dell, previously discussed throughout this book, explained to the Court that her husband, Patrick:

> was yelling & crusing [sic] at me in front of my six children .... He put up video camera up in the house without my neglect [sic]. I am afraid for my life and my children [sic] life .... My children are being affective [sic]. They hear him call me name, crusing [sic] at one & hitting me. My 13 year son only tries to defend me when I have to get between them both. I am really afriad [sic] for myself and my children. I do not know what my husband will do next.[173]

She was granted a temporary injunction on the same day she filed her petition and was awarded a final injunction on April 17, 2008, that remained in effect until October 17, 2008.[174] Even so, on December 20, 2009, Patrick was arrested and probable cause was found for aggravated assault with a deadly weapon and criminal mischief against Natasha and one of her friends.[175] The case was settled with Patrick being released from jail on his own recognizance.[176] He was ordered not to possess any type of weapons or firearms, not to have any violent contact with the victims in the case, and to have a mental health evaluation.[177]

About two years later, on May 18, 2010, Natasha filed another petition for injunction requesting protection from Patrick because she was "afraid for my life and my children [sic] life because he keep telling me my last days are going to be bitter."[178] She continued to explain that she had information that he was attempting to purchase a gun and explained about the previous incident in December 2009 whereby he chased her with knives.[179] She was not provided a temporary hearing for this petition, but the court awarded her a final injunction on May 28, 2010, that was to remain in full force until November 28, 2010.[180]

With that final injunction still in effect, on September 27, 2010, Patrick followed through with his threat against Natasha when he killed her and four of her children before killing himself.[181] He spared two children he and Natasha had in common, one and three years old, who were also in the home at the time of the killings but were unharmed.[182] A fifteen-year-old boy was shot in the neck but survived.[183] The night before the killings, Patrick told the family he would kill them after he argued with Natasha about his belief that she was cheating on him.[184] However, according to news reports, police were called to the home thirty-four times in the prior four years; so, this threat was not taken overly seriously by the family.[185]

The father of the surviving fifteen-year-old boy and the brother of one of the four children killed blamed Florida Department of Children and Families (DCF) for not having done more to prevent the killings because they were preceded by so many police calls to the home.[186] They each filed wrongful death suits against DCF for inadequately protecting the children in the home, and the father included a claim of negligence.[187] Both men acted as personal representatives for the estates of the deceased children as well.[188] The brother specifically alleged:

> "DCF failed to implement any safety plan that would or could address the violent and volatile situation existing within the Dell home. DCF did not recommend, suggest, or require any services or actions to address the domestic violence permeating the Dell home.

DCF's only recommendation was for Natasha and her children to call 911 should any future domestic violence occur."[189]

In fact, DCF closed its investigation of the Dell household in February 2010 after determining the children were at a low risk of significant harm, citing "No Indicators' of Family Violence Threatens Child," even though there were five different calls to police between July 2009 and November 2009; and Patrick had been arrested for aggravated assault with a deadly weapon and criminal mischief for acts against Natasha that included threatening her with a knife.[190] A long court battle ensued, making its way to the Florida Supreme Court, which ultimately determined that a cap for damages of $200,000 for all the deaths was all that could be imposed against the state of Florida.[191]

Damas v. Damas

On September 29, 2000, Mesac Damas called the sheriff's department to complain that his girlfriend, Guerline Dieu, with whom he had a seven-week-old son, was upset and "throwing some lamps and other things around."[192] He also stated that she "held onto [his] clothing to keep him from leaving her."[193] They had been together two years, and she believed he was out with another woman.[194] Mesac was leaving the apartment they shared and told her he did not want to see her anymore.[195] He called the sheriff because he wanted to get some clothes.[196] Neither of them had any injuries or wanted to press charges, and they both agreed he would leave without incident.[197]

On December 16, 2001, Guerline reported an incident in which Mesac "became angry at her because she did not tell him where she was going."[198] He threw food around the kitchen, and they got into a verbal argument.[199] In his fit of rage, furniture throughout their apartment was broken.[200] When Guerline attempted to call the sheriff's, she realized Mesac took the phone.[201] He later explained to sheriff's deputies that he broke the items throughout the apartment to make Guerline angry.[202] Sheriff's provided her with DV information, and she stayed with her brother for the night.[203]

The next report to authorities or the court from either Guerline or Mesac came on June 7, 2005, when Guerline filed her first petition for injunction.[204] She explained that Mesac committed aggravated sexual assault on her and that he always makes her have sex when she does not want to have it.[205] She detailed that he takes the car from her to prevent her from going out and that he takes her money from the bank.[206] But she also told the court, "If I live he will take the kids .... He told [me] if he not going to see to [sic] kids he will do something bad. Please help me to save my life and my kids life's [sic]."[207] She was issued a temporary injunction for protection against Mesac with a final hearing scheduled for June 16, 2005;

and he was served with the temporary injunction on June 9, 2005.[208] Also on June 9, 2005, Mesac filed his own petition for injunction against Guerline.[209] In his petition, he discussed his concern of her taking their kids away from him.[210] He explained about a new girlfriend he had and that he did not want her to leave him because of Guerline calling him.[211] He alleged that Guerline slapped her own face or cut herself to accuse him of causing her injuries.[212] He was not issued a temporary injunction, but his case was set to be heard on June 16, 2005, at the same time as Guerline's and in front of the same judge.[213] After the final hearing on June 16, 2005, Guerline was provided a final injunction for ninety days against Mesac with supervised visitation for the children, but he did not receive any type of injunction against her.[214] However, Guerline and Mesac filed motions to dismiss their injunctions for protection (although he did not have one issued by the court) on June 20 and June 23, 2005, respectively.[215] The dismissal in Guerline's case was issued after a hearing on July 14, 2005.[216]

On January 5, 2006, sheriff's deputies issued a report stating that they met with Guerline because she "is becoming increasingly afraid of Mesac."[217] At the time of this report, the couple was living together, and he "threatened to trash their apartment if Guerline did not come home before" a certain time.[218] When she was not able to make it home by the time set by Mesac, she found "items from the china [sic] cabinet in the trash can."[219] Because he had done this before and had a history of DV, she was advised to stay with a friend or relative and to file a petition for injunction.[220] However, she did not do so after this occurrence.[221]

But on November 27, 2006, Mesac filed a petition for injunction against Guerline because she "came to my job with all my four kids and treating [sic] me. She will have somebody take care of me and my new girlfriend."[222] He complained that he did not want her to come by his place of work, a popular restaurant, ever again.[223] According to his petition, they were no longer living together because she threw him out four months prior; and she was not allowing him to speak to the children over the phone.[224] He was requesting joint custody and a peaceful life.[225] But he claimed that Guerline "wants to kill, she wants to do this and that."[226] His petition was not granted a temporary injunction, and Mesac did not appear at the hearing for the final injunction although Guerline did appear.[227] As a result, his request for an injunction was denied.[228]

On April 14, 2007, Guerline and Mesac were married.[229] By May 27, 2007, a witness to another physical altercation between the couple was called into the sheriff's office.[230] The witness explained that he saw Mesac hitting Guerline and then kicking her while she was on the ground in the parking lot of an apartment building.[231] The witness approached Guerline and advised her to leave, so she drove away.[232] When sheriff's deputies questioned Mesac, he denied any type of physical violence between them, only stating that they were arguing.[233] He also referred to Guerline as "his soon to be ex-wife."[234] Further, deputies reported that he "became uncooperative and agitated;" so, he was placed in a patrol car for the remainder of the investigation.[235] He also complained of medical problems for which medical personnel were called to treat.[236] However, after exhaustive efforts, deputies were not able to locate Guerline for questioning; so, Mesac was free to leave.[237] On June 6, 2007, deputies spoke to Guerline and Mesac, who both denied any physical altercation between them taking place on May 27, 2007.[238] They each accused the witness to the event as being "'high' or 'drunk'" for having placed the call to authorities.[239] When deputies followed-up with the witness, he explained that he was woken up by loud yelling and saw Mesac hitting Guerline.[240] However, due to a lack of another independent witness, the case was suspended.[241]

The next call to the sheriff's office was made on November 21, 2008, and Guerline made it herself, stating that "Mesac slaps her constantly. The last incident occurred four (4) months ago. [She] has not reported any incidents of physical abuse because she is in fear of her husband. The physical abuse has occurred in the presence of the children."[242] The couple had five small children together at this point; and Guerline's mother was staying with them, who had witnessed the abuse.[243] Guerline's mother also explained that he threatened to kill Guerline if she left him, which caused her fear because of the abuse she witnessed.[244] Guerline echoed the fear of being killed by Mesac if she left him.[245] However, the report was for informational purposes only, so no action by the authorities was taken.[246]

On January 5, 2009, Guerline called the sheriff's office because Mesac physically attacked her for arriving home late from work.[247] While she was holding their infant child, he tore her shirt off her body and struck her in the face multiple times.[248] As he continued attacking her, he "choked her by holding her by the throat with his hand(s)."[249] During this physical altercation, Guerline lost her grip on the baby, causing her to fall on the concrete floor.[250] Guerline had several visible injuries and told the deputies that "Mesac 'cut off my air' with his hand(s).'"[251] The baby was assessed for injuries and did not require further medical treatment; however, DCF was contacted and provided information related to the incident.[252]

On January 6, 2009, Mesac was arrested for domestic battery, and a criminal misdemeanor case against him was filed for the incident described above.[253] The court issued a no contact order against Mesac, preventing him from having any contact of any type with Guerline until further order of the court.[254] He was also prevented from returning to his residence, except for removing some of his personal belongings within seventy-two hours of his release from jail.[255] Additionally, to visit his children, he had to do so under supervised conditions at the local child advocacy center.[256]

On January 16, 2009, Guerline wrote a letter to the judge in the case requesting that the no contact order be lifted because "all my kids miss their dad, they asked for him every day."[257] She explained that they made a mistake and asked the judge to "let him alone to come home."[258] However, the court did not provide the relief to Mesac that Guerline requested in her letter; so, on January 30, 2009, she wrote another letter to the judge.[259] In this letter, she explained how sorry she was for what happened.[260] She explained that it was a little argument and that she called the sheriff's office to scare Mesac.[261] She went on to explain that the kids miss him and that she does not know what to tell them about where he is and what is taking place.[262] She also detailed her difficulties with taking care of five small children on her own, including trying to work full-time, afford child care, etc.[263] She wrote, "I know he made a mistake and I do make one also by calling 911."[264] On the same day, prosecutors filed an information for the incident as battery (DV), a first degree misdemeanor.[265]

On February 9, 2009, Mesac's public defender filed a motion to set aside the no contact order, which referred to the letters Guerline sent to the court requesting the judge remove the no contact order.[266] This motion was denied after a hearing on February 25, 2009, so Mesac's new defense attorney filed a renewed motion to set aside the no contact order on March 11, 2009.[267] In his motion, Mesac cited that a "material change in circumstances had occurred" since the denial of the previous motion, which was the fact that DCF initiated a dependency action and was "now involved [in] supervising all parties."[268] As a result, after a hearing on the motion on April 2, 2009, an order removing the no contact order was granted; however, the battery case itself against Mesac progressed.[269] On June 1, 2009, he plead no contest to the charge of battery and was adjudicated guilty.[270] He was sentenced to twelve months' probation, two hundred hours community service, a batterers intervention program, a parenting class, and was working under a case plan in the dependency case.[271]

On September 19, 2009, the sheriff's office received a call from Guerline's brother who was concerned because he had not seen or heard from her since around 2:00 p.m. on September 17, 2009, which was very unusual.[272] Another one of Guerline's siblings had last heard from her on September 17, 2009, when she told her that she and Mesac had gotten into a fight.[273] The brother was additionally concerned due to the history of DV between the couple, the fact that he had gone to their home and found a DCF card at the door, and the fact that the children missed school on September 18, 2009.[274] Sheriff's deputies conducted their own welfare checks on September 18, 2009, and on September 19, 2009, at about 5:49 p.m. at the couple's home but did not receive any response at the door.[275] Further investigation determined that Mesac did not report to work on September 18 or 19, 2009.[276] Guerline did not report to work for the past few day prior to September 19, 2009, as well.[277] It was unusual for either of them to miss work; and "due to the domestic volatility" between the couple and the "lack of common communication between siblings," deputies considered the seven member family to be "missing endangered."[278]

By 6:24 p.m. on September 19, 2009, sheriff's deputies were, again, dispatched to the Damas home to conduct another welfare check, only this time they obtained "a key for the residence [] from the landlord who granted permission to enter the residence."[279] Upon entry, deputies discovered blood in the kitchen area of the home.[280] They also observed an area rug that looked out of place in front of a closed closet door under the stairwell off the kitchen.[281] When they first attempted to open the door, it was locked; but once opened, they discovered Guerline's body lying on the floor of a small bathroom.[282] Her torso and hands were loosely wrapped "with what appeared to be a white extension cord," and her arms were bound by copious amounts of duct tape.[283] She had a black trash bag over her head.[284] The upper portion of her body, including her neck and mouth, had been bound with duct tape, so much so "that it was impossible to discern what she was wearing from the waist up."[285] Her legs were also bound with duct tape from just over her ankles to just above her knees and including her thighs.[286] In all, to prevent her from fighting back, she was bound with "nearly fifty-five yards of duct tape[,]" enough to exceed the distance of half a football field when stretched from one end to the other.[287] "Her throat had been cut through the duct tape."[288]

Once upstairs, deputies discovered the deceased bodies of all five of Guerline and Mesac's small children, all under the age of ten, still in their bedrooms.[289] The wounds to all the children were horrifying and indicated they were not all unconscious before their first major injuries.[290] They were all killed by lacerations around their necks, but their deaths were not instantaneous.[291] Some were worse than others, and it was clear the older ones fought back.[292] One was nearly decapitated.[293] Another's bed was broken, indicative of a struggle; and he had "knife wounds [that] nearly encircled his neck."[294] The local sheriff at the time "called the killings 'the most horrific and violent event' in county history."[295]

Mesac was not found inside the home, so a nationwide Be-On-the-Look-Out (BOLO) was put out for him and his vehicle.[296] During the homicide investigation, it was learned that he called his father the morning of September 18, 2009, explaining that "he had a fight with Guerline, hit her, and he did not think she was going to wake up."[297] Also on September 18, 2009, Mesac purchased with cash a one-way airline ticket that departed at 9:50 a.m. for Haiti.[298] On September 21, 2009, he was apprehended in Haiti and interviewed by the FBI after being given his Miranda warning.[299] He signed a confession and the Miranda warning while in Haiti.[300]

As part of his confession given in Haiti on September 21, 2009, Mesac stated that "bad spirits" made him commit the murders and that he flew to Haiti to say goodbye to his family.[301] He believed "he deserved death for what he did and if he had a gun he would take his own life."[302] He was extradited back to the United States on September 23, 2009, by U.S. Marshals and was indicted for six counts of first degree murder on October 14, 2009.[303] While first back in the United States, he provided another statement about the murders to the local sheriff's office that was recorded and transcribed rather than only summarized by the investigating agent as was done with the prior statements.[304]

In that last interview in the United States taken on September 23, 2009, he explained about the battery case in January 2009 and about the no contact order, as well as DCF's involvement with the family.[305] He detailed how he would watch Guerline without her knowing and borrow a friend's car so he would not be detected when doing so.[306] Once the no contact order was lifted, he moved back in with Guerline; but she had not forgiven him and wanted a divorce.[307] Guerline's mother told her if she took him back, she would never speak to her again; and she was beginning to think her "mom [was] probably right" about needing to leave him.[308] He told her if she did he would kill her, her mom, and himself.[309]

By September 16, 2009, Guerline told Mesac that if he hit her again, she would ensure he went to prison for the rest of his life and never see his children again.[310] It was at that point that he considered killing himself and her, explaining that "the devil start[ed] coming out of [him]" telling him, "'Oh, why don't you just kill yourself? Kill her and then kill yourself' you know, 'Let your parents, whatever, take care of the kids.' But I was like, 'But I love the kids and when I die how am I going to know if they [are] okay.'"[311] That same day she also met with a DCF employee about their case without Mesac, causing him to believe "[t]hey were setting me up for failure. [Guerline] was asking her how she can divorce me …. I was so pissed off … the fact [that] she betrayed me like that."[312] But later that night, she promised to help him finish his probation classes prior to divorcing him.[313]

The morning of September 17, 2009, Mesac followed Guerline to work, leaving the children at home alone.[314] When she and her store manager threatened to call authorities he said, "If you call the cops they're going to arrest me, they're going to arrest you too because both of us left the kids alone at the house. They're going to take the kids away from us. I know you love the kids too, right?"[315] When Guerline took her next work break, she went home and asked Mesac to sign some immigration papers that just arrived in the mail.[316] She also explained she would not be coming home after work for fear of Mesac physically harming her; however this was the same night that Mesac left work early, complaining he did not feel well.[317] Also, in his Haiti confession, he described the events of September 17, 2009, as a day in which he and Guerline were arguing during the afternoon; and prior to his leaving for work that evening, she told him she was leaving him and taking their children with her.³¹⁸ His response to her was "NEVER!"³¹⁹

At about 8:42 p.m. on September 17, 2009, Mesac left work early, telling his employer he "wasn't feeling well and had a pounding headache."³²⁰ On his way home, he considered his options:

> I said I would go and kill her and myself. But if I kill her[,] custody of the kids would go [to] her mom. So I wanted to kill her mom so my mom would have custody. I [was] talking to myself in my car. I said what if I kill my kids and myself? But what about her? She will marry again! What if I just kill her? But if they find me[,] they will take my kids away from me.³²¹

Around 9:00 p.m., after driving by his home to observe Guerline with his friend who was helping watch the children, he thought she was with another man.³²² "At approximately 10:30 p.m., [he] purchased duct tape, a filet knife, and chewing gum."³²³ Once he returned to the home he shared with his family, he spent about an hour outside observing Guerline while she spoke on the phone, laughing and looking happy.³²⁴ Around 12:30 a.m. on September 18, 2009, he entered the home by tearing off the screen door to the lanai and making his way through the sliding glass door that he knew was malfunctioning.³²⁵

Guerline screamed when she saw him and told him not to touch her.³²⁶ He punched her, and they began fighting in the kitchen.³²⁷ She was trying to call for help, and he knew he was going to jail.³²⁸ She was making a lot of noise, slapping Mesac, and pushing the wall.³²⁹ So, he duct taped her body extensively to prevent her from calling out, and told her that "he was going to let her live but he was going to kill all the children in front of her."³³⁰ "He encircled her mouth, neck, upper torso, arms, forearms, hands, and legs with duct tape."³³¹ He explained to her that his plan was to burn the house down with the children and him in it.³³² When Guerline asked to speak, he removed the duct tape from her mouth.³³³ She told him she loved him and begged for the children's lives.³³⁴ He reconsidered, but "realized if he let her go, she would call the police and his kids would get taken away from him."³³⁵ At that point, he took the knife, killed Guerline, and engage in the following thought process:

> "What am I going to do? Run, call the cops? Say I killed my wife or something."
>
> ....
>
> I love my children to death. I'm going to jail for life.
>
> ....

Death penalty, whatever, electric chair. I'm thinking, thinking. One o'clock in the morning, two o'clock in the morning. I'm thinking. I got the knife in my hand still. I said, "Uh I'm to slice my throat too." I said, "I'm gonna suffer before I f[***]ing die. I can do it." I wasn't going to kill the kids, man. I still had them to survive, you know, let them live. So the devil come to me and say, "Who's going to taking care of kids?"[336]

So, he went upstairs to kill the children.[337] As he described it, "he cut the children's throats 'one by one.'"[338] He explained that as he was killing each child, he heard voices encouraging him to "[k]eep doing it."[339] As he told the story of the killings, he described how he was going to leave the youngest and the oldest alive; but when he got back downstairs and saw the blood from killing Guerline, he could not leave them alive for her mother to raise.[340] Then he explained how the baby was "the easiest one to die[;]" and how the oldest one struggled and fought back.[341] Then, Mesac watched his oldest son bleed to death.[342]

He stayed in the house all night trying to figure out how to kill himself; but, ultimately, "he didn't have the nerve [] after killing his family."[343] So, he changed his clothes, packed a suitcase, and placed the filet knife he used for the killings, now substantially bent from having completed the killings, in a nightstand in the master bedroom, which was ultimately recovered by authorities.[344] Apparently, he considered suicide again before leaving the home but could not cut his own throat.[345] He took the cash he used to purchase his airplane ticket to Haiti from Guerline's wallet and drove to the airport.[346] When he first spoke to the special agent in Haiti, he stated, "I know what I did was wrong. Bad sprits made me do it."[347]

On December 3, 2009, the state of Florida filed its notice of intent to seek the death penalty in the pending criminal felony case against him.[348] On September 5, 2017, Mesac pled guilty to six counts of first-degree murder, provided a waiver of his right to a penalty-phase jury, as well as a waiver of his right to a presentation of mitigation.[349] But before the case concluded and six death sentences were imposed, a torturous, eight-year-long criminal proceeding for Guerline's family resulted due to many delays caused by questions of Mesac's competency, various requests by Mesac to represent himself that were denied, several changes in judges, and multiple changes of Mesac's defense counsel.[350] And on December 28, 2018, the Florida Supreme Court upheld all six convictions and sentences of death.[351]

Judicial Terrorism® Revisited

As discussed in Chapter 3, litigation between an IPV victim and their abuser can often become a forum for the continuation of the non-violent tactics of coercive control whereby the IPV victim is virtually helpless in thwarting the abuser's efforts at nonstop isolation, intimidation, harassment, and power and control.[352] However, when isolation is further exacerbated due to issues such as English not being the IPV victim's first language or when she leaves all of her loved ones behind to join her husband in a foreign land, the filing of multiple police reports and petitions for injunction against her may be so devastating that she does not know how to handle the immediate situation at the time of arrest, let alone how to properly defend herself in a court of law. Indeed, when her abuser is a well-educated professional, who can effectively maneuver through the court system and has assumed control over her earning potential (or prevented her from having any) and personal assets, it becomes even more difficult to withstand his power and control. Finally, when child custody issues become the forefront to a dissolution of marriage action (DOM) whereby the IPV abuser is prepared to do anything to prevent his victim from obtaining or retaining custody of the children, the lethality risk to the victim is imminent whether prior physical violence or the threat thereof has occurred or not. Indeed, the following case, like others before it in this book, exemplifies the aspects of judicial terrorism® as described in Chapter 3 even though the intimate partner couple was not involved in any one court case for an extraordinary length of time.

Frasch v. Frasch

Adam and Samira Frasch met in Paris, France in August 2006 at a fashion show where she was working as a model.[353] After a long-distance courtship, they married in Las Vegas on November 15, 2009; but Samira returned to Paris to finalize her work obligations before returning to the United States in March 2010.[354] Upon her arrival, she learned she was pregnant but also learned Adam fathered another child in her absence, causing her to miscarry.[355] At that point, contemplating whether she would divorce Adam, Samira planned to fly back to Paris and went to stay at a hotel for solitude; however, he followed her.[356] On May 27, 2010, after her lack of forgiveness and continued desire for a divorce, Adam grabbed Samira and explained she needed to go to jail for a lesson.[357] However, local authorities saw it differently; and Samira, who spoke and wrote very little English, was arrested and charged with domestic battery based on Adam's allegation that she hit and scratched him, which was supported by his limo chauffeur.[358] While she was in jail, Adam took her passport and other belongings.[359] She was also ordered to have no contact with Adam through the pending criminal proceeding against her.[360] On July 22, 2010, the information was amended to add a second count against Samira for breach of the peace or disorderly conduct, allowing the state of Florida to enter a nolle prosequi on the battery charge against her and for her to plead nolo contendere to the disorderly conduct charge.[361] As a result, the court withheld adjudication for the disorderly conduct offense and the case concluded on July 22, 2010.[362]

By the time Samira was cleared, Adam was apologetic for having fathered a baby out of wedlock while Samira was in Paris and for causing her arrest, promising a future of faithfulness and honesty in return for her forgiveness.[363] Because she made such drastic changes in her life to marry Adam, including giving up her career, she agreed to a reconciliation; and they renewed their vows oversees before her family and friends.[364] Soon thereafter in 2011, Samira gave birth to their first daughter; however, Adam began to distance himself from the family by being gone for long weekends, continuing his "passion for gambling, fast cars and women."[365] Over time, the couple grew apart; and their relationship became "tumultuous and even violent."[366] One incident that occurred in mid-November 2012, involved Adam slamming Samira against the wall, then "encircl[ing] her torso with this arms and squeez[ing] her until she blacked out" before throwing her to the floor.[367] And on July 14, 2013, Adam made a police report that Samira rammed his vehicle with hers.[368] But from there, the incidents of Adam's reports to law enforcement and the court quickly escalated.

On the evening of August 1, 2013, Adam called local sheriff's deputies to his home to report that Samira came home at 2:30 a.m. the morning of July 31, 2013, from "a night out at the club" and "jumped on him and hit him in the chest with a bottle of contact solution."[369] He continued to explain that she hit him with a large glass vase in the back of the head but eventually calmed down, leaving him alone.[370] However, he refused to allow deputies to take any photographs of a small cut on his chest and a knot on the back of the left side of his head.[371] During his interview with deputies, Adam described Samira as being "extremely violent towards him" throughout their four year marriage.[372] He explained that she is known to injure herself so that when law enforcement arrives on scene from him making the call, they take her side and are not helpful toward him.[373]

But when asked by deputies to make a sworn, written statement, Adam refused, stating "he would rather not due to the fact he was in fear [Samira] would retaliate."[374] He went on to explain that he was concerned she might be suffering from some type of mental illness and that he was going to file for an injunction for protection the following day.[375] But there is no evidence he filed for any injunction for protection, at least at the beginning of August 2013. In fact, Samira later alleged that on August 1, 2013, at 2:00 a.m., Adam grabbed her and yanked her hair when she was not interested in his sexual advances.[376] As part of Adam's explained fear of Samira to deputies, he described how he was concerned for the safety of the couple's two young daughters, ages two months and two years, because she rammed her vehicle into his with the children inside of her car.[377] He had a close friend, who also worked for him, present when the deputies took his statement, who also

Physical Violence, the Ultimate in Power and Control? 235

detailed the fact that he witnessed several incidents in which Samira was "being extremely violent towards [Adam]."[378] This friend expressed concern for Adam and the children's safety as well.[379] As a result, DCF was contacted and advised that a report would be generated.[380] Nevertheless, on September 6, 2013, "due to [Adam's] lack of cooperation at the time he made the report[,]" this particular case was closed due to lack of evidence for a crime of domestic battery against Samira.[381]

On August 30, 2013, Adam contacted local sheriff's deputies to meet him at a nearby location regarding a domestic disturbance that had already occurred.[382] He began by explaining that he and Samira were having marital difficulties over the past four months, that they had two young children together, and that he filed a DV report against her on August 1, 2013.[383] Then he explained that she had violent tendencies that were worsening, that she likes rough sex but that he was concerned he would be blamed as a batterer for having sex that way if she bruised, and that he had a previous marriage in which he was accused of DV so the divorce did not go well for him.[384] He continued to detail his marital troubles with Samira as stemming from her accusations of infidelity and the fact that she becomes physically violent toward him when the issue comes up.[385] He also stated that when he threatens to call law enforcement on her for the physical violence she threatens to accuse him of rape.[386] He told deputies that believed "she is extorting him for his money."[387] In fact, he was a very wealthy professional who also bragged about being a very successful gambler "who wins substantial monies at casinos" and "never loses."[388]

He continued to explain that he was not living at home but went home to change his clothes.[389] He stated that this is when she physically attacked him, but the deputy did not see any sign of recent injury that coincided with his story.[390] When asked why he waited five hours to call authorities, his answers changed from "he needed to get ready for work" to "he decided to call later when she would not talk to him about it."[391] When deputies met with Samira, she was surprised and upset to learn they had been called because she viewed herself as the victim of both physical and mental abuse at the hands of Adam.[392] She explained:

> He has brought her to America from France and has held her back from a good career. She knows little English and has only one friend with no other outlets. He has pulled her hair, punched and raped her in the past. In doing so he tells her he can do this in America and get away with it.[393]

Samira was in the process of filing for divorce, and Adam was trying to make up with her the night before.[394] She showed deputies texts from him that brought up good memories and "refers to their sex as being magical and that it is always better after an argument."³⁹⁵ When he came to their home the morning of August 30, 2013, after she would not speak to him, he threatened that "he would bruise himself, call law enforcement, and blame it on her."³⁹⁶ She explained they had no physical contact and denied scratching or hitting him in the head.³⁹⁷ She further explained, without deputies telling her he said anything about a knot on the left side of his head, that he was born with it.³⁹⁸ She recounted how he attempted to blame her for the same knot on August 1, 2013, which deputies confirmed from the prior report.³⁹⁹ Also, she had no physical injuries to her body that indicated she would have done to Adam what he alleged.⁴⁰⁰ She also showed deputies a text after Adam left, stating he wanted her back and mentioning nothing about a physical altercation between them.⁴⁰¹ As a result of the lack of independent witnesses to his allegations, the inconsistent statements between the couple, and the inconsistent injuries to Adam based on his statement, no arrests were made related to Adam's report against Samira.⁴⁰²

On August 30, 2013, and, then again, on August 31, 2013, Adam filed petitions for injunction related to his allegations against Samira as described above, only with additional allegations and information in each of his petitions.⁴⁰³ The first petition for injunction filed on August 30, 2013, was very similar to the police report in that he explained about the hitting, scratching, and hitting him on the back of the head.⁴⁰⁴ Indeed, he emphasized her hitting him in the head several times during this incident and in the past.⁴⁰⁵ He also accused her of poking him in the eyes while he is driving with the children in the car.⁴⁰⁶ He continued to state that she threatened to kill him or have others kill him and that she would claim self-defense, making it look like he tried to rape her.⁴⁰⁷ This petition was not provided a temporary injunction but was set to be heard on September 13, 2013.⁴⁰⁸ So, on August 31, 2013, Adam filed another petition for injunction that had very similar facts to the one he filed the day before; but it had more emphasis on the "bleeding" and quoted the statements Samira said to him, such as "go ahead and I'll tell them you raped me."⁴⁰⁹ He also underlined the word "kill" every time he used it in his narrative when he explained that she threatened to kill him; and this time he told the court she threatened to kill the children as well.⁴¹⁰ As a result, Adam was provided a temporary injunction for this petition, which was also scheduled for a final hearing on September 13, 2013.

When Adam was provided with the temporary injunction based on his August 31, 2013, petition, the court ordered custody of the couple's minor children to him even though Samira was still breastfeeding their two-month old daughter.⁴¹¹ When he came to their home to take it over, an altercation between the couple took place in which Samira was accused of grabbing Adam by the neck, scratching it, and saying "I'll kill you."⁴¹² However, Samira told deputies that Adam scratched himself because she did not touch him.[413] The only witness to the incident was the same friend Adam had to the August 1, 2013, incident report.[414] But after a simple misdemeanor domestic battery case was initiated, the state attorney determined that, although probable cause existed for an arrest, there was "insufficient admissible evidence to prove elements of the crime beyond a reasonable doubt" so no information was filed on October 4, 2013.[415]

Meanwhile, the two pending injunction cases Adam had against Samira, originally set for hearing on September 13, 2013, were reset on September 13, 2013, for hearing on November 6, 2013.[416] The temporary injunction Adam was awarded on August 31, 2013, against Samira was extended while they awaited the final hearing.[417] However, in mid-September 2013, Samira started filing her own papers to begin to tell her side of the story to the court, which caused things to begin to work in her favor.[418] First, on September 16, 2013, she filed a motion for reconsideration in the August 31, 2013, injunction case.[419] Then, on September 17, 2013, she filed her petition for DOM, which included Adam's friend/employee as a defendant to a civil conspiracy count for depriving her of her right to her children, getting her arrested, and causing her severe emotional distress.[420] As a result, on or about September 27, 2013, an order was entered in the August 31, 2013, injunction case that granted custody back to Samira even though that case continued to wait for the November 6, 2013, final hearing.[421]

During that time, "she and her children stayed for three months in a rental townhouse owned by [her divorce attorney and his wife] that [was] next door to their home."[422] The couple had to take out a no-trespass order against Adam for both their business and their home.[423] But Samira's attorney explained, "'She had nowhere else to go and no money at that time.' ... 'She didn't have anybody to help her.'"[424] Then, a hearing in the August 31, 2013, case took place on October 3, 2013, at 1:00 p.m. on an emergency basis (it is unclear as to why the hearing was set).[425] An order denying a motion for reconsideration filed by Adam was denied at this hearing.[426] At 4:44 p.m. the same day, Adam filed yet another petition for injunction alleging the same facts against Samira that occurred in August 2013, but adding facts about her taking knives out and having thrown them at him, as well as another incident in September 2013 in which he claimed she broke another vase over his head and other various acts he typically accused her of in the previous petitions for injunction.[427] The October 3, 2013, injunction case was not awarded a temporary injunction and was set for hearing on October 16, 2013.[428] It was dismissed at that hearing.[429]

On November 5, 2013, a motion to consolidate the two injunction cases, i.e., the August 30 and 31, 2013, cases, was filed, causing the November 6, 2013, final injunction hearing to be reset to December 4, 2013, with the temporary injunction Adam had against Samira being extended again.[430] Once more, the December 4, 2013, hearing was reset to December 19,

2013.⁴³¹ However, this time, on December 13, 2013, through the DOM action, the court provided Samira "temporary exclusive possession of the marital residence[,]" financial support through a myriad of forms, and rule that "[a]t this time the Court will not award any parenting time to Husband, however he can file a motion to address same."⁴³² The August 31, 2013, injunction case reflects that an "order modifying temporary injunction of August 31, 2013" was entered that same day.⁴³³ Although the hearing for December 19, 2013, remained set and the motion for consolidation was granted on December 16, 2013, Adam's August 31, 2013, injunction case was not heard on December 19, 2013, for reasons unknown.⁴³⁴ It was dismissed for failure to prosecute on June 22, 2015.⁴³⁵

On February 3, 2014, the court issued an order in the DOM action relating to the various financial support obligations to Samira and the children it provided for in its December 13, 2013, order.⁴³⁶ Samira filed a motion for enforcement, contempt, and for attorney's fees because Adam was not timely making his financial support obligation payments.⁴³⁷ As a result of Adam's failure to make timely payments, the court issued an order stating that if he failed to make timely payments in the future he would face "an Order to Show Cause … as to why he should not be incarcerated or another sanction imposed for the failure to comply with the Order of this Court."⁴³⁸

On February 7, 2014, Samira went to Adam's professional office to retrieve her vehicle.⁴³⁹ On the way back to her home, Adam ran Samira's vehicle off the road.⁴⁴⁰ Later that day, at the security gate of the community where the marital home was located, Adam and Samira got into an argument.⁴⁴¹ The video footage from the community surveillance shows Samira backing her vehicle into Adam's.⁴⁴² The next day, Adam sent a text to Samira that read "I love you, Sam, but if you push this divorce and injunction, thing [sic] will get bad to worse and then we both suffer, and the babies."⁴⁴³ On February 21, 2014, Adam breached the security gate to the marital home's community by tailgating Samira's car after they had an argument at the security gate before she entered the secured subdivision.⁴⁴⁴

During the early morning hours of February 22, 2014, while their two young children slept, after confronting Adam about information she found on his cell phone, Samira was beaten, hit over the head with a golf club until she was incapacitated, and placed into the family pool (she could not swim).⁴⁴⁵ She was found later that morning by a maintenance man who worked for the Frasch's, naked (other than a scant cloth wrapped around her waist) at the bottom of the deep end of the pool.⁴⁴⁶ She had "significant blunt trauma injuries to her head and a massive skull fracture, which the medical examiner testified could not have come from tripping and falling, nor from a single blow with a fist."⁴⁴⁷ She had "swelling on the right cheek and the right eye, on the right side of her face …. [O]n the left side, there was a [severe] skull fracture and hemorrhaging inside – in the brain."⁴⁴⁸

Initially, on February 22, 2014, Adam was arrested for interference with child custody based on the fact that, when Samira' body was found, information came to light and he was found with the couple's two daughters, whom he did not have legal authority to have in his custody.[449] As a result and because of a Medicare fraud case against him as well, he was held in the local jail for months while the murder investigation took place, during which time his competency was questioned in the interference with custody case.[450] On August 1, 2014, it was determined that Adam was "suffer[ing] from a major mental illness" and "[was] incompetent to proceed" with the criminal case related to the interference with child custody until he received treatment.[451] And, after additional competency evaluations, on October 22, 2014, the court found Adam competent to proceed in the interference with custody case.[452] On October 30, 2014, he pled nolo contendere to both counts of interference with child custody pending against him; and the court withheld adjudication, providing him credit for time already served.[453]

On November 7, 2014, the Grand Jury indicted Adam for first degree murder because it concluded he killed Samira "by inflicting trauma to the head or drowning."[454] One detail that came out during the murder investigation and pendency of the case was that Adam gave investigators details about the circumstances surrounding Samira's death, such as the fact that she was found in a pool and had flip-flops on, before anyone from law enforcement released those details to the public.[455] These were facts that Adam could not have learned at that time without having been at the crime scene.[456] Also, Samira was found to have Adam's DNA underneath her fingernails, as well as "off vaginal and anal swabs."[457] While in jail awaiting trial, he admitted to his cellmate that he killed her, providing details of the murder that were consistent with the evidence including information about the fact that he hit her with a golf club prior to throwing her in the pool.[458] Based on this information, law enforcement located a golf club inside the marital home that had Samira's DNA on the striking portion of the club.[459] He was initially held with no bond due to the fact that it was a "high profile case" and because he was considered a flight risk; but, by the end of 2015, that condition was modified to a more restricted pretrial release.[460]

The murder trial took many twists and turns, including two judges recusing themselves *sua sponte* in December 2014 and January 2016.[461] The state filed a notice to seek the death penalty in November 2014, only to waive its right to pursue it in October 2015 when Adam waived his right to a twelve-person jury trial.[462] Instead, he agreed to a six-person jury in exchange for the state agreeing to not seek the death penalty; however, that deal seemed to change in August 2016 when the state filed another notice of intent to seek the death penalty.[463] As a result, because his charge was for first degree murder, Adam faced the death penalty or life in prison without the possibility of parole.[464] The case went to trial in January 2017, and he was convicted of first degree murder by a six-member jury.[465] He was sentenced to life in prison, and his conviction and sentence was upheld on appeal at the state district court level.[466] The Florida Supreme Court denied further review of the district court's decision, and the U.S. Supreme Court denied his request for a writ of certiorari as well.[467]

Notes

1. *See* Mary Ann Dutton & Lisa A. Goodman, *Coercion in Intimate Partner Violence: Toward a New Conceptualization*, 52 SEX ROLES 743 (2005) https://doi.org/10.1007/s11199-005-4196-6; Donna J. King, *Naming the Judicial Terrorist: An Exposé of an Abuser's Successful Use of a Judicial Proceeding for Continued Domestic Violence*, 1 TENN. JOURNAL OF RACE, GENDER, & SOCIAL JUSTICE 153 (2012); EVAN STARK, COERCIVE CONTROL: HOW MEN ENTRAP WOMEN IN PERSONAL LIFE (2007).
2. *See* H. Douglas, *Battered Women's Experiences of the Criminal Justice System: Decentring the Law*, 20 FEM. LEG. STUD. 121 (2012) https://doi.org/10.1007/s10691-012-9201-1; STARK, *supra* note 1.
3. Redd v. Redd, 05-119DR, 5 (2005) (Pet. for Inj. for Prot. Against Dom. Viol.).
4. *Id.*
5. *See* Jensen, 2000020428 at 1; Everett, 2003061099, at 1; Jensen, 2005040500, at 1.
6. *See* Jensen-428, *supra* note 5.
7. *See Id.*
8. *See* Everett, *supra* note 5.
9. *See Id.*
10. *See Id.*
11. *See Id.*
12. *See* Jensen-500, *supra* note 5.
13. *See Id.*; Redd v. Redd, 05-119DR, 5 (2005) (Pet. for Inj. for Prot. Against Dom. Viol.).
14. *See* Jensen-500, *supra* note 5.
15. *See Id.*
16. *See Id.*
17. *See* Hightower, 2005040850, at 1.
18. *See Id.*
19. Butler, 2005091071, at 1.
20. *Id.*
21. *Id.* at 20.
22. *See Id.*
23. *See Id.*
24. *Id.*
25. *See Id.*
26. *See Id.* at 15.
27. *Id.* at 20.
28. *See Id.*
29. *Id.*
30. *See Id.*

31 *See Id.*
32 *See Id.*
33 *See Id.*
34 *See Id.* at 12.
35 *See Id.*
36 *See Id.* at 16.
37 *See generally* Heinemann, 12-119301, at 1–15.
38 *See generally Id.*
39 *See Id.* at 2.
40 *See Id.*
41 *See Id.*
42 *See Id.* at 3.
43 *See Id.* at 14.
44 State of Florida v. Grindrod, 12-MM-021623 (2012) (Notice to the Clerk).
45 Grindrod v. Grindrod, 12-000494DR, 3 (2012) (Pet. for Inj. for Prot. Against Dom. Viol.).
46 *See* Heinemann, *supra* note 37 at 11.
47 Grindrod v. Grindrod, 12-000494DR (2012) https://matrix.leeclerk.org/Case/CaseView (last visited May 16, 2023).
48 Grindrod v. Grindrod, 12-000494DR, 1 (2012) (Final J. of Inj. for Prot. Against Dom. Viol. with Minor Child(ren) (after notice)).
49 *Id.* at 3.
50 *Id.* at 4.
51 *See* Beck, 12-197552 at 4.
52 *See Id.*
53 *See Id.*
54 *See Id.*
55 *See Id.*
56 *See Id.*
57 DeJesus v. Aguilar, 2000-DR-003150 (2000) https://appsgp.mypalmbeachclerk.com/eCaseView/search.aspx (last visited May 17, 2023).
58 *See* Hussey, 11101214 at 1.
59 *See Id.*
60 *See Id.* at 2.
61 *See Id.*
62 *See Id.*
63 *See Id.*
64 *See generally* Aguilar v. DeJesus, 2011DR009914 (2011) (Pet. for Inj. for Prot. Against Dom. Viol.).
65 *Id.*
66 *See* Aguilar v. DeJesus, 2011DR009914 (2011) https://appsgp.mypalmbeachclerk.com/eCaseView/search.aspx (last visited May 17, 2023).
67 *See Id.*; Cynthia Roldan, *Lake Worth Man Shoots Wife, then is Slain by Stepson in Self-Defense, Sheriff Says*, THE PALM BEACH POST (September 1, 2011).
68 *See* Desmond, 11116609, at 1; Roldan, *supra* note 67.
69 Roldan, *supra* note 67 AT ¶ 7; Desmond, *supra* note 68 at 3.
70 *See* Roldan, *supra* note 67.
71 *See Id.*
72 *See* Santiago Nunez v. Nunez, 2007DR014851, 4 (2007) (Pet. for Inj. for Prot. Against Dom. Viol.).

73 *See Id.* at 3. See also Santiago Nunez v. Nunez, 2007-DR-007364 (2007) https://appsgp.mypalmbeachclerk.com/eCaseView/search.aspx (last visited May 18, 2023).
74 Santiago Nunez, 2007DR014851 at 3.
75 *See Id.*
76 *See Id.*
77 *See Id.*
78 *Id.* at 4.
79 *See* Santiago Nunez v. Nunez, 2007DR014851 (2007) https://appsgp.mypalmbeachclerk.com/eCaseView/search.aspx (last visited May 18, 2023).
80 *See* McDaniel, 08022939, at 1–2. *See also* Santiago Nunez v. Nunez, 2007DR014851 (2007) https://appsgp.mypalmbeachclerk.com/eCaseView/search.aspx (last visited May 18, 2023).
81 *See* Schneider, 08022997, at 3.
82 *See* McDaniel, *supra* note 80 at 2. *See also Teen Finds His Parents Dead,* ORLANDO SENTINEL (August 3, 2021).
83 Brunson v. Brunson, 98-977 CA, 3 (1998) (Pet. for Inj. for Prot. Against Dom. Viol.).
84 *See Id. See supra* Chapter 7, Resistance to Abuse.
85 Brunson, 98-977 CA at 4.
86 *See* State of Florida v. Brunson, 2000MM1666, 3 (2000) (Court Disposition).
87 *See Id.*
88 *See Id.*
89 *See Id.*
90 *See Id.* at 1.
91 *See Id.*
92 *See* Carswell, 2015-001502 at 3; Gatehouse Media Services, *Update: Victim in Jackson County Murder-Suicide had Chipley Ties,* PANAMA CITY NEWS HERALD (November 24, 2015).
93 *See* Carswell, *supra* note 92.
94 *See* Gatehouse, *supra* note 92.
95 *See* Carswell, *supra* note 92; Gatehouse, *supra* note 92.
96 *See* Carswell, 2015-001502 at 3.
97 Marriage Record Florida, Application No. 92 6110, Adult Control No. 557619.
98 *Id.*
99 *See generally* Pierson v. Pierson, 93-7484-FD-R (1993) (Pet. for Inj. for Prot. Against Dom. Viol.).
100 *Id.* at 1.
101 *See* Pierson v. Pierson, 93-7484-FD-R (1993) https://ccmspa.pinellascounty.org/PublicAccess/CaseDetail.aspx?CaseID=1463127 (last visited May 17, 2023); Laura C. Morel, *Largo Man Accused of Killing Wife has Long History of Violence,* TAMPA BAY TIMES (October 1, 2013).
102 *See* Morel, *supra* note 101. *See also* Pierson, Richard L, https://ccmspa.pinellascounty.org/PublicAccess/Search.aspx?ID=300&NodeID=11000%2c11100%2c23001%2c11101%2c11102%2c11103%2c11104%2c11105%2c11106%2c11107%2c11108%2c11114%2c11109%2c23002%2c23003%2c11110%2c11111%2c11112%2c11113%2c11200%2c11201%2c11202%2c11203%2c11204%2c11205%2c11206%2c11207%2c11208%2c23004%2c11209%2c11210%2c11300%2c11301%2c11302%2c11303%2c11304%2c11305%2c11400%2c11410%2c11411%2c11412%2c11450%2c

11451%2c11452%2c11453%2c11600%2c11601%2c11602%2c11603%
2c11604%2c12000%2c12100%2c12101%2c12102%2c12103%2c12104
%2c12105%2c12106%2c12107%2c12108%2c12109%2c12110%2c1211
1%2c12113%2c12112%2c12114%2c12200%2c12201%2c12202%2c12
203%2c12204%2c12205%2c12206%2c12207%2c12208%2c12209%2c
12300%2c12310%2c12311%2c12312%2c12320%2c12321%2c12322%
2c12400%2c14000%2c14100%2c14200%2c14300%2c14400%2c14500
%2c14600%2c13000%2c13100%2c13200&NodeDesc=Pinellas+County (last visited May 18, 2023).

103 See Morel, *supra* note 101. *See also* Pierson, *supra* note 102.
104 See State of Florida v. Pierson, 1993MM003283 (1993) https://ccmspa.pinellascounty.org/PublicAccess/CaseDetail.aspx?CaseID=10210428 (last visited May 18, 2023); State of Florida v. Pierson, 2006CF026487 (2006) https://ccmspa.pinellascounty.org/PublicAccess/CaseDetail.aspx?CaseID=7929190 (last visited May 18, 2023); State of Florida v. Pierson, 2009CF007421 (2009) https://ccmspa.pinellascounty.org/PublicAccess/CaseDetail.aspx?CaseID=8021525 (last visited May 18, 2023); State of Florida v. Pierson, 2009CF016369 (2009) https://ccmspa.pinellascounty.org/PublicAccess/CaseDetail.aspx?CaseID=8030435 (last visited May 18, 2023). In Florida, when the state attorney files a "No information," it is a document notifying the court that the prosecutor has decided not to pursue formal charges, causing the case to terminate. (*See Anatomy of a Criminal Case*, THE KILFIN LAW FIRM, P.C., https://www.kilfinlaw.com/criminal-defense/anatomy-of-a-criminal-case/#:~:text=In%20Florida%2C%20a%20charging%20document,Release%22%20and%20prosecution%20is%20terminated. (last visited June 9, 2023)).
105 *See* Pierson, 2006CF026487; Pierson, 2009CF007421; Pierson, 2009CF016369.
106 *See* State of Florida v. Pierson, 2009CF007421, 1 (2009) (Complaint & Advisory).
107 *See* State of Florida v. Pierson, 2009CF007421, 1 (2009) (Request Not to Prosecute/Request for Contact).
108 *See* State of Florida v. Pierson, 2009CF007421, 1 (2009) (Order Allowing Contact); State of Florida v. Pierson, 2009CF007421, 1 (2009) (No Information).
109 *See* State of Florida v. Pierson, 2010CF010930 (2010) (Complaint & Advisory).
110 *Id.* at 1.
111 *See Id.*
112 *See* State of Florida v. Pierson, 2010CF010930 (2010) (Request Not to Prosecute/Request for Contact); State of Florida v. Pierson, 2010CF010930 (2010) (No Information).
113 *See* State of Florida v. Pierson, 2012CF013494 (2012) https://ccmspa.pinellascounty.org/PublicAccess/CaseDetail.aspx?CaseID=8130647 (last visited May 18, 2023).
114 *See* State of Florida v. Pierson, 2012CF013494 (2012) https://ccmspa.pinellascounty.org/PublicAccess/CaseDetail.aspx?CaseID=8130647 (last visited May 18, 2023); Morel, *supra* note 101.
115 *See* Morel, *supra* note 101 at ¶ 9.
116 *See* State of Florida v. Pierson, 2012CF013494 (2012) https://ccmspa.pinellascounty.org/PublicAccess/CaseDetail.aspx?CaseID=8130647 (last visited May 18, 2023).
117 *See Id.*; Morel, *supra* note 101.
118 *See* Lake, 13-009530 at 7. *See also* Pierson, 2012CF013494.
119 *See* Lake, *supra* note 118 at 8.
120 *See Id.* at 7.

121 *See Id.*
122 *See Id.* at 8.
123 *See Id.* at 7.
124 *See Id.*
125 *See Id.*
126 *See Id.*
127 *See Id.*
128 State of Florida v. Pierson, 2013CF016502 (2013) (Indictment).
129 State of Florida v. Pierson, 2013CF016502 (2015) (Judgment).
130 Dieu v. Damas, 05-1723-DR, 3 (2005) (Pet. for Inj. for Prot. Against Dom. Viol.).
131 Huss v. Huss, 03-485 DV, 2 (2003) (Pet. for Inj. for Prot. Against Dom. Viol.).
132 *See* Tewmey, 12-140716 at 16.
133 *See Id.*
134 *See Id.*
135 *See Id.* at 19.
136 Allen v. Allen, 12-15371, 4 (2012) (Pet. for Inj. for Prot. Against Dom. Viol.).
137 *Id.*
138 *Id.*
139 *Id.*
140 *Id.*
141 *Id.*
142 *See* Allen v. Allen, 12-15371, 4 (2012) https://hover.hillsclerk.com/html/case/caseSummary.html (last visited May 18, 2023).
143 *See* Bonefont, SC# HS 2013-2555 at 4.
144 *See Id.*
145 *See Id.*
146 *See Id.*
147 *See Id.*
148 *See* Dan Sullivan, *Couple's Unstable Relationship Ends in Murder-Suicide, Hillsborough Deputies Say*, TAMPA BAY TIMES (April 27, 2013).
149 *See Id.*
150 *See Id.*
151 *Id.* at ¶ 11.
152 *See Id.*
153 *See* RICHARD M. HOUGH & KIMBERLY D. MCCORKLE, AMERICAN HOMICIDE (2017).
154 *Id.* at 90; Sonia Salari & Carrie LeFevre Sillito, *Intimate Partner Homicide-Suicide: Perpetrator Primary Intent Across Young, Middle, and Elder Adult Age Categories*, 26 AGGRESSION AND VIOLENT BEHAVIOR 26, 27 (2016) https://doi.org/10.1016/j.avb.2015.11.004.
155 HOUGH & MCCORKLE, *supra* note 118 at 90.
156 *See Id.*
157 *See Id.*
158 *See Id.*
159 Brown v. Brown, 15-DR-4900-06D-W, 4, 7 (2015) (Pet. for Inj. for Prot. Against Dom. Viol.).
160 *Id.* at 4–7.
161 *Id.* at 4.

162 Id. at 7.
163 Id.
164 Brown v. Brown, 15-DR-4900-06D-W (2015) (Temporary Inj. for Prot. Against Dom. Viol. with Minor Child(ren)); Brown v. Brown, 15-DR-4900-06D-W (2015) (Final Judgment of Inj. for Prot. Against Dom. Viol. with Minor Child(ren) (after Notice)).
165 Brown v. Brown, 15-DR-4900-06D-W, 1 (2015) (Final Judgment of Inj. for Prot. Against Dom. Viol. with Minor Child(ren) (after Notice)).
166 *See generally* Brown, 201600002927 at 1–48. *See also* Tom Cleary, *Henry Ramone Brown: 5 Fast Facts You Need to Know*, HEAVY (April 19, 2016); Edward Lawson, *Slain Wife Warned Police that Husband Threatened to Kill Her*, THE DAYTONA BEACH NEWS-JOURNAL (April 19, 2016).
167 *See* Hannah Parry, *Florida Man Hides in Trunk of Wife's Car at Chili's, Stabs Her to Death and Runs Her Over, Before Shooting Their Two Kids and Himself Dead*, DAILY MAIL.COM (April 18, 2016). *See also* Brown, *supra* note 166.
168 *See generally* Brown, *supra* note 166. *See also* Lawson, *supra* note 166.
169 *See generally* Brown, *supra* note 166. *See also* Lawson, *supra* note 166.
170 *See generally* Brown, *supra* note 166. *See also* Lawson, *supra* note 166.
171 *See generally* Brown, *supra* note 166. *See also* Lawson, *supra* note 166.
172 *See generally* Brown, *supra* note 166. *See also* Lawson, *supra* note 166.
173 Whyte v. Dell, 2008DR003807, 3–4 (2008) (Pet. for Inj. for Prot. Against Dom. Viol.).
174 *See* Whyte v. Dell, 2008DR003807 (2008) https://appsgp.mypalmbeachclerk.com/eCaseView/search.aspx (last visited May 19, 2023).
175 *See* State of Florida v. Dell, 09CF015967 (2009) (Arrest/Notice to Appear); State of Florida v. Dell, 09CF015967 (2009) (Order).
176 *See* State of Florida v. Dell, 09CF015967 (2009) (Reporting Conditions of Supervision).
177 *See Id.*
178 Whyte-Dell v. Dell, 2010DR006153, 4 (2010) (Pet. for Inj. for Prot. Against Dom. Viol.).
179 Id.
180 *See* Whyte-Dell v. Dell, 2010DR006153 (2010) https://appsgp.mypalmbeachclerk.com/eCaseView/search.aspx (last visited May 19, 2023).
181 *See* Vance, 10-10106 at 3–16; Marimer Matos, *Police, Florida Blamed for Family Massacre*, COURTHOUSE NEWS SERVICE (February 2, 2012).
182 *See* Vance, *supra* note 181; Matos, *supra* note 181.
183 *See* Vance, *supra* note 181; Matos, *supra* note 181.
184 *See* Vance, *supra* note 181.
185 *See Id.*; Matos, *supra* note 181.
186 *See* Matos, *supra* note 181; *Father of Dead Children Sues DCF in Riviera Beach Murder-Suicide*, ABC 25WPBF NEWS (March 7, 2010).
187 *See* Matos, *supra* note 181; *Father of Dead Children Sues DCF in Riviera Beach Murder-Suicide*, *supra* note 186.
188 *See* Barnett v. State Dept. of Fin. Serv., SC19-87, 3–4 (Fla. 2020).
189 Matos, *supra* note 181 at ¶ 13–14; *accord Father of Dead Children Sues DCF in Riviera Beach Murder-Suicide*, *supra* note 186.
190 Matos, *supra* note 181 at ¶ 16; *accord* Barnett, SC19-87 at 3–4.
191 *See generally* Barnett, SC19-87. Because of the number of deaths through gun violence at the hands of Patrick Dell on September 27, 2010, this act

is considered a mass shooting or mass murder because four or more people were killed, not including the shooter (*See Id.*); Wyatte Grantham-Philips, *What is a Mass Shooting?: There's No Consensus Definition, but Here's What You Should Know*, USA TODAY (June 11, 2022)). The trial level court heard motions for partial summary judgment by the father and brother regarding the issue of sovereign immunity the State of Florida raised as an affirmative defense to the lawsuit, arguing "whether the $200,000 aggregate cap applied to all claims arising out of the mass shooting committed at Whyte-Dell's residence" (Barnett, SC19-87 at 4). The trial court found in favor of the father and brother, determining that each death was eligible for an individual claim; however, Florida's Fourth District Court of Appeal reversed the trial court, concluding that DCF's negligence created only one single claim from which each estate or the injured child could recover. As a matter of great public importance, the question regarding the limitation on the waiver of sovereign immunity and the liability cap of state agencies at $200,000 for all resulting injuries or deaths when there are multiple claims for negligence arising out of the same negligent act(s) committed by a state agency or actor arising out of the same incident or occurrence was certified by the Florida Supreme Court. The Florida Supreme Court upheld the Fourth District Court of Appeal by determining that the controlling Florida Statute did not allow for a waiver of sovereign immunity above the liability cap in cases against state agencies and actors, preventing the father and son from recovering more than the $200,000 aggregate cap. This case has since affected the recovery for other families in mass shooting cases, including those from the February 14, 2018 mass murder at Marjory Stoneman Douglas High School in Parkland, Florida (*See* Scott Powers, *Supreme Court Caps Sovereign Claims at $200K, Even for Parkland*, FLORIDA POLITICS (September 24, 2020)).

192 *See* Davis, 0000033189 at 5.
193 *See Id.*
194 *See Id.*
195 *See Id.*
196 *See Id.*
197 *See Id.*
198 *See* Raines, 0100038928 at 4.
199 *See Id.*
200 *See Id.*
201 *See Id.*
202 *See Id.* at 4–5.
203 *See Id.* at 5.
204 *See generally* Dieu v. Damas, 2005-DR-001723 (2005) (Pet. for Inj. for Prot. Against Dom. Viol.).
205 *See Id.* at 3.
206 *See Id.*
207 *Id.*
208 *See* Dieu v. Damas, 2005-DR-001723 (2005) https://cms.collierclerk.com/CMSWeb/#!/casedetails (last visited May 20, 2023).
209 *See generally* Damas v. Dieu, 2005-DR-001753 (2005) (Pet. for Inj. for Prot. Against Dom. Viol.).
210 *See generally Id.*
211 *See Id.*
212 *See Id.*

213 *See* Dieu v. Damas, 2005-DR-001723 (2005) https://cms.collierclerk.com/CMSWeb/#!/casedetails (last visited May 21, 2023); Damas v. Dieu, 2005-DR-001753 (2005) https://cms.collierclerk.com/CMSWeb/#!/casedetails (last visited May 21, 2023).
214 *See* Dieu v. Damas, 2005-DR-001723 (2005) https://cms.collierclerk.com/CMSWeb/#!/casedetails (last visited May 21, 2023); Damas v. Dieu, 2005-DR-001753 (2005) https://cms.collierclerk.com/CMSWeb/#!/casedetails (last visited May 21, 2023).
215 *See* Dieu v. Damas, 2005-DR-001723 (2005) https://cms.collierclerk.com/CMSWeb/#!/casedetails (last visited May 21, 2023); Damas v. Dieu, 2005-DR-001753 (2005) https://cms.collierclerk.com/CMSWeb/#!/casedetails (last visited May 21, 2023).
216 *See* Dieu v. Damas, 2005-DR-001723 (2005) https://cms.collierclerk.com/CMSWeb/#!/casedetails (last visited May 21, 2023).
217 *See* Ward, 0600000613 at 5.
218 *See Id.*
219 *See Id.*
220 *See Id.*
221 *See* Damas, Mesac, https://cms.collierclerk.com/CMSWeb/#!/search-results (last visited May 21, 2023).
222 Damas v. Dieu, 2006-DR-003595, 3 (2006) (Pet. for Inj. for Prot. Against Dom. Viol.).
223 *See Id.*
224 *See Id.*
225 *See Id.*
226 *Id.* at 3.
227 *See* Damas v. Dieu, 2006-DR-003595 (2006) https://cms.collierclerk.com/CMSWeb/#!/casedetails (last visited May 22, 2023).
228 *See Id.*
229 *See* State of Florida, Marriage Record, Application No. 07-0443, Dept. of Health, Vital Statistics (March 27, 2007).
230 *See* Forth, 0700017695 at 8.
231 *See Id.*
232 *See Id.*
233 *See Id.*
234 *Id.*
235 *Id.*
236 *See Id.*
237 *See Id.*
238 *See Id.*
239 *Id.* at 10.
240 *See Id.*
241 *See Id.*
242 Acres, 0800033320 at 6.
243 *See Id.*
244 *Id.*
245 *Id.*
246 *Id.* at 1.
247 *See* Comings, 0900000461 at 7.
248 *See Id.*
249 *Id.* at 7.

250 See Id.
251 Id. at 7–8.
252 See Id. at 8–9.
253 See Id.; State of Florida v. Damas, 2009-MM-000056 (2009) https://cms.collierclerk.com/CMSWeb/#!/casedetails (last visited May 22, 2023); State of Florida v. Damas, 2009-MM-000056 (2009) (Booking Sheet for Battery).
254 See State of Florida v. Damas, 2009-MM-000056 (2009) (No Contact Order).
255 See Id.
256 See Id.; State of Florida v. Damas, 2009-CF-002298, 11–12 (2009) (Sentencing Order).
257 State of Florida v. Damas, 2009-MM-000056 (2009) (Correspondence from Victim to Judge).
258 Id.
259 See State of Florida v. Damas, 2009-MM-000056 (2009) https://cms.collierclerk.com/CMSWeb/#!/casedetails (last visited May 22, 2023); State of Florida v. Damas, 2009-MM-000056 (2009) (Correspondence from Victim to Judge).
260 See State of Florida v. Damas, 2009-MM-000056 (2009) (Correspondence from Victim to Judge).
261 See Id.
262 See Id.
263 See Id.
264 Id. at 2.
265 See State of Florida v. Damas, 2009-MM-000056 (2009) (Information For).
266 See State of Florida v. Damas, 2009-MM-000056 (2009) (Mt. to Set Aside No Contact Order).
267 See State of Florida v. Damas, 2009-MM-000056 (2009) (Renewed Mt. to Set Aside No Contact Order).
268 Id.
269 See State of Florida v. Damas, 2009-MM-000056 (2009) (Order); State of Florida v. Damas, 2009-MM-000056 (2009) https://cms.collierclerk.com/CMSWeb/#!/casedetails (last visited May 22, 2023).
270 See State of Florida v. Damas, 2009-MM-000056 (2009) (Plea of Guilty or No Contest); State of Florida v. Damas, 2009-MM-000056 (2009) (Judgment).
271 See State of Florida v. Damas, 2009-MM-000056 (2009) (Judgment); State of Florida v. Damas, 2009-CF-002298, 11–12 (2009) (Sentencing Order).
272 See Ward, 0900025053 at 5; Ellis, 0900025085 at 9.
273 See Ward, supra note 272.
274 See Id.; State of Florida v. Damas, SC17-2062, 8 (Fla. 2020).
275 See Ward, supra note 272; Ellis, supra note 272; State of Florida v. Damas, 2009-CF-002298, 1 (2009) (Aff. For Criminal Offense).
276 See Ward, supra note 272.
277 See Id.; Ellis, supra note 272.
278 Ward, supra note 272.
279 Ellis, supra note 272.
280 See Id.
281 See Id.; State of Florida v. Damas, 2009-CF-002298, 1 (2009) (Aff. For Criminal Offense).
282 See Ellis, supra note 272; State of Florida v. Damas, SC17-2062, 8 (Fla. 2020).
283 Damas, 2009-CF-002298 at 1; accord Damas, SC17-2062 at 8; Ellis, supra note 272.
284 See Damas, SC17-2062 at 8.

285 Id.
286 See Id. at 9; State of Florida v. Damas, 2009-CF-002298, 7 (2009) (Sentencing Order).
287 See Damas, SC17-2062 at 22; State of Florida v. Damas, 2009-CF-002298, 26 (2009) (Sentencing Order).
288 See Damas, SC17-2062 at 8–9.
289 See Ellis, *supra* note 272 at 10; State of Florida v. Damas, 2009-CF-002298, 6 (2009) (Sentencing Order).
290 See Damas, SC17-2062 at 9, 14.
291 See Id.
292 See Id. at 14.
293 See Id. at 9.
294 See Id.
295 See Brooke Baitinger, *Supreme Court Affirms Six Death Sentences for Mesac Damas in Killing of Wife and Five Kids*, NAPLES DAILY NEWS ¶ 6 (January 3, 2019).
296 See Ellis, *supra* note 272 at 10–11.
297 State of Florida v. Damas, 2009-CF-002298, 2 (2009) (Aff. For Criminal Offense).
298 See Id.; State of Florida v. Damas, SC17-2062, 9 (Fla. 2020).
299 See State of Florida v. Damas, 2009-CF-002298, 2–3 (2009) (Aff. For Criminal Offense); State of Florida v. Damas, 2009-CF 002298, 12–13 (2009) (Sentencing Order).
300 See State of Florida v. Damas, 2009-CF-002298, 3 (2009) (Aff. For Criminal Offense).
301 Id.; *accord* State of Florida v. Damas, 2009-CF-002298, 12–13 (2009) (Sentencing Order).
302 State of Florida v. Damas, 2009-CF-002298, 3 (2009) (Aff. For Criminal Offense).
303 See generally State of Florida v. Damas, 2009-CF-002298, 3 (2009) (Booking Sheet Capias/Warrant); State of Florida v. Damas, 2009-CF-002298, 3 (2009) (Indictment); State of Florida v. Damas, 2009-CF-002298, 1 (2009) (Sentencing Order).
304 See State of Florida v. Damas, SC17-2062, 2 (Fla. 2020).
305 See Id. at 3.
306 See Id. at 4.
307 See Id.
308 See Id. at 4–5.
309 See Id. at 5.
310 See Id.
311 Id.
312 Id.
313 See Id. at 6.
314 See Id.
315 See Id.
316 See Id.; State of Florida v. Damas, 2009-CF-002298, 14 (2009) (Sentencing Order).
317 See State of Florida v. Damas, 2009-CF-002298, 3 (2009) (Aff. For Criminal Offense); State of Florida v. Damas, SC17-2062, 6–7 (Fla. 2020).
318 See State of Florida v. Damas, 2009-CF-002298, 3 (2009) (Aff. For Criminal Offense).
319 Id.

320 State of Florida v. Damas, 2009-CF-002298, 12 (2009) (Sentencing Order); *accord* State of Florida v. Damas, 2009-CF-002298, 3 (2009) (Aff. For Criminal Offense); Damas, SC17-2062 at 7.
321 Damas, SC17-2062 at 7.
322 *See Id.*
323 *Id.*
324 *Id.* at 10.
325 *See Id.*
326 *See Id.*
327 *See Id.*
328 *See Id.*
329 *See* State of Florida v. Damas, 2009-CF-002298, 26 (2009) (Sentencing Order).
330 State of Florida v. Damas, 2009-CF-002298, 3 (2009) (Aff. For Criminal Offense); State of Florida v. Damas, 2009-CF-002298, 26 (2009) (Sentencing Order).
331 State of Florida v. Damas, 2009-CF-002298, 26 (2009) (Sentencing Order).
332 *See* State of Florida v. Damas, 2009-CF-002298, 3 (2009) (Aff. For Criminal Offense).
333 *See Id.*
334 *See Id.*
335 *Id.* Because his statements to agents in Haiti and to authorities in the United States are inconsistent on these facts, it is unclear as to the series of events whether Mesac killed Guerline before dragging her into the bathroom and whether he cut her throat prior to the duct tape being applied to her neck (*See* State of Florida v. Damas, SC17-2062, 10, n.9 (Fla. 2020)). Crime scene and forensic evidence suggests she was killed after she was in the bathroom and after the duct tape was fully applied (*See* State of Florida v. Damas, SC17-2062, 10, n.9 (Fla. 2020)).
336 Damas, SC17-2062 at 11; *accord* State of Florida v. Damas, 2009-CF-002298, 3 (2009) (Aff. For Criminal Offense).
337 *See* Damas, SC17-2062 at 12.
338 *Id.*
339 *Id.*
340 *See Id.*
341 *Id.*; *accord* State of Florida v. Damas, 2009-CF-002298, 17 (2009) (Sentencing Order).
342 *See* State of Florida v. Damas, 2009-CF-002298, 17 (2009) (Sentencing Order).
343 State of Florida v. Damas, 2009-CF-002298, 3 (2009) (Aff. For Criminal Offense); *accord* State of Florida v. Damas, 2009-CF-002298, 17 (2009) (Sentencing Order).
344 *See* State of Florida v. Damas, SC17-2062, 12, 15 (Fla. 2020); State of Florida v. Damas, 2009-CF-002298, 19 (2009) (Sentencing Order).
345 *See* Damas, SC17-2062 at 13.
346 *See Id.* at 12–13.
347 *Id.* at 13.
348 *See* State of Florida v. Damas, 2009-CF-002298 (2009) (Notice of Intent to Seek Death Penalty).
349 *See* State of Florida v. Damas, 2009-CF-002298, 6 (2009) (Sentencing Order); Damas, SC17-2062 at 13.

350 *See generally* State of Florida v. Damas, 2009-CF-002298 (2009) (Sentencing Order).
351 *See generally* Damas, SC17-2062.
352 *See supra* Chapter 3, Litigation Abuse or Judicial Terrorism®? *See also* King, *supra* note 1.
353 *See* Frasch v. Frasch et al., 2013-DR-4158, 4 (2103) (Verified Petition for Dissolution of Marriage and Other Relief).
354 *See Id.* at 2, 4.
355 *See Id.* at 5.
356 *See Id.*
357 *See Id.* at 6.
358 *See Id.*; State of Florida v. Mbotizafy, 2010-MM-005852, 1 (2010) (Information).
359 *See* Frasch v. Frasch et al., 2013-DR-4158, 6 (2103) (Verified Petition for Dissolution of Marriage and Other Relief).
360 *See* Mbotizafy, 2010-MM-005852 at 1.
361 *See* State of Florida v. Mbotizafy, 2010-MM-005852, 1 (2010) (Amended Information); State of Florida v. Mbotizafy, 2010-MM-005852, 1 (2010) (Nolle Prosequi); State of Florida v. Mbotizafy, 2010-MM-005852, 1 (2010) (Judgment).
362 *See* State of Florida v. Mbotizafy, 2010-MM-005852, 1 (2010) (Judgment).
363 *See* Frasch v. Frasch et al., 2013-DR-4158, 6 (2103) (Verified Petition for Dissolution of Marriage and Other Relief).
364 *See Id.* at 3, 6.
365 Jennifer Portman, *Frasch Murder Investigation Reveals Couple's Torrid Existence*, PENSACOLA NEWS JOURNAL ¶ 8 (March 1, 2015); *accord* Frasch et al., 2013-DR-4158 at 6–7.
366 Frasch v. State of Florida, 1D17-754, 6 (Fla. 1st DCA 2019); *accord* Frasch et al., 2013-DR-4158 at 6–7.
367 Frasch et al., 2013-DR-4158 at 14.
368 *See* State of Florida v. Frasch, 2014CF003426, 8 (2015) (Transcript of Hearing on Motion to Set Bond).
369 Farcas, 130133844 at 3.
370 *See Id.*
371 *Id.*
372 *Id.*
373 *See Id.*
374 *Id.*
375 *See Id.*
376 *See* Frasch v. Frasch et al., 2013-DR-4158, 14 (2103) (Verified Petition for Dissolution of Marriage and Other Relief).
377 *See* Farcas, *supra* note 369.
378 *Id.*; *accord* Frasch et al., 2013-DR-4158 at 16.
379 Farcas, *supra* note 369.
380 *Id.*
381 *Id.* at 4.
382 *See* Morgan, 130152169 at 3.
383 *See Id.*
384 *See Id.*
385 *See Id.*
386 *See Id.*
387 *Id.*

388 *See* Frasch v. Frasch et al., 2013-DR-4158, 3–4 (2103) (Verified Petition for Dissolution of Marriage and Other Relief).
389 *See* Morgan, *supra* note 382.
390 *See Id.*
391 *Id.*
392 *See Id.*
393 *Id.*
394 *See Id.*
395 *Id.*
396 *See Id.*
397 *See Id.*
398 *See Id.*
399 *See Id.*
400 *See Id.*
401 *See Id.*
402 *See Id.*
403 *See generally* Frasch v. Frasch, 2013DR003946 (2013) (Pet. for Inj. for Prot. Against Dom. Viol.); Frasch v. Frasch, 2013DR003955 (2013) (Pet. for Inj. for Prot. Against Dom. Viol.).
404 *See* Frasch v. Frasch, 2013DR003946, 4 (2013) (Pet. for Inj. for Prot. Against Dom. Viol.).
405 *See Id.*
406 *See Id.*
407 *See Id.*
408 *See* Frasch v. Frasch et al., 2013-DR-4158, 11 (2103) (Verified Petition for Dissolution of Marriage and Other Relief).
409 Frasch v. Frasch, 2013DR003955, 4 (2013) (Pet. for Inj. for Prot. Against Dom. Viol.).
410 *Id.*
411 *See* Frasch et al., 2013-DR-4158 at 11–12.
412 State of Florida v. Frasch, 2013MM3605, 2 (2013) (Probable Cause Aff.).
413 *See Id.*
414 *See Id.*
415 State of Florida v. Frasch, 2013MM3605 (2013) (No Information).
416 *See generally* Frasch v. Frasch, 2013DR003946 (2013); Frasch v. Frasch, 2013DR003955 (2013).
417 *See generally* Frasch, 2013DR003955.
418 *See* State of Florida v. Frasch, 2014CF003426, 10 (2015) (Transcript of Hearing on Motion to Set Bond).
419 *See generally* Frasch, 2013DR003955.
420 *See* Frasch v. Frasch et al., 2013-DR-4158, 16 (2103) (Verified Petition for Dissolution of Marriage and Other Relief).
421 *See generally* Frasch, 2013DR003955. *See also* State of Florida v. Frasch, 2014CF003426, 10 (2015) (Transcript of Hearing on Motion to Set Bond).
422 Jennifer Portman & Sean Rossman, *Attorney not Shocked by His Client's Death*, Tallahassee Democrat ¶ 17 (February 25, 2014).
423 *See Id.*
424 *Id.* at ¶ 18.
425 *See generally* Frasch, 2013DR003955.
426 *See generally Id.*
427 *See* Frasch v. Frasch, 2013DR004302, 4 (2013) (Pet. for Inj. for Prot. Against Dom. Viol.).

428 *See generally Id.*
429 *See generally Id.*
430 *See generally* Frasch v. Frasch, 2013DR003946 (2013) (Pet. for Inj. for Prot. Against Dom. Viol.); Frasch, 2013DR003955.
431 *See generally* Frasch, 2013DR003946; Frasch, 2013DR003955.
432 Frasch v. Frasch, 2013DR004158, 1–2 (2013) (Order on Wife's Emergency Mt. for Temp. Alimony, Child Support, Attorney's Fees, Suit Money and Costs, Temp. Parenting Plan and Exclusive Use and Possession of Marital Home).
433 *See generally* Frasch, 2013DR003955.
434 *See generally* Frasch, 2013DR003946; Frasch, 2013DR003955.
435 *See generally* Frasch, 2013DR003955.
436 *See generally* Frasch v. Frasch, 2013DR004158 (2013) (Order on Wife's Emergency Mt. for Enforcement, Contempt, and for Attorney's Fees).
437 *See generally Id.*
438 *Id.* at 2.
439 *See* State of Florida v. Frasch, 2014CF003426, 1 (2014) (Notice Pursuant to Florida Statues 90.404(2)).
440 *See Id.*
441 *See Id.*
442 *See Id.*
443 State of Florida v. Frasch, 2014CF003426, 14 (2015) (Transcript of Hearing on Motion to Set Bond).
444 *See* McConnaughhay v. Frasch et al., 2014CA001421, 3–5 (2015) (Second Amended Complaint).
445 *See* Frasch v. State of Florida, 1D17-754, 6–7 (Fla. 1st DCA 2019); McConnaughhay v. Frasch et al., 2014CA001421, 3–5 (2015) (Second Amended Complaint); State of Florida v. Frasch, 2014CF003426, 48 (2015) (Transcript of Hearing on Motion to Set Bond).
446 *See* Portman, *supra* note 365.
447 Frasch v. State of Florida, 1D17-754, 6 (Fla. 1st DCA 2019).
448 *See* State of Florida v. Frasch, 2014CF003426, 20 (2015) (Transcript of Hearing on Motion to Set Bond).
449 *See* State of Florida v. Frasch, 2014CF000557, 1 (2014) (Summary of Offense and Probable Cause Aff.).
450 *See* Portman, *supra* note 365; State of Florida v. Frasch, 2014CF000557 (2014) (Order to Appoint Mental Health Expert to Determine Defendant's Competency to Proceed); State of Florida v. Frasch, 2014CF000557 (2014) (Mt. to Quash Order Appointing Mental Health Expert); State of Florida v. Frasch, 2014CF000557 (2014) (Amended Order Appointing Mental Health Expert to Determine Defendant's Competency to Proceed); State of Florida v. Frasch, 2014CF000557 (2014) (Order Appointing Expert for Competency Evaluation and Notice of Hearing); State of Florida v. Frasch, 2014CF000557 (2014) (Order Granting Defendant's Motion to Quash Order Appointing Mental Health Expert); State of Florida v. Frasch, 2014CF000557 (2014) (Order Appointing Expert for Competency Evaluation and Notice of Hearing). *See generally* State of Florida v. Frasch, 2014CF003426 (2015) (Transcript of Hearing on Motion to Set Bond).
451 State of Florida v. Frasch, 2014CF000557, 2 (2014) (Order Adjudging Defendant Incompetent to Proceed).
452 *See* State of Florida v. Frasch, 2014CF000557, 2 (2014) (Order Finding Defendant Competent [Mental Illness]).

453 *See* State of Florida v. Frasch, 2014CF000557 (2014) (Plea and Acknowledgement of Rights); State of Florida v. Frasch, 2014CF000557 (2014) (Judgment).
454 State of Florida v. Frasch, 2014CF003426, 1 (2014) (Indictment); *accord* State of Florida v. Frasch, 2014CF003426, 1 (2014) (Arrest/Probable Cause Aff.).
455 *See* State of Florida v. Frasch, 2014CF003426, 33–34 (2015) (Transcript of Hearing on Motion to Set Bond).
456 *See Id.* at 33–34, 84.
457 *See Id.* at 35–36.
458 *See* Frasch v. State of Florida, 1D17-754, 7 (Fla. 1st DCA 2019).
459 *See* State of Florida v. Frasch, 2014CF003426, 49 (2015) (Transcript of Hearing on Motion to Set Bond); Frasch, 1D17-754 at 7.
460 State of Florida v. Frasch, 2014CF003426, 3 (2014) (Arrest/Probable Cause Aff.); *accord* State of Florida v. Frasch, 2014CF003426 (2015) (Order Granting Renewed Motion for Pretrial Bond); State of Florida v. Frasch, 2014CF003426, 87–89 (2015) (Transcript of Hearing on Motion to Set Bond).
461 *See* State of Florida v. Frasch, 2014CF003426 (2014) (Order of Recusal); State of Florida v. Frasch, 2014CF003426 (2016) (Order of Recusal). "*Sua sponte* means of their own will or motion, without prompting or suggestion." (*Sua sponte* definition, LAW INSIDER, https://www.lawinsider.com/dictionary/sua-sponte (last visited May 31, 2023)).
462 *See* State of Florida v. Frasch, 2014CF003426 (2014) (Nt. of Intent to Seek the Death Penalty); State of Florida v. Frasch, 2014CF003426 (2015) (Nt. of Waiver of Twelve Person Jury).
463 *See* State of Florida v. Frasch, 2014CF003426 (2015) (Nt. of Waiver of Twelve Person Jury); State of Florida v. Frasch, 2014CF003426 (2016) (Nt. of Intent to Seek the Death Penalty).
464 *See* State of Florida v. Frasch, 2014CF003426, 88 (2015) (Transcript of Hearing on Motion to Set Bond).
465 *See* State of Florida v. Frasch, 2014CF003426 (2015) (Verdict); State of Florida v. Frasch, 2014CF003426 (2015) (Trial Record).
466 *See generally* State of Florida v. Frasch, 2014CF003426 (2015) (Judgment); Frasch v. State of Florida, 1D17-754 (Fla. 1st DCA 2019).
467 *See generally* Frasch v. State of Florida, 2020 Fla. LEXIS 1023 (Fla. 2020); Frasch v. State of Florida, 2021 U.S. LEXIS 185 (2021).

Part III
Regulating Coercive Control
Lessons from Intimate Partner Violence and Intimate Partner Homicide Data

This part begins with a review of the study's data that includes a comprehensive explanation of its qualitative and quantitative results. Demographics of the intimate partner homicide (IPH) victims is discussed, which includes a closer look at Native Americans as well as Asian Americans and Pacific Islanders. Results of cases with multiple petitions for injunction for protection against domestic violence (DV) are provided, as well as those related to the intimate partner violence (IPV) victim's resistance to abuse. The significance of the theme of abuser mental illness is discussed; and the results of the theme of resistance of abuse are provided. Statistics on the effectiveness of orders of injunctions for protection against DV are provided to help the reader understand from the study's data whether the IPV victims, who filed for protection from the court, were able to obtain orders of protection at all or had orders of protection at the time of their deaths. The quantitative results for this study are provided to present further details about the entirety of the data collected and analyzed.

9 The Frequencies of Coercive Control

The population used for this study is the total population of intimate partner homicide (IPHs) between heterosexual spouses in the state of Florida from January 1, 2006, to June 30, 2016, according to the Florida Department of Law Enforcement's (FDLE's) Uniform Crime Report Supplemental Homicide Report (UCR-SHR), as more thoroughly described in Chapter 4.[1] Table 9.1 explains the coding coverage percentages of all the themes and subthemes as discussed in Part II. The first results column, N = 493, states the coding coverage percentage for each theme and subtheme when the petitions for injunction are considered against all the cases in the study. The second column, N = 62, states the coding coverage percentage for each theme and subtheme when the petitions for injunction are considered against all the cases in the qualitative portion of the study. The third column, N = 100, states the coding coverage percentage for each theme and subtheme when the petitions for injunction are considered as part of this content analysis for the qualitative portion of the study.

In the first column, physical violence had the highest overall coding coverage with 10.7% (Table 9.1). Resistance to abuse was the second highest coding coverage with 10.3%. The third highest coding coverage for the first column was threats with 8.9%. The lowest coding coverage for this column included three different subthemes which were: (1) animal abuse, (2) violent acts toward family and friends, and (3) pregnant. In the second column, as with the first, physical violence had the highest overall coding coverage with 84.1%. Resistance to abuse was also the second highest coding coverage with 80.9%. Similarly, threats came in third with 69.8% coding coverage. Also, as with the first column, animal abuse, violent acts toward family and friends, and pregnant had the same lowest coding coverage at 3.1%. The third column is the most indicative of the content analysis coding coverage percentages for the themes and subthemes of this qualitative portion of the study. Here, at 75%, physical violence was matched with threats as the highest coding coverage. Resistance to abuse has the second highest percentage at 51.0%, with power and control in third at 48.0%. The lowest

Table 9.1 Coding Coverage Percentages

Code Name		Cases, N = 493	Cases[a] w/Petition for Injunction, N = 62	Petition for Injunction, N = 100
Theme	Subtheme			
Intimidation		1.6%	12.6%	10.0%
	Animal abuse	0.4%	3.1%	2.0%
	Harassment	3.4%	26.9%	21.0%
	Surveillance	2.8%	22.2%	15.0%
	Threats	8.9%	69.8%	75.0%
	Threatens family and friends	2.8%	22.2%	14.0%
	Weapons	2.4%	19.0%	12.0%
Isolation		3.4%	26.9%	22.0%
	Economic control	2.0%	15.8%	10.0%
	False imprisonment	2.0%	15.8%	11.0%
	Financial control	2.2%	17.4%	13.0%
Humiliation		1.4%	11.1%	10.0%
	Degradation	1.8%	14.2%	11.0%
	Name Calling	4.6%	36.5%	23.0%
Power and control		7.3%	57.1%	48.0%
	Child abuse	3.4%	26.9%	23.0%
	Violent acts toward family and friends	0.4%	3.1%	2.0%
	Taking children from victim	1.2%	9.5%	7.0%
	Deprivation of necessities	1.0%	7.9%	5.0%
	Psychologically controlling	2.8%	22.2%	17.0%
	Verbal abuse	2.8%	22.2%	18.0%
	Household, clothes, and personal belongings destroyed	3.4%	26.9%	22.0%
Fearful of the future		7.0%	55.5%	42.0%
	Fear for child(ren)'s safety	2.8%	22.2%	16.0%
	Pregnant	0.4%	3.1%	2.0%
Resistance to abuse		10.3%	80.9%	51.0%
	Helping abuser	1.4%	11.1%	10.0%
	Separated or estranged	5.8%	46.0%	37.0%
Abuser mental illness		1.8%	14.2%	11.0%
	Drinking alcohol	3.0%	23.8%	19.0%
	Drug use	0.8%	6.3%	5.0%
	Paranoia	3.4%	26.9%	17.0%
Physical violence		10.7%	84.1%	75.0%
	Non-fatal strangulation	2.6%	20.6%	14.0%
	Rape and sexual abuse	1.6%	12.6%	9.0%

Note: Physical violence was used as a dependent variable in quantitative analysis.
[a] Cases may have more than one petition for injunction.

coding coverage percentages, i.e., animal abuse, violent acts toward family and friends, and pregnant, still tied at 2.0%.

The coercive control themes described throughout this book, i.e., intimidation, isolation, humiliation, power and control, fearful of the future, resistance to abuse, abuser mental illness, and physical violence, can all be analyzed in terms of their frequencies within the petitions for injunction, keeping in mind that all subthemes are incorporated within the themes. Table 9.2 explains the definitions and coding of the variables utilized for the frequencies presented in Table 9.3. IBM SPSS®, an advanced statistical software analysis program, was utilized for the frequencies analyses for this portion of the quantitative methods phase of the study.

Table 9.2 Definitions and Coding of Coercive Control Variables

	Variable	Variable Coding
Result of Abuse		
Intimidation	No (reference category)	0
	Yes	1
	Missing	9
Isolation	No (reference category)	0
	Yes	1
	Missing	9
Humiliation	No (reference category)	0
	Yes	1
	Missing	9
Power and Control	No (reference category)	0
	Yes	1
	Missing	9
Fearful of the Future	No (reference category)	0
	Yes	1
	Missing	9
Response to Abuse		
Resistance to Abuse	No (reference category)	0
	Yes	1
	Missing	9
Attribute of the Abuser		
Abuser Mental Illness	No (reference category)	0
	Yes	1
	Missing	9
Result of Abuse		
Physical Violence	Yes (reference category)	0
	No	1
	Missing	9

Note: Physical violence was used as a dependent variable in quantitative analysis.

Table 9.3 The Characteristics and Frequencies of Coercive Control

	Frequency, N = 100		Valid Percent	
Theme	No	Yes	No	Yes
Result of Abuse				
Intimidation	22	78	22.0%	78.0%
Isolation	62	38	62.0%	38.0%
Humiliation	67	33	67.0%	33.0%
Power and Control	25	75	25.0%	75.0%
Fearful of the Future	57	43	57.0%	43.0%
Response to Abuse				
Resistance to Abuse	25	75	25.0%	75.0%
Attribute of the Abuser				
Abuser Mental Illness	60	40	60.0%	40.0%
Result of Abuse				
Physical Violence	24	76	24.0%	76.0%

Note: Physical violence was used as a dependent variable in quantitative analysis.

Of all the coercive control themes, intimidation had the highest frequency with a 78.0% positive response for it being discussed in the petition for injunction by the victim. Power and control, as well as resistance to abuse, had the second highest positive response rate at 75% for the themes with "no" as their reference category. Fearful of the future had a frequency of 43% positive response, and isolation had a 38% positive response. Abuser mental illness had a frequency of 40% positive response for this theme that is unique to the attribute of the abuser. Humiliation had the lowest frequency with a 33.0% positive response for it being mentioned by the victim in the petition for injunction. Physical violence, with its reference category as "yes," had a high positive response rate of 76.0%; but it was not the highest overall.

Other frequencies of note for the qualitative portion of this study include the rate at which temporary injunctions and final injunctions were granted by the court as well as a determination as to whether any IPH victims were killed during the time these court protections were in place. $N = 107$ for these frequencies because, of the total 108 petitions for injunction collected, all but one was able to be used for these statistics. Table 9.4 provides the definitions and coding of these variables utilized for their frequencies presented in Table 9.5.

The frequency with the highest positive response rate shown in Table 9.5 is for Temporary Injunction Granted, which has a rate of 73.8% and describes temporary injunctions granted by the court to petition for injunction

Table 9.4 Definitions and Coding of Temporary Injunction and Final Injunction Variables

	Variable	Variable Coding
Temporary Injunction Granted	No (reference category)	0
	Yes	1
	Missing	9
Temporary Injunction in place at time of IPH	No (reference category)	0
	Yes	1
	Missing	9
Final Injunction Granted	No (reference category)	0
	Yes	1
	Missing	9
Final Injunction in place at time of IPH	No (reference category)	0
	Yes	1
	Missing	9

victims for protection against intimate partner violence (IPV). Final Injunction Granted had a frequency of 32.7% rate for a positive response relative to the court granting protection against IPV. When looking at the frequency rate of the IPH occurring during the time a protective order is in place, final injunctions had the higher rate of killing occurrence with a 15.9% positive rate than a temporary injunction, which had a 4.7% positive rate.

The variables IPH victim race, IPH offender race, petition for injunction victim race, and petition for injunction offender race have frequencies that are of importance to this qualitative portion of the study because certain minorities, i.e., Native Americans and Asians, who have dissimilarities with Black and White American cultures, often disappear in the statistics of quantitative analysis. Table 9.6 explains the definitions and coding of the variables utilized for victim/offender race in this study and their frequencies are presented in Table 9.7. $N = 493$ for IPH Race of Victim/Offender and $N = 108$ for Petition for Injunction Victim/Offender Race.

Table 9.5 Temporary Injunction and Final Injunction Variable Frequencies

	Frequency, $N = 107$			Valid Percent	
	No	Yes	Total	No	Yes
Temporary Injunction Granted	28	79	107	26.2%	73.8%
Temporary Injunction in place at time of IPH	102	5	107	95.3%	4.7%
Final Injunction Granted	72	35	107	67.3%	32.7%
Final Injunction in place at time of IPH	90	17	107	84.1%	15.9%

Table 9.6 Coding and Definitions of IPH and Petition for Injunction Victim/Offender Race

Variable		Variable Coding
IPH Race of Offender		
	White (reference category)	0
	Black	1
	Native Americans	2
	Asian	3
IPH Race of Victim		
	White (reference category)	0
	Black	1
	Native Americans	2
	Asian	3
Petition for Injunction Victim Race		
	White (reference category)	0
	Black	1
	Native Americans	2
	Asian	3
Petition for Injunction Offender Race		
	White (reference category)	0
	Black	1
	Native Americans	2
	Asian	3

Table 9.7 IPH and Petition for Injunction Victim/Offender Race Variable Frequencies

	Frequency								
Variable	White	Black	Native Americans	Asian	Total	White	Black	Native Americans	Asian
IPH Race of Victim	400	83	1	9	493	81.1%	16.8%	0.2%	1.8%
IPH Race of Offender	395	92	1	5	493	80.1%	18.7%	0.2%	1.0%
Race of Petition for Injunction Victim	68	36	3	1	108	63.0%	33.3%	2.8%	0.9%
Race of Petition for Injunction Offender	65	40	3	0	108	60.2%	37.0%	2.8%	0.0%

Whites had the highest positive response rate for all the race categories, with IPH race of victim as the highest at 81.1%; and race of petition for injunction offender as the highest at 60.2%. IPH race of offender for whites had a positive response rate of 80.1%; and race of petition for injunction victim had a positive response rate of 63.0%. Blacks had the second highest overall positive response rate for all categories, with race of petition for injunction offender as the highest at 37.0%; and IPH race of victim as the lowest rate for Blacks at 16.8%. Race of petition for injunction victim for Blacks had a positive response rate of 33.3%, and IPH race of offender had a positive response rate of 18.7%. Asians had the next highest positive response rate for the IPH category with a 1.8% rate for IPH race of victim and a 1.0% rate for IPH race of offender. Native Americans had the lowest positive response rate for IPH race of victim/offender with just 0.2% for both categories; however, this race category changes against Asians when looking at the petition for injunction victim/offender categories. Native Americans had a higher positive response rate for petition for injunction victim/offender race at 2.8% as opposed to Asians at 0.9% for petition for injunction victim race and 0.0% for petition for injunction offender race.

The final frequency for the qualitative portion of this study focuses on an analysis between the petition for injunction victim and the IPH victim. Because the IPH victim may not necessarily be the same as the petition for injunction victim, a variable was created to analyze whether there is a difference between the two victim types, if any. The dummy variable "Petition for Injunction Victim was IPH Victim," with a nominal level of measurement, is no = 1, yes = 0. With $N = 108$, it has a positive response rate of 67.6%, meaning 67.6% of the petition for injunction victims were the same as the IPH victims. Or stated a different way, 32.4% of the petition for injunction victims were not the IPH victims.

Demographics of Intimate Partner Homicide Victims

Although this is a scientific study and the data analyzed in this qualitative phase of the study were viewed through a scientific lens, it is important to remember that the 100 petitions for injunction examined for the content analysis represent sixty-two (62) IPHs, i.e., sixty-two (62) lives lost of people who were involved in a court process of asking for court protection prior to their deaths, not including others who lost their lives during the killing event.[2] Even though 32.4% of the petitions for injunction filed were not filed by the IPH victim, meaning the IPH offender asked the court for protection from IPV prior to killing their spouse, the remaining 67.6% of the petitions for injunction were filed by the IPH victim. Thus, the cases discussed below are about people who are no longer fighting for their lives. Indeed, they lost their battles against their abusers.

Native Americans

The first case of focus is on the only Native American IPH case in this study. For many reasons it is of interest, the most noticeable is race. During pre-Colonial times, Native Americans did not tolerate violence against women.[3] Their culture was one of gender equality whereby each saw the other as contributing equally to the overall good of society.[4] If harm came to a woman through sexual or physical violence, it was dealt with by the community swiftly.[5] Now, however, much has changed for Native American women, who are no longer safe on their native soil.[6] American Indian and Alaskan Native women experience lives filled with risk of violent crime, including IPV, at higher rates than other races.[7] Native American women should not feel safe in today's America; and when they seek a court's protection from domestic violence (DV), it is not necessarily the same process for them as it is for the rest of American women, making it even more difficult to stay safe.[8]

The fact that Native Americans constitute only 0.2% of the race basis of this study is surprising given the racial diversity in the state of Florida (Table 9.7). At the time of this study, Native Americans made-up 0.38% of Florida's total population.[9] In 2014, Native Americans make up about 2% of the total population in the United States, and Roberts (2015) explains that the national average for Native Americans for spousal homicide is 1.55%, highlighting the exceptionally low rate of 0.2% for Native American IPHs in this study.[10] Additionally, of the 100 petitions for injunction utilized for the content analysis for this study, there were two (2) petition for injunction generated from this same Native American couple.[11] These two (2) petitions for injunction were coded with ten (10) codes and twelve (12) codes respectively; thus, the details of the narrative were fairly rich. This is important in understanding that, although this single case may not have much of an impact for quantitative purposes, it did play a role in the qualitative voice of the victims. This Native American's voice is not lost.

Asian Americans and Pacific Islanders

The Asian population in this study is the other minority group of focus. There is little research regarding Asian Americans and Pacific Islanders and violence, but that does not mean that these minority groups are not at risk of experiencing IPV at the same rate as their White counterparts.[12] Indeed, the Asian population is known to under-report IPV because of the cultural stigma it brings based on the patriarchal norms of Asian culture.[13] Because of these deep-rooted cultural ideals of women's place in society, where men are the breadwinners and women stay home, it is important to analyze any data available where Asians reach out for assistance from the judicial system.[14]

Out of the 493 IPH cases, there were nine (9) Asian victims and five (5) Asian offenders, which means there are couples of different racial combinations in this study (Table 9.7). The Asian IPH victims and offenders constituted only 1.8% and 1.0% of the race basis of this study, respectively. Asians made-up 2.0% of Florida's total population at the time of this study; so, for the IPH cases, the average of 1.4% Asian IPH death rate is slightly lower than its population in Florida.[15] Roberts (2015) provides detailed explanations of male-on-female and female-on-male national averages for Asian spousal homicide rates based on the varying racial combinations he examined.[16] However, these rates are not comparable to this study since this study's frequencies were determined based on victim/offender rates; and the different racial combinations of Asians in this study. Thus, averaging Roberts (2015) results across all Asian categories of racial combinations, i.e., Asian killing Asian, Asian killing White, Asian killing Black, and Asian killing Native Americans allows for a gross comparison of the national averages for Asian spousal homicides, which are 1.80% for male-on-female and 1.02% for female-on-male.[17] These averages from the Roberts (2015) study help to explain that Florida's average Asian IPH rate determined by this study is in line with the national average when taking both national rates provided by Roberts (2015) into consideration.[18]

Only one of the nine (9) Asian IPH victims sought court protection prior to their death, and none of the five (5) Asian IPH offenders chose to initiate any court proceedings regarding petitions for injunction prior to a killing. The one IPH victim who did file a petition for injunction was involved in a mixed-race marriage with a White spouse. The petition for injunction alleged nonfatal strangulation as part of the physical violence, which is a marker for increased risk of IPH. Also, because the coding coverage percentage was the lowest for the subtheme of violent acts toward family and friends, the allegation of slashing the tires of the victim's brother due to an argument the offender had with the brother begs the question of race-based motives that might have been directed toward the brother (Table 9.1).

Multiple Petitions for Injunction for Protection Against Domestic Violence

Of the sixty-six (66) cases with filed petitions for injunction, some have multiple filings ranging from two (2) to six (6) petitions for injunction in one case; and 13.6% of the cases have petitions for injunction from both spouses as shown in Table 9.8.[19] The multiple filings, as well as the filings from both spouses, provide interesting dynamics to the qualitative portion of this study in addition to the overall perspective of IPH. To begin with, these multiple filings, as well as many of the single petition for injunction filings, reveal the behavior of law and the IPV victim's decision to mobilize the law. Black's (2010) theory of the behavior of law explains that intimates will not mobilize the law against each other even when IPV is present; and when the law is mobilized, he states that it is ineffective because intimates,

Table 9.8 Petition for Injunction Filing Frequencies

	Frequency							Valid Percent					
	1	2	3	4	5	6	Total	1	2	3	4	5	6
Petition for Injunction Case Filings	43	12	6	3	1	1	66	65.2%	18.2%	9.1%	4.5%	1.5%	1.5%

such as spouses, are less likely to follow through on participating in prosecutions or civil actions against each other.[20] However, when viewing the many cases with multiple petitions for injunction filings in this study, i.e., 34.8% in all, Black's (2010) notion that intimates will not mobilize the law when IPV is present does not seem to hold true.[21] In fact, the relational distance of the spouses in this study does not appear to matter overall given that 46.0% of the cases with petitions for injunction had a coding coverage percentage for the separated or estranged subtheme (Table 9.1). As a result, based on this qualitative portion of the study, not only do intimates mobilize the law against each other, Black's (2010) notion that intimates are inactive when it comes to the law is fallible.[22]

At first, one might assume that the IPH victim would be the only one to file all the petitions for injunction asking for protection from the court; but given that almost a third of the petitions for injunction in this study, i.e., 32.4% were filed by the killer, this assumption does not follow conventional wisdom. Perhaps this is because the petition for injunction victim is a battered spouse who just cannot take it anymore and becomes so frustrated with their situation because relief from the ongoing IPV is not provided by the court even though multiple requests were made. Thus, the IPV victim who has sought relief from the court, i.e., mobilized the law to no avail, takes the matter into their own hands and kills their abusive spouse, as was seen in several cases in Part II of this book. Additionally, when reviewing the content analysis for the qualitative portion of this study, it is important to remember that not all the words and phrases come from the IPH victim, meaning that some of the words and phrases analyzed came from the person who was the killer in the case. This perspective, although it is not known at the time the words are analyzed, is important because, once again, conventional wisdom is to assume that the petition for injunction victim was ultimately killed; but, for almost one third of the petitions for injunction, this is not the case.

Abuser Mental Illness Disclosed

One very important disclosure the petitions for injunction provide is about the abuser's mental illness.[23] As discussed in Chapter 3, IPHSs are killings that are generally not unexpected but are, rather, events that culminate after IPV relationships experience turmoil and conflict. Among the turmoil and conflict that exists within these IPV relationships that were disclosed in the petitions for injunction that ended in IPHSs were details of abuser mental illness. As stated in the results section of this study, many petition for injunction victims mentioned their spouses having mental health problems or diagnoses from professionals, as well as others stating that their spouse was Baker Acted. The significance in the Baker Act reference is that this often is the result of a threat against one's own life, which is a known risk factor for IPHS when IPV and depression are present.

A pronounced subtheme of abuser mental illness was paranoia. The petition for injunction narratives provided throughout Part II exemplify the lengths at which some abusers will go to accuse victims and hold them accountable. Many of the petitions for injunction had accounts of the abuser accusing the victim of cheating on them by simply texting, phoning, speaking, or talking to someone they did not approve of whether they had proof or not. Indeed, many of the narratives expressed the abuser's willingness to go to extremes to expose the victim's infidelity, meaning they would place themselves, the victim, their children, or others in harm's way. Amy Daley described her abuser accusing her of cheating on him and getting into her email to send threatening messages to people she knew. And Pamela Allen was sexually assaulted because her abuser accused her of infidelity. Then she was held against her will, i.e., false imprisonment, while her texts were read by her abuser. Finally, her abuser threatened her life. He killed her six (6) months later in an IPHS, which helps to prove that these events are not sudden, unexpected events that come out of the blue but are predictable, preventable murders.

The Intimate Partner Violence Victim's Resistance to Abuse

As discussed in Chapter 1, a term coined by Kelly and Johnson (2008), violent resistance, describes the violence an IPV victim may use in reaction to physical violence against oneself for the primary purpose of self-protection.[24] However, in this study, the resistance to abuse theme coded in the content analysis specifically excluded all references to physical violence because this study's focus is on the coercive control tactics exclusive of physical violence. Additionally, each petition for injunction was coded as its own individual data source, regardless of who filed it; so, this study did not determine whether violent resistance, as defined by Kelly and Johnson (2008), had taken place between the spouses.[25] Thus, physical violence was coded separately from any references to resistance to abuse, meaning the resistance to abuse definition for this study did not include the violent resistance as defined by Kelly and Johnson (2008).[26]

The resistance to abuse theme had an 80.9% coding coverage percentage for the sixty-two (62) cases, which was the second highest percentage next to physical violence (Table 9.1).[27] This high percentage juxtaposed against physical violence's coding coverage percentage of 84.1%, however, does seem to support Kelly and Johnson's (2008) proposition that IPV victims "fight" back against their abusers, although support for this is derived from this study's data which are based on non-violent tactics rather than from the violent resistance Kelly and Johnson (2008) espouse.[28] Indeed, as Stark (2007) explains and this study's data tend to prove, the coercive control victim will work through their victimization and find their agency through their resistance to the abuse.[29] Additionally, the IPV victims' narratives highlighted in this study, Chapter 7: When the Intimate Partner Violence Victim Resists the Abuse, Resistance to Abuse, reflect women who explicitly mobilized the law for their own protection, once again seemingly refuting Black's (2010) contention that intimates will not utilize the law for assistance when IPV is present in the relationship.[30]

The Effectiveness of Orders of Injunctions for Protection Against Domestic Violence

Chapter 3, the "The Disillusionment of the Protections of an Injunction for Protection against Domestic Violence: Why and When Are They Important to IPV Victims?" section discusses the willingness of IPV victims to jump through legal hoops to obtain a temporary injunction and/or final injunction to prevent their abuser from having legal access to them, which may include jail time for the abuser if the order is violated.[31] Indeed, often, IPV victims will file multiple petitions for injunction and obtain multiple temporary injunctions and/or final injunctions in the process of trying to protect themselves from multiple occurrences of abuse. The multiple petitions for injunction discussed throughout this book illuminate this willingness of IPV victims and the fact that some will tirelessly fight for their safety.[32] But even after these extraordinary efforts by IPV victims to ask for court protection, 95.3% of the IPH victims did not have a temporary injunction order in place when they were killed and 84.1% of the IPH victims did not have an final injunction in place at the time of their death (Table 9.5). Although these percentages mean that only 4.7% of the IPH victims were killed when a temporary injunction was in place and 15.9% were killed when a final injunction was active, these IPH victims had mobilized the law and asked the court to protect them as much as possible before they were killed. However, it is important to discuss the fact that many IPV victims had their injunction cases dismissed after their temporary injunctions were issued.

Throughout Chapters 5–8 of this book, case after case illustrates the difficulty the IPV victim faces once a temporary injunction is in place. First, when they are unable to attend the final injunction hearing, the case is dismissed. For some of the cases, it was apparent that the IPV victim was not able to attend the final injunction hearing for reasons such as work or previous obligation, at least those were the reported causes of them having missed their final hearings. For others, it was unclear why they did not return to court to attempt to obtain a final injunction. Second, it became very clear throughout many of the cases that the IPV victims repeatedly filed voluntary motions to dismiss their injunction cases prior to their final injunction hearings. Often, these motions to dismiss were almost immediately filed as soon as the abuser was served with notice of the injunction against them. In many cases where criminal actions ran concurrently with the civil injunction cases, the victims filed motions in the criminal cases asking prosecutors not to move forward with the prosecutions of their abusers. In fact, some experts estimate that the number of victims who drop charges against their abusers may be 50% or more.[33]

Some of the cases included concurrent dissolution of marriage action (DOM) litigation in which the IPV victim voluntarily dismissed that action as well. This pattern of the IPV victim dropping injunction cases, requesting criminal actions to not be prosecuted, or voluntarily dismissing DOM proceedings is palpable, is of concern given the outcome of these cases, and should be viewed as a red flag for lethality, which is another reason to view the IPV victim and abuser's case wholistically rather than in a vacuum within each individually filed injunction case proceeding. Finally, in a few of the cases, the court dropped the injunction case for reasons that were unclear, which may be due to the IPV victim not being able to attend the final hearing and not having an attorney there in their stead. Indeed, when an unrepresented IPV victim is not able to attend a final hearing for a legitimate reason, they have no one in court to explain to the judge the reason for their absence. As a result, the case will be dismissed; but with proper representation, the case might be continued.

The IPH victims, who had filed petitions for injunction and who were killed without any type of protective order in place at the time of their death, were left to their own devices even though they had mobilized the law and asked the court for protection. They did everything they legally could to protect themselves by, at least, beginning the legal process to request the court's protection from their abuser. In furtherance of the fact that IPV victims mobilize the law well, 73.8% of the petitions for injunction received a temporary injunction and 32.7% obtained a final injunction. This means that almost one third of the IPV victims followed through with their petitions for injunction to the final hearing to obtain a final injunction. Given the obstacles IPV victims face when attempting to obtain a final injunction, including the fact that many of them are not represented by an attorney, this success rate is commendable.

The analysis of the petition for injunction narratives in this study help prevent turning the focus from the IPH victim when they are killed with a protective order in place. Indeed, the perspective that the victim tried everything to protect themselves is lost in the rhetoric when such an occurrence happens because family, friends, and the media often look to the court and the judicial system for blame. However, people who work for these institutions did not do the killing; the IPH offender committed the crime. The "piece of paper" that must be strengthened are the laws that the courts must follow so that they have more choices to protect IPV victims when facing the fact patterns before them, including those that rely more heavily on coercive control without physical violence. It is important that state laws allow for judges to review people's lives and the continuum of behavior presented before them in petitions for injunction other than just having to parse out the simple battery or aggravated assault that may be before them. In fact, many lives might be saved if judges were not bound to only the acts of physical violence and threats to personal safety as the standard by which they must have evidence to grant a temporary injunction or final injunction. Instead, the petition for injunction narratives in this study present rich details of important non-violent coercive control events that courts could, and indeed should, be able to consider under the law as valid evidence for issuance of a temporary injunction or final injunction regardless of any evidence of physical violence.

The Interactions of Coercive Control Tactics

Qualitative Frequency Interactions

Coercive control tactics work together against its victim to ensure that the ongoing continuum of abuse maintains its effectiveness. In this study, the non-violent tactics of intimidation and power and control had the most efficacy against the petition for injunction victim with 78.0% and 75.0% positive frequency rate in the sixty-two (62) cases examined for content analysis, respectively (Table 9.3). The fact that intimidation and power and control rate the highest of the tactics that are a result of abuse is reasonable because these abusive behaviors are comparable. Again, these themes are not mutually exclusive, and some of the actions the petition for injunction victims described in their narratives are analogous to many other themes or subthemes.

Physical violence had a positive frequency rate of 76.0% (Table 9.3). With that said, resistance to abuse had a positive frequency rate of 75.0%, which is a direct result of, or response to, the abuse. For example, when a petition for injunction victim described being attacked, many of the narratives detailed responses that included calls to 911, speaking to the police, or the fact that the petition for injunction had been filed. These same reactions happened when petition for injunction victims described interactions with abusers who were intimidating and controlling to the point that the victim felt threatened. Also, although the positive frequency rate for the theme fearful of the future was not as high with a rate of 43.0%, often, the victim described feeling fearful of the future when such threats from the abuser would occur (Table 9.3).

Isolation and humiliation, both with lower positive frequency rates than the previously discussed coercive control tactics at 38.0% and 33.0% respectively, function to strip the coercive control victim of their personhood (Table 9.3). In this study, the petitions for injunction reveal details of victims feeling trapped in their own homes with no means of transportation to visit friends or family, as well as any way to call for help when abuse has occurred. These themes also work to ensure that the victims lose their sense of self-worth; so, over time, all the coercive control tactics begin to take their toll on the victim to where they lose their autonomy. However, the high positive frequency rate of resistance to abuse for this qualitative portion of the study is interesting because it indicates that many of the petition for injunction victims, who were focused on requesting protection from IPV from the court, did not allow the coercive control in their lives to prevent them from being completely stripped of their autonomy. This is a testament to the strength of these victims.

Quantitative Methods Results

As previously stated, it is important to remember that every case in this study represents an IPH between heterosexual spouses. Often, in scientific studies, among all the data and abbreviations, the people and the stories behind the data get lost. For a moment, it is appropriate to recognize that this study began with 665 homicide cases as provided by the FDLE's UCR-SHR that was subsequently divided into two data sets each with 493 and sixty-two (62) cases, respectively. In the following quantitative discussion, data set A represents the data set with 493 cases; and data set B represents the data set with sixty-two (62) cases.[34] Through quantitative data, it is possible to learn from these cases and to predict the risk of lethality to reduce the number of IPHs in the future, especially as it pertains to the non-violent tactics of coercive control.

Discussion: Data Set A – Frequencies

The purposive sample of 493 cases for data set A was drawn from the total population of 665 cases for this study due to the various reasons as described in detail in Chapter 4, including ensuring that the cases met the requirement of a heterosexual spousal IPH.[35] The following is a list and description of the variables used in the logistic regression model for data set A

Table 9.9 Explanation of Quantitative Variables for Data Set A

Predictor Variables	Coding	Dependent Variable	Coding
Weapon Used		Prior Report of Physical Violence to Law Enforcement	
Not a Handgun	0		
Handgun	1	IPH with a Prior Report of Physical Violence to Law Enforcement (reference category)	0
Not Other Firearms	0		
Other Firearm	1	IPH without a Prior Report of Physical Violence to Law Enforcement	1
Not Knife/Cutting Instrument	0		
Knife/Cutting Instr.	1	Missing	9
Not Hands/Fist/Feet	0	**Predictor Variables**	**Coding**
Hands/Fist/Feet	1		
Not Other Weapon	0	IPHS	
Other Weapon	1	Killing was not an IPHS (reference category)	0
		Killing was an IPHS	1
		Missing	9
		Record of Petition for Injunction	
		IPH with a Record of Record of Injunction (reference category)	0
		IPH without a Record of Petition for Injunction	1

in this exploratory study, which are also shown in Table 9.9.[36] The dependent variable measures whether there was a prior report of physical violence to law enforcement between the heterosexual spouses before the IPH.

The first variable for discussion, "prior report of physical violence to law enforcement," was used as the dependent variable throughout this study. Although the predominant viewpoint is that recidivism, which must come from some form of reporting to or interaction with the police, is one of the greatest risk factors for lethality assessment for IPV victims, data set A's dependent variable indicates that only 15.3% of the victims of IPH reported any physical violence to the police prior to their death (Table 9.10).[37] Indeed, because the outcome variable for this study is IPH, it is surprising to learn that this simple frequency turns the notion of recidivism and prearrest policies on their head. Stated another way, 84.7% of the IPH heterosexual

Table 9.10 Dependent Variable Frequencies (Data Set A)

	Frequency, N = 493			Valid Percent	
	Yes	No	Total	Yes	No
Prior Report of Physical Violence to Law Enforcement	66	365	431	15.3%	84.7%

Note: N = 493; there are sixty-two (62) missing records for this variable.[39]

Table 9.11 IPHS Variable Frequencies (Data Set A)

	Frequency, N = 493			Valid Percent		
	No	Yes	Total	No	Yes	Total
IPHS	247	245	492	50.2%	49.8%	100%

Note: N = 493; there is one (1) missing record for this variable.[46]

spouses in this study were not previously involved with law enforcement regarding their intimate relationship and physical violence prior to the killing. To say the least, numbers this low were not expected. Based on these results, Black's (2010) behavior of law theory is supported by the empirical research, suggesting that intimates do not mobilize the law against each other.[38]

The next variable for discussion is IPHS. The percentage of IPHs, 49.8%, that resulted in an IPHS was not expected but was not completely surprising either (Table 9.11). Velopulos et al. (2018) reported a 35% success rate of male suicides after killing female intimate partners.[40] The Violence Policy Center reported that in 2019, "Sixty-five percent of all murder-suicides involved an intimate partner. Of these, 95 percent were females killed by their intimate partners. Of these, 92 percent involved a gun."[41] In fact, the most common type of murder-suicide is one that takes place between two intimate partners.[42] The results from this study are much higher than the Velopulos et al. (2018) study, and the Violence Policy Center statistics do not completely comport with this study because they are strictly compared to other murder-suicides.[43] It is important to note that Velopulos et al. (2018) stated "[t]he high rate of 35% of completed suicide is staggering, and this argues for addressing and studying both IPV and suicidality together."[44] With this study's result of 49.8% completed IPHSs, one should be rather stunned with this statistic, further supporting Velopulos et al. (2018) call for additional IPHS research.[45]

The variable record of petition for injunction had only 13.4% of the cases with a filed petition for injunction, which is commensurate to the number of cases having a petition for injunction for analysis in this study (Table 9.12). It is interesting that less than 15% of the IPH victims sought

Table 9.12 Record of Petition for Injunction Variable Frequencies (Data Set A)

	Frequency, N = 493			Valid Percent		
	Yes	No	Total	Yes	No	Total
Record of Petition for Injunction	66	427	493	13.4%	86.6%	100%

protection from the court prior to their death because victims are generally referred to the court by social workers, clergy, friends, neighbors, etc., especially when all other sources of assistance have failed. However, through the cases presented in Part II, it became evident that, even though there were slightly more interactions with law enforcement, i.e., 15.3% (Table 9.10) than there were with the court, IPV victims often chose not to pursue the route of filing for an injunction for protection when they were presented with the option to do so (Table 9.12). Thus, based on this variable, it is logical to conclude that Black's (2010) behavior of law theory is upheld because intimates did not mobilize the law against each other at a high occurrence rate.[47]

Weapon used involves five variables that ranked in order of the most used to least used weapon the IPH offender utilized in the killing. Handgun and other firearms are the top two weapons used in an IPH with a combined percentage of 72.7% (Table 9.13). This is interesting because, 80% to 94% of IPHSs are accomplished with some type of firearm, and approximately half of the IPHs in this study resulted in an IPHS.[48] Indeed, women are most killed by firearms in the United States, which is typically carried out by an intimate partner whether current, estranged, or former.[49]

Throughout Part II, cases indicated that the court might have ordered the abuser in the injunction case to relinquish their weapons once they were served with the temporary injunction. If a temporary injunction was not issued, but a final injunction was issued, the order to relinquish weapons might be issued at that time. However, some cases revealed that an IPV victim was concerned about their abuser continuing to maintain weapons after the injunction order issues. Indeed, IPHs occurred when these orders were in place, which included relinquishment of weapons orders. Webster et al. (2010) report that only "26% (21 of 82) of victims whose abuser possessed a firearm reported that the judge ordered that these firearms

Table 9.13 Weapon Used Variable Frequencies (Data Set A)

	Frequency, N = 493			Valid Percent		
	Not the Weapon Used	Weapon Used	Total	Not the Weapon Used	Weapon Used	Total
Handgun	261	232	493	52.9%	47.1%	100%
Other Firearms	367	126	493	74.4%	25.6%	100%
Knife/Cutting Instrument	418	75	493	84.8%	15.2%	100%
Hands/Fist/Feet	450	43	493	91.3%	8.7%	100%
Other Weapon	476	17	493	96.6%	3.4%	100%

be surrendered or removed from the abusers."[50] A lesser 12% of the participants in the Webster et al. (2010) study "believed that the court order resulted in the removal of all the abusers' firearms." [51] Given the known factor of firearms causing such death and destruction throughout families in which IPV is present, it is unconscionable that more care is not taken to ensure firearms are not removed from the abuser's care, custody, and control.

Table 9.13 explains that knife/cutting instrument was the third most common weapon used in this study, at 15.2%, which could mean anything from a common kitchen knife to a machete or anything in between. The next type of weapon in common usage for this study was hands/fist/feet at 8.7%, which most likely includes strangulation, although not specifically identified by UCR-SHR. As discussed in Chapter 2, Coercive Control's Impact on the Intimate Partner Violence Victim, Physical Violence, Nonfatal Strangulation, nonfatal strangulation is a well-known indicator for IPH; and it carries a greater risk of death than those who have not been previously strangled.[52] The last most common weapon was the other weapon category at 3.4%, which includes all other types of forms in which the IPH victim died by the offender, such as by an intentional drug overdose, by an intentional vehicular homicide, by an intentional fire set, or by blunt force trauma.

Discussion: Data Set A – Logistic Regression

Data set A addresses the research question using one dependent variable, i.e., prior report of physical violence to law enforcement, in this exploratory study. The following research question was tested in this quantitative phase of this exploratory quantitative study for data set A: What influences do the independent variables, such as IPHS, record of petition for injunction., and weapon used, have on an IPH with a prior report of physical violence to law enforcement for heterosexual spouses in Florida from 2006 to June 30, 2016?

The independent variables utilized for this logistic regression model are IPHS, record of petition for injunction, handgun, knife/cutting instrument, hands/fist/feet, other firearm, and other weapon.[53] The logistic regression model, as shown in Table 9.14, yielded a statistically significant model and statistically significant variable results. The full model was statistically significant, χ^2 (df = 6, N = 493) = 307.946, $p < 0.001$.[54] 68.2% of the variance is explained by the independent variables.

There were three independent variables of significance in the model (Table 9.14). For the first variable, the log odds of an IPH with a prior report of physical violence to law enforcement was positively related to an IPH with a record of petition for injunction.[55] The odds of an IPH with a prior report of physical violence to law enforcement are 14.245 times

Table 9.14 Data Set A: Logistic Regression Analysis of Prior Reporting of Physical Violence to Law Enforcement for IPH between Heterosexual Spouses in Florida, N = 493

Variable	B	Exp(B)
IPHS	0.382	1.465
Record of Petition for Injunction	2.656	14.245****
Knife/Cutting Instrument	−0.843	0.430**
Hands/Fist/Feet	−0.136	0.873
Other Firearms	−0.912	0.402***
Other Weapon	−0.748	0.473
χ^2	307.946****	
R^2	0.682	

Notes: * $p < 0.1$; ** $p < 0.05$; *** $p < 0.01$; **** $p < 0.001$; there are sixty-three (63) missing cases in this model; the variable "handgun" was used as the reference category in this model.

higher for IPHs with a record of petition for injunction compared to IPHs without a record of petition for injunction ($p < 0.001$).[56] For the second statistically significant variable, according to the model, the log odds of an IPH with a prior report of physical violence to law enforcement was negatively related to an IPH being carried out with a knife/cutting instrument. The odds of prior physical violence reported to law enforcement before an IPH are 57% lower when knife/cutting instruments are used compared to when handguns are used ($p < 0.05$).[57] For the third statistically significant variable, the log odds of an IPH with a prior report of physical violence to law enforcement was negatively related to an IPH being accomplished with a firearm that is not a handgun, i.e., other firearms. The odds of prior physical violence reported to law enforcement before an IPH are 59.8% lower when other firearms are used compared to when handguns are used ($p < 0.05$).[58]

Because the logistic regression model is statistically significant at $p < 0.001$, indicating that at least one of the independent variables are statistically significant, it is important to identify which independent variables are statistically significant to determine which hypotheses to reject.[59] The first independent variable tested, IPHS, was not statistically significant (Table 9.14). It was determined that IPHS does not influence an IPH with a prior report of physical violence to law enforcement.[60] The percentage of IPHSs in data set A were split 50.2% for "was not an IPHS" to 49.8% for "was an IPHS" (Table 9.11). As discussed in Chapter 3, The Role of Intimate Partner Homicide-Suicide in Intimate Partner Homicide, IPHSs are not often something that occurs without warning; rather, they take place after a long course of abusive behavior and struggle whereby the IPV victim may attempt to leave the relationship, signifying an undeniable urge for the abuser to maintain control over the victim.[61] However, here because of such a close split in the frequency of the occurrence of these events of IPH to IPHS, these results seem to support but, also, might contradict this contention. It is important to note the lack of its statistical significance to prior reporting of physical violence to law enforcement. This could further support the notion that IPHSs may be the most difficult class of IPHs to predict and prevent.

The next independent variable, record of petition for injunction, was statistically significant at $p < 0.001$; thus, the null hypothesis for record of petition for injunction was rejected (Table 9.14).[62] It can be determined that an IPH with a record of petition for injunction positively influences an IPH with a prior report of physical violence to law enforcement. These findings are interesting when considering the processes of the legal system an IPV victim must endure to ensure their safety. As discussed in Chapter 3, The Disillusionment of the Protections of an Injunction for Protection against Domestic Violence: Why and When are They Important to IPV Victims?, IPV victims must jump through many legal hoops to try to obtain a court order that provides them the hope for some type of formal protection from their abuser.[63] Nevertheless, generally, once they choose to enter the legal system to ask for assistance or protection, they will continue to try to obtain resources. In fact, the odds of an IPH with a prior report of physical violence to law enforcement are 14.245 times higher for IPHs with a record of a filed petition for injunction compared to IPHs without a record of a filed petition for injunction. Therefore, based on these results, it is reasonable that the IPV victim would also contact law enforcement if physical violence were one of the tactics of abuse that is being wielded against them. Thus, Black's (2010) behavior of law theory regarding an IPV victim's lack of mobilization of the law is not upheld when an IPV victim chooses to protect themselves from physical violence by filing a petition for injunction.[64] These results indicate that intimates effectively mobilize the law against each other when physical violence is present in the relationship and the legal system is engaged.

Two weapon used variables tested were statistically significant (Table 9.14). The null hypothesis for knife/cutting instrument is rejected.[65] An IPH carried out by a knife/cutting instrument negatively influences an IPH with a prior report of physical violence to law enforcement. The null hypothesis for other firearms was rejected.[66] An IPH carried out by a gun other than a handgun, i.e., other firearms, negatively influences an IPH with a prior report of physical violence to law enforcement. As explained above, the odds of prior physical violence reported to law enforcement before an IPH are 57% and 59.8% lower compared to when handguns are used for knife/cutting instruments and other firearms, respectively. This result is most interesting when put into the context of an issued temporary injunction and/or final injunction, whereby the abuser should have already had their handgun confiscated.[67] Although there are fewer cases in this study that had both a prior report of physical violence to law enforcement and a record of a filed petition for injunction, an order for an injunction for protection typically comes with an order to turn over all handguns or firearms. It is possible that the handguns were removed from the offenders in these cases due to the prior report of physical violence to law enforcement and the success of a filed petition for injunction; so, they used other weapons for the IPH, such as a knife/cutting instrument or other firearms purchased after the issuance of the protective order.

Discussion: Data Set B – Frequencies

The purposive sample of sixty-two (62) cases for data set B was drawn from the total population of 665 cases for this study since these cases had filed petitions for injunction for content analysis that were subsequently able to be utilized for exploratory quantitative analysis. Table 9.15 provides a list and description of the variables used in the logistic regression model for data set B. The first dependent variable measures whether there was a Prior Report of Physical Violence to Law Enforcement between the heterosexual spouses before the IPH. The second dependent variable measures whether physical violence was reported to the court by the IPV victim through the petition for injunction.

The following research questions were tested in the quantitative phase of this exploratory study for data set B:

1 What influences do the independent variables, such as resistance to abuse, fearful of the future, and abuser mental illness, have on an IPH with a prior report of physical violence to law enforcement for heterosexual spouses in Florida from 2006 to June 30, 2016?
2 What influences do the independent variables, such as humiliation, intimidation, isolation, power and control, resistance to abuse, fearful of the future, and abuser mental illness, have on an IPH with a prior report of physical violence to the court for heterosexual spouses in Florida from 2006 to June 30, 2016?

The following two tables explain the frequencies for each of the variables used in the logistic regression model for data set B. Table 9.16 explains that, of the fifty-five (55) cases of data collected regarding whether the heterosexual couple involved in the IPH had a prior report of physical violence to law enforcement before the killing, 61.8% of the cases have a prior report of physical violence to law enforcement, regardless of who made the report, i.e., the victim or the offender of the IPH. Additionally,

Table 9.15 Explanation of Quantitative Variables for Data Set B

Predictor Variable	Coding	Dependent Variables	Coding
Intimidation		Prior Report of Physical Violence to Law Enforcement – *Dichotomous Variable*	
IPH with No Presence of Intimidation (reference category)	0		
IPH with Presence of Intimidation	1	IPH with Prior Report of Physical Violence to Law Enforcement (reference category)	0
Missing	9	IPH without Prior Report of Physical Violence to Law Enforcement	1
Isolation			
IPH with No Presence of Isolation (reference category)	0	Missing	9
		Prior Report of Physical Violence to the Court – *Dichotomous Variable*	
IPH with Presence of Isolation	1	IPH with Prior Report of Physical Violence to the Court (reference category)	0
Missing	9		
Humiliation		IPH without Prior Report of Physical Violence to the Court	1
IPH with No Presence of Humiliation (reference category)	0	Missing	9
IPH with Presence of Humiliation	1	Predictor Variable	Coding
Missing	9	*Fearful of the Future*	
Power and Control		IPH with No Presence of Fearful of the Future (reference category)	0
IPH with No Presence of Power and Control (reference category)	0	IPH with Presence of Fearful of the Future	1
IPH with Presence of Power and Control	1	Missing	9
Missing	9	*Abuser Mental Illness*	
Resistance to Abuse		IPH with No Presence of Abuser Mental Illness (reference category)	0
IPH with No Presence of Resistance to Abuse (reference category)	0	IPH with Presence of Abuser Mental Illness	1
IPH with Presence of Resistance to Abuse	1	Missing	9
Missing	9		

of the sixty-two (62) cases analyzed in data set B, 69.4% of the IPV victims reported violence to the court through the filed petitions for injunction prior to the IPHs.

Table 9.17 explains the percentages of non-violent coercive control tactics reported by the IPV victim in the petition for injunction filed with the court prior to the IPH.[69] Resistance to abuse, considered an IPV victim's reaction to abuse, has the highest percentage of affirmative reporting at

Table 9.16 Dependent Variable Frequencies (Data Set B)

	Frequency, N = 62			Valid Percent		
	Yes	No	Total	Yes	No	Total
Prior Report of Physical Violence to Law Enforcement	34	21	55	61.8%	38.2%	100%
Prior Report of Physical Violence to the Court	43	19	62	69.4%	30.6%	100%

Notes: N = 62; there are seven (7) missing records for the variable "Prior Report of Physical Violence to Law Enforcement."[68]

87.1%. The second highest percentage, at 82.3%, is power and control, which is considered an abuser's tactic used against the IPV victim. Third highest is intimidation, another abusive tactic, with a percentage of 77.4%. The fourth highest reporting percentage, at 58.1%, is fearful of the future, which describes the IPV victim's state of mind in reaction to the abuse they have or are experiencing. Fifth is abuser mental illness at 51.6%, which describes the abuser's state of mind as understood by the IPV victim. With 46.8%, isolation is another abusive tactic that was reported by IPV victims through the injunctions for protection and ranks sixth out of the seven variables in Table 9.17. Finally, humiliation, with 44.3%, is the last abusive tactic to be reported affirmatively by IPV victims to the court through the petitions for injunction prior to the IPH taking place.

Data set B addresses three research questions utilizing the first dependent variable, i.e., prior report of physical violence to law enforcement, in this exploratory study.[70] There is a total of seven independent variables used in data set B. However, although there are no specific rules regarding adequacy of sample size for logistic regression, a minimum ratio of 10 to 1 is recommended.[71] Thus, the non-violent coercive control tactic

Table 9.17 Non-Violent Coercive Control Variable Frequencies (Data Set B)

	Frequency, N = 62			Valid Percent		
	No	Yes	Total	No	Yes	Total
Humiliation	34	27	61	55.7%	44.3%	100%
Intimidation	14	48	62	22.6%	77.4%	100%
Isolation	33	29	62	53.2%	46.8%	100%
Power and Control	11	51	62	17.7%	82.3%	100%
Resistance to Abuse	8	54	62	12.9%	87.1%	100%
Fearful of the Future	26	36	62	41.9%	58.1%	100%
Abuser Mental Illness	30	32	62	48.4%	51.6%	100%

Notes: N = 62; there is one (1) missing record for the variable "Humiliation."

independent variables for the logistic regression models in data set B are divided into two groups: (1) Victims' Reactions and (2) Abusers' Tactics. The group titled "victims' reactions" has three independent variables, i.e., resistance to abuse, fearful of the future, and abuser mental illness. "Abusers' Tactics" has four independent variables, humiliation, intimidation, isolation, and power and control.

The first logistic regression model explored the first dependent variable, prior report of physical violence to law enforcement, and applied three independent variables, i.e., resistance to abuse, fearful of the future, and abuser mental illness.[72] The logistic regression model, as shown in Table 9.18, yielded statistically significance and statistically significant variable results. The full model was statistically significant, χ^2 (df = 3, N = 62) = 6.530, $p < 0.1$, and 14.9% of the variance is explained by the independent variables. Abuser mental illness was the one variable of significance in the model. According to the model, the log odds of IPH with a prior report of physical violence to law enforcement was positively related to IPH with abuser mental illness. The odds of an IPH with a prior report of physical violence to law enforcement are 3.121 times higher for an IPH with abuser mental illness compared to an IPH with no abuser mental illness ($p < 0.05$) (Table 9.18).

Data set B addresses seven hypotheses utilizing the second dependent variable, i.e., prior report of physical violence to the court. There are two logistic regression models with this variable, which uses seven independent variables.[73] These independent variables are intimidation, isolation, humiliation, power and control, resistance to abuse, fearful of the future, and abuser mental illness. The recommended minimum ratio of 10 to 1 for adequacy of sample size for logistic regression was followed for the second dependent variable as well; thus, the independent variables were divided into the two groups, i.e., victims' reactions and abusers' tactics.[74]

Table 9.18 Data Set B: Logistic Regression Analysis of Prior Reporting of Physical Violence to Law Enforcement for IPH between Heterosexual Spouses in Florida, Including Non-Violent Coercive Control (Victim Reaction Tactics), N = 62

Variable	B	Exp(B)
Resistance to Abuse	−0.457	0.633
Fearful of the Future	−0.836	0.433
Abuser Mental Illness	1.138	3.121**
χ^2	6.530*	
R^2	.149	

Notes: * $p < 0.1$; ** $p < 0.05$, *** $p < 0.01$, **** $p < 0.001$; there are seven (7) missing cases in this model.

Table 9.19 Data Set B: Logistic Regression Analysis of Prior Reporting of Physical Violence to the Court for IPH between Heterosexual Spouses in Florida, Including Non-Violent Coercive Control (Victim Reaction Tactics), N = 62

Variable	B	Exp(B)
Resistance to Abuse	−0.913	0.401*
Fearful of the Future	0.905	2.472
Abuser Mental Illness	−0.620	0.538
χ^2	7.855**	
R^2	0.159	

Notes: * $p < 0.10$; ** $p < 0.05$, *** $p < 0.01$, **** $p < 0.001$.

The first logistic regression model for the dependent variable, prior report of physical violence to the court, used three independent variables, resistance to abuse, fearful of the future, and abuser mental illness (Table 9.19). The full model was statistically significant, χ^2 (df = 3, N = 62) = 7.855, $p < 0.05$, and 15.9% of the variance is explained by the independent variables. IPH with resistance to abuse was the one variable of approaching statistical significance in the model. According to the model, the log odds of an IPH with a prior report of physical violence to the court was negatively related to an IPH with resistance to abuse. An IPH with resistance to abuse reduces the odds of having prior physical violence reported to the court before the killing by 59.9% ($p < 0.10$).

The second logistic regression model for the second dependent variable in data set B has four independent variables, humiliation, intimidation, isolation, and power and control (Table 9.20). The full model was

Table 9.20 Data Set B: Logistic Regression Analysis of Prior Reporting of Physical Violence to the Court for IPH between Heterosexual Spouses in Florida, Including Non-Violent Coercive Control (Abuser Tactics), N = 62

Variable	B	Exp(B)
Humiliation	−0.237	0.789
Intimidation	0.761	2.141
Isolation	−0.548	0.578
Power and Control	−1.202	0.301*
χ^2	11.888**	
R^2	0.236	

Notes: * $p < 0.1$; ** $p < 0.05$, *** $p < 0.01$, **** $p < 0.001$; there is one (1) missing case in this model.

statistically significant, χ^2 (df = 4, N = 61) = 11.888, $p < 0.05$, and 23.6% of the variance is explained by the independent variables. IPH with power and control was the only variable of approaching statistical significance in the model. According to the model, the log odds of IPH with a prior report of physical violence to the court was negatively related to IPH with power and control. An IPH with power and control reduces the odds of having prior physical violence reported to the court before the killing by 69.9% ($p < 0.10$).

As with data set A, the first data set B variable for discussion, prior report of physical violence to law enforcement, was used as one of data set B's dependent variables. However, quite differently than data set A, which had only 15.3% of the victims of IPH report any physical violence to the police prior to their death (Table 9.10), data set B had 61.8% of the victims of IPH report any physical violence to the police prior to their death (Table 9.16). Additionally, for the second dependent variable in data set B, prior report of physical violence to the court, 69.4% of the victims of IPH reported physical violence to the court prior to their death (Table 9.16). These higher data set B percentages may be explained by the fact that all the cases in data set B are petition for injunction cases; thus, they derive from IPH cases whereby the victim and offender were engaged in court proceedings, meaning the legal system and available victim resources, prior to the killing. As a result, these cases would tend to mobilize the law for their own self-protection more readily, which does not support Black's (2010) behavior of law theory regarding mobilization of the law.[75]

This study focuses on seven non-violent tactics of coercive control, which were analyzed in data set B.[76] As explained throughout this book, resistance to abuse, as used in this study, does not refer to any type of physical violence, as this variable represents a non-violent tactic of coercive control. Because data set B's cases are IPHs with at least one filed petition for injunction, it is not surprising that resistance to abuse had the highest percentage frequency, i.e., 87.1% among this study's non-violent coercive control variables (Table 9.17). Indeed, IPV victims who are willing to mobilize the law, such as filing a petition for injunction, are actively working to resist the abuse they are experiencing. They have consciously made the decision to resist their abuser, knowing the cost may very well be an escalation in physical violence or possible death; however, some realize that this option is better than the alternative of living with the abuse any longer. As such, Black's (2010) behavior of law theory regarding mobilization of the law is fallible based on this frequency because it shows that intimates effectively mobilized the law against each other.[77]

Power and control, with 82.3%, was the next highest frequency, explaining the overarching theme of non-violent coercive control (Table 9.17). As explained throughout this book, generally, coercive control tactics are not deployed in a vacuum, nor are they deployed one at a time. Indeed, coercive control tactics are not mutually exclusive and are often utilized in a combination of complex means in which the abuser manifests certain tactics that are most beneficial within the context of the circumstances of the interaction with their victim. An abuser may rely on many coercive control tactics for effectiveness to keep their victim "in line" and under their power and control. Thus, the fact that power and control ranked so high among the tactics is not surprising because it is the most common tactic to result from many of the other tactics' implementation.

As with power and control, intimidation works with the other coercive control tactics to produce an overall effect upon the victim. At a 77.4% frequency, intimidation is deployed often and is most likely very effective for the abuser, explaining the fact that IPH victims described this type of behavior in their petitions for injunction at such a high frequency (Table 9.17). As previously explained in Chapter 2, Intimidation, as well as Isolation, is one of the most effective non-violent tactics of coercive control because it compares to torture experienced by someone who was a prisoner of war.[78] However, for the IPV victim, coercive control's intimidation can inflict much worse psychological harm because the abuser was intimate with the victim rather than being an unknown assailant as in the prisoner of war scenario.[79]

Culminating from the first three coercive control tactics' frequencies discussed above is the next highest frequency at 77.4% for fearful of the future (Table 9.17). The ranking for fearful of the future after (1) resistance to abuse, (2) power and control, and (3) intimidation can be explained by the fact that many of the IPH victims, when expressing their fears of the future in the petitions for injunction, were reacting to the other tactics of coercive control they were experiencing, such as resistance to abuse, power and control, and intimidation. This reaction to coercive control tactics is an excellent example of how abusers can commingle their tactics to ensure compliance from their victims. However, it is also a good example of the fact that, even though IPV victims are fearful of the future, they are willing to do what it takes to resist the abuse they are facing. Indeed, resistance to abuse had the highest frequency percentage; and fearful of the future had the fourth highest frequency percentage. Keeping in mind that, generally, IPH victims were facing power and control and intimidation as well, they withstood their fears and some of the most difficult forms of non-violent coercive control to resist the abuse and live their lives while working to protect themselves and, usually, their children.

IPH victims reported in their petitions for injunction that their abusers had some type of mental illness at a 51.6% frequency (Table 9.17). Although this variable does not fundamentally represent a non-violent coercive control tactic whereby the abuser commits an act against the IPV victim, based on its frequency, it indicates that many IPHs had a spouse of questionable mental health, at least as far as one of the spouses was concerned.[80] The subthemes in this theme are important to remember as they are described in Chapter 7, Abuser Mental Illness, especially as it pertains to drinking alcohol and paranoia.[81] These subthemes play a major role in the lives of abusive heterosexual marriages on a day-to-day basis, which helps to explain the frequency percentage for abuser mental illness. Although drinking alcohol is self-explanatory, paranoia needs clarification. As described in detail in Chapter 7, some of the most significant results from this abusive behavior were jealousy and possessiveness.[82] In fact, as jealousy and possessiveness escalated, so did the power and control, as well as the intimidation. Abuser mental illness is one non-violent coercive control tactic that helps make clear that these behaviors work together to maintain the abusive relationship that is desired by the offender, without the need for physical violence.

Isolation is the next non-violent coercive control tactic, at 46.8%, in order of percentage of frequency (Table 9.17). It is surprising that the frequency for isolation was not higher, as it would be expected to be at the same level as intimidation based on the literature. However, it is possible that many IPH victims did not believe reporting such behavior to the court was important enough to document on their petitions for injunction because it is not as aligned with physical violence or the threat thereof, i.e., the typical legal standard for a successful petition for injunction in Florida. As such, this would explain the lower frequency percentage compared to intimidation. Nevertheless, overall, the 46.8% frequency percentage for this study indicates that many IPH victims, almost half, were able to communicate in their petitions for injunction some form of isolation that they were experiencing during their abusive relationship with their heterosexual spouse. Indeed, many of the IPH victims experienced isolation in the form of being kept from their family and friends or false imprisonment. Others told the court about economic control they experienced, such as interference with their job or school. Still, others experienced isolation in the form of financial control whereby their personal bills were not paid by their abusers and money for essential living expenses was withheld, evidencing the importance these victims placed on these non-violent tactics.

Humiliation had the lowest percentage frequency of all the non-violent coercive control tactics with 44.3% (Table 9.17). The fact that humiliation ranked the lowest of all the coercive control variables is surprising because it is very powerful when utilized by the abuser against the IPV victim. However, it may be the simple fact that the IPV victim is too embarrassed to explain in a petition for injunction the humiliation they have experienced at the hands of their abuser that this tactic ranked so low. Indeed, considering the humiliating facts an IPV victim would have to write in a petition for injunction, such the ones delineated in this book, it is quite remarkable that the victims had the courage to report the humiliation that they did experience to the court through their petitions for injunction. Allowing the court to understand the degrading names their abuser called them for an extensive period or time or to explain the humiliating actions of the abuser through a petition for injunction is impressive and is a testament to the fact that this tactic's frequency percentage is as high as 44.3%.

Discussion: Data Set B – Logistic Regression

For data set B, the first logistic regression model, using prior report of physical violence to law enforcement as its dependent variable, was approaching statistical significance at $p < 0.10$, indicating that at least one of the three independent variables were statistically significant.[83] Table 9.18 indicates that the first independent variable tested, IPH with resistance to abuse, was not statistically significant. It is determined that an IPH with resistance to abuse does not influence an IPH with a prior report of physical violence to law enforcement.[84] The second independent variable tested, IPH with fearful of the future, was not statistically significant. It is determined that an IPH with fearful of the future does not influence an IPH with a prior report of physical violence to law enforcement.[85]

The third independent variable tested, IPH with abuser mental illness, was statistically significant at $p < 0.05$; thus, the null hypothesis for an IPH with abuser mental illness is rejected (Table 9.18).[86] So, it can be determined that an IPH with abuser mental illness positively influences an IPH with a prior report of physical violence to law enforcement. Keeping in mind that the variable, abuser mental illness, includes drinking alcohol and paranoia, i.e., jealousy and possessiveness, it seems likely that physical violence between the spouses might result. The odds of an IPH with a prior report of physical violence to law enforcement are 3.121 times higher for an IPH with abuser mental illness compared to an IPH with no abuser mental illness. Is it possible that the IPH victims did not want to report the physical violence they were experiencing for fear of some type of retaliation from their abusers they feared had or they knew were suffering from a mental illness? Is this an indication that an abuser's mental illness prevents a victim from seeking law enforcement's assistance?

The second logistic regression model for data set B uses prior report of physical violence to the court as its dependent variable and is statistically significant at $p < 0.05$, indicating that at least one of the three independent variables are statistically significant.[87] Table 9.19 explains that the first independent variable tested, IPH with resistance to abuse, was approaching statistical significance at $p < 0.10$. The null hypothesis for an IPH with resistance to abuse is rejected; however, the hypothesized relationship is different than expected, meaning it was negative rather than the hypothesized positive direction.[88] So, it can be determined that an IPH with resistance to abuse negatively influences an IPH with a prior report of physical violence to the court. This result is logical because the IPH victim works hard at protecting themselves once they determine it is time to stand up to their abuser in court. In fact, as this model found, an IPH with resistance to abuse reduces the odds of having prior physical violence reported to the court before the killing by 59.9%. Thus, it seems that once the law is mobilized within the judicial system, the IPV victim will continue to exhaust all judicial resources available to them to attempt to maintain their safety and well-being.

The third logistic regression model for data set B uses prior report of physical violence to the court as its dependent variable and is statistically significant at $p < 0.05$, indicating that at least one of the four independent variables are statistically significant. The first three independent variables in the model, humiliation, intimidation, and isolation, were not statistically significant (Table 9.20). The fourth independent variable tested in the third logistic regression model for data set B, IPH with power and control, was approaching statistical significance at $p < 0.10$; thus, the null hypothesis for an IPH with power and control is rejected.[89] So, it can be determined that an IPH with power and control negatively influences an IPH with a prior report of physical violence to the court. The causal relationship between these variables is not surprising due to the commingling of coercive control tactics as described throughout this book. Indeed, it is no surprise that IPHs with power and control influences IPHs with prior reports of physical violence to the court because it is a frequent form of coercive control to describe, meaning the abuser will prevent the IPV victim from mobilizing the law if there is physical violence to report. An IPH with power and control reduces the odds of having prior physical violence reported to the court before the killing by 69.9%. Having said this, it is remarkable that so many IPV victims resisted the power and control deployed by their abuser and mobilized the law to file their petitions for injunction to ask the court for protection.

Notes

1 See supra Chapter 4.
2 Note that 108 petitions for injunction were utilized for the frequencies and other statistical measurements as discussed throughout this chapter.
3 See Shelby Settles Harper & Christina Marie Entrekin (Barbara Hart ed., 2006), *Violence Against Native Women: A Guide for Practitioner Action*, OFFICE ON VIOLENCE AGAINST WOMEN, https://www.bwjp.org/assets/documents/pdfs/ncpoffc_violence_against_native_women.pdf.
4 See Id.
5 See Id.
6 See Id.
7 See Id.

8 See Id.
9 See *Population Demographics for Florida 2017, 2018*, SUBURBAN STATS (2018) https://suburbanstats.org/population/how-many-people-live-in-florida (last visited April 24, 2019).
10 See John M. Roberts, *U.S. Spousal Homicide Rates by Racial Composition of Marriage*, 25 ANNALS OF EPIDEMIOLOGY 668 (2015) https://doi.org/10.1016/j.annepidem.2015.04.004; Profile America Facts for Features, *American Indian and Alaska Native Heritage Month: November 2015*, U.S. CENSUS BUREAU (2015) https://www.census.gov/content/dam/Census/newsroom/facts-for-features/2015/cb15-ff22_AIAN_month.pdf. The national average for Native American on Native American spousal homicide is 1.55% (*See* Roberts, *supra* note 10). This average was used because in this study, the IPH victim and offender were the Native American couple of interest for this analysis.
11 Table 9.7 indicates a frequency of three (3) petitions for injunction; however, one petition for injunction was not analyzed as it was destroyed by the clerk of court through administrative procedures and was not available for data collection. The same person filed both petitions for injunction in this case.
12 See Shu-wen Wang, *Intimate Partner Violence Among Asian American and Pacific Islander Women: What is Intimate Partner Violence (IPV)?*, AAPA (2014) https://aapaonline.org/wp-content/uploads/2014/06/AA_IPV-final-web.pdf.
13 See Id.
14 See Id.
15 See *Population Demographics for Florida 2017, 2018*, *supra* note 9.
16 See Roberts, *supra* note 10.
17 See Id.
18 See Id. The national average for Asian spousal homicide for the Roberts (2015) study is 1.41% when taking the 1.80% male-on-female and 1.02% female-on-male rate into consideration. Florida's average Asian IPH rate determined by this study is 1.4% when taking the 1.8% rate for IPH race of victim and 1.0% IPH race of offender rates into consideration.
19 These sixty-six (66) cases derive from the online search of the court records for all 493 cases. The difference between the sixty-two (62) cases with petitions for injunction and the sixty-six (66) cases is the four (4) cases that had their petitions for injunction destroyed by administrative process by the appropriate clerk of court for the county within which the records were kept.
20 See DONALD BLACK, THE BEHAVIOR OF LAW: SPECIAL EDITION (2010). Black (2010) suggests the relational distance is similar in measurement to stratification. (*See Id.*).
21 See Id.
22 See Id.
23 Note that the theme abuser mental illness includes the subthemes drinking alcohol, drug use, and paranoia.
24 See Joan B. Kelly & Michael P. Johnson, *Differentiation Among Types of Intimate Partner Violence: Research Update and Implications for Interventions*, 46 FAMILY COURT REVIEW 476 (2008) https://doi.org/10.1111/j.1744-1617.2008.00215.x. *See supra* Chapter 1, The Gender Asymmetry of Coercive Control.
25 See Kelly & Johnson, *supra* note 24.
26 See Id.
27 This excludes the subthemes of helping the abuser and separated or estranged.
28 See Kelly & Johnson, *supra* note 24.

29 See EVAN STARK, COERCIVE CONTROL: HOW MEN ENTRAP WOMEN IN PERSONAL LIFE (2007).
30 See BLACK, *supra* note 20. See *supra* Chapter 7, Resistance to Abuse.
31 See *supra* Chapter 3, The Disillusionment of the Protections of an Injunction for Protection against Domestic Violence: Why and When are They Important to Intimate Partner Violence Victims?
32 Note that 86.6% of the cases in this study did not have petition for injunction filings; sixty-six (66) of the 493 cases in this study had petitions for injunction, leaving 427 cases without a filed petition for injunction.
33 Heather Allen, *Troubled Marriage Ends in Death*, HERALD-TRIBUNE, ¶ 16 (April 27, 2007).
34 The original data set for this study was separated into two distinct data sets due to the extraordinarily high Variance Inflation Factors [hereinafter VIFs] and excluded variables that resulted when all the variables in the original data set were run in an OLS model to check for multicollinearity. All the results of the OLS model checking for multicollinearity for each data set can be found in Appendix C: V.I.F. Tables of Study Variables.
35 See *supra* Chapter 4.
36 Because this is an exploratory study, values approaching significance at $p < 0.10$ for data set A are included.
37 See R. Emerson Dobash et al., *"Out of the Blue:" Men Who Murder an Intimate Partner*, 4 FEMINIST CRIMINOLOGY 194 (2009) http://dx.doi.org/10.1177/1557085109332668 (discussing the fact that "the best predictor of subsequent intimate partner violence is general criminal recidivism"); Laurie M. Graham et al., *The Danger Assessment: An Instrument for the Prevention of Intimate Partner Homicide*, *in* HANDBOOK OF INTERPERSONAL VIOLENCE ACROSS THE LIFESPAN (R. Geffner at al. eds., 2019) https://doi.org/10.1007/978-3-319-62122-7_145-1; David Hirschel & Eve Buzawa, *Understanding the Context of Dual Arrest with Directions for Future Research*, 8 VIOLENCE AGAINST WOMEN 1449 (2002) https://doi.org/10.1177%2F107780102237965; Andrew R. Klein, *Lethality Assessments and the Law Enforcement Response to Domestic Violence*, 12 J. OF POLICE CRISIS NEGOTIATIONS 87 (2012) https://doi.org/10.1080/15332586.2012.720175; N. Zoe Hilton et al., *An Indepth Actuarial Assessment for Wife Assault Recidivism: The Domestic Risk Appraisal Guide*, 32 LAW HUM. BEHAV. 150 (2008) https://doi.org/10.1007/s10979-007-9088-6.
38 See BLACK, *supra* note 20.
39 One of the reasons for the sixty-two (62) missing cases is because, as explained in Chapter 4, Methodology for Data Collection: Sourcing Public Records, Florida Local Law Enforcement Agencies, sixty (60) cases were affected by a lack of response by twenty (20) agencies during the second request for records from law enforcement. See *supra* Chapter 4, Methodology for Data Collection: Sourcing Public Records, Florida Local Law Enforcement Agencies.
40 See Catherine G. Velopulos et al., *Comparison of Male and Female Victims of Intimate Partner Homicide and Bidirectionality: An Analysis of the National Violent Death Reporting System*, 87 J. TRAUMA ACUTE CARE SURG. 331 (2019) https://doi.org/10.1097/TA.0000000000002276.
41 *American Roulette: Murder-Suicide in the United States*, VIOLENCE POLICY CENTER 2 (2020) https://vpc.org/studies/amroul2020.pdf.
42 See Velopulos et al., *supra* note 40; Shilan Caman et al., *Trends in Rates and Characteristics of Intimate Partner Homicides Between 1990 and 2013*, 49 J. OF

CRIMINAL JUSTICE 14 (2017) https://doi.org/10.1016/j.jcrimjus.2017.01.002; *American Roulette: Murder-Suicide in the United States*, *supra* note 41.
43 *See* Velopulos et al., *supra* note 40; *American Roulette: Murder-Suicide in the United States*, *supra* note 41.
44 *See* Velopulos et al., *supra* note 40.
45 *See Id. See infra* Chapter 11, Future Directions for Research. Explaining that the frequency for IPHS in data set B is 50% and discussing the need for additional research into IPH and IPHS.
46 The missing case for this variable is due to a sealed case whereby the information regarding whether the case was an IPHS was not available.
47 *See* BLACK, *supra* note 20.
48 *See American Roulette: Murder-Suicide in the United States*, *supra* note 41.
49 *See* Daniel W. Webster et al., *Women with Protective Orders Report Failure to Remove Firearms from Their Abusive Partners: Results from an Exploratory Study*, 19 J. OF WOMEN'S HEALTH 93 (2010) https://doi.org/10.1089/jwh.2007.0530.
50 *Id.* at 96.
51 *Id.* at 97.
52 *See supra* Chapter 2, Coercive Control's Impact on the Intimate Partner Violence Victim, Physical Violence, Nonfatal Strangulation.
53 Additional independent variables were not utilized in this logistic regression model due to their high VIF levels.
54 *See* SPSSisFun, *Binary Logistic Regression: Part 3-Interpreting Output (model significance and variance)*, YOUTUBE (Sept. 25, 2016) https://www.youtube.com/watch?v=MybWvtRYEg4 (last visited June 12, 2023).
55 *See* Peng et al., *An Introduction to Logistic Regression Analysis and Reporting*, 96 THE JOURNAL OF EDUCATIONAL RESEARCH 3 (2010) https://doi.org/10.1080/00220670209598786.
56 *See* Hui Bian, *Logistic Regression Analysis: Using SPSS*, OFFICE FOR FACULTY EXCELLENCE (2018) https://www.scribd.com/document/140797247/Logistic-Regression-Analysis (last visited June 12, 2023).
57 *See Using Logistic Regression in Research*, STATISTICS SOLUTIONS (2019) https://www.statisticssolutions.com/using-logistic-regression-in-research/ (last visited Jun 22, 2019).
58 *See Id.*
59 *See* Bian, *supra* note 56.
60 The null hypothesis for the variable IPHS was "IPHS does not positively influence an IPH with a prior report of physical violence to law enforcement."
61 *See* Emma Morton et al., *Partner Homicide-Suicide Involving Female Homicide Victims: A Population-Based Study in North Carolina*, 1988–1992, 13 VIOLENCE AND VICTIMS 91 (1998). *See supra* Chapter 3, The Role of Intimate Partner Homicide-Suicide in Intimate Partner Homicide.
62 The null hypothesis for the variable record of petition for injunction was "record of petition for injunction does not positively influence an IPH with a prior report of physical violence to law enforcement."
63 *See supra* Chapter 3, The Disillusionment of the Protections of an Injunction for Protection against Domestic Violence: Why and When are They Important to Intimate Partner Violence Victims?
64 *See* BLACK, *supra* note 20.
65 The null hypothesis for the variable knife/cutting instrument was "knife/cutting instrument does not negatively influence an IPH with a prior report of physical violence to law enforcement."

66 The null hypothesis for the variable other firearms was "other firearms does not negatively influence an IPH with a prior report of physical violence to law enforcement."
67 See supra Chapter 9, The Interactions of Coercive Control Tactics, Quantitative Methods Results, Discussion: Data Set A – Frequencies. (discussing relinquishment of firearms policies).
68 One reason for the seven (7) missing cases is because sixty (60) cases were affected by a lack of response by twenty (20) agencies during the second request for records from law enforcement. See supra Chapter 4, Methodology for Data Collection, Sourcing Public Records, Florida Local Law Enforcement Agencies.
69 The coding coverage percentages referred in Table 9.1 were derived from NVivo Pro 12 and are not commensurate with the coercive control frequency percentages shown in Table 9.17 because SPSS was used for Table 9.17. The frequencies of coercive control analyzed in the qualitative phase of this study were based on the petitions for injunction rather than the IPH reports collected in this study, which were not utilized for content analysis (Table 9.3). See supra Chapter 4, Methodology for Data Collection" Sourcing Public Records, Florida Local Law Enforcement Agencies.
70 Because this is an exploratory study, values approaching significance at $p < 0.10$ for data set B are included.
71 See Peng et al., supra note 55.
72 Additional independent variables were not utilized in this logistic regression model due to their high VIF levels. Of the independent variables that qualified for the model based on their VIF levels, not more than four (4) variables were used in a model at a time due to the number of cases, i.e., $N = 62$.
73 Additional independent variables were not utilized in either logistic regression model due to their high VIF levels. Of the independent variables that qualified for the model based on their VIF levels, not more than four (4) variables were used in a model at a time due to the number of cases, i.e., $N = 62$.
74 See Peng et al., supra note 55.
75 See BLACK, supra note 20.
76 The coding coverage percentages referred in Table 9.1 were derived from NVivo Pro 12 and are not commensurate with the coercive control frequency percentages shown in Table 9.17 because SPSS was used for Table 9.17. The frequencies of coercive control analyzed in the qualitative phase of this study were based on the petitions for injunction rather than the IPH reports collected in this study, which were not utilized for content analysis (Table 9.3). See supra Chapter 4, Methodology for Data Collection" Sourcing Public Records, Florida Local Law Enforcement Agencies.
77 See BLACK, supra note 20.
78 See supra Chapter 2, Coercive Control's Impact on the Intimate Partner Violence Victim, Isolation, Financial Control.
79 See STARK, supra note 29.
80 Because 32.4% ($N = 108$) of the petitions for injunction were not filed by the IPH victim, it is important to refrain from accusing the IPH offender of possibly having a mental illness because it is possible that the IPH victim was the IPV offender.
81 See supra Chapter 7, Abuser Mental Illness.
82 See supra Chapter 7, Abuser Mental Illness.
83 See Using Logistic Regression in Research, supra note 57. As previously stated, this is an exploratory study; thus, values approaching significance at $p < 0.10$ for data set B are included.

84 The null hypothesis for the variable resistance to abuse was "resistance to abuse does not positively influence an IPH with a prior report of physical violence to law enforcement."
85 The null hypothesis for the variable fearful of the future was "fearful of the future does not negatively influence an IPH with a prior report of physical violence to law enforcement."
86 The null hypothesis for the variable abuser mental illness was "abuser mental illness does not positively influence an IPH with a prior report of physical violence to law enforcement."
87 As previously stated, this is an exploratory study; thus, values approaching significance at $p < 0.10$ for data set B are included.
88 The null hypothesis for the variable resistance to abuse was "resistance to abuse does not positively influence an IPH with a prior report of physical violence to the court."
89 The null hypothesis for the variable power and control was "power and control does not negatively influence an IPH with a prior report of physical violence to the court."

10 Coercive Control Legislation and Reimagining Lethality Risk Assessment for Intimate Partner Violence

Coercive Control Legislation in the United States

Most U.S. state laws, intended to protect intimate partner violence (IPV) victims from their abusers, do not adequately account for coercive control's non-violent tactics.[1] Without such protections, an IPV victim who seeks legal assistance might be turned away without any evidence of physical violence or threat thereof; however, the results of this study suggest the lethality risk for intimate partner homicide (IPH) is as great whether the physical violence is present, as long as coercive control is present.[2] Progress has been made in some U.S. states toward the inclusion of coercive and controlling behaviors into existing legislation or through new legislation to account for the non-violent tactics of coercive control.[3] However, there is much work to be done to protect victims. Indeed, domestic violence (DV) advocates emphasize that new legislation, inclusive of protection for coercive control, could help change the status quo with how cases are handled by law enforcement and the courts.[4]

Addressing the Legislative Gaps of Coercive Control

Non-violent abuse is less regulated by U.S. state statutes, as the legislature, law enforcement, and the judicial system do not view such abuse as meeting the same "immediate and present danger" criteria or burden of proof that is typically required to obtain a temporary injunction or other protections that physical violence, or threats thereof, tend to meet.[5] The non-violent forms of abuse are minimized, overshadowed, and misunderstood when they are combined with physical acts of violence, causing the non-physical behavior to be normalized by the victim, society, and the judicial system.[6] Abusers understand that civil and criminal courts, which are regularly gender-biased and apathetic to violence against women, may view women negatively for reporting any form of IPV they experience.[7] These gender-biased courts reward abusers with their IPV victims' failed

DOI: 10.4324/9781003097488-14

petitions for injunction.[8] Often, because the victim must report the IPV when applying for the injunction for protection, it angers and empowers the abuser because they are emboldened when the court denies the petition.[9] Coupled with a lack of official response or assistance to the IPV victim, filing the petition for injunction may become deadly for the victim.[10] Most U.S. state laws focus on addressing each discrete act of physical violence, rather than attempting to regulate the ongoing, continuous pattern of mental abuse that typically manifests in the more covert, torturous nonviolent acts of IPV that may turn just as deadly.[11]

The criminal court's rational for punishment is based solely on the idea that IPV occurs in discrete and insular acts of physical violence rather than on the notion that it is comprised of a continuum of actions; actions that may *never* involve physical violence.[12] By treating multiple acts of physical abuse as a separate and distinct act of violence, for which the offender is charged with a separate and distinct crime when each occurrence takes place, the criminal justice system restricts itself by only assessing each of the multiple acts one incident at a time rather than viewing the abuse as a continuum of behavior.[13] Instead, when escalating abusive behaviors occur between the same IPV offender and victim, the criminal justice system needs to become more nimble to provide the comprehensive adjudication of an overarching pattern of controlling and abusive behaviors, which include, but is not exclusive of, physical violence.[14] Barlow and Walklate (2021) discuss the fact that, to deal with coercive control, criminal law should move away from its current "incident-led" approach and adopt a "process-led" approach that would take into account the abuser's course of conduct.[15] This process-led approach that would "focus on the cumulative effect of the minutiae of everyday behaviours, some visible, some not, the total effect of which are abusively controlling" is an approach that is desperately needed to begin to prevent the type of IPHs detailed throughout this book.[16]

McMahon et al. (2020) assert that "a new law should generally only be introduced if there is a 'gap' that needs filling."[17] Historically, criminal and civil laws have looked to various categories to provide protections to victims from their abusers, such as DV, dating violence, stalking, and elder abuse.[18] However, in most states, as previously discussed throughout this book, these laws do not adequately protect victims from the non-violent tactics of coercive control.[19] The more complex version of the non-violent tactics of coercive control, deployed through a judicial proceeding, i.e., judicial terrorism®, is even more problematic to legislate and regulate; but some U.S. states are instituting laws against this form of abuse.[20] Nevertheless, stalking laws have been enacted and enforced for non-violent behaviors that have similar attributes and effects on its victims to coercive control.[21] There is a link between the non-violent tactics of coercive control and stalking, making criminal and civil stalking laws a launching platform for the legislation of the non-violent tactics of coercive control.[22] However, when implementing and regulating stalking laws, there is disagreement among experts and professionals in the field as to whether these tactics are only utilized by the IPV abuser when the intimate relationship has ended or whether the relationship is ongoing.[23] Still, criminal stalking laws and civil injunctions for protection against stalking may be a blueprint for coercive control legislation.[24]

Based on the results of this study, this chapter specifically addresses the opportunity for borrowing from existing civil stalking laws to develop a new category of civil injunction for protection against IPV and IPH that includes the non-violent forms of coercive control, which a small few U.S. states have accomplished.[25] Although some states within the United States have made great strides in employing coercive control language to attempt to further protect IPV victims, several of these laws have very specific applications as written.[26] In other words, the coercive control language does not apply to all aspects of civil or criminal law within the respective states that have included the coercive control language.[27] Unfortunately, despite the tireless efforts of advocates for change, some of these few laws are rather narrowly written; but others are more broadly applied.[28]

Members of state legislatures, who are attempting to strengthen their laws by adding more inclusive language for coercive control, are running into strong headwinds. For example, Florida, the state in which this study's data were collected, passed a bill known as Greyson's Law, effective on July 1, 2023, that is intended to increase protections for children subjected to child custody issues where DV and/or child abuse is a concern.[29] Originally, the law was intended to "add 'coercive control' to Florida's definition of domestic violence" in its state statutes.[30] The proposed coercive control definition read as follows:

> [A] pattern of threatening, humiliating, or intimidating actions by one family or household member against another family or household member, which actions are used to harm, punish, or frighten the family or household member and make him or her dependent on the other family or household member by isolating, exploiting, or regulating him or her.[31]

However, as approved, Greyson's Law does not include any definition of coercive control and continues to "leave[] much of the decision-making to a judge's discretion rather than outlin[ing] steps the court must take in various circumstances."[32] But the approved bill does require the court to consider whether a parent has engaged in a pattern of behavior over a period of time, which includes intimidating or controlling behavior (harkening back to coercive control language).[33] The bill also strengthens the factors a court must consider when reviewing a petition for injunction by adding "whether the respondent has or had engaged in a pattern of abusive, threatening, intimidating, or controlling behavior that is composed of a series of acts, not matter how short a period of time, which demonstrates a continuity of purpose ..."[34] Indeed, this language does provide for the continuing course of conduct that an abuser, who utilizes coercive control, relies upon whether physical violence is employed or not. Although Greyson's Law provides hope that children in Florida, who are the subject of custody battles, will be more protected and the application of DV injunctions should be less focused on discrete acts of physical violence, there is currently no outlook providing a future expansion of Florida's DV definition.[35]

The Link between Stalking and the Non-Violent Tactics of Coercive Control

Stalking or harassment are considered indicators of "high risk of escalation and harm" in terms of DV and IPH.[36] Attempting to legislate or regulate stalking when it occurs within the context of an intimate partner relationship is difficult because such efforts tend to become skewed toward the typical DV response.[37] In other words, when the stalking occurs between intimates, law enforcement may not recognize the stalking behavior, is less likely to charge the offender with stalking, and is more likely to send the victim to family court for protection rather than initiating any criminal action for the stalking.[38] One reason for this may be the fact that IPV victims might be less likely to report the abusive behavior they are experiencing as stalking, especially if they want to continue the relationship.[39] Another reason this occurs is because prosecutors and courts are hesitant to consider certain acts from a *current* intimate as stalking behaviors, perhaps because they are concerned about cooperation from the victim who wants to maintain the relationship or who is afraid to testify; or the victim, as well as the professionals involved, are not able to identify certain acts as stalking.[40] However, law enforcement and prosecutors are more likely to move forward with a stalking case once the intimate relationship has ended.[41] This is because stalking is generally identified with an intimate partner relationship that has ended, i.e., post-separation as opposed to one that is ongoing, which is typically referred to as family violence, DV, or domestic abuse.[42]

Stalking laws were created with broad provisions to deal with a course of conduct that exceeds an individual event and address that of mental harm, the scope of which is traditionally outside of criminal law.[43] These laws do not require much in the way of physical harm, if any, and the mental harm can typically be imputed to an alleged offender if the mental harm cannot be proven.[44] Depending on the jurisdiction, stalking laws either specify short and narrowly construed behaviors constituting stalking; or, others provide long and broadly construed behaviors, as well as a catch-all provision to include any behavior that could reasonably cause mental harm, apprehension, or fear.[45] Still, it is argued that, especially in light of the catch-all provisions, the regulated behaviors *must* be understood within the context they are acted upon, tying them back to the list of narrowly construed behaviors.[46] To do so, essentially, causes the catch-all provisions to become ineffective without the narrowly construed behaviors with which they must be contextualized.[47]

But another argument states that, in order to adequately ensure that legislation will protect victims into the future, the catch-all provisions should stand separate from the preceding narrowly construed lists.[48] This is because it is incredibly limiting to attach the catch-all provisions to the narrowly construed behaviors, essentially stripping the catch-all behaviors of any true protections for stalking victims.[49] However, the fact that the catch-all provisions exist alongside the narrowly tailored lists of behaviors suggests that these laws recognize that, even under stalking laws, prohibited behaviors for non-violent harms that cause mental anguish and fear in its victims are extensive and need to be broadly construed to ensure the criminal acts are regulated.[50] Yet, it is argued that stalking laws should not be viewed as the sole source of criminal and civil relief for those mental harms that result from the myriad of non-violent coercive control tactics.[51]

When shifting the focus of developing criminal and civil laws from stalking to the non-violent tactics of coercive control, it is important to consider whether the intimate partners are still cohabitating at the time the non-violent tactics are deployed.[52] Generally, with stalking laws, they can be applied in varying situations whereby the victim may not be an intimate partner of the offender or may not know the offender, which is not the case with IPV or coercive control.[53] Thus, it is counterintuitive for those who do not have a clear understanding of stalking and IPV that a current intimate partner would be able to stalk their intimate partner, especially one they live with.[54] One reason for this is because there is a limited understanding among professionals and academics, who influence those working in the field, that staking only occurs once the intimate partner relationship ends.[55] This is understandable given the fact that an extensive amount of definitions for stalking ultimately utilize a previous intimate partner relationship in their description.[56] However, research is slowly emerging that details the concepts of stalking, harassment, and coercive control as behaviors occurring between intimate partners who have an ongoing relationship.[57]

When the intimate partner relationship is ongoing, the forms that the type of intimate partner stalking take on are not commonplace stalking behaviors.[58] They typically take on the non-violent forms of coercive control discussed throughout this book.[59] Moreso, the general public may not appreciate criminalizing the non-violent tactics of coercive control, as its tactics and effects on its victims may seem too abstract and intangible for a clear appreciation of how legislation should be enacted and interpreted.[60] But such legislative efforts should be attempted when valid.[61] But by doing so, it is imperative to ensure that a narrative of a *well enforced and prosecuted* intimate partner relationship with physical violence is not conveyed because the physical acts of IPV are *still often overlooked and under prosecuted*.[62] In other words, it is extremely important to ensure that the current efforts at mitigating the deleterious effects of physical violence between intimates are not undone. To the contrary, simply by attempting to legislate and enforce the non-violent tactics of coercive control within existing legislation, the impacts of physical violence experienced between intimates must not be minimized; and the non-violent tactics of coercive control may become lost in the larger narrative of the violence.

For that reason, a new category of civil protective order, i.e., injunction for protection is recommended to alleviate the conflict between existing stalking laws and existing laws that protect IPV victims, which typically only look to physical violence or the threat thereof for their implementation. Indeed, as this study has shown, there is a need for enacting further legislation, criminal or civil, regarding non-violent coercive control to enhance the current laws that protect IPV victims rather than lessening existing protections that are currently afforded to them. However, by simply adding coercive control language to existing civil injunction statutes, there is a risk of running into the same "physical violence fixation" with which legislators, courts, and law enforcement currently operate.

Cross (2022) "argues that criminalizing coercive control will do far more harm than good."[63] She explains that the criminal legal system is incapable of distinguishing between the motive behind a physical act of IPV that is intended as a one-off moment of lashing out from a physical act in which the abuser intends to invoke power and control over their victim.[64] She also suggests that the criminal justice system is not capable of understanding the difference between physical acts of violence stemming from the IPV abuser as the primary aggressor and those from the IPV victim as "reactive/resistance."[65] In doing so, Cross (2022) "call[s] for the scaling back of both the scope of domestic violence criminal laws and overall reliance on the criminal legal system."[66] She cites three main reasons why coercive criminalizing control should not be commonplace in the United States: (1) studies show criminal laws do not have a positive impact on DV, (2) coercive control laws will face constitutional challenges, (3) even if passed and enforced, coercive control laws will work against IPV survivors who do not appear as sympathetic to those they rely upon for assistance.[67] Instead, Cross (2022) calls for a mitigation of criminal interventions for IPV and a pivot to programs and policies that improve IPV survivors lives without the risks of criminal interventions.[68]

But there is a reason the IPV victims and abusers, either of which might have activated law enforcement or the court prior to the killing, are not referred to as IPV survivors in this book. One or the other of them either died or committed the killing; and in 49.8 percent of the cases, both spouses died because of an intimate partner homicide-suicide (IPHS). Contrary to Cross' (2022) argument that there is no need for additional coercive control legislation, the results of this study show that the IPV victim, who died from an IPH, mobilized the law 67.6 percent of the time while attempting to protect themselves from IPV whether they disclosed physical violence or not. Perhaps more of the victims in this study would have mobilized the law if they had known law enforcement or the court could have protected them if physical violence was not the overwhelming criteria for assistance. Over eighty percent of the IPV victims in this study resisted the abuse with which they were confronted, *without physical violence in return*, refuting Cross' (2022) contention that criminal law is incapable of determining whether a victim's actions vary from that of the primary aggressor.[69] Indeed, it is possible to take a holistic approach to reviewing cases of IPV; and its victims and abusers deserve nothing less, which is why coercive control should be written into U.S. state statutes. With the overwhelming evidence that coercive control exists, is measurable, and is lethal without the precursor of physical acts of violence, it is necessary to ensure that the entirety of the intimate partner relationship is reviewed by the court to safeguard the proper protections are afforded the proper parties to the case. Without such analyses, the judicial system is failing the intimate partners, their children, their family and friends, and society as a whole.

By creating a new category of civil protective order specific to coercive control, which has been done in a few U.S. states, the limitations of stalking laws being enforced only when the intimate partner relationship has ended, i.e., post-separation, can have a better application in law.[70] It is well researched, including in this study, that coercive control can operate effectively and efficiently within an existing and ongoing intimate partner relationship, as well as one in which the relationship has ended.[71] This compares to the application of that of a civil DV injunction, which requires physical violence, that recognizes the violence at any stage of the intimate relationship.[72] Indeed, a coercive control injunction for protection would comport with the notion of a civil DV injunction relative to the status of the intimate relationship and would borrow from a civil stalking injunction for its non-violent underpinnings.[73] The legislature, courts, and law enforcement would more fundamentally understand this new category of civil injunction because the non-violent tactics occur during any time within the intimate relationship, i.e., whether it is ongoing or post-separation but could more readily apply the non-violent tactics as it already does to stalking.[74] What is more, as this new category of injunction for protection becomes mainstream, coercive control would become more well recognized through training of law enforcement, court personnel and advocates, allowing IPV victims to more readily self-identify as victims of coercive control as well.

Reimagining Intimate Partner Violence Lethality Risk Assessments

There is a widely accepted belief that, to accurately assess a victim's risk of becoming a casualty of an IPH, previous evidence of physical violence or direct threats of physical violence must exist between the abuser and victim.[75] This belief is based on the notion of recidivism, meaning those who are repeatedly arrested for IPV or violent crimes are the most at risk for committing re-abuse or IPH.[76] However, recidivism is reliant upon the IPV victim's reporting of the original offense, meaning the physically violent act by the abuser.[77] Sheehan et al. (2015) assert that previous abuse is considered "one of the most important risk factors of IPH."[78] In their discussion, Sheehan et al. (2015) explain the danger of separation for the IPV victim due to the abuser's loss of control over their victim and the fact that women were three times more likely to become a victim of IPH if separated from their abuser rather than living with them.[79] Additionally, stalking, the presence of weapons, especially handguns, as well as the abuser's consumption of drugs and alcohol contribute to the heightened risk of lethality for the IPV victim.[80]

Campbell et al. (2003) state that "[t]he majority (67%-80%) of intimate partner homicides involve physical abuse of the female by the male before the murder, no matter which partner is killed."[81] They draw the conclusion that intervening in intimate partner relationships where physical abuse exists will reduce the number of IPHs but seek to find additional risk factors beyond physical abuse to enhance their knowledge of risk factors.[82] They raise unemployment as an important risk factor leading to IPH; and, similar to Sheehan et al. (2015), Campbell et al. (2003) state that the availability of guns increases the risk of IPH.[83] Reckdenwald et al. (2020) explain that another less commonly recognized but very significant risk factor for IPH is nonfatal strangulation.[84] In fact, prior nonfatal strangulation carries an estimated seven and a half times higher risk of IPH than for IPV victims who have not experienced nonfatal strangulation.[85] Indeed, many of the cases detailed throughout this book help to explain that this is an indicator of lethality.[86]

Aldridge and Browne (2003) acknowledge that IPV research has been a vigorous endeavor without an IPH empirical research counterpart.[87] But, they explain that "[t]here is a large body of evidence that links spousal homicide to domestic violence."[88] In their literature review, they explain that the data on IPH risk factors are limited because the victim, the key witness to the homicide to which one is trying to collect the data, is unavailable.[89] However, other sources of data, with potential self-serving agendas, provide a picture of risk factors to assess.[90] Aldridge and Browne (2003) agree with and echo many of the risk factors determined by Sheehan et al. (2015) and Campbell et al. (2003); and they determine others as well.[91] These risk factors include age disparity between the IPV victim and their abuser, possessiveness and sexual jealousy by the abuser, and personality disorder.[92]

Myhill and Hohl (2016) explain that some risk assessment tools currently in use have a physical violence bias, as they were developed by statistical manipulation to "prioritize factors associated with physical violence."[93] They also contend that several of the available risk assessment tools follow "the violence model" in which the IPV victim is screened at a "higher danger" protocol if they answer affirmatively to questions concerning threats to kill and the use of weapons.[94] Indeed, current risk assessment tools and the statistical models that helped develop them may not be able to account for the continuum of behaviors that is coercive control, especially when those behaviors interact simultaneously, because the models are only able to account for each behavior one at a time.[95] Myhill and Hohl (2016) support this study's contention that viewing coercive control's continuum of behaviors, including the themes and subthemes as described throughout this book, holistically will better identify the IPV victim's risk of IPH.[96]

Reallocating Intimate Partner Violence Resources

There are many different needs and risk assessment tools available within the context of IPV for evaluating the needs and risks of both the IPV offender and victim to mitigate future violence and the potential for lethality.[97] But many of these tools may never reach their intended targets because, as this study shows, IPV victims who become victims of IPH do not often report the physical abuse they might be experiencing if they are experiencing physical abuse prior to the IPH at all. What if the first time the physical violence occurs is at the time of the killing? If this occurs under the current violence-based system, the IPV victim and abuser would not be identified;[98] and based on this study's results, over eighty-four percent of the IPH victims would not have been identified because they did not report physical violence prior to the killing. Therefore, when conducting lethality risk assessments, is it an injustice to those IPH victims that so much emphasis is being placed on physical violence in the intimate partner relationship? Absolutely.

Barlow and Walklate (2021) argue that the best risk assessment is that offered by the IPV victim themselves.[99] Their study echoes the sentiment of Myhill and Hohl (2016) in that most risk assessment tools are the product of statistical measurement limited in their ability to adapt to coercive control's complexities.[100] And this study helps to show that it is possible to collect, measure, and analyze data that is generalizable, both for qualitative and quantitative purposes, to develop better risk assessment tools specifically for the purposes of identifying coercive control beyond that of physical violence. Indeed, the IPV victim who suffers the torment of coercive control's daily intrusion is the most capable of describing its torturous effects and the abusive behaviors that are implemented against them. But IPV victims have reported that police officers do not adequately "allow their own perceptions of risk and safety to be heard and fully considered" when it comes to coercive control.[101]

There is a plethora of resources available for an IPV victim to find information related to DV.[102] But, as this study shows, obtaining assistance for protection from their abuser is not as easy; and if they are confronted with a risk assessment tool that is focused on physical violence, they most likely will slip through the cracks even if they managed to find an advocate that takes the time to listen to their plight. This is because, as explained above, risk assessment tools that are slanted toward ensuring physical violence, or the threat thereof, are met with a heightened sense of urgency. But providing IPV victims with their full voice is of the utmost importance if the battle against DV, inclusive of IPV and coercive control, is going to be won. The victims are the true heroes of this war and must be listened to as the ambassadors of the data, not the statistical models that have made the risk assessments what they are today. With such an approach, an emphasis on outreach for education to the community about the tactics of coercive control and how it is deployed is essential.

IPV victims and their abusers must understand what the full extent of coercive control is and what its effects are to the family at large so that some relief might come to those who are suffering in silence. Through this study, the torment of coercive control's tactics was shown to affect its victims, as well as their children, other family members, and friends. If IPV victims are better educated on coercive control, then they should be able to self-identify as victims of abuse whether they are physically abused or not. This is not currently happening within the United States' understanding of DV. A broad scale educational program that dovetails with a reimagined risk assessment program should become the new focus of the United States' coercive control program to ensure these senseless IPH killings do not continue to occur.

Notes

1 E.g., Lisa A. Fontes, *Domestic Violence Isn't About Just Physical Violence – and State Laws are Beginning to Recognize That*, THE CONVERSATION (May 12, 2021); Kristy Candela, *Protecting the Invisible Victim: Incorporating Coercive Control in Domestic Violence Statutes*, 54 FAMILY COURT REVIEW 112 (2016) https://doi.org/10.1111/fcre.12208; *Coercive Control Codification Matrix*, BATTERED WOMEN'S JUSTICE PROJECT (2022) http://bwjp.org/wp-content/uploads/2022/08/CC_MATRIX.pdf.
2 See supra Chapter 9. See also Fontes, supra note 1.
3 See Fontes, supra note 1. See also Coercive Control Codification Matrix, supra note 1.
4 See Fontes, supra note 1. See also Coercive Control Codification Matrix, supra note 1.

5 OFFICE OF THE STATE COURTS ADMINISTRATOR, FLORIDA INSTITUTE ON INTERPERSONAL VIOLENCE, CONTRACT NO. LJ990, FLORIDA'S DOMESTIC VIOLENCE BENCHBOOK 105 (2020); *accord* EVAN STARK, COERCIVE CONTROL: HOW MEN ENTRAP WOMEN IN PERSONAL LIFE (2007).
6 *See* Margaret E. Johnson, *Redefining Harm, Reimagining Remedies and Reclaiming Domestic Violence Law*, 42 U.C. DAVIS L. REV. 1107 (2009).
7 *See* H. Douglas, *Battered Women's Experiences of the Criminal Justice System: Decentring the Law*, 20 FEMINIST LEGAL STUDIES 121 (2012) https://doi.org/10.1007/s10691-012-9201-1; Donna J. King, *Naming the Judicial Terrorist: An Exposé of an Abuser's Successful Use of a Judicial Proceeding for Continued Domestic Violence*, 1 TENN. JOURNAL OF RACE, GENDER, & SOCIAL JUSTICE 153 (2012); SUSAN WEITZMAN, "NOT TO PEOPLE LIKE US:" HIDDEN ABUSE IN UPSCALE MARRIAGES (2000).
8 *See* Joan Zorza, *Batterer Manipulation and Retaliation Compounded by Denial and Complicity in the Family Courts*, in DOMESTIC VIOLENCE, ABUSE, AND CHILD CUSTODY: LEGAL STRATEGIES AND POLICY ISSUES (Mo Therese Hannah & Barry Goldstein eds., 2010).
9 *See* Radha Inyengar, *Does the Certainty of Arrest Reduce Domestic Violence?: Evidence from Mandatory and Recommended Arrest Laws*, 93 JOURNAL OF PUBLIC ECONOMICS 85 (2009) https://doi.org/10.1016/j.jpubeco.2008.09.006.
10 *See* Mike Brigner, *Why Do Judges Do That?*, in DOMESTIC VIOLENCE, ABUSE, AND CHILD CUSTODY: LEGAL STRATEGIES AND POLICY ISSUES (Mo Therese Hannah & Barry Goldstein eds., 2010).
11 *See* Candela, *supra* note 1; STARK, *supra* note 5; Claire Wright, *Torture at Home: Borrowing from the Torture Convention to Define Domestic Violence*, 24 HASTINGS WOMEN'S LAW JOURNAL 457 (2013).
12 *See* MOLLY DRAGIEWICZ, EQUALITY WITH A VENGEANCE: MEN'S RIGHTS GROUPS, BATTERED WOMEN, AND ANTIFEMINIST BACKLASH (2011); Joanna Birenbaum & Isabel Grant, *Taking Threats Seriously: Section 264.1 and Threats as a Form of Domestic Violence*, 59 CRIMINAL LAW QUARTERLY 1 (2013); Cheryl Hanna, *The Paradox of Progress: Translating Evan Stark's Coercive Control Into Legal Doctrine for Abused Women*, 15 VIOLENCE AGAINST WOMEN 1458 (2009) https://doi.org/10.1177%2F1077801209347091; David Hirschel & Eve Buzawa, *Understanding the Context of Dual Arrest with Directions for Future Research*, 8 VIOLENCE AGAINST WOMEN 1449 (2002) https://doi.org/10.1177%2F107780102237965.
13 *See* Marilyn McMahon et al., *An Alternative Means of Prosecuting Non-Physical Domestic Abuse: Are Stalking Laws an Under-Utilised Resource?*, in CRIMINALISING COERCIVE CONTROL: FAMILY VIOLENCE AND THE CRIMINAL LAW (Marilyn McMahon & Paul McGorrery eds., 2020).
14 *See* Candela, *supra* note 1; Courtney K. Cross, *Coercive Control and the Limits of Criminal Law*, 56 UC DAVIS LAW REVIEW 195 (2022); McMahon et al., *supra* note 13; Julia Quilter, *Evaluating Criminalisation as a Strategy in Relation to Non-Physical Family Violence*, in CRIMINALISING COERCIVE CONTROL: FAMILY VIOLENCE AND THE CRIMINAL LAW (Marilyn McMahon & Paul McGorrery eds., 2020).
15 Charlotte Barlow & Sandra Walklate, *Gender, Risk Assessment and Coercive Control: Contradictions in Terms?*, 61 BRIT. J. CRIMINOL. 887, 892 (2021) https://doi.org/10.1093/bjc/azaa104.
16 *Id.*
17 McMahon et al., *supra* note 13 at 95.

18 See Cross, *supra* note 14.
19 *E.g.*, Fontes, *supra* note 1; Candela, *supra* note 1; *Coercive Control Codification Matrix*, *supra* note 1.
20 *See Coercive Control Codification Matrix*, *supra* note 1. *See also* WASH. REV. CODE §§ 26.51.010-26.51.070; *29-41-101. Definitions, Statutes: Tennessee*, WOMENSLAW.ORG (last visited March 7, 2023 https://www.womenslaw.org/laws/tn/statutes/29-41-101-definitions).
21 *See* McMahon et al., *supra* note 13.
22 *See Id.*
23 *See Id.*
24 *See Id.*
25 *See* Cross, *supra* note 14.
26 *See Id.*; *Coercive Control Codification Matrix*, *supra* note 1. *See also* WASH. REV. CODE §§ 26.51.010-26.51.070; *29-41-101. Definitions, Statutes: Tennessee*, *supra* note 20.
27 *See* Candela, *supra* note 1; Cross, *supra* note 14. *See also Coercive Control Codification Matrix*, *supra* note 1.
28 *See* Candela, *supra* note 1; Cross, *supra* note 14. *See also Coercive Control Codification Matrix*, *supra* note 1.
29 *See* H.B. 97, 117th Gen. Assemb., Reg. Sess. (Fla. 2023). Greyson's Law is named after Greyson Kessler, a four-year-old boy who was killed by his father in a murder-suicide. His mother desperately attempted to seek protection from the court for Greyson in the days immediately leading up to his death, but Florida law was inadequate to assist. (*See* Greyson's Law, *Greyson's Law Passed!*, GREYSON'S CHOICE https://greysonschoice.org/greysons-law (last visited June 15, 2023)).
30 Jesse Scheckner, *Michael Grieco Files "Greyson's Law" to Add Protections for Children at Risk of Parental Harm*, FLORIDA POLITICS ¶ 17 (December 1, 2021).
31 *Id.*
32 Jesse Scheckner, *Streamlined Bill Safeguarding Children at Risk of Parental Harm Refiled for 2023 Session*, FLORIDA POLITICS ¶ 14 (January 4, 2023).
33 *See* H.B. 97, 117th Gen. Assemb., Reg. Sess. (Fla. 2023).
34 S.B. 130, 117th Gen. Assemb., Reg. Sess. (Fla. 2023).
35 *See* Greyson's Law, *supra* note 29. *See also* Cross, *supra* note 14.
36 Chris Todd et al., *Technology, Cyberstalking and Domestic Homicide: Informing Prevention and Response Strategies*, 31 POLICING AND SOCIETY 82, 83 (2021) https://doi.org/10.1080/10439463.2020.1758698.
37 *See* McMahon et al., *supra* note 13.
38 *See Id.*
39 *See Id.*
40 *See Id.*
41 *See Id.*
42 *See Id.*
43 *See Id.*
44 *See Id.*
45 *See Id.*
46 *See Id.*
47 *See Id.*
48 *See Id.*
49 *See Id.*
50 *See Id.*

51 See Id.
52 See Id.
53 See Id.
54 See Id.
55 See Id.
56 See Id.
57 See Todd et al., *supra* note 36; McMahon et al., *supra* note 13.
58 See McMahon et al., *supra* note 13.
59 See *supra* Part II: Voices of Intimate Partner Homicide Victims. See also McMahon et al., *supra* note 13.
60 See McMahon et al., *supra* note 13.
61 See Quilter, *supra* note 14.
62 E.g., Id.
63 Cross, *supra* note 14 at 195.
64 See Id.
65 Cross, *supra* note 14 at 216.
66 Id.
67 See Id.
68 See Id.
69 See Id.
70 See Id.; McMahon et al., *supra* note 13.
71 See *supra* Part II: Voices of Intimate Partner Homicide Victims.
72 See FLA. STAT. § 741.30 (2023).
73 See Cross, *supra* note 14.
74 See FLA. STAT. § 784.048 (2023).
75 See NATIONAL INSTITUTE OF JUSTICE, U.S. DEPARTMENT OF JUSTICE, QUESTIONS AND ANSWERS IN LETHAL AND NON-LETHAL VIOLENCE: PROCEEDINGS OF THE SECOND ANNUAL WORKSHOP OF THE HOMICIDE RESEARCH WORKING GROUP (1992); R. Emerson Dobash et al., *Lethal and Nonlethal Violence Against an Intimate Female Partner: Comparing Male Murderers to Nonlethal Abusers*, 13 VIOLENCE AGAINST WOMEN 329 (2007) https://doi.org/10.1177/1077801207299204; Brynn E. Sheehan et al., *Intimate Partner Homicide: New Insights for Understanding Lethality and Risks*, 21 VIOLENCE AGAINST WOMEN 269 (2015) https://doi.org/10.1177/1077801214564687.
76 See R. Emerson Dobash et al., *"Out of the Blue:" Men Who Murder an Intimate Partner*, 4 FEMINIST CRIMINOLOGY 194 (2009) http://dx.doi.org/10.1177/1557085109332668 (discussing the fact that "the best predictor of subsequent intimate partner violence is general criminal recidivism"); Laurie M. Graham et al., *The Danger Assessment: An Instrument for the Prevention of Intimate Partner Homicide*, in HANDBOOK OF INTERPERSONAL VIOLENCE ACROSS THE LIFESPAN (R. Geffner et al. eds., 2019) https://doi.org/10.1007/978-3-319-62122-7_145-1; Hirschel & Buzawa, *supra* note 12; Andrew R. Klein, *Lethality Assessments and the Law Enforcement Response to Domestic Violence*, 12 J. OF POLICE CRISIS NEGOTIATIONS 87 (2012) https://doi.org/10.1080/15332586.2012.720175; N. Zoe Hilton et al., *An Indepth Actuarial Assessment for Wife Assault Recidivism: The Domestic Risk Appraisal Guide*, 32 LAW HUM. BEHAV. 150 (2008) https://doi.org/10.1007/s10979-007-9088-6; Radha Iyengar, *Corrigendum to "Does the Certainty of Arrest Reduce Domestic Violence? Evidence from Mandatory and Recommended Arrest Laws" [JPubEc 93(1–2), pp. 85–89]*, 179 J. OF PUBLIC ECONOMICS 1 (2019) https://doi.org/10.1016/j.jpubeco.2019.104098.

77 *See* Iyengar, *supra* note 77.
78 Sheehan et al., *supra* note 75 at 271.
79 *See Id.*
80 *See Id.*
81 Jacquelyn C. Campbell et al., *Risk Factors for Femicide in Abusive Relationships: Results from a Multisite Case Control Study*, 93 AMERICAN JOURNAL OF PUBLIC HEALTH 1089, 1089 (2003) https://doi.org/10.2105/ajph.93.7.1089.
82 *See Id.*
83 *See Id.*; Sheehan et al., *supra* note 75.
84 *See* Amy Reckdenwald et al., *Prosecutorial Response to Nonfatal Strangulation in Domestic Violence Cases*, 35 VIOLENCE AND VICTIMS 160 (2020) https://doi.org/10.1891/VV-D-18-00105.
85 *See Id.*
86 *See supra* Part II: Voices of Intimate Partner Homicide Victims.
87 *See* Mari L. Aldridge & Kevin D. Browne, *Perpetrators of Spousal Homicide: A Review*, 4 TRAUMA, VIOLENCE, & ABUSE 265 (2003) https://doi.org/10.1177/1524838003004003005.
88 *Id.* at 267.
89 *See Id.*
90 *See Id.*
91 *See Id.*; Campbell et al., *supra* note 81; Sheehan et al., *supra* note 75.
92 *See* Aldridge & Browne, *supra* note 87.
93 Andy Myhill & Katrin Hohl, *The "Golden Thread": Coercive Control and Risk Assessment for Domestic Violence*, 34 J. OF INTERPERSONAL VIOLENCE 4477, 4481 (2016) https://doi.org/10.1177/0886260516675464.
94 *Id.* at 4482.
95 *See Id.*
96 *See Id. See supra* Part II: Voices of Intimate Partner Homicide Victims.
97 *See* Barlow & Walklate, *supra* note 15; Myhill & Hohl, *supra* note 93.
98 *See* Barlow & Walklate, *supra* note 15.
99 *See Id.*
100 *See Id.*; Myhill & Hohl, *supra* note 93.
101 Barlow & Walklate, *supra* note 15 at 899.
102 *See, e.g., Resources*, NCADV, https://ncadv.org/RESOURCES (last visited June 16, 2023).

11 Conclusion

The Introduction to this book began with a focus on a family, the Davenport's, whereby the abuser, Joseph, employed several non-violent tactics of coercive control against Deborah, while exposing their children to them as well. His acts were so egregious that he held a gun to each family member's head. Immediately thereafter, Deborah engaged in resistance to abuse by mobilizing the law when she filed a petition for injunction and was granted a temporary injunction by the court. In fact, after a hearing, she was awarded a final injunction that was not scheduled to expire without further order from the court. But Deborah asked the court to modify the final injunction in favor of Joseph, which lead to the injunction being dismissed. Following this incident, the Davenport's continued to live together for eight years without any apparent reports of physical violence to law enforcement or the court. Except once Deborah informed Joseph that she was considering a divorce, he kidnapped her and killed her in an intimate partner homicide-suicide (IPHS).

Unfortunately, cases such as *Davenport v. Davenport*, as detailed throughout this book, are all too familiar. This study contains 493 individual cases of heterosexual spouses with their own story to tell of their intimate partner homicide (IPH). Of these 493 cases, there were sixty-two (62) wherein the intimate partner violence (IPV) victim detailed their story through a petition for injunction narrative that was coded and analyzed in NVivo Pro 12, which allowed for the contextualization and operationalization of coercive control for this study. Because one of the goals of this study was to determine whether emphasizing physical violence for lethality assessment in high risk IPV cases is appropriate, the IPV victims' perspectives helped to achieve this goal, as coercive control was operationalized; and it was determined that the major emphasis on physical violence in lethality risk assessments should change.

The empirical literature chasm, which did not have any direct IPH victim data prior to this study, began to be filled through the analyses of the data from the IPV victims who filed their petitions for injunction.

DOI: 10.4324/9781003097488-15

Although it is important to remember that one-third of the petitions for injunction were written by the IPH offender, this study provides empirical data from the IPH victim for analysis and study. Indeed, without the petition for injunction narratives from the victims and offenders in this study, it would have been very difficult to determine the non-violent tactics of coercive control's role in heterosexual spousal relationships prior to an IPH from the point of view of the IPH victim.

In the qualitative phase of the study, the question asked was: "What role do the non-violent tactics of coercive control play in IPV compared to physical violence prior to the IPH?" This question was answered by the coercive control frequencies in Table 9.3, where it was discovered that physical violence was not the most reported coercive control tactic by the IPV victims in their petition for injunction narratives. In fact, physical violence, at 76%, came close to a second-place tie with power and control, as well as resistance to abuse.[1] Additionally, the narratives of the IPV victims are quite revealing as to the role the non-violent tactics of coercive control play in IPV compared to physical violence prior to the IPH. Indeed, many of the IPV victims described in great detail the non-violent tactics of coercive control they were enduring prior to their deaths, whether the IPH occurred almost immediately after the narrative was written or years after the narrative was filed with the court.

In assessing whether the non-violent tactics of coercive control should be legislated and how such laws can be implemented, as Hanna (2009) argues, it is important to consider the IPV victim's willingness to participate in the legal process.[2] Unlike physical violence that is possible to litigate without a victim's participation, non-violent coercive control is more difficult to prosecute or argue against without the IPV victim's involvement, especially if they are the only person who is witness to these tactics of abuse. For example, this study shows that IPH victims who experience the non-violent tactic of power and control are less likely to report physical violence to the court by 69.9% than those IPH victims who do not experience power and control. As a result, IPV victims are silenced due to a possibility of a variety of reasons that may include the fear of retribution from their abuser, an inability to mobilize the law due to the extreme power and control their abuser invokes upon them, or the fact that physical violence is not present in the abusive relationship. It is the last reason that is the focus of this study.

A significant result from this study is the challenge to the notion that reported physical violence is always present in an intimate partner relationship prior to an IPH, including the likelihood that implementing non-violent coercive control is extremely effective until the time of death. In other words, based on a prior report of physical violence to law enforcement, this study showed that the first occurrence of physical violence between the couple was at the time of the IPH in 84.7% of the cases. Thus, for power and control to be a non-violent coercive control tactic that, potentially, works in the abuser's favor so much so to the point that physical violence is not necessary for a victim's compliance is remarkable but not entirely unexpected. This result supports the policy implications discussed throughout this book regarding legislative change and the inclusion of the non-violent tactics of coercive control as indicators for IPH on lethality risk assessments.

Limitations to the Study

This study found its rewards but also its challenges. To properly discuss a path forward for future research, it is important to recognize this study's limitations. The data collected were limited to the jurisdictions in which the IPHs occurred. In other words, it is possible that some of the heterosexual spousal couples had a history of prior reports of physical violence in other jurisdictions than where the IPH happened. Based on time and resources, the data collection efforts were limited to the specific locale in which the IPH took place rather than being able to determine whether the couples had any prior reports of physical violence in their relationship in other jurisdictions. Future studies would benefit from expanding outward from the IPH jurisdiction to determine whether law enforcement or the court were contacted in other jurisdictions.

Another issue with data collection related to jurisdiction protocols, which affected the richness of the data obtained. This is because each law enforcement agency's procedures in providing public records may have differed from the other. Also, each law enforcement officer's writing of the reports might have been more, or less, informative depending on the law enforcement agencies' report writing requirements. Some missing data in this study were because each law enforcement agency has autonomy throughout the state of Florida with their policies for fulfilling public records requests from the public. Additionally, the incident reports themselves are not standardized throughout the state of Florida. Thus, one report might provide very detailed information regarding the events of the IPH or the IPV incident, but another may provide very limited information. Also, the data collection was dependent upon each agency's rules of disclosure. Although Florida is governed by the Sunshine Law, many agencies followed their own jurisdictional rules which made it difficult, if not impossible, to obtain their records.[3] When pushed to provide the information, citing the Sunshine Law, some agencies responded positively with the requested information; however, other agencies were unresponsive, even with repeated efforts over an extended period of time. Thus, the decision to terminate attempting to collect data from the unresponsive agencies was necessary based on the completion time for this study. The effect of which was explained in detail in Chapter 4.[4]

The data collected for this study were limited to law enforcement agencies and court documents, limiting the scope of this study to publicly accessible data. However, with additional time and funding for future research, there are other means of obtaining details of an IPV victim's life and willingness to disclose abuse. Covictims and proxies, such as family, friends, neighbors, coworkers, and clergy are valuable resources, in addition to the IPH victim, to obtain data for an in-depth study regarding physical violence, as well as non-violent tactics of coercive control.[5] These resources for data collection may have details about prior physical violence, as well as non-violent coercive control tactics, that were not accessed in this study. Another source for determining the existence of physical violence in an abusive relationship, whether the IPV victim reports it or not, is by accessing medical records. Indeed, accessing these resources for an expanded study regarding whether an IPH victim divulged to their family, friends, neighbors, coworkers, clergy, doctors, etc., the physical abuse and/or the non violent tactics of coercive control they were enduring would be similar to the type of case study a fatality review board conducts but on a much larger scale.[6] It is important to keep in mind that maintaining generalizability for further coercive control empirical studies is critical.

The notion that IPV victims do not report to law enforcement or the court for fear of retaliation from their abuser is valid and should be considered with the results of this study.[7] It is possible the IPH victims reported physical abuse and/or non-violent tactics of abuse to family, friends, neighbors, coworkers, etc., which would cause the results of a study that included such data to be quite different from this one. With such intimate details, it would be possible to understand what the victims endured prior to the killings. It would shed light into the extent of the coercive control that was not understood in this study because so many cases from this study, i.e., 86.6% did not have filed petitions for injunction. Although this book provides insight into the IPH victims and offenders lives leading up to and after the killings, an empirical study about the details of these lives with such data analyses about the actions the IPV victims took would be quite helpful in learning more about IPV, coercive control and IPH. Truly, an expansive, generalizable study that provides details surrounding the lives of IPH victims and offenders, as well as the individuals they were before the killings, is one of the best ways to begin to stop the scourge of these types of deaths.

It is possible that some IPV victims are not as inclined to explain in their petition for injunction narratives all the non-violent tactics of coercive control they are experiencing because most state laws focus on physical violence or threats of physical violence for the issuance of an injunction for protection. Indeed, the instructions on many applications for an injunction for protection against domestic violence direct the affiant to provide details about physical violence and threats thereof rather than asking for information relating to non-violent coercive control tactics as well; but they may indicate to the affiant to provide supplementary information that includes some non-violent coercive control tactics. It is only when an IPV victim is willing to elaborate on their abusive relationship to the court that data regarding non-violent coercive control is collected. Thus, the results of this study, with the high percentage and emphasis of the non-violent coercive control tactics, are remarkable and indicate a need for further investigation into the role they play in IPH.

Future Directions for Research

This study is exploratory and is intended to lay the groundwork for future studies of this nature; thus, this discussion of future directions for research is essential. A study that can incorporate the type of details, on a case-by-case basis, similar to a fatality review board would be one way to expand the existing research from this study, as well as the Fatality Review Team's information, to generalizable findings.[8] Such findings may, in fact, increase the ability for policy change to provide IPV victims protections from the non-violent tactics of coercive control because this study's findings suggest non-violent coercive control tactics influence the reporting of physical violence to law enforcement or the court, especially when viewed in light of the comparison of the frequencies of physical violence to resistance to abuse at 76% to 75%, respectively.[9]

The timing of any reporting of physical violence to law enforcement or the court compared to when the IPH occurred is an area for future research that deserves attention. Indeed, during data collection for this study, one law enforcement agency indicated that there was a "3-week window of danger" that the IPH victim would be in if there were to be any reports of physical violence to law enforcement prior to the IPH, suggesting that an IPH victim is *only in danger from their abuser three weeks prior to the killing* [emphasis added]. However, many of the IPHs in this study had police reports of physical violence and/or petitions for injunction with reports of physical violence long before and, some, decades before the IPH. Thus, a study regarding the length of time between contact with law enforcement and/or the court regarding physical violence, the non-violent tactics of coercive control, and the IPH is warranted. The results of this type of study would be especially useful for law enforcement, judicial training, and policy review purposes. Indeed, a collective review of the cases in this book, and others like them, may shed light on the fact that the predominant policy of the six-month time frame for prior physical violence or the threat thereof for courts to consider in issuing an injunction for protection may be misguided.

The high percentages of IPHS frequencies for data set A and B indicate the need for further research into this topic, i.e., 49.8% and 50%, respectively, especially because this study is one of the few that determines the rate of IPHS from IPH itself rather than from murder-suicide.[10] Indeed, most studies report about IPHS stemming from murder-suicide.[11] However, similar to this study, Caman et al. (2017) and Velopulos et al. (2019) are two of the few studies that report IPHS rates from IPH cases; and Caman et al. (2017) consider, on average for their twenty-three-year study, that a 15.5% IPHS rate was profound.[12] Also, at a rate of 35% success for completed IPHSs, Velopulos et al. (2019) assert that this rate is staggering and warrants further research into both IPV and suicidality.[13] Thus, with this study's 49.8% success rate for completed IPHS for data set A and 50% for data set B, it is irresponsible to do anything but conclude that further research into IPHS and IPH, especially as it relates to the non-violent tactics of coercive control as well as the prior reporting of physical violence to law enforcement and the court and IPV in general, is warranted.

The concept of an order for protection just being a "piece of paper" is continuously challenged but is not rigorously tested.[14] However, future directions from this study suggests that determining the efficacy of orders for protection, as well as the judicial process IPV victims must go through, is possible and necessary. The data set for this study contains information regarding certain aspects of the process for obtaining and maintaining a protective order, such as whether the IPV victim had an order for protection at the time of the IPH. As a result, there are several topics surrounding this field of study that are suggested for future research.

The first topic details whether the IPH victim applied for and received a temporary injunction and/or final injunction. The frequency rate for the success of an IPV victim obtaining a temporary injunction was 73.8%; however, it dropped to 32.7% for final injunctions [Table 9.5]. This discrepancy warrants further research because an apparent reason for this discrepancy is the varying success rate, or lack thereof, in an IPV victim's ability in obtaining a final injunction as opposed to a temporary injunction, which should be analyzed further. Second, for those cases with multiple petition for injunction filings, even if the IPV victim was denied any type of injunction the first time a petition for injunction was filed, it is possible another one was filed by the same IPV victim for the same occurrence or for another abusive episode days, months, or years later as explained throughout Part II.[15] Third, these multiple filings could be from both spouses, which warrants further investigation rather than assuming the IPV victim is always one and the same as the person who becomes the IPH victim. Finally, there does not appear to be another study that focuses on the prevalence of multiple filings of petitions for injunction by the same IPV victim or between the same set of victim/offender. Thus, additional research into this topic is imperative, especially if it is coupled with the efficacy of orders of protection.

Another topic regarding petitions for injunctions emerges as one in which, if the petition was denied or dismissed, determining and understanding why it had that outcome is of the utmost importance. As previously discussed in Chapter 9, The Effectiveness of Injunctions for Protection against Domestic Violence, there are many possible reasons a temporary injunction and/or final injunction is denied or dismissed, such as the fact that the victim does not appear at the final hearing, the judge determines there is not enough evidence to justify the issuance of a temporary injunction and/or final injunction, or the parties reconcile.[16] What is more, it became apparent in some of the cases throughout Part II of this book that injunctions for protection might not be issued even handedly, as the study by Agnew-Brune et al. (2017) in Chapter 3, Litigation and Coercive Control: Not Every Petition for Injunction for Protection against Domestic Violence is the Same explains.[17] For example, in the case of *Olms v. Olms*, each spouse accused the other of physical violence in their respective petitions for injunction; but only Frank Olms was awarded any type of injunction.[18] In fact, he was awarded a temporary and final injunction; but Nancy Olms was not awarded any type of injunction.[19] But Frank killed Nancy and attempted to kill himself.[20] Although it is unclear as to why the court did not issue any protection for Nancy, it is this type of discrepancy that the cases in this book and Agnew-Brune et al. (2017) raise that warrant further research.[21]

Finally, a future study on IPV and IPH offenders and their sentencing is a much-needed topic for further empirical research. As throughout this book, most IPV studies related to harms against IPV victims focus on arrest rates and offenders' interactions with police. Indeed, it is rare, if not at all possible, to find these types of studies that follow IPV cases and/or IPH cases through to sentencing. But it is important to understand how the IPV and IPH offender is sentenced, especially due to the percentage of IPHSs found in this study and the potential risk of bias it brings to such research.[22] Indeed, because IPHS cases are often, if not every time, closed without investigation and are not charged or convicted because there is no living defendant to prosecute, it is important to ensure that these cases are included in the research.[23] This study, compared to the Velopulos et al. (2019) and the Caman et al. (2017) studies, has the highest rate of IPHSs for analysis and includes known victim-offender relationships, which Caman et al. (2017) explain is less common within the scientific field of IPH.[24] Thus, such a study is ideal for future directions for research because the IPV and IPH offenders, as well as those who committed IPHS, are already identified.

One Final Word

The comprehensive goal for this study was to determine whether the nonviolent tactics of coercive control affect IPH without interference from physical violence, i.e., reports of physical violence to law enforcement or the court. In developing this study's methodology to collect the required data, there was no motive to create a study that would forge new territory in the areas of IPH, IPHS, and IPV research as explained above; however, there is a certain, exceptional responsibility that comes with the data that resulted from this study. The homicide reports reviewed for the data collection for this study were gut-wrenching to read. The police reports that were reviewed for reports of physical violence were, often, just as difficult to read because there was a known outcome between the parties to the reports. The petitions for injunction were heartbreaking, especially the ones where the IPV victims *absolutely knew with certainty* their lives were in danger; and they helplessly begged the court for protection.

The experience working with this study has been rewarding and well worth the heartache because there is such a need for research that views IPH from the IPV victims' viewpoint. IPV victims desperately need their voices heard, especially the ones who do not survive. But it should be said that these IPH events occur because the offenders have a certain "voice" that they must need to have heard as well. Carl Martin, an IPHS offender who left a note, made it clear that he and his estranged wife "never were divorced we die together."[25] Perhaps with a better focus for listening to all of those involved, these deadly events can be mitigated. These cases, these decedents have the most to teach us. Through innovative research methods and a willingness to provide resources toward this type of data collection, IPH victims may explain what we do not already know but *must* learn if we are going to save the lives of those who beg to be saved.

Notes

1. See *supra* Chapter 9. Power and control and resistance to abuse equaled 75%.
2. See Cheryl Hanna, *The Paradox of Progress: Translating Evan Stark's Coercive Control Into Legal Doctrine for Abused Women*, 15 VIOLENCE AGAINST WOMEN 1458 (2009) https://doi.org/10.1177%2F1077801209347091.
3. See Attorney General, *Open Government – The "Sunshine" Law*, STATE OF FLORIDA, https://www.myfloridalegal.com/open-government/the-quotsunshinequot-law (last visited June 2, 2023).
4. See *supra* Chapter 4.
5. See Jacquelyn C. Campbell et al., *Risk Factors for Femicide in Abusive Relationships: Results From a Multisite Case Control Study*, 93 AM. J. PUBLIC HEALTH 1089 (2003) https://doi.org/10.2105/ajph.93.7.1089; Brynn E. Sheehan et al., *Intimate Partner Homicide: New Insights for Understanding Lethality and Risks*, 21 VIOLENCE AGAINST WOMEN 269 (2015) https://doi.org/10.1177%2F1077801214564687.
6. See *supra* Introduction, Significance of the Research.
7. See Radha Iyengar, *Does the Certainty of Arrest Reduce Domestic Violence?: Evidence from Mandatory and Recommended Arrest Laws*, 93 J. OF PUBLIC ECONOMICS 85 (2009) https://doi.org/10.1016/j.jpubeco.2008.09.006.
8. See *supra* Introduction, Significance of the Research.
9. See *supra* Chapter 9.

10 *See supra* Chapter 9.
11 *See American Roulette: Murder-Suicide in the United States*, VIOLENCE POLICY CENTER (2020) https://vpc.org/studies/amroul2020.pdf.; Emma Morton et al., *Partner Homicide-Suicide Involving Female Homicide Victims: A Population-Based Study in North Carolina, 1988–1992*, 13 VIOLENCE AND VICTIMS 91 (1998); Tara N. Richards et al., *Reporting Femicide-Suicide in the News: The Current Utilization of Suicide Reporting Guidelines and Recommendations for the Future*, 29 J. FAM. VIOL. 453 (2014) https://doi.org/10.1007/s10896-014-9590-9; Sonia Salari & Carrie LeFevre Sillito, *Intimate Partner Homicide-Suicide: Perpetrator Primary Intent Across Young, Middle, and Elder Adult Age Categories*, 26 AGGRESSION AND VIOLENT BEHAVIOR 26 (2016) https://doi.org/10.1016/j.avb.2015.11.004.
12 *See* Shilan Caman et al., *Trends in Rates and Characteristics of Intimate Partner Homicides Between 1990 and 2013*, 49 J. OF CRIMINAL JUSTICE 14 (2017) https://doi.org/10.1016/j.jcrimjus.2017.01.002; Catherine G. Velopulos et al., *Comparison of Male and Female Victims of Intimate Partner Homicide and Bidirectionality: An Analysis of the National Violent Death Reporting System*, 87 J. TRAUMA ACUTE CARE SURG. 331 (2019) https://doi.org/10.1097/TA.0000000000002276.
13 *See* Velopulos et al., *supra* note 12.
14 *See* Lorena Garcia et al., *Homicides and Intimate Partner Violence: A Literature Review*, 8 TRAUMA, VIOLENCE, & ABUSE 370 (2007) https://doi.org/10.1177/1524838007307294.
15 *See supra* Part II: The Intimate Torture of Coercive Control.
16 *See supra* Chapter 9, The Effectiveness of Injunctions for Protection against Domestic Violence.
17 *See* Christine Agnew-Brune et al., *Domestic Violence Protective Orders: A Qualitative Examination of Judge's Decision-Making Processes*, 32 J. OF INTERPERSONAL VIOLENCE 1921 (2017) https://doi.org/10.1177/0886260515590126. *See supra* Chapter 3, Litigation and Coercive Control: Not Every Petition for Injunction for Protection against Domestic Violence is the Same.
18 *See generally* Olms v. Olms, 2009DR21006SC (2009) (Pet. for Inj. for Prot. Against Dom. Viol.); Olms v. Olms, 2007DR000005SC (2007) (Pet. for Inj. for Prot. Against Dom. Viol.). *See* Olms v. Olms, 2007DR000005SC (2007) https://secure.sarasotaclerk.com/CaseInfo.aspx (last visited Dec. 28, 2022).
19 *See* Olms v. Olms, 2009DR21006SC (2009) https://secure.sarasotaclerk.com/CaseInfo.aspx (last visited Dec. 28, 2022).
20 *See* David Miller, 201100058034 at 2, 6; *See generally* State of Florida v. Olms, 2011CF010399NC (2011) (Amended Probable Cause Aff.).
21 *See* Agnew-Brune et al., *supra* note 17.
22 *See* Caman et al., *supra* note 12.
23 *See Id.*
24 *See Id.*; Velopulos et al., *supra* note 12.
25 Purtis, 2009-00058067 at 4.

Appendix
Codebook – Coercive Control Themes and Subthemes

Intimidation	Narrative describes acts by the abuser that are meant to create fear in the intimate partner violence (IPV) victim in general, such as threatening suicide or making the IPV victim afraid, including creating fear for their safety, by using certain behaviors and gestures.
Animal Abuse	Narrative describes acts the abuser has committed, or threatens to commit, that are, or would be, harmful, neglectful, or of a physically or sexually abusive nature toward animals that are loved by the IPV victim.
Harassment	Narrative describes the abuser continuously contacting the IPV victim or doing something the victim has asked the abuser to stop doing.
Surveillance	Narrative describes acts by the abuser intended to maintain constant information about what the IPV victim is doing and with whom they are doing it.
Threats	Narrative describes acts or words by the abuser toward the IPV victim that are meant to evoke immense fear of imminent danger or worry of something to occur in the future.
Threatens Friends and Family	Narrative describes acts or words by the abuser toward the IPV victim's friends and/or family that are meant to evoke immense fear in the IPV victim that there is imminent danger of something terrible happening to their friends or family.
Weapons	Narrative describes the abuser's possession of weapons, threat to use a weapon against the IPV victim, or intent to purchase a weapon.

(*Continued*)

Isolation	Narrative describes acts by the abuser that causes the IPV victim to feel alone or secluded.
Economic Control	Narrative describes the abuser preventing the victim from going to work or school, as well as interfering with the IPV victim's work or school activities.
False Imprisonment	Narrative describes the abuser confining or restraining the IPV victim against their will.
Financial Control	Narrative describes the abuser's ability to control certain aspects of the IPV victim's financial resources, such as money, shelter, car, etc.
Humiliation	Narrative describes acts the abuser did to the IPV victim to evoke feelings of mortification.
Degradation	Narrative describes a range of non-violent tactics used by the abuser to disrespect or show contempt for the IPV victim, whether in public or private.
Name Calling	Narrative explains situations in which the abuser calls the IPV victim humiliating and/or degrading names either in public or in private.
Power and Control	Narrative describes acts of authority and regulation the abuser maintains over the IPV victim to obtain compliance from the victim.
Child Abuse	Narrative indicates the abuser has committed acts of child maltreatment and/or neglect or has threatened to commit acts of child maltreatment and/or neglect, including physical violence, sexual abuse, or psychological abuse against the children and/or step-children of, or those in common with, the abuser and the IPV victim, including committing acts of IPV or coercive control by the abuser against the IPV victim in front of the children.
Violent Acts toward Family and Friends	Narrative describes violence by the abuser toward family and friends of the IPV victim.
Taking Children from Victim	Narrative explains situations in which the abuser either did take the children from the IPV victim or threatened to take the children from the victim.
Deprivation of Necessities	Narrative explains non-violent tactics the abuser uses to deprive the IPV victim of necessities such as food, medicine, showering, toileting, etc.

(*Continued*)

Psychologically Controlling	Narrative explains acts by the abuser whereby non-violent tactics are used for maintaining a form of mental control over the IPV victim.
Verbal Abuse	Narrative describes verbal acts of vitriol and invective spewed by the abuser toward the IPV victim.
Household, Clothes, and Personal Belongings Destroyed	Narrative describes the abuser destroying property including the home, household furnishings, and the IPV victim's personal belongings.
Fearful of the Future	Narrative indicates the IPV victim has expressed a fear or dread of something happening in the future due to the abuser's actions.
Fear of Children's Safety	Narrative describes the IPV victim's fear of the abuser's ability to harm the children and/or stepchildren of or those in common with the abuser and the IPV victim.
Pregnant	Narrative explains that the victim was pregnant at the time of the incident.
Resistance to Abuse	Narrative describes acts by the IPV victim that constitute resistance to the abuser's tactics of abuse, including resisting a physical altercation without violence, calling the police, filing the petition for injunction, leaving the abuser, etc.
Helping Abuser	Narrative contains a description by the IPV victim whereby the victim helped the abuser, even though the victim also described being abused in the same narrative.
Separated or Estranged	Narrative explains that the IPV victim and the abuser are no longer living together or are living together but in different quarters of the marital home.
Abuser Mental Illness	Narrative indicates the abuser has a history of, or tendency toward, a wide range of conditions that affect mood, thinking, and behavior, i.e., mental disorder or is dealing with some type of mental disorder.
Drinking Alcohol	Narrative indicates the abuser drinks alcohol in excess or to the point that the IPV victim believed it necessary to raise this fact.

(Continued)

Drug Use	Narrative indicates the abuser uses illegal drugs or prescription drugs other than as prescribed.
Paranoia	Narrative describes "1. mental illness characterized by systematized delusions of persecution or grandeur usually without hallucinations; 2. A tendency on the part of an individual or group toward excessive or irrational suspiciousness and distrustfulness of others" that manifests in statements or acts by the abuser, such as threats to kill themselves or accusing the IPV victim of seeing another person.[1]
Physical Violence	Narrative describes acts of physical violence by the abuser against the IPV victim; these acts may be simple battery not resulting in the IPV victim claiming cuts or bruising, such as having their shirt pulled.
Non-fatal Strangulation	Narrative explains the IPV victim having their normal breathing or blood flow to the brain obstructed during violent acts committed by the abuser against the IPV victim.
Rape and Sexual Abuse	Narrative describes various forced sexual acts and other types of unwanted sexual violence forced on the IPV victim by the abuser.

Note

1 Dictionary, Paranoia, Merriam-Webster.com, https://www.merriam-webster.com/dictionary/paranoia (last visited March 5, 2023).

Index

Note: Pages in *italics* represent figures and **bold** indicates tables in the text. Page numbers followed by "n" refer to end notes.

abuser mental illness 45, 85, 183–184; disclosure 266–267; *Dunn v. Dunn* 186–188; *Finn v. Finn* 184–186
Agnew-Brune, Christine 59, 313
Aguilar v. Martinez 216–217
alcohol *see* drinking alcohol
Aldridge, Mari L. 52, 69, 300
Allen v. Allen 221–222
animal abuse 34–35, 91; *Cloaninger v. Colley* 91–93
Asian Americans and Pacific Islanders 264–265
Astacio v. Astacio 182
Avakame, Edem F. 75–77

Bailey v. Bailey 168–170
Barlow, Charlotte 3, 294, 301
battered woman syndrome (BWS) 14n67
behavior of law (Black) 64, 74–75
Belcher v. Belcher 129–130
Bellew, Kara 75–76
Be-On-the-Look-Out (BOLO) 133, 229
Berns, Nancy 28
Biden Administration 22
Bitch 128
Black 263
Black, Donald 266, 268, 288n20; behavior of law theory 64, 73–77, 265, 273–274, 277, 283; propositions 74, 80n66
Block, Carolyn Rebecca 8, 70
Browne, Kevin D. 52, 69, 300

Brown v. Brown 223
Brunson v. Brunson 218–219

Caman, Shilan 10, 312–313
Campbell, Jacquelyn C. 65, 70–71, 300
child abuse 40–41, 134; *Caso v. Caso* 135; *Marshall-Burkhart v. Marshall* 135–137
children from the IPV victim 41, 137–138; *Strong v. Fulgham* 138–142
children's safety 44
Christakos, Antigone 8, 70
coding coverage percentage 257, **258**, 259, 265–268, 291n69, 291n76
coercive control 3, 34, 64, 85, **86**, 259–260; abuser mental illness 45–46; characteristics and frequencies **260**; definitions and coding **259**; fearful of the future 43–44; gender asymmetry of 28–29; humiliation 39–40; intimidation 34–37; isolation 37–39; legislation 293–299; litigation and 59–60; The Maze of Coercive Control 19, 23, *25*, 87; non-violent 280–282, 280–285, 287; physical violence 46–47; power and control 40–43; qualitative frequency interactions 270–271; resistance to abuse 44–45; stalking and the non-violent

tactics 296–299; themes and subthemes 316–319; victim-survivors of 8; *see also* quantitative methods results
Constitutional Rights 193–194
content analysis 7–8, 68, 85, 87, 257, 266–267
conversely genderasymmetry 3
covictim 69, 72–73, 78n17, 310
Craft-Enzor v. Enzor 174–175
criminal law 5, 76–77, 294–296, 298–299
Cross, Courtney K. 298–299
The Cycle Theory of Violence (Walker) 23

Damas v. Damas 225–232
Davenport v. Davenport 1–8, 307
Davies, Lorraine 51
Declaration on the Elimination of Violence against Women (1994) 22
degradation 39, 126; *Diller v. Diller* 127–128; *Olms v. Olms* 126–127
DeKeseredy, Walter S. 38
Department of Children and Families (DCF) 139, 169–170, 194, 224–225, 227–228, 230, 235, 246n191
dependent variable frequencies 272, **272, 278, 280**
deprivation of necessities 41, 142; *Hawkins v. Hawkins* 142–143
Diller v. Diller 127–128
dissociation 63n67
Dissolution of Marriage Action (DOM) 102, 106, 127, 129, 150, 181, 183, 186, 191–193, 215, 217, 233, 237–238, 269
divorce 76, 97, 106, 135, 187
Dobash, R. Emerson 3, 9, 71–72, 195
Dobash, Russell P. 3, 9, 71–72, 195
Domestic Abuse Intervention Project 23, 87
domestic violence (DV) 21–22, 33; filing frequencies 265, **266**; history of 71, 73; injunction for protection 54–55; IPH and **262**, 263; litigation and coercive control 59–60; multiple petitions for injunction 265–266, **266**; orders of injunctions for 268–270; variable coding 261, 262; variable frequencies **273, 273–274**
Dragic v. Dragic 167–168
Dragiewicz, Molly 28
drinking alcohol 46, 188; *Vargas-Brevick v. Brevick* 188–190; *White v. White* 190–192
drug use 46, 192; *Peacock v. Peacock* 192–195
Dunn v. Dunn 186–188
Dutton, Mary Ann 28
DV protection system 55

economic control 37–38, 107; *Hogan-McCarthren v. McCarthren* 108–109
ex parte 2, 54, 61–62n38, 108, 185

false imprisonment 38, 109; *Martin v. Martin* 110–112; *Rimmer v. Rimmer* 109–110
familicide and the family annihilator 222; *Brown v. Brown* 223; *Damas v. Damas* 225–232; *Whyte-Dell v. Dell* 223–225
Fatality Review Team 9–10, 311
fearful of the future 43–44, 165; *Mantrana v. Mora* 165–166
fear of children's safety 44, 166–167; *Bailey v. Bailey* 168–170; *Dragic v. Dragic* 167–168
financial control 38–39, 112; *Jackson v. Jackson* 112–113
Finn v. Finn 184–186
first-degree murder 93, 112, 135, 141, 175, 183, 232
Florida county courthouses 68–69
Florida Department of Law Enforcement (FDLE) 7, 9, 11, 65, 257, 271
Florida Local Law Enforcement Agencies 66–68
Florida Supreme Court 93, 141, 225, 232, 240, 246n191
Frasch v. Frasch 233–240
frequencies 271–275, **272–273**, 278–286, **279–282**,

gender bias 10, 58–59, 293–294
gender-symmetry 3
Goodman, Lisa A. 28
Goraya v. Goraya 147–149
Gordon v. Gordon 125–126
Green v. Green 150–151
Greyson's Law 295–296, 304n29
Grindrod v. Grindrod 215–216
Gwinn, Casey G. 33

Hanna, Cheryl 27
harassment 35, 56–57, 93–94; *Jodi Wood v. William Wood* 94–95
Harp v. Harp 196–197
Hawkins v. Hawkins 142–143
helping abuser 45, 177; *Morrow v. Morrow* 180–181; *Welch v. Welch* 178–180
Herbert v. Herbert 131–132
heterosexual spousal relationship 3, 5, 7–8, 64–66, 271–272, **276**, **282**, 285
Hohl, Katrin 301
household, clothes, and personal belongings 43, 149–150; *Green v. Green* 150–151; *Tinsley v. Tinsley* 151–152
humiliation 39, 125, 260, 285–286; degradation 39; *Gordon v. Gordon* 125–126; name calling 39–40
Huss v. Huss 144–147
hyperarousal 52

IBM SPSS® 7, 259
injunction court 7, 92, 170–171
intimate partner homicide (IPH): Asian Americans and Pacific Islanders 264–265; coding and definitions 261, **262**; comparison of 69–73; demographics of 263–265; mental illness 286; native americans 264; power and control 287; race 263; risk factors 72; theoretical framework for 73–77
intimate partner homicide-suicide (IPHS) 53; murder-suicide 311–312; Native American 264; potential prevalence of 10; role of 52–53; variable frequencies 273, **273**
intimate partner violence (IPV) 21–22; definitions 22; gender and 23–27; resistance to abuse 267–268; resources 301–302; risk of lethality 300–302; socioeconomic divide 75–76; *see also* coercive control
intimidation 34, 89; animal abuse 34–35; *Dhani v. Dhani* 90–91; harassment 35; surveillance 35; threatens friends and family 36; threats 36; *Torres v. Torres* 89–90; weapons 36–37
isolation 37, 103–104, 285; *Alvarez v. Alvarez* 106–107; economic control 37–38; false imprisonment 38; financial control 38–39; *Romero v. Romero* 104–105

Johnson, Michael P. 3, 8, 29, 76, 267–268
Jones, Kathy 23–24
judicial terrorism® 10, 19, 58, 232–233, 294; *Frasch v. Frasch* 233–240

Kelly, Joan B. 29, 267–268

Lininger, Tom 22
litigation: abuse 57–58; and coercive control 59–60
logistic regression 275–278, **276**, 286–287

Mantrana v. Mora 165–166
Marchman Act Florida 189, 207–208n421
marriage 37, 52, 89, 104, 147, 165, 219, 269
Marshall-Burkhart v. Marshall 135–137
masculinity 28
Mattaini v. Lennon 137
The Maze of Coercive Control 19, 23, 25, 87
McMahon, Marilyn 294
mental illness 45–46, 183, 195, 266–267, 281, 285–286

Index 323

mobilization of law 74
Morocco, Kathryn E. 70–71
Morrow v. Morrow 180–181
Morton, Emma 53
murder 6; first-degree 93, 112, 135, 141, 175, 183, 232; second-degree 108, 129, 134–135, 147
The Murder in Britain Study (Dobash et al.) 71–72
Music v. Music 175–177
Myhill, Andy 301

name calling 39–40, 128; *Belcher v. Belcher* 129–130; *Nicholson v. Nicholson* 128–129
National Crime Victimization Survey (NCVS) 76
National Domestic Violence Fatality Review Initiative 9
National Family Violence Surveys (NFVS) 76
National Judicial Education Program 58
native americans IPH 264
Nicholson v. Nicholson 128–129
nonfatal strangulation 47, 217; *Brunson v. Brunson* 218–219; *Pierson v. Pierson* 219–220; *Santiago Nuñez v. Nuñez* 217–218
non-violent abuse 55, 293
null hypothesis 277, 286–287
NVivo 12 Pro 7, 83, 87, 113n3, 291n69, 291n76, 307

O'Dell, Anne 33
Office of Violence Against Women (OVW) 5, 22
Olms v. Olms 126–127, 313

paranoia 46, 195; *Harp v. Harp* 196–197
Payne, Brian K. 74–75
Peacock v. Peacock 192–195
petition for injunction *see* domestic violence
physical abuse 26, 42, 47, 52–53, 134, 227, 294, 300–301, 310
physical violence 46–47, 213; *Aguilar v. Martinez* 216–217; *Grindrod v. Grindrod* 215–216; *Redd v. Redd* 213–215

Pierson v. Pierson 219–220
power and control 40, 130–131, 260, 283–284; child abuse and violent acts 40–41; children from the IPV victim 41; deprivation of necessities 41; *Herbert v. Herbert* 131–132; household, clothes, and personal belongings 43; psychological control 41–42; *Shook v. Shook* 132–134; verbal abuse 43
Power and Control Wheel 19, 23, 24, 87
pregnant 44, 170; *Wilkerson v. Wilkerson* 170–172
process-led approach 294
proxy 71, 78n17
psychological abuse 40–41, 43, 134
psychological control 41–42
psychologically controlling 143–144; *Huss v. Huss* 144–147

quantitative methods results 271; frequencies 271–275, 272–273, 278–286, 279–282; logistic regression 275–278, 276, 286–287

rape and sexual abuse 47, 220–221; *Allen v. Allen* 221–222
Reckdenwald, Amy 300
Redd v. Redd 213–215
resistance to abuse 44–45, 172–174, 267–268; *Craft-Enzor v. Enzor* 174–175; *Music v. Music* 175–177
Richards, Tara N. 53
Roberts, John M. 265, 288n18
Romero, Fabiana 125

Salari, Sonia 53
Santiago Nuñez v. Nuñez 217–218
Schwartz, Martin D. 38
screaming obscenities 39, 126
second-degree murder 108, 129, 134–135, 147
separated/estranged 45, 181–182; *Astacio v. Astacio* 182; *Wallace-Taylor v. Taylor* 182–183
separation assault 52

Sev'er, Aysan 22, 52
sex 182, 195, 220–222, 235
sexual abuse *see* rape and sexual abuse
Sheehan, Brynn E. 72–73, 78n17, 300
Shook v. Shook 132–134
Sillito, Carrie LeFevre 53
societal failure 51
stalking 35, 57, 94, 294–300
Stark, Evan 26, 268
Strong v. Fulgham 138–142
substantial emotional distress 35, 48n20, 116n112
suicide 10, 34, 53, 186, 194
Sunshine Law 69, 78n13, 309
surveillance 35, 95; *Daley v. Benevides* 95–96
survival mode 88

threatens friends and family 36, 99–100; *Garvin-Williams v. Williams* 101; *Warren v. Warren* 100
threats 36, 96–97; *Davis v. Davis* 98–99; *Donna Wood v. William Wood* 97–98; *Thomas v. Thomas* 99
Tinsley v. Tinsley 151–152
Triplett, Ruth 74–75
Trump Administration 22
Tuerkheimer, Deborah 26

Uniform Crime Report Supplemental Homicide Report (UCR-SHR) 7, 11, 64–67, 257, 275
United Kingdom 26, 72
The United States 2–3, 5–6, 53, 55, 72, 147, 149, 230, 233; coercive control legislation 293–299
U.S. judicial system 56–58

Vargas-Brevick v. Brevick 188–190
Variance Inflation Factor (VIF) 289n34, 290n53, 291n72–291n73
Vatnar, Solveig K. B. 53
Velopulos, Catherine G. 53, 273, 312–313
verbal abuse 43, 147; *Goraya v. Goraya* 147–149
violence perpetration 28, 32n80
Violence Policy Center 273
violent acts toward family and friends 40–41, 137; *Mattaini v. Lennon* 137
violent resistance 29, 267–268

Walker, Lenore E. 23
Walklate, Sandra 3, 294, 301
Wallace-Taylor v. Taylor 182–183
Waller, Garland 28
weapons 36–37, 101–102; *Curry v. Curry* 102–103; *Reddick v. Jackson* 103
weapon used variable frequencies 274, **274**, 277
Websdale, Neil 9
Webster, Daniel W. 274–275
Welch v. Welch 178–180
White v. White 190–192
Whyte-Dell v. Dell 223–225
Wilkerson v. Wilkerson 170–172
women: disempowerment of 58; marriage 37, 52, 89, 104, 147, 165, 219, 269; rape and sexual abuse 47, 220–222; sex 182, 195, 220–222, 235; violence against 22, 28, 264
Women's Rights Movement 23
Wood v. Wood 134
Wright, Claire 5

For Product Safety Concerns and Information please contact our EU
representative GPSR@taylorandfrancis.com
Taylor & Francis Verlag GmbH, Kaufingerstraße 24, 80331 München, Germany

www.ingramcontent.com/pod-product-compliance
Lightning Source LLC
Chambersburg PA
CBHW051349290426
44108CB00015B/1942